"We no longer teach psychoanalysis, in the singular. These days, we teach psychoanalyses, in the plural. There is now a wide ranging diversity of psychoanalytic schools and perspectives, each featuring their own terms, traditions, principles, and technical implications. With Marilyn Charles' superb collection: *Introduction to Contemporary Psychoanalysis: Defining Terms and Building Bridges*, we have a single text that introduces the major orientations. Each chapter is written by an expert in the approach, and a unique feature is that many chapters discuss how the schools relate to each other and how they may be combined by the individual practitioner to suit that clinician's individual personality and idiom."

– Lewis Aron, Ph.D., Director, New York University Postdoctoral
Program in Psychotherapy & Psychoanalysis

"Psychoanalysis has gone from being a monolithic Truth to a loose congeries of positions that have agreed to disagree—and maybe sometimes agree. How and in what way these contemporary positions align themselves with each other, theoretically, clinically and politically, remains obscure. In this brilliantly edited volume, Dr. Charles allows a series of distinguished authors to explicate their positions, including an assessment of its limitations—a thematic that postulates that every position ultimately becomes a countertransference; and that our success depends more on integrating positions that establishing some new superordinate Truth. This thoughtful, well-organized and informative volume should be indispensable to anyone, in or out of the field, in search of some coherence in our current disorder."

– Edgar A. Levenson, Fellow Emeritus, Training,
Supervisory Analyst and Faculty at the William Alanson White Institute.
Adjunct Clinical Professor of Psychology at the New York University Graduate
Studies Division, Honorary Fellow at the Postgraduate Center for Mental Health,
Honorary Member of the American Psychoanalytic Association, Life Fellow of
the American Academy of Psychoanalysis, and Distinguished Life Fellow of the
American Psychiatric Association

"This book respects all the contemporary schools of thought; psychoanalysis is tribal territory, where controversy is rife and not always respectful. It brings together in the palm of the hand all the strands that currently exist, but which head off in their own direction without concern for the whole. The field of view is also strewn with obstacles as words and ideas subtly change their exact meanings in the course of migration over time. So, such a project is not easy. Nor is it usual, as one frequent answer is a simplistic pluralism; anything goes, and the more ideas the merrier we shall be. Less frequent is the much more important stance we find here. Specialists survey their own frame of reference and deliver the reader the wherewithal to make our own assessments and comparisons."

– Bob Hinshelwood, Emeritus Professor, Centre for
Psychoanalytic Studies, University of Essex, UK

INTRODUCTION TO CONTEMPORARY PSYCHOANALYSIS

This book provides a clear introduction to the main contemporary psychoanalytic theoretical perspectives. Psychoanalysis is often thought of as an obscure and outdated method, and yet those familiar with it recognize the profound value of psychoanalytic theory and technique. Part of the obscurity may come from psychoanalytic language itself, which is often impenetrable. The complexity of the subject matter has lent itself to a confusion of tongues, and yet, at base, psychoanalysis remains an earnest attempt to make sense of and ease human distress.

Introduction to Contemporary Psychoanalysis seeks to make this rich wealth of information more accessible to clinicians and trainees. Psychoanalytic clinicians from various schools here describe the key ideas that underlie their particular perspective, helping the reader to see how they apply those ideas in their clinical work. Inviting the contributors to speak about their actual practice, rather than merely providing an overview, this book helps the reader to see common threads that run across perspectives, but also to recognize ways in which the different lenses from each of the perspectives inform interventions. Through brief vignettes, the reader is offered an experience-near sense of what it might be like to apply those ideas in their own work. The contributors also note the limits or weaknesses of their particular theory, inviting the reader to consider the broader spectrum of these diverse offerings so that the benefits of each might be more visible.

Introduction to Contemporary Psychoanalysis offers readers the richness and diversity of psychoanalytic theory and technique, so that the advantages of each particular lens might be visible and accessible as a further tool in their clinical work. This novel, comparative work will be an essential text for any psychoanalyst or psychoanalytically inclined therapist in training, as well as clinicians and those who teach psychoanalytic theory and technique.

Marilyn Charles is a psychologist and psychoanalyst at the Austen Riggs Center, in Stockbridge, Massachusetts, and on faculty at Harvard Medical School, Boston Graduate School of Psychoanalysis, and the University of Monterrey. She serves as Contributing Editor of *Psychoanalysis, Culture and Society* and has published over one hundred articles and book chapters and six books, including *Psychoanalysis and Literature: The Stories We Live* (2015).

INTRODUCTION TO CONTEMPORARY PSYCHOANALYSIS

Defining Terms and Building Bridges

Edited by Marilyn Charles

LONDON AND NEW YORK

First published 2018
by Routledge
2 Park Square, Milton Park, Abingdon, Oxon OX14 4RN

and by Routledge
711 Third Avenue, New York, NY 10017

Routledge is an imprint of the Taylor & Francis Group, an informa business

© 2018 selection and editorial matter, Marilyn Charles; individual chapters, the contributors

The right of the editor to be identified as the author of the editorial material, and of the
authors for their individual chapters, has been asserted in accordance with sections 77 and 78
of the Copyright, Designs and Patents Act 1988.

All rights reserved. No part of this book may be reprinted or reproduced or utilised
in any form or by any electronic, mechanical or other means, now known or
hereafter invented, including photocopying and recording, or in any information
storage or retrieval system, without permission in writing from the publishers.

Trademark notice: Product or corporate names may be trademarks or registered trademarks,
and are used only for identification and explanation without intent to infringe.

British Library Cataloguing in Publication Data
A catalogue record for this book is available from the British Library

Library of Congress Cataloging in Publication Data
Names: Charles, Marilyn, editor.
Title: Introduction to contemporary psychoanalysis : defining terms
and building bridges / edited by Marilyn Charles.
Description: Abingdon, Oxon ; New York, NY : Routledge, 2018. |
Includes bibliographical references and index.
Identifiers: LCCN 2017014357 | ISBN 9781138749870 (hardback : alk. paper) |
ISBN 9781138749887 (pbk. : alk. paper) | ISBN 9781351718400 (web pdf) |
ISBN 9781351718387 (mobi/kindle)
Subjects: LCSH: Psychoanalysis.
Classification: LCC BF173 .I4745 2018 | DDC 150.19/5–dc23
LC record available at https://lccn.loc.gov/2017014357

ISBN: 978-1-138-74987-0 (hbk)
ISBN: 978-1-138-74988-7 (pbk)
ISBN: 978-1-315-18012-0 (ebk)

Typeset in Bembo
by Out of House Publishing

This book is dedicated to Grant Justin King and to Carson Laura King, whose indefatigable love, curiosity and joy renew my spirit and give me hope for the future.

CONTENTS

Acknowledgments	*xi*
List of contributors	*xii*

Introduction: Comparative psychoanalysis: Defining terms, building bridges   1
Marilyn Charles

PART I
Conceptual underpinnings   **7**

1 Contemporary Freudian approaches   9
   Danielle Knafo and Seymour Moscovitz

2 Jungian approaches to psychotherapy   33
   Lionel Corbett

3 Lacan and the evolution of Hermes   53
   David Lichtenstein

PART II
Object relations   **73**

4 A contemporary Kleinian/Bionian perspective   75
   Marilyn Charles

x Contents

5 D. W. Winnicott: Holding, playing and moving toward
mutuality   97
Joyce Slochower

PART III
Building bridges   **119**

6 Toward a new Middle Group: Lacan and Winnicott
for beginners   121
Deborah Luepnitz

PART IV
Field theories   **143**

7 Psychoanalytic field theory   145
Montana Katz

8 Self-experience within intersubjectivity: Two clinicians'
use of self psychology   165
Jeffrey Halpern and Sharone Ornstein

9 Interpersonal psychoanalysis   191
Eugenio Duarte

10 Relational psychoanalysis: Not a theory but a framework   208
Johanna C. Malone

Afterword   227
Marilyn Charles

Index   *229*

ACKNOWLEDGMENTS

I acknowledge with gratitude all who have contributed to this volume. Each chapter is enlivened by all the theorists, patients, supervisors and students who have challenged and enriched the thinking and being of the author.

On a more personal note, I would like to thank my friends and family and all the individuals who have shared their lives, struggles and stories with me over the years. I hope that I have been worthy of your trust.

In this work, we are truly all in it together.

CONTRIBUTORS

Marilyn Charles, PhD, ABPP, is a staff psychologist at the Austen Riggs Center and a psychoanalyst in private practice in Stockbridge, Massachusetts; a training and supervising Analyst with the Chicago Center for Psychoanalysis; and on faculty at Harvard Medical School, Boston Graduate School of Psychoanalysis, and the University of Monterrey. A member of the editorial boards of numerous psychoanalytic journals, she serves as a Contributing Editor of *Psychoanalysis, Culture and Society*. Dr. Charles has presented her work nationally and internationally, publishing over 100 articles and book chapters and six books: *Patterns: Building Blocks of Experience* (2002); *Constructing Realities: Transformations through Myth and Metaphor* (2004); *Learning from Experience: A Guidebook for Clinicians* (2004); *Working with Trauma: Lessons from Bion and Lacan* (2012); *Psychoanalysis and Literature: The Stories We Live* (2015); and an edited volume with Michael O'Loughlin: *Fragments of Trauma and the Social Production of Suffering* (2014).

Lionel Corbett, M.D., is a psychiatrist and Jungian analyst. He is a Professor of Depth Psychology at Pacifica Graduate Institute in Santa Barbara, California, where he teaches depth psychology. He is the author of numerous professional papers and four books: *The Religious Function of the Psyche* (1996); *Psyche and the Sacred: Spirituality beyond Religion* (2007); *The Sacred Cauldron: Psychotherapy as a Spiritual Practice* (2011); and, most recently, *The Soul in Anguish: Psychotherapeutic Approaches to Suffering* (2015). He is the co-editor of four sets of collected papers: *Psyche's Stories* (two volumes: 1991, 1992); *Depth Psychology: Meditations in the Field* (2000); *Psychology at the Threshold* (2001); and *Jung and Aging: Possibilities and Potentials for the Second Half of Life* (2014).

Eugenio A. Duarte, Ph.D., is Chair of the LGBTQ Study Group at the William Alanson White Institute, in New York City, and an Associate Editor for the journal *Contemporary Psychoanalysis*. He is adjunct faculty at New York University's Department of Applied Psychology. He also serves as host of the podcast "New Books in Psychology" on the New Books Network. He is a licensed psychologist and psychoanalyst in private practice seeing LGBTQ patients and couples in downtown Manhattan.

Jeffrey Halpern, M.D., is a training and supervising analyst at the Columbia University Center for Psychoanalytic Training and Research, in New York City. He is Clinical Assistant Professor of Psychiatry at Columbia University College of Physicians and Surgeons. He teaches and supervises. He has a private practice in New York City.

Danielle Knafo, Ph.D., is a clinical psychologist and psychoanalyst. She is a professor at Long Island University – Post in its Clinical Psychology Doctoral Program; she is also a supervisor and faculty member at New York University's Postdoctoral Program in Psychotherapy and Psychoanalysis, at which she has taught courses on the evolution of Freud's thought and working (and playing) with the unconscious. Dr. Knafo has published extensively, and her books include *Dancing with the Unconscious: The Art of Psychoanalysis and the Psychoanalysis of Art* (2012). Her most recent book (with Rocco Lo Bosco) is *The Age of Perversion: Desire and Technology in Psychoanalysis and Culture* (2016).

S. Montana Katz, Ph.D., LP, is a training and supervising analyst and senior faculty member at the National Psychological Association for Psychoanalysis, New York City. She is an associate faculty member at the Erikson Institute of the Austen Riggs Center and on the editorial boards of *Psychoanalytic Inquiry* and *The Psychoanalytic Review*. Montana Katz is a founding Co-Director of the International Field Theory Association and Co-Editor of the Routledge Psychoanalytic Field Theory Book Series. She is the editor of *Metaphor and Fields: Common Ground, Common Language, and the Future of Psychoanalysis* (Routledge, 2013); co-editor of *Advances in Contemporary Psychoanalytic Field Theory: Concept and Future Development* (Routledge, 2016); and author of *Contemporary Psychoanalytic Field Theory: Stories, Dreams, and Metaphor* (Routledge, 2017). She has a private practice in New York City.

David Lichtenstein, Ph.D., is a psychoanalyst in private practice in New York City. A co-founder of the Après-Coup Psychoanalytic Association, he is on the faculty at the New York University Postdoctoral Program in Psychoanalysis and Psychotherapy and at the City University of New York Graduate Program in Clinical Psychology. He is Editor of *DIVISION/Review: A Quarterly Psychoanalytic Forum*, author of numerous articles and book chapters and co-editor of a forthcoming book: *The Lacan Tradition*.

Deborah Anna Luepnitz, Ph.D., is a Clinical Associate in the Department of Psychiatry at the Perelman School of Medicine at the University of Pennsylvania,

xiv List of contributors

in Philadelphia. She is the author of three books, including *The Family Interpreted: Psychoanalysis, Feminism, and Family Therapy* (1988) and *Schopenhauer's Porcupines: Intimacy and Its Dilemmas: Five Stories of Psychotherapy* (2002), which has been translated into six languages. She was also a contributing author to *The Cambridge Companion to Lacan* (2003). She has worked to foster a conversation between the British and French traditions in psychoanalysis, and her article "Thinking in the Space between Winnicott and Lacan" was published in the *International Journal of Psychoanalysis* in 2009. In 2005 Dr. Luepnitz launched IFA (Insight For All), a pro bono program that connects psychoanalysts with homeless and formerly homeless adults. She maintains a private practice in Philadelphia.

Johanna C. Malone, Ph.D., is a Lecturer of Psychiatry at Harvard Medical School and Cambridge Health Alliance, Massachusetts, where she supervises psychology interns and collaborates on research. She is an Associate Editor of *Psychoanalytic Psychology*, the journal of the American Psychological Association (APA), Division 39 (Psychoanalysis). She served as co-editor for both the child and adolescent personality sections of the revised edition of the *Psychodynamic Diagnostic Manual, PDM-2* (2017). She is a faculty member at the Massachusetts Institute for Psychoanalysis (MIP). Her published work uses developmental frameworks to understand dynamic processes of personality, creativity and self-experience. She has a private practice in Cambridge.

Seymour Moscovitz, Ph.D., is a faculty member at the New York University Postdoctoral Program in Psychotherapy and Psychoanalysis and the Institute for Psychoanalytic Training and Research (IPTAR). He is also an Assistant Clinical Professor at Columbia University and the Director of Education and Training of the New York City Family Court Mental Health Service. He is in the private practice of psychoanalysis and forensic psychology in New York City.

Sharone Ornstein, M.D., is a training and supervising analyst and former Curriculum Chair at the Columbia University Center for Psychoanalytic Training and Research. She is Clinical Assistant of Psychiatry at Weill Cornell Medical College, New York City, where she teaches and supervises. She is in private practice in psychiatry and psychoanalysis in New York City.

Joyce Slochower, Ph.D., ABPP, is Professor Emerita of Psychology at Hunter College and the Graduate Center, City University of New York. She is faculty and supervisor at the New York University Postdoctoral Program in Psychotherapy and Psychoanalysis, the Steven Mitchell Relational Study Center, the National Training Program of the National Institute for the Psychotherapies (NIP) (all in New York), the Philadelphia Center for Relational Studies and the Psychoanalytic Institute of Northern California (in San Francisco). She is on the editorial boards of *Psychoanalytic Dialogues*, *Ricerca Psicoanalitica* and *Perspectives in Psychoanalysis* and is on the board of the International Association for Relational Psychoanalysis and

Psychotherapy (IARPP). Joyce has published over 80 articles on various aspects of psychoanalytic theory and technique. Second editions of her two books *Holding and Psychoanalysis: A Relational Perspective* (1996) and *Psychoanalytic Collisions* (2006) were released in 2014 by Routledge. She is co-editor, with Lew Aron and Sue Grand, of the forthcoming books *De-Idealizing Relational Theory: A Critique from Within* and *Decentering Relational Theory: A Comparative Critique*. She is in private practice in New York City, where she sees individuals and couples.

INTRODUCTION

Comparative psychoanalysis: Defining terms, building bridges

Marilyn Charles

This volume is written for those individuals interested in developing their understanding of psychoanalytic technique and theory. The reader will find an array of psychoanalytic "languages" offered, affirming the idea that diversity of perspectives is an important underpinning of good clinical practice. Contributors were asked to describe the basic theory underlying their particular perspective, giving a few key conceptualizations for that perspective, and then to briefly illustrate how they apply those ideas in clinical practice. Contributors were also asked to describe the weaknesses of their particular vantage point and what they do when they hit that limit. I was hoping, in this way, to offer the reader a felt sense of the conceptualizations and techniques that guide each of these lenses, and also the weaknesses inherent in each. My idea is that each lens affords an important perspective on the puzzle of how to conceptualize the human struggles that underlie intensive clinical work and therefore guide the techniques that are brought to bear. My own experience is that no single perspective is sufficient, that I need to draw from the various theories in order to most effectively work through the variety of clinical dilemmas that present themselves.

The reader will note that each of the chapters not only delineates a different theoretical orientation but also bears the mark of the person writing it. I hope that this fact will invite the reader to consider ways in which a particular theory might call to us precisely because it is consistent with the way we think, feel and work. Inherent, then, is the recognition of the inevitability of character as it plays itself out in our lives, choices, writings and values, and in our very beings. Part of the strength of a psychoanalytic sensibility is to be able to recognize the multiple ways in which character is formed by and then, in turn, forms experience. As Grotstein (2000) notes, "What we call perception is more often apperception" (p. xxi). Our lenses are inevitably colored by previous experience; transference is ubiquitous and inescapable, though potentially observable.

The reader should be on the alert for themes running through the text that become familiar in spite of the variety of dialects through which they are spoken. For example, Winnicott's (1971) stress on object usage, which highlights the importance of the analyst tolerating and surviving aggression or narcissistic injury, first encountered in Chapter 5 and is then picked up again in Chapter 8 in terms of shame, narcissistic rage and selfobject functions. In his descriptions of what he terms *binocular vision*, Bion (1977) marks the value of having diverse perspectives, suggesting that we obtain a more differentiated picture of whatever we are looking at when we can see it from more than one vantage point. This binocular perspective also helps us to recognize key essential dilemmas that are part of the psychoanalytic journey. Viewing those elements from different orientations helps to sharpen our thinking and to augment our technical tools.

We begin, of course, with Freud, whose indefatigable curiosity and depth and breadth of vision form the cornerstone of psychoanalytic theory and technique. In Chapter 1, Danielle Knafo and Seymour Moscovitz lay the groundwork for our explorations with their introduction to contemporary Freudian approaches. In their chapter, the authors offer a brief outline of the history of contemporary Freudian theory and introduce key terms that continue to be integral to this approach, marking unconscious fantasy and the centrality of psychic conflict as crucial organizing principles, along with the emphasis on sexuality as a primary force in development, defense mechanisms as a means to grapple with psychic pain, and transference and resistance as essential elements of the analytic process. Also offered are key clinical concepts and descriptions of the technical tools most relevant to the Freudian tradition.

We turn next to Jung, in Chapter 2. Although Freud excluded Jung from his psychoanalytic canon, we would be remiss in not attending to those aspects of human experience and clinical work that have been elaborated through the Jungian lens. Lionel Corbett offers us a cogent and articulate picture of the Jungian perspective, in which the analyst's own personality and level of psychological development are seen as more important than any technical considerations. From this perspective (similar to themes that will emerge again in our considerations of Lacan, in Chapter 3), the analyst needs to refrain from *imposing* theory so that the patient is able to derive his or her own theory. Corbett notes that Jungian analysis may be viewed as an early form of field theory, in which meanings are derived from both transference/countertransference experiences and also the transpersonal self in which the pair are embedded. Key Jungian concepts include a view of the unconscious suffused by a transpersonal, universal dimension, through which archetypal forms represent important processes within the individual psyche. Archetypal structures and processes include the transpersonal Self, the shadow, anima and animus, and persona, or mask. Much as in the Freudian perspective, dreams and the unconscious play important roles in a working-through process that, from a Jungian perspective, aims toward greater individuation.

I include Lacan in this first part because of Lacan's (1953) explicit intention to align his own thinking and technique in relation to Freud's "Promethean

Introduction: Comparative psychoanalysis **3**

discovery" (p. 34) of "the function and field of speech and language in psychoanalysis" (p. 30) and the method aligned with it. In that important paper, Lacan explicitly insists that psychoanalysis "can only survive by maintaining itself at the level of an integral experience" (p. 31). In line with this insistence on *experience* over *authorized knowledge* (a theme also stressed by Bion), David Lichtenstein highlights ways in which Lacan offers us both a return to and a complicating of Freud that, importantly, resists the tendency to oversimplify complexities inherent in the human condition. Lichtenstein embeds his chapter in the character of Hermes, whose dual functions of representation and interpretation he likens to the craft of psychoanalysis, which is governed by principles not of science but, rather, of truth and meaning. Lacan, in pointing toward the paradox at the heart of meaning and of speech, insists on meaning as something that *must be made* rather than merely learned, and that this learning can occur only through the recognition of limit and of lack through which one might recognize one's own desire. In line with the Jungian perspective, Lacan asserts the importance of the subject's own desire as the orienting point of the exploration.

We turn next to object relations theories in Chapters 4 and 5. Opposing the drive model in which much psychoanalytic work had been cast, object relations perspectives reconceptualize the human dilemma not as driven primarily by internal physiological processes but, rather, by social and affiliative needs. In these theories, we encounter various conceptualizations regarding the collision that occurs between self and other. In Chapter 4, I offer a perspective informed by the work of Klein and Bion. Klein added to the psychoanalytic canon through her conjectures about the processes at play in early development in the negotiation between primary needs and limits. Recognizing early hostility and aggression, Klein delineates concepts such as splitting and projective identification that have become part of the larger psychoanalytic canon. Her ideas were informed by her work with young children whose development had been waylaid, leaving them enacting largely unsymbolized experiences. Klein's and Bion's attempts to elucidate such inchoate meanings have important ramifications for our work with adults as well. Contemporary Kleinians have offered rich and useful ways of looking at the ubiquity of transference in the clinical encounter. Their metaphors help to highlight primary defenses and to suggest ways of working with those defenses as they manifest in the treatment.

In Chapter 5, Joyce Slochower offers us the developmental perspective of Winnicott, a pediatrician who came at this issue of self in relation to other from the perspective of his observations of infants and mothers. In contrast to Klein, who worked with very disturbed young children, Winnicott was a pediatrician, affording him a more normative view. In this way, Winnicott's work helps us to track some of the essential developmental milestones that must be successfully negotiated in order to become a separate and viable self in relation to others. Slochower leads us through some of his key conceptualizations of holding, play and object usage, showing us how profoundly Winnicott provides a foundation for a more relational view of psychoanalytic clinical work.

4 Marilyn Charles

In Part III, Building Bridges, we pause to think about how the theories we have already considered might fit together to condition and augment one another. Deborah Luepnitz' chapter offers us a perspective that makes use of ideas from both Winnicott and Lacan and explains how these dual vantage points inform her own clinical work. Luepnitz begins with her stance that Winnicott represents the more humanistic aspects of Freud and his work, whereas Lacan represents the skeptic, radical, truth-teller aspect. Luepnitz notes a few key concepts that are seen very differently from these two perspectives. Lacan, for example, views the mirror stage as an important moment because it marks an essential alienation between the person and the image, whereas, for Winnicott, the mirror afforded by the maternal gaze is essential for healthy development. She notes ways in which André Green located himself between these two frameworks, emphasizing the importance of both a Winnicottian attention to transference, as it evolves in the relationship between two people, and a Lacanian emphasis on language and meaning. Most important, stresses Luepnitz, is the engagement, itself, through which psychoanalysis is invented anew with each patient.

We then turn to contemporary theories that might all be seen to cohere within the general rubric of Part IV's title: Field Theories. In Chapter 7, Montana Katz introduces us to the concept of field theory, first giving an historical overview, noting ways in which developments in science demanded recognition of the inevitable effects of interaction upon the individual. She then elaborates three trends in field theory that have emerged. The first theory described is that of the Barangers in Argentina, who reformulated Freud's structural model in bi-personal terms. She then describes field theory as it evolved in North America, three variations of which, self psychology and relational and interpersonal theories, are then each explicated in the following chapters. Finally, she describes the field theory that evolved in Italy based upon the work of Bion, in which the goal is to expand the thinking/feeling/dreaming capacity of the patient.

In Chapter 8, Jeffrey Halpern and Sharone Ornstein describe the self psychology perspective. Contextualizing their ideas in the work of Kohut, they highlight four particular contributions to clinical work from this perspective, notably the use of empathy as a method of observation; a view of narcissism as a force in healthy development; Kohut's discovery of selfobject functions and selfobject transferences; and a heightened appreciation of shame and rage. From this perspective, self-experience is seen as deeply embedded in and inextricable from intersubjectivity, making recognition by the other essential for self-development. We see in this perspective an alliance with Winnicott, in the recognition of how important it is that the analyst be able to recognize, tolerate and work through his or her own complicated feelings about the patient so that, through sequences of disruption and repair, both learn to survive the encounters more fully alive.

In Chapter 9, Eugenio Duarte introduces us to the interpersonal approach to psychoanalysis. Key ideas include the assumption of participant observation: that we inevitably have an impact on whatever we observe; the analyst's role as *riding the wave* rather than steering the ship; and the detailed inquiry as a core way of marking our curiosity and willingness to engage further beyond the surface detail. Duarte reviews some key implications of the interpersonal approach, including the importance of humility and of multicultural competence. He stresses that this is a perspective that fundamentally recognizes and values the differences between individuals that color and enliven experience.

In Chapter 10, Johanna Malone importantly notes that relational psychoanalysis is not so much a theory but, rather, a framework that emphasizes the primacy of relationships in the development and experience of the psyche. She suggests that the relational psychoanalyst uses self-experience as a lens through which to reflect on and consider tensions between past and present and between fantasy and reality, and also, perhaps most importantly, how the analyst him- or herself is affecting the therapeutic process. We encounter again the idea that each psychoanalytic encounter must be invented anew but, unlike Lacan's emphasis on logos (Chapter 3) or Bion's admonition to enter the room without memory or desire (Chapter 4), the relational perspective explicitly asks the analyst to recognize his or her own desire and to pay attention to the impact of his or her needs, feelings and character upon the analytic field. The relational perspective has been notable in its explicit attention to issues of race, culture and social justice, in some ways reminiscent of Freud's hope for psychoanalysis to have broad accessibility through free clinics.

I end this introduction with a few final thoughts to invite an active engagement with the text. My hope is that the reader will find common themes along with differences in emphasis and technique that will usefully inform his or her clinical work. These themes may be most useful when seen as metaphors that hold some of the complexities of human experience and engagement. Psychoanalytic theory is dense enough that we can work at learning the jargon rather than recognizing the metaphors that point to clinical difficulties and ways we might work with them. Bion, in his famous – or infamous – grid, helps us to recognize ways in which it is the function of the word or behavior that most informs the process. Paying close attention to the process invites the patient to engage in a more finely-tuned analysis as well. Recognizing that our jargon holds dense conceptualizations at the level of metaphor helps us to hold less tightly to these theory-driven metaphors and, rather, work with those metaphors that emerge in the work with a particular individual.

Metaphors provide a link between primary and secondary process, aiding in the translation between experience and the words we use to communicate those experiences with one another. The psychoanalytic process is dense, layered and elusive, and psychoanalytic terms can be seen as condensed metaphors that reference very complicated meaning structures. Much like the myth, which can hold complexities of relationships because the story contains it, metaphors hold a story in ways that enable us to unpack pieces of the whole without entirely losing sight of the context. Winnicott's (1971) *object usage* or Klein's *projective identification* are good examples of metaphors that have found their way into the clinical canon – metaphors that expand and enrich along with the clinician's growing experience.

I hope that metaphors will emerge in these pages that will enliven your own process in this very challenging work that we do. Because of the difficulty of holding hope and also of communicating experience that is largely ineffable and beyond words, metaphors are particularly important in our work with people whose development has been impeded by trauma. Metaphors breathe life into the work because they are, of essence, *playful*: they cannot be taken in directly but, rather, must be *played with*. Such playfulness requires the ability to regulate one's affect so that grief can be faced rather than denied. Coming back to life can be painful. One young woman, whose creative engagements had increasingly become the type of fantasying Winnicott (1971) alludes to, noted: "I've been living in a hallucination of what's outside the window. I made up life. I made up the truth. But this is where I am. And it hurts."

In sharing her metaphors, I try to participate with her in the enterprise of meaning-making, trying to dream through the sessions along with her in the fashion described by Bionian field theorists such as Ferro (2009) and Civitarese (2005). Allowing the veneer to slip has enabled this young woman to encounter more of herself – and, with it, her pain – through which process she is beginning to come alive sufficiently to feel anything at all beyond the abject and nameless pain she was suffering when we first met. She worries that she is getting worse, but also has the sense that she is getting better. "You've been numb," I say. "And it hurts to come back to life."

References

Bion, W. R. (1977). *Seven Servants*. New York: Jason Aronson.

Civitarese, G. (2005). Fire at the theatre: (Un)reality of/in the transference and interpretation. *International Journal of Psychoanalysis*, 86(5): 1299–1316.

Ferro, A. (2009). Transformations in dreaming and characters in the psychoanalytic field. *International Journal of Psychoanalysis*, 90(2): 209–230.

Grotstein, J. S. (2000). *Who Is the Dreamer Who Dreams the Dream? A Study of Psychic Presences*. Hillsdale, NJ: Analytic Press.

Lacan, J. (1953 [1977]). The function and field of speech and language in psychoanalysis. In *Écrits: A Selection* (A. Sheridan, Trans.), pp. 30–113. New York: W. W. Norton.

Winnicott, D. W. (1971). *Playing and Reality*. London: Tavistock Publications.

PART I
Conceptual underpinnings

1

CONTEMPORARY FREUDIAN APPROACHES

Danielle Knafo and Seymour Moscovitz

Each generation of psychoanalysts returns to Freud, not simply to study the origins of psychoanalysis, but because his writings are so profound that one discovers a paragraph here or a sentence there that will provoke a rethinking of contemporary assumptions. It is an odd thing indeed – and for some quite embarrassing – to find on returning to Freud a future train of thought that was originally considered abandoned by him (probably for lack of time) and by his followers (probably for lack of genius).

(Bollas, 2009, p. 13)[1]

Introduction: basic tenets and principles

Every few years, over the past half century, an article has appeared announcing Freud's death – such as "Sigmund Freud is dead" (Davids, 1972) – along with the demise of the psychoanalytic enterprise he created. These announcements are found in scholarly journals as well as popular media, and the critiques take many forms, most of them attempts to discredit the founder of psychoanalysis and point out the unscientific basis of his constructs. Just as frequently, articles appear questioning whether Freud is indeed dead: "Why Freud isn't dead" (Horgan, 1996); "Is Freud really dead?" (Westen, 1999). Some even revive Freud from the dead: "Freud returns" (Solms, 2007). If Freud were alive today and tried to apply his own theory to understand the pervasive need to repeatedly kill and resurrect him, he might deduce that what he had to say was very threatening indeed. One thing is clear: if people are still arguing whether Freud's thought is dead or not, then it most certainly is not. In this chapter, we present the ways contemporary Freudian psychoanalysis reflects both continuity with Freud's pioneering contributions and significant change and evolution, as new developments in theory, research and clinical practice have been gradually incorporated into the Freudian model. Many

10 Danielle Knafo and Seymour Moscovitz

of Freud's foundational ideas remain part of contemporary Freudian practice: the ubiquity of unconscious fantasies that inform conscious experience; the centrality of psychic conflict; the myriad of defense mechanisms employed to reduce psychic pain; the importance of sexuality in development; and the therapeutic handling of transferences and resistances as they appear in the here-and-now process of treatment are all examples of this continuity. Added to this foundation, as we will show, are newer concepts, such as intersubjectivity, enactment, pre-Oedipal development and the internalization of interactions with others.

A brief history of the post-Freudian era

Following Freud's actual death in 1939 and the end of World War II, an ego psychological paradigm dominated American psychoanalysis and was prominent throughout the 1950s and 1960s. The theoretical origins of this paradigmatic change can be traced to Freud's positing of his structural theory in *The Ego and the Id* (1923) and *Inhibitions, Symptoms and Anxiety* (1926), setting forth the familiar tripartite division of the mind into an id, ego and superego. Seminal contributions by Anna Freud (e.g., *The Ego and the Mechanisms of Defense*, 1937) and the monumental work of Heinz Hartmann (1939) and his collaborators, Ernst Kris and Rudolf Lowenstein, extended Freud's structural model to encompass a normal psychology of the ego.

We shall call this post-Freudian period (c. 1939 to 1980) the "modern era" rather than "traditional," "mainstream" or "post-classical," as it shares several aspects of modernity in general (e.g., a belief in the separateness of the observer and observed). While many great advances occurred during this time, the period was characterized by an unwarranted degree of certitude in its theorizing (e.g., the assigning of fixed meanings to psychosomatic disorders: Alexander, 1950). An acultural presumption of the universality of the complexes, conditions and developmental pathways that psychoanalysis had uncovered ignored diversity. During these decades the institutes of the American Psychoanalytic Association enjoyed hegemonic control over the political and intellectual landscape of psychoanalysis, and their influence continued through the 1970s. A degree of authoritarianism infiltrated its training institutes and inhibited creativity (Kernberg, 1996). The last nearly 40 years (c. 1980 to 2018) may be described as a time of contemporary pluralism during which many of the other viewpoints presented in this volume emerged, such as self psychology, relational psychoanalysis, feminist psychoanalysis, intersubjectivity theory, attachment theory, two-person psychologies, contemporary Kleinian theory and other developments in the widening world of psychoanalysis. In this period of expansion, contemporary Freudian psychoanalysis has been characterized by an openness and receptivity to theoretical viewpoints and clinical practices that previously had been foreclosed.

Given its assimilation of ideas from other schools of thought, contemporary Freudian psychoanalysis can no longer be said to be monolithic, and several branches in the Freudian tree have developed. Some contemporary Freudian analysts have extended the implications and technical applications of Freud's structural model, while making important revisions to it, an approach described now as modern conflict theory and discussed in more detail below. Other contemporary Freudians, such as Paul Gray and Fred Busch, have refined a way of working close to the conscious awareness of the patient, addressing the ego's defensive operations at a microscopic level – a procedure known as "close process analysis" (Gray, 1994; Busch, 1995). From our perspective, Charles Brenner's reformulation of structural theory and Gray's applications of defense analysis represent refinements in, rather than fundamental revisions of, classical psychoanalysis.

Another group of contemporary Freudians (e.g., Salman Akhtar, Sheldon Bach, Nancy Chodorow, Judith Chused, Steven Ellman, Theodore Jacobs, Fred Pine) have incorporated recent developments in a spirit of pluralism. Sometimes referred to as "self and object Freudians" (Ellman, 2010) or "intersubjective ego psychologists" (Chodorow, 2004), these contemporary Freudians have modified and integrated many different ideas into their clinical practice: the origins and vulnerability of the self, early object relations and trauma, and the interactional and enacted aspects of the analytic relationship. Their focus incorporates both one-person and two-person psychologies and has widened the scope of psychoanalysis to include the intersubjective and interpsychic, bridging classical intrapsychic and interpersonal models. The therapeutic relationship as well as interpretation and insight are viewed as central mutative factors. While adhering to certain tenets of the classical tradition, these contemporary Freudians have attempted to shed some of the constraints and dogmatic attitudes of the modern era. In a similar discussion of these historical trends, Andrew Druck (2011) has referred to these theorists as representing a "modern structural theory" (as distinct from "modern conflict theory") that emphasizes the role of early development and internalization in constituting "an inner world and inner structure" (p. 26).

Key Freudian concepts

In the sections that follow, key concepts of contemporary Freudian psychoanalysis will be summarized, indicating areas of continuity with Freud's thought as well as important new developments. This review will encompass classical, modern and contemporary perspectives as we have defined these periods, and it will also include contributions from the two variants of contemporary Freudian theory outlined above.

Unconscious fantasy

The unconscious stands as a pillar in psychoanalytic thought. Morris Eagle (in press) observes that, until recently, it would have been difficult to imagine psychoanalytic theory without the concept of unconscious processes at its center.

Unconscious processes are not directly observed but are inferred from material provided by the patient. The Freudian analyst pays attention to the timing and sequencing as well as the content of the patient's associations, as contiguity of ideas

12 Danielle Knafo and Seymour Moscovitz

may reflect connection. The analyst makes use of seemingly extraneous remarks, which may likewise open up interconnected pathways.

Jacob Arlow (1969) surmised that aberrations in conscious experience often reveal unconscious fantasies. He cites a patient who reported an experience of *déjà vu* while waiting for an appointment with his employer, which he feared might go badly. He was greeted by an attractive female secretary and, as he looked out the window of the waiting room, had the uncanny sense he had experienced all of this before. From associations provided by the patient, Arlow surmised that the secretary represented the sexually tempting yet reassuring mother, protecting him from a castrating father figure. This unconscious fantasy explained the patient's experience of *déjà vu* and served the defensive and adaptive functions of reassuring the man that he had mastered this potential trauma in the past. Dream reports, slips of the tongue, bodily postures and nonverbal behavior all allow the analyst to penetrate the surface of socially constructed communications and presentations.

Unconscious fantasy may even underlie veridical perceptions of reality by enhancing attunement to selected aspects of the external world. An example was provided in a play session with a six-year-old girl whose parents were involved in a contentious divorce. The girl astutely noticed that a vase on the therapist's bookshelf was chipped. The vase had been turned to avoid exposure of this flaw, which did not escape the perceptive notice of this child, whose heightened but unconscious concern with broken and damaged objects was an expression of both fantasy and reality.

Often, patients report on events in their life outside the consulting room as if they were unconstructed "realities," and not infrequently analysts do not explore further and attend only to these "real" contemporary experiences and relationships, without acknowledging the contribution of unconscious fantasy on the patient's perceptions.

Freud (1915) considered some unconscious fantasies so widespread within a given culture as to be considered universal. He postulated the existence of several such fantasies – the primal scene, childhood seduction and the threat of castration – that continue to be relevant in contemporary Freudian psychoanalytic views of development. Children still wonder about their parents' lives and relationships, are especially curious about the secret activities that take place behind closed doors, tend to be worried about being punished for transgressive thoughts, and are concerned about their bodies, especially their genitals, comparing them with others' (Knafo & Feiner, 2006a). All these anxieties are expressed in primal fantasies.

Unconscious fantasies may be described as ubiquitous, complex psychic phenomena that exist outside awareness yet exert an influence on motivation, overt behavior and conscious experience. They combine cognition and affect, wishes and defense, and self and object representations and identifications and involve the most basic, primal, intimate predilections that determine what we perceive, experience and feel (Knafo & Feiner, 2006a). Unconscious fantasies are increasingly regarded as internalized relationships that have a protagonist in a scenario relating to others

Contemporary Freudian approaches **13**

in specific ways (Knafo & Feiner, 2006a). The manner in which the self is portrayed defines the relationship, and the relationship, in turn, determines the experience of the self.

From a contemporary Freudian perspective, an appreciation of unconscious fantasy – both as process and as content – is needed to understand how a patient's experience is shaped by internal and external events. Without this perspective, the therapeutic process may become excessively reality-bound and unwittingly foster repetitive enactments. When the value of unconscious fantasy is recognized and obstacles to its playful use removed, the analytic process may be enlivened.

Unlike Freud (1908), who regarded fantasy as pathological and indicative of dissatisfaction, the contemporary Freudian regards access to fantasy as a sign of healthy commerce between conscious and unconscious mental states (Loewald, 1960), imbuing psychic reality with richness and vitality. The ability to engage in play, imagination and fantasy is now considered a sign of a more flexible, adaptive and healthy mental life (Winnicott, 1971; Bollas, 1987).

Psychosexual development

Another of Freud's contributions that continues to be central in contemporary Freudian practice is his elaboration of sexuality and the effect of fantasies about the body on normal and pathological functioning and development. Although later theorists in the modern era developed a heteronormative bias, Freud's original "hypothesis of the universal influence of sexuality as belonging to the general structure of human nature" (Green, 1995, p. 872), and his progressive views that we are all bisexual beings and that homosexuality is a natural stage in all human development, were groundbreaking.

Freud was the first to bring attention to the infantile aspect of sexuality (1905), and his writings (1905, 1927) stressed the perverse aspects that are present in all sexuality. Sexuality, for Freud, is much more than a drive; sexuality is an "emotionally charged experience" that organizes psychic life and fantasy (Lemma & Lynch, 2015, p. 6). Indeed, much of Freud's legacy involves the attention he brought to the body ("The ego is first and foremost a bodily ego": Freud, 1923, p. 26).

Contemporary Freudian analysts (Knafo & Feiner, 2006b) attend to fantasies about the body that aim to answer the following questions: What do I possess inside and outside of my body? What do I envy in others? Who is like me/different from me? What fears do I have about my body? What does it mean to be male/female (Knafo & Feiner, 2006b)? These are questions involving potentially shifting paradigms that all children and adults engage in their fantasies and in their object choices throughout their lifetime.

Freud's (1905) psychosexual theory and his conceptualization of the psychoneuroses centered largely on his postulation of the Oedipal complex. Today adherence to the Oedipus complex, even by contemporary Freudians, is a hotly debated topic, with some insisting that it is central while others believing the concept needs to be revised or discarded. Although Freud did postulate a negative Oedipus, in which the child desires the same-sex parent and competes with the opposite-sex parent, the Oedipus complex limits the way one is left thinking about sex and gender (Barden, 2015). Fantasies about castration and penis envy abound but so do those involving womb envy, the phallic mother, the "vaginal father" (Lorand, 1939), the body as phallus (Lewin, 1933), hermaphroditism and bisexual completeness (Fast, 1984). The phallic woman fantasy, for example, is invoked not merely to allay castration fears in the boy but also to act as a bridge between male and female, a symbol of sexual intercourse between mother and father, and a unification declaring that one can have it all. These fantasies, while centering on anatomical features and their limitations, or the overcoming of these limitations, also involve narcissistic and object relational concerns as well as issues of aggression and omnipotent control.

Memory, repetition and enactment

From the beginning of his psychoanalytic writings up until his death, Freud was fascinated with the function that memory played, both in the formation of symptoms and in their treatment. Many contemporary Freudians have replaced Freud's goal of memory retrieval and insight with one that places greater emphasis on relationships in the here and now. What Freud found to be vital was the liberation of mental contents from the unconscious, whether due to repression or dissociation, both of which result in memories that are unintegrated into one's life and unavailable for assimilation into the "ego core" (Loewald, 1962). The centrality of working with memory is illustrated in the following vignette from the patient of one of us (D.K.):

> Mr. H., a bespectacled man in his fifties, presented with extremely negative memories of his childhood from which time he apparently also suffered from very poor vision. He had severed ties with his family forty years prior to seeking treatment. It was literally impossible for Mr. H to "see" any positive aspect to his childhood for several years into his analysis. Eventually, however, Mr. H's analysis, which improved his "in-sight," allowed for a softening of his stance toward his family members. As he began to entertain the possibility of possessing positive memories of his parents, he faced the pain of not having had his emotional needs met by them. Although this made him feel very vulnerable, it was a state that he was now able to tolerate. Interestingly, as Mr. H faced his past in a more open way that allowed for both positive and negative memories to emerge, his vision cleared up remarkably to the point of being able to see without his glasses – the first time since childhood – for most of the time. He stated it simply: "The more I feel better, the more I can see." He equated his "breakthrough in vision" with his parallel "breakthrough in consciousness." In this case, insight had a direct effect on sight.
>
> *(Knafo, 2009)*

Whereas Freud initially (Breuer & Freud, 1893–95) insisted that repressed memories had to be uncovered through verbal representation, he later (1914) appreciated that memories are often *enacted* rather than verbalized. When memory is repressed, the person is "obliged to repeat the repressed material as a contemporary experience instead of... remembering it as something belonging to the past" (1920, p. 18). In other words, many of us remain unaware of critical memories but, in analysis, we can become conscious of them by paying attention to repetitions in our behavior and relationship patterns. Freud anticipated contemporary interest in the importance of enactments in psychoanalysis.

A dramatic example of a memory enacted rather than remembered is that of Mr. Z, a patient treated by the supervisee of one of the authors (D.K.). Mr. Z found himself facing the termination of a very prestigious military career that had lasted decades when he suddenly developed a hysterical symptom: several times throughout the day, his general lethargy and visibly depressed affect were violently interrupted by sudden, uncontrolled behavior. Seemingly out of the blue, this large and imposing man soared out of the chair he had otherwise planted himself in, shook his hands in frenzied motions above his head and shouted at the top of his lungs for minutes at a time. No one knew what to make of this behavior, which was clearly both extremely disturbed and disturbing. Mr. Z was so debilitated by his behavior that his wife began to treat him like an infant and to tend to all his needs. The therapist had to make home visits in order to treat Mr. Z as well as his decompensating family situation. Mr. Z had created a state of emergency in all around him, including in the student/therapist.

What emerged from this case involved the discovery that Mr. Z had witnessed his mother's suicide as a child. She had leapt to her death from a balcony before his very eyes. Although he had never reacted emotionally to the crisis, he had clearly retained this traumatic memory in his body (van der Kolk, 2014, has noted that "the body keeps score"). His dramatic symptoms entailed a clear reenactment of how he felt while witnessing the gruesome suicide of his mother, a reenactment that he needed to repeat. It took the ending of his prestigious military career, a career that had bolstered his masculinity and defenses, to revisit the most traumatic memory of his life. The key to his behavior was in Mr. Z's eyes, which had a glazed quality to them, as if he were witnessing a disaster *in the present moment*.

The "termination" of his career was a kind of suicide to Mr. Z. The meaning of this current event was signified by the association to his earlier trauma and to the feeling that he was now witnessing something disastrous. Interestingly, his decompensation turned his wife into the mother he had lost. Although Mr. Z was entirely unaware of the repressed memory at the time of his dramatic reenactment, or of its tie to the present, he was helped to piece together the missing links to his past so that he could finally integrate them, mourn them and move beyond them.

Repetition and enactment are often ways we show that we remember (Freud, 1914). The greater the resistance, the greater is the tendency to act out rather than to remember. In addition, the more affect is attached to the memory, the greater the likelihood of its being acted out rather than remembered. This is because the more intense affect impairs the required distance needed for representational memory. Loewald (1976) described this dynamic well when he wrote: "[T]he patient, instead of *having* his past, *is* his past; he does not distinguish himself as rememberer from the content of his memory" (p. 165, emphasis in original).

The fate of traumatic memories, the nature of childhood memories and the role of repressed or dissociated memory in psychopathology continue to inform contemporary Freudian theory and practice.

Psychic conflict and compromise formation

Freud's pioneering discovery (Breuer and Freud, 1893–95) that hysterical symptoms resulted from a conflict between sexual wishes and fantasies that are incompatible with the patient's self-image or societal expectations proved to be a very protean concept, which he applied in rapid succession to a variety of psychic phenomena, such as dreams (Freud, 1900a, 1900b), parapraxes (1901) and wit (1905). All these overt phenomena represent a manifest expression of underlying, unconscious and contradictory wishes and defenses.

Freud originally viewed repression as the main or only defense employed in situations of conflict but subsequent contributors, such as Anna Freud (1937), described an assortment of mechanisms – repression, denial, undoing, reaction formation, altruism, identification with the aggressor, turning against the self, to name a few – that may be used to avoid experiencing painful emotional states.

As noted in our introduction, Freud's model of psychic conflict has been further refined by a group of contemporary Freudians (Sandor Abend, Jacob Arlow and Charles Brenner, among others) into what is now known as modern conflict theory. The tripartite division into separate agencies, each charged with specialized functions, is no longer seen as a viable account of how the mind works by some (Brenner, 1979, 2002), but not all (Boesky, 1994), conflict theorists. Brenner (1979, 2002) has argued that there are no separate parts of the mind devoted solely to rational or irrational thought, no separate mechanisms dedicated solely to defense. What has been retained from Freud's structural model are the following components of conflict and compromise formation.

- *Drive derivatives*. Drives are not experienced or expressed in pure form but appear in consciousness as derivatives of these hypothetical entities. As used in Freudian theory, drive derivatives are essentially synonymous with wishes for gratification to be fulfilled by and through an object. Many Freudians consider sexual/libidinal and aggressive drives as primary, though other kinds of motivating influences have been recognized, such as wishes for merger or preservation of self-esteem and self-cohesion. Contemporary Freudians do not limit all motivation to a dual drive theory (Pine, 1989).
- *Danger situations*. Central to all models of conflict is the idea that the fulfillment of certain wishes may, at least in fantasy, lead to calamitous outcomes. Freud

(1923) identified four such situations: fear of loss of the object, fear of loss of the object's love, fear of castration and fear of superego condemnation. Some Freudian analysts (Hurvich, 1989) have added other calamities, such as fear of annihilation, to this list.

- *Dysphoric affect*: Whereas a conscious fear may be aroused by real external danger and prompt behavior to ward off the danger (such as fight or flight), unconscious anxiety also serves as a signal of the presence of internal danger. Freud (1926) considered anxiety as the sole alarm that sets in motion self-protective action. Later theory has differentiated between the fear that a catastrophe is about to happen in the future (anxiety) and the perception that the calamity has already occurred (depression) (Brenner, 1979). Since the psyche is geared to ward off pain and seek pleasure, either form of dysphoric affect, anxiety or depression, can serve a signal function.
- *Defense*: The intrapsychic sounding of an alarm triggers mechanisms of defense to ward off dysphoric affect. Defense mechanisms are enlisted to avoid unpleasurable affective states, whether adaptively or maladaptively. Some defenses (e.g., sublimation, humor) may be regarded as mature (Vaillant, 1992) while others (e.g., splitting, projective identification, denial) are considered developmentally more primitive. Modern conflict theory does not posit a finite set of mechanisms of defense but, rather, views any psychic process that can be employed for the purpose of warding off dysphoric affect to be a defense. The primary function of defense is protection against a range of unpleasurable affect states, including anxiety and depression. Some contemporary Freudians also consider emptiness, shame, low self-esteem, self-fragmentation, threats to one's self-image and loss of identity to be motives for defense.
- *Compromise formation*: The resultant overt behavior and conscious experience deriving from this interplay of conflicting unconscious mental processes are considered a compromise formation. All the psychic phenomena that are observable in the clinical situation – symptoms, transference reactions, resistances, enactments, free associations – may be considered compromise formations.

Modern conflict theory has proved to be a versatile model for clinical use. Viewing the analysand's material as a series of compromise formations calls the analyst's attention to the complex makeup and "multiple functions" (Waelder, 1936) of any psychic act. A simple example might be a patient's silence. Should this be considered a defense, an expression of hostility, a means of coercing the analyst to speak and thereby gratify the patient's wish to be cared for, or a psychic retreat or a moment of adaptive self-reflection, a passive rebellion or an active assault? Modern conflict theory enjoins the analyst to consider all the above possible functions as underlying the overt behavior demonstrated by the patient. It would therefore be a technical error to view the patient's silence solely as a defense or resistance, as that is only one component of the conflict and compromise formation.

18 Danielle Knafo and Seymour Moscovitz

Faced with this complexity, technical precepts help the analyst choose a place to start, such as beginning with the defense before interpreting the impulse or addressing surface phenomena before interpreting underlying depths (Fenichel, 1941). Modern conflict theory suggests that interpretations addressing defensive, adaptive and affective components of a compromise formation may be particularly helpful. For example, an analyst might say: "I wonder if you are worried [defensive component] what might happen [adaptive component] if you allowed yourself to speak your mind [impulse/affective component] right now?" Freudian technical precepts urge analysts to be alert to the multiple possibilities that overt behavior serves and not be content to identify only one function it may serve.

A clinical example illustrating the utility of conflict and compromise formation theory has been discussed by the authors (Knafo & Moscovitz, 2006) in a volume on anger-related disorders (Feindler, 2006). The case involves a 48-year-old white male named Anthony, who expressed periodic upsurges of unpredictable and intense anger that led to serious social consequences, such as his wife's wishing to divorce him. The precipitating event leading to the referral occurred while Anthony was coaching his daughter's softball team and berated the players at one practice for their lack of competitive drive. His tirade culminated in his hurling bats and other gear at the backstop, leaving the girls in tears and other parents shocked by this display of explosive anger.

Viewed as a compromise formation, Anthony's behavioral and emotional outburst represents many conflicting components in his psychology. Central to Anthony's background was an experience of having been sexually abused as an adolescent, an experience he recalled with much humiliation and rage. The failure of his daughter's team to play competitively seemed to have aroused unconscious fears of being humiliated once again. Anthony's berating a team of girls for their lack of competitive drive apparently reflected a defensive need to externalize this undesirable part of himself and to coerce change in the objects of his projection to ward off a sense of castrated/feminized humiliation (dysphoric affect).

What is central to this illustration is that the focus on the patient's behavior as a compromise formation leads to uncovering an array of conflicting factors underlying the symptom. Modern conflict theory does not seek the elimination or resolution of conflict but, rather, a more adaptive compromise formation, one that results in less misery and greater opportunity for fulfillment in reality of one's needs, wishes, ambitions and ideals.

Internalization and relations with others

One persisting confusion about Freudian psychoanalysis concerns the role of relations with others in psychic development. In their classic work, Jay Greenberg and Stephen Mitchell (1983) present a dichotomous choice between what they label "drive/structure" and "relational/structure" models. In both theories, "structure" refers to the relatively enduring consistencies in motivation, personal identity and psychic processes that have "a slow rate of change" (Rapaport & Gill, 1959, p. 157).

The former model, attributed to Freud and subsequent Freudian theorists, views psychic structure as developing in response to efforts to gratify instinctual drives (libido and aggression), as distinct from alternative models (e.g., those of Harry Stack Sullivan or Ronald Fairbairn) that view structure as evolving from the individual's relations with other people (Greenberg & Mitchell, 1983). Greenberg and Mitchell then endeavor to show the theoretical entanglements of attempting to mix models, ultimately favoring the relational/structure model as the richer explanatory paradigm. Contemporary Freudian psychoanalysts have rejected this dichotomy, with its implication of a relative neglect or diminution in the importance of relations with others, insisting that both drives *and* relations are needed to account for human development, motivation, psychopathology and mental functioning in general.

Although beyond the scope of this chapter, an object relations theory was evident in Freud's work (Freud 1917, 1920). In "Mourning and melancholia," written in 1917, Freud brought our attention to the interpersonal nature of depression and the close relationship that exists between the maintenance of self-esteem and a successful relationship. The "lost" object is retained in the form of an internalization: the ego is the "precipitate of abandoned object cathexes," containing the history of its "object choices" (Freud, 1923, p. 28) and forming the first "identifications" of the ego. The superego, likewise, was described as the "heir to the Oedipus complex," preserving "the character given to it by its derivation from the father-complex – namely, the capacity to stand apart from the ego and to master it" (Freud, 1923, p. 47). By processes of internalization, variously described by Freud as introjection or identification, relations with others form the basic building blocks of psychic structure.

Following Freud's death, interest in early object relations and the pre-Oedipal period deepened, exploring the dyadic relationship of mother and child (e.g., Mahler, Pine & Bergman, 1975; Jacobson, 1964). These investigations referred to a period of development when the boundaries of self and other have not yet been differentiated. Although developmental research (Stern, 1985; Beebe & Lachman, 2002) has shown self–other differentiation at birth, Pine (1984, 1992) has countered that there are nonetheless "moments" of merger that are developmentally significant, even if the infant is alert and attentive at other times.

Systematic efforts have been made by ego psychologists in the modern era (e.g., Schafer, 1968) to explicate the various processes and outcomes by which the external world of objects is taken in (via incorporation, introjection or identification) and used to develop schemas of self and others in interaction. These internalized object relations – comprising an image of the self, object and the affective quality of the interaction – ultimately become the constituents of the developed ego and superego (Kernberg, 1966).

This formulation has been useful in describing the extreme polarizations of behavior observed in borderline and psychotic patients, as the person alternates, sometimes rapidly, in relating to others as all-good or all-bad. Defense mechanisms such as splitting and projective identification, originally described within the

Kleinian literature, have made their way into contemporary Freudian discourse, though some Freudians (e.g., Abend, Porder & Willick, 1988; Porder, 1987) have objected to the importation and argue that the observed phenomena could be explained by the more familiar notion of identification with the aggressor.

Clinical experiences with more disturbed patients have increasingly challenged the one-person, intrapsychic model and called into play the subjectivity of the analyst, not just in occasional moments of interference by countertransference but, rather, as a regular if not ubiquitous occurrence. Owen Renik (1993) argues that the subjectivity of the analyst is an "irreducible" and unavoidable aspect of the analytic situation. "Every aspect of an analyst's clinical activity," Renik maintains, "is determined in part by his or her personal psychology" (p. 553).

These criticisms from within and without Freudian psychoanalysis have heralded a shift from one- to two-person models in contemporary theory.

Intersubjectivity: one- and two-person psychologies in a Freudian model

Freud's account of the unconscious communication between patient and analyst was a prologue to contemporary discussions of intersubjectivity. Freud (1912) advised the analyst to listen to the patient by attuning his or her unconscious to that of the patient. This form of attunement – *evenly hovering attention* – represents an early account of a realm of communication and interaction that may be considered "interpsychic."

These modes of relatedness are an essential aspect of therapeutic action. Hans Loewald (1970) noted the "re-externalization of internal relationships and conflicts" during the course of analysis (p. 53). The re-externalization Loewald is referring to is a form of *enactment* that involves both patient and analyst attuned at an unconscious level to each other. A contemporary analyst, Stefano Bolognini (2016), has also written of an "interpsychic" level of relatedness and communication, describing this as a transitional space that occurs in moments of therapeutic regression.

An example of this form of relatedness has been described by Gil Katz (1998) in his treatment of a young man, Jimmy, who had suffered significant object loss. For long periods Jimmy did not show up for his sessions, contact his therapist or pay his bills, though he later revealed that on some of those occasions he had remained in his car, parked across from the analyst's office, just to see if the light remained on. Katz tells us of the resonance of the themes of loss and waiting in his own life, which contributed to his engagement and forbearance in this prolonged enactment of a scenario of damage and reparation. The relatedness existing between patient and analyst, not mediated by words, illustrates the realm of interpsychic communication.

The therapeutic potential of such enactments ultimately resides in, and returns to, the patient's self-understanding, which is facilitated and made vivid by its dramatization and actualization in the matrix of transference/countertransference actions. The "co-creation" of transferential dramas is a transitory phenomenon, a merging of the psychologies of analyst and patient, but therapeutic action must ultimately foster the *patient's* emotional growth. Intersubjectivity as an ontological position is also questionable from a Freudian perspective, as it suggests that mind itself is co-created (Stolorow & Atwood, 1992). As much as the specific interaction with a patient may be influenced by subjective aspects of the analyst's personality, the adult patient is seen as having a pre-formed personality independent of others, although requiring interaction with others in order to emerge.

Clinical concepts

In what follows, we will explore the contemporary Freudian position on core technical precepts.

Free association, even hovering attention and reverie

When a patient speaks to the analyst in an atmosphere of safety and trust about "whatever comes to mind," he or she is expressing thought and meaning that are largely woven together and determined unconsciously. Such content, though not necessarily evident in the text itself, and against which the patient may be defended, is the hidden narrative nurturing the dialogue, keeping it alive and moving it forward.

Freud's discovery of the free association method heralded the advent of psychoanalysis as a distinctive treatment modality. Rather than attempting to induce the patient to give up symptoms (as in the hypnotic method) or recover repressed memories (as in the cathartic method), the psychoanalyst instructs the patient to observe his or her train of thoughts and candidly report them without censorship. Free association promised to liberate the patient from the constraints of interpersonal influence and to obviate the analyst's need to overcome the patient's resistance through suggestion. The analysand who follows this "fundamental rule" of free association would learn to traverse the complex and intertwined pathways of the trivial, the everyday and the forbidden. Relieved of the social responsibility of maintaining coherent, polite and sequential communication, the analysand would be free to describe the stream of passing thoughts, sensations, affects, fantasies and memories, from which the analyst could discern the patient's latent conflicts, patterns of thought, unacknowledged wishes and covert defenses.

In exchange for the analysand's candor, the analyst offers a confidential setting and listens receptively and without judgment, with an "evenly suspended attention" (Freud, 1912, p. 111) rather than a focused or strained effort to concentrate on selected content. The analyst's special kind of listening puts consciousness in brackets while heightening unconscious receptivity to the more secluded, disguised or inaccessible dimension of the patient's and the analyst's communications. This type of listening attends to what has remained silent, the voice of the other that has been denied, rendered quiet or disguised in the language of the body, affect, symbol or action. It is listening that allows the hidden to emerge, what Theodor Reik (1965) called "listening with the third ear" or "perceiving what has not yet been said" (p. 17). Such listening establishes the basis of connectivity, not only among the disparate thoughts of the analysand but also between the analytic couple.

The contemporary Freudian analyst makes extensive use of Freud's idea of unconscious communication between patient and analyst, in which the analyst is attuned to the patient's unconscious fantasy life (Freud, 1912). But free association is no longer the task assigned only to the patient. Like Thomas Ogden (1994), who has written about the analyst's reverie states as corollaries to the patient's free associations, many contemporary Freudians (Paul Gray may be a notable exception) tap into their reverie states for guidance about what is occurring in the treatment. This bidirectional connectivity allows transmission and reception, while it encourages continued and deepening exploration. The analyst is often *right there* with the patient in a state of openness and unknowing, or "affective interpenetration" (Ellman, 2010), allowing links to form on their own without yet applying the shaping force of analysis. Both analyst and analysand are like the artist who, in the act of creation, *always stands on the threshold of the unknown*. Working associatively, and teaching the patient to do so, is a major way the analyst invites creativity into the sessions (Knafo, 2012).

Dream interpretation

The clinical use of dreams is yet another key Freudian technical precept that has evolved in its application. Once considered "the royal road to a knowledge of the unconscious activities of the mind" (Freud, 1900b, p. 608), dreams are viewed by some contemporary Freudian analysts (e.g., Brenner) as but one pathway to exploring psychic conflict along with many others. Other Freudian analysts (e.g., Gray) even consider the report of a dream as a resistance if it serves to move attention away from the emergence of drive derivatives. Despite these considerations, many continue to believe that dreams deserve a unique place in the analytic process and offer perhaps the most direct communication of unconscious fantasy. An analysis without report of the analysand's dream life would appear to be a very sterile one.

Like graphic artworks, dreams utilize an economy of visual expression to articulate one's inner life. Dreams occur prior to the intervention of conscious thought and frequently present themselves as riddles to consciousness. Often, the more incoherent dreams appear, the more their revelatory value, for the condensation of their symbolism contains a plethora of meaning. The creative aspect of working with dreams involves the art of interpretation, which includes asking the questions that will lead the analytic dyad deeper into the dream's hidden meanings.

When working with dreams one accesses an intimate and mysterious language, often uncovering repressed memories, hidden fears, gnawing anxiety and destructive assumptions as well as unseen solutions. The dream is less governed by theory, censorship or convention than is conscious thought. But it is more than a site of repressed content. It unites layers of memory, imagination and desire, and its architecture encrypts crucial elements of our psychic life.

Dreams, like associations and transference, are now thought to be bidirectional in nature. They express unconscious thoughts as well as attempts to modify and understand them. When dreams engage the analysis – and, among other things, dreams reported while in analysis are doing just that (Mancia, 2004) – analytic work gains the power to counteract or undo repression, to expand the limitations of conscious minds and to unite in a profound and multidimensional encounter with the other.

Resistance: the clinical manifestation defense

Another pillar of classical technique is the analysis of resistance. The method of free association described above inevitably encounters opposition by the analysand. Clinically, defense mechanisms are manifested in a variety of ways, such as lateness, silence, missed sessions, failure to pay the fee or lack of progress (Greenson, 1967).

Analysis of resistance has remained the focal point of the close process monitoring advocated by Gray (1994) and Busch (1995, 2013), but it has waned in contemporary practice, as the term has pejorative connotations and ignores the adaptive value of many seeming resistances (Schafer, 1973). There are many reasons why patients may oppose the analyst's technical preferences or thwart therapeutic change. Some, such as Ogden (1989), consider all patients to be naturally resistant to analysis; he advises analysts to be attuned to a patient's "cautionary tales" regarding the reasons why an analysis is likely to fail. In a two-person model, moreover, resistance is viewed as a joint collusion by patient and analyst to prevent disruption of the dyad (LaFarge, 2012).

The transference/countertransference matrix

Along with unconscious fantasy and free association, transference is another foundational concept in the Freudian lexicon. Its meaning within the Freudian literature has focused on two aspects: *transference as a repetition* of earlier relationships transposed onto figures in the present, especially the analyst; and *transference as a distortion* of present-day reality resulting from this superimposition, much as unconscious fantasy may distort conscious perception and experience (Greenson, 1967).

In other usages of the term, especially among relational analysts (Bass, 2001), the patient's experience of the analyst is but one part of an interwoven "matrix" or "field" without any implication that this mode of cognition either repeats the past or distorts the present. Attributions the patient makes are viewed as plausible alternatives to the analyst's perspective (Gill, 1984; Hoffman, 1983), so that the analyst cannot assume a privileged place as the arbiter of reality. As Eagle (in press) has pointed out, transference merely as a way of organizing experience obviates the need for the term "transference" and, more importantly, fails to account for how past experiences shape or influence the patient's perceptual-cognitive activity.

While contemporary Freudians acknowledge that the analyst is neither a completely blank slate nor an empty container, the role of past object relations in imbuing the patient's schemas of present-day relationships remains a critical concept.

Just as the patient's free associations reveal multiple perspectives and meanings, so do transference reactions express meaning in action within the context of the therapeutic relationship. Katz (1998) has referred to these two aspects of treatment as the "verbal dimension" and the "enactive dimension." The patient unconsciously enacts and repeats (early) relational patterns within the therapeutic context, and the analyst, if truly engaged in the process, functions as a "co-actor on the analytic stage" (Loewald, 1960), unwittingly participating in the process and inevitably activating his or her own (counter)transferences. Because the transference relationship is bidirectional and co-created, it functions as a malleable context into which layers of identifications, projections, enactments and symbolizations can come to light and potentially be explored and worked through.

Transference repetition or enactment is therapeutically most useful when the meaning and significance of the patient's experience are rendered in words, a process Freud (1915) originally referred to as the joining of "thing representation" and "word representation." Contemporary Freudians also use the analyst's unwitting fulfillment of the patient's role expectations, what Joseph Sandler (1976) has referred to as "role responsiveness." With the linking of the enacted dimension and verbal dimension (Katz, 1998), experiential insight may emerge, leading to therapeutic change. The analyst may not initially realize he or she has actualized a pattern of object relations from the patient's past, as no one can know the extent of his or her own transference as it applies to a specific individual. Because transference/countertransference involves the relationship of two unconscious minds, it is the most unknown and exciting aspect of the work.

The transference is creatively handled by allowing the relationship to flow and change, by guiding, through free and spontaneous dialogue, the growing insight of the patient and by becoming aware of the multiple transference dimensions arising in oneself. This process requires that the analyst engage multiple meanings while taking on multiple identities – a highly fluid process fraught with potential difficulty and requiring a loosening of boundaries between the self and the other, between what is inside and what is outside.

The concept of a transference neurosis – an unfolding of a pre-patterned set of reactions to the analyst – has waned in its significance. Contemporary Freudian analysts have expanded this model within a two-person framework to include ideas such as "transitional space" (Winnicott, 1971), "analytic third" (Ogden, 1994), "interpsychic" communication (Loewald, 1970; Bolognini, 2016) and "affective interpenetration" (Ellman, 2010) to refer to an "analytic space" beyond the boundaries of either the patient's or analyst's private experience.

Significant changes have been made to the understanding and use of the analyst's *countertransference*. Originally considered a blind spot to be overcome, today countertransference is regarded as a major avenue affording access to the patient's

Contemporary Freudian approaches **25**

unconscious as well as one's own. Understanding one's own subjectivity, potential for enactment, role responsiveness and projective identification all highlight this new awareness (Gabbard, 1999).

Contemporary Freudian analysts at times disclose their countertransference feelings in order to advance the treatment (Jacobs, 2013). Christopher Bollas (1987) states, "I establish my subjectivity as a useful and consistent source of material in the psychoanalytic situation" (p. 210).

The analytic frame

A psychoanalytic process is set in motion by the parameters that define the situation, such as the frequency of sessions, the position of the patient vis-à-vis the analyst (recumbent or face to face) and the agreed-upon tasks and roles of patient and analyst (free association, fundamental rule). Ever mindful of potential exploitation or abuse of the patient in a vulnerable situation, Freud also established constraints on the analyst's behavior and emotional position vis-à-vis the patient. These classical injunctions – neutrality, anonymity and abstinence – have been the source of much controversy and critique. They have also underscored the importance of self-care and privacy – all present to protect both analyst and analysand from the temptations, pitfalls and potential abuses of the intense relationship that develops. Ultimately, these guidelines are in the service of fostering the analysis of the transference (Knafo, 2013).

Rigid adherence to these technical parameters has led to analytic situations that were recognized as authoritarian and ritualistic by Freudians long before Relational critiques of these principles emerged (e.g., Greenson, 1965, 1967). No doubt many analysts practiced in a more humane and warm manner (Stone, 1954) despite these precepts, which were originally intended to avoid manipulating the patient in a state of heightened suggestibility.

From a contemporary Freudian viewpoint, these principles have been modified but not entirely discarded, and they need to be applied with flexibility and attention to the patient's developmental needs.

Technical tools of the Freudian analyst

Accounts of analytic practice that stress the "irreducible subjectivity" of the analyst (Renik, 1993) minimize the role of deliberate and conscious technique. While the contemporary Freudian recognizes that the analyst is moved by forces that are personally unconscious and not deliberate or technical, there is nonetheless a place for the skillful, well-timed, empathic and accurate use of clarification, confrontation and interpretation. To be effective, the analyst's technique must occur within the context of a relationship that is experienced as helpful and humane.

Interpretation in contemporary discourse is also given a broader meaning than simply making the unconscious conscious. The analyst's ability to formulate the patient's inchoate experience in words provides a function similar to the mother's ability to understand and respond empathically to the infant's nonverbal cues (Loewald, 1960).

Therapeutic action

The therapeutic action of psychoanalysis is a topic that has become increasingly popular since Loewald's groundbreaking paper in 1960, which articulated a developmental model of analytic change and mutative factors (Moscovitz, 2014). In overly simplified terms, therapeutic action has been seen either as deriving from interpretation, leading to insight, or as interaction, creating a corrective emotional experience. A contemporary Freudian view attempts to integrate both these positions, which need to be intertwined to achieve optimal results. As noted above, the therapeutic action of psychoanalysis often entails an unplanned repetition in action of the patient's unconscious conflicts, which ultimately must be verbalized to allow for a higher-order integration.

The widening scope of psychoanalysis

A driving force in the modification of Freudian psychoanalysis has been the expansion of indications for psychoanalytic psychotherapy as well as psychoanalysis proper. While some distinction is maintained between these two modalities, they are now viewed as more on a continuum, with greater or lesser focus on transference, reliance on interpretation as the main technical tool, and maintenance of the position of neutrality (Kernberg, 1999).

The concept of analyzability (Tyson & Sandler, 1971) – a diagnostic assessment of the patient's personality structure and amenability to unmodified psychoanalytic procedures – has become a less prominent component in selecting patients for analysis. The concept implies that the success of the analysis depends largely, if not solely, on the patient's internal character structure rather than on the particular mesh between a given patient and analyst. Whereas personality structure remains an important consideration, the contemporary Freudian analyst attempts to fit the treatment to the patient's needs. Today, psychoanalytic treatment – therapy or analysis – has been expanded to include patients with severe personality disorders (Kernberg, 1984) and psychotic disorders (Bollas, 2015; Knafo, 2016).

Limitations and weaknesses of the contemporary Freudian perspective

A weakness that remains in contemporary Freudian psychoanalysis is the acultural assumption of the universality of its discoveries. Postmodern critiques object to the positing of universal or absolute truth and advocate an epistemology that is perspectival, fluid and changing (Aron, 1996). Moreover, the particular historical period in which a theory is developed and the embedded assumptions it might

Contemporary Freudian approaches **27**

contain need to be acknowledged (Aron & Starr, 2012; Ellman, 2010). For example, ego autonomy as the endpoint of development represents a particular Western value system. This hidden assumption points to the lack of integration of a cultural perspective within Freudian psychoanalysis (Cushman 1996).

To take one example, a candidate from an Asian country reported in supervision that her patient, also from Asia, frequently apologized for "burdening" the analyst with her problems. The candidate reported that she had repeatedly been told by a previous supervisor that she was not sufficiently confrontational, a criticism she accepted, even though her patient was showing deference toward an individual whom she considered to be an authority figure, an attitude adopted in parallel process by the candidate. Other minority candidates have expressed concern that specific actions may be interpreted through a lens that ignores their unique perspective and cultural background, customs and mores (Akhtar 2005; Roland, 1996).

Endnote

To conclude this chapter on contemporary Freudian approaches, we return to Greenberg and Mitchell's (1983) dichotomy of drive/structure and relational/structure models. In contrast to either/or propositions, the contemporary Freudian is inclined toward a "both/and" point of view that incorporates conflict and deficit, insight and relationship, need and wish, past and present, conscious and unconscious, discovered and created, therapy and analysis, the intrapsychic and the interpersonal.

From a comparative psychoanalytic perspective, this insistence on the inclusion of polarities may mean that it is harder to draw bright red lines between contemporary Freudian and non-Freudian orientations. There may even be sharper distinctions between contemporary Freudian and classical or traditional ego-psychological perspectives. This chapter has attempted to make the delineations as clear as possible for heuristic purposes, even though in clinical practice these lines of demarcation are often blurred. What is clear is that Freud's thought lives on, because he created a profound and useful therapeutic method that continues to evolve.

Note

1 Reprinted as an epigraph by permission of the author and of Taylor & Francis, LLC.

References

Abend, S., Porder, M. S., and Willick, M. (1988). A response. *Psychoanalytic Inquiry*, 8(3): 438–455.

Akhtar, S. (Ed.) (2005). *Freud along the Ganges: Psychoanalytic Reflections on the People and Culture of India*. New York: Other Press.

Alexander, F. (1950). *Psychosomatic Medicine: Its Principles and Applications*. New York: W. W. Norton.

Arlow, J. A. (1969). Unconscious fantasy and disturbances of conscious experience. *Psychoanalytic Quarterly*, 38(1): 1–27.

Aron, L. (1996). *A Meeting of Minds: Mutuality in Psychoanalysis*. Hillsdale, NJ: Analytic Press.

Aron, L., & Starr, K. (2012). *A Psychotherapy for the People: Toward a Progressive Psychoanalysis*. New York: Routledge.

Barden, N. (2015). Disrupting Oedipus: The legacy of the Sphinx. In A. Lemma & P. E. Lynch (Eds.), *Sexualities: Contemporary Psychoanalytic Perspectives*, pp. 81–100. London: Routledge.

Bass, A. (2001). It takes one to know one; or, Whose unconscious is it anyway? *Psychoanalytic Dialogues*, 11(5): 683–702.

Beebe, B., & Lachmann, F. M. (2002). *Infant Research and Adult Treatment: Co-Constructing Interactions*. Hillsdale, NJ: Analytic Press.

Boesky, D. (1994). Dialogue on the Brenner paper between Charles Brenner, M.D., and Dale Boesky, M.D. *Journal of Clinical Psychoanalysis*, 3(4): 509–522.

Bollas, C. (1987). *The Shadow of the Object: Psychoanalysis of the Unthought Known*. London: Free Association Books.

Bollas, C. (2009). *The Evocative Object World*. London: Routledge.

Bollas, C. (2015). *When the Sun Bursts: The Enigma of Schizophrenia*. New Haven, CT: Yale University Press.

Bolognini, S. (2016). The interpsychic dimension in the psychoanalytic interpretation. *Psychoanalytic Inquiry*, 36(1): 102–111.

Brenner, C. (1979). The components of psychic conflict and its consequences in mental life. *Psychoanalytic Quarterly*, 48(4): 547–567.

Brenner, C. (2002). Conflict, compromise formation, and structural theory. *Psychoanalytic Quarterly*, 71(3): 397–417.

Breuer, J., & Freud, S. (1893–95 [1955]). Studies on hysteria. In J. Strachey (Ed. & Trans.), *The Standard Edition of the Complete Psychological Works of Sigmund Freud*, Vol. II, pp. 1–306. London: Hogarth Press.

Busch, F. (1995). *The Ego at the Center of Clinical Technique*. Hillsdale, NJ: Jason Aronson.

Busch, F. (2013). *Creating a Psychoanalytic Mind: A Psychoanalytic Method and Theory*. Hove, UK: Routledge.

Chodorow, N. J. (2004). The American independent tradition. *Psychoanalytic Dialogues*, 14(2): 207–232.

Cushman, P. (1996). *Constructing the Self, Constructing America: A Cultural History of Psychotherapy*. Boston: Da Capo Press.

Davids, A. (1972). Sigmund Freud is dead. *Contemporary Psychology*, 17(12): 652–655.

Druck, A. B. (2011). Modern structural theory. In A. B. Druck, C. Ellman, N. Freedman and A. Thaler (Eds.), *A New Freudian Synthesis: Clinical Process in the Next Generation*, pp. 25–50. London: Karnac Books.

Eagle, M. N. (in press). *Core Concepts in Classical Psychoanalytic Theory: Evidence and Critique*. London: Routledge.

Ellman, S. J. (2010). *When Theories Touch: A Historical and Theoretical Integration of Psychoanalytic Thought*. London: Karnac Books.

Fast, I. (1984). *Gender Identity: A Differentiation Model*. Hillsdale, NJ: Analytic Press.

Feindler, E. L. (Ed.) (2006). *Anger-Related Disorders: A Practitioner's Guide to Comparative Treatments*. New York: Springer.

Fenichel, O. (1941). *Problems of Psychoanalytic Technique* (D. Brunswick, Trans.). Oxford: Psychoanalytic Quarterly.

Freud, A. (1937 [1966]). *The Ego and the Mechanisms of Defense*. New York: International Universities Press.

Freud, S. (1900a [1953]). The interpretation of dreams (first part). In J. Strachey (Ed. & Trans.), *The Standard Edition of the Complete Psychological Works of Sigmund Freud*, Vol. IV, pp. 1–338. London: Hogarth Press.

Freud, S. (1900b [1953]). The interpretation of dreams (second part). In J. Strachey (Ed. & Trans.), *The Standard Edition of the Complete Psychological Works of Sigmund Freud*, Vol. V, pp. 339–622. London: Hogarth Press.

Freud, S. (1901 [1960]). The psychopathology of everyday life. In J. Strachey (Ed. & Trans.), *The Standard Edition of the Complete Psychological Works of Sigmund Freud*, Vol. VI, pp. 1–280. London: Hogarth Press.

Freud, S. (1905 [1953]). Three essays on the theory of sexuality. In J. Strachey (Ed. & Trans.), *The Standard Edition of the Complete Psychological Works of Sigmund Freud*, Vol. VII, pp. 135–243. London: Hogarth Press.

Freud, S. (1908 [1960]). Creative writers and day-dreaming. In J. Strachey (Ed. & Trans.), *The Standard Edition of the Complete Psychological Works of Sigmund Freud*, Vol. IX, pp. 141–153. London: Hogarth Press.

Freud, S. (1912 [1958]). Recommendation to physicians practising psycho-analysis. In J. Strachey (Ed. & Trans.), *The Standard Edition of the Complete Psychological Works of Sigmund Freud*, Vol. XII, pp. 109–120. London: Hogarth Press.

Freud, S. (1914 [1958]). Remembering, repeating and working-through (further recommendations on the technique of psycho-analysis II). In J. Strachey (Ed. & Trans.), *The Standard Edition of the Complete Psychological Works of Sigmund Freud*, Vol. XII, pp. 145–156. London: Hogarth Press.

Freud, S. (1915 [1957]). The unconscious. In J. Strachey (Ed. & Trans.), *The Standard Edition of the Complete Psychological Works of Sigmund Freud*, Vol. XIV, pp. 166–215. London: Hogarth Press.

Freud, S. (1917 [1957]). Mourning and melancholia. In J. Strachey (Ed. & Trans.), *The Standard Edition of the Complete Psychological Works of Sigmund Freud*, Vol. XIV, pp. 243–258. London: Hogarth Press.

Freud, S. (1920 [1955]). Beyond the pleasure principle. In J. Strachey (Ed. & Trans.), *The Standard Edition of the Complete Psychological Works of Sigmund Freud*, Vol. XVIII, pp. 7–64. London: Hogarth Press.

Freud, S. (1923 [1961]). The ego and the id. In J. Strachey (Ed. & Trans.), *The Standard Edition of the Complete Psychological Works of Sigmund Freud*, Vol. XIX, pp. 12–66. London: Hogarth Press.

Freud, S. (1926 [1959]). Inhibitions, symptoms and anxiety. In J. Strachey (Ed. & Trans.), *The Standard Edition of the Complete Psychological Works of Sigmund Freud*, Vol. XX, pp. 87–172. London: Hogarth Press.

Freud, S. (1927 [1961]). Fetishism. In J. Strachey (Ed. & Trans.), *The Standard Edition of the Complete Psychological Works of Sigmund Freud*, Vol. XXI, pp. 152–157. London: Hogarth Press.

Gabbard, G. O. (Ed.) (1999). *Countertransference Issues in Psychiatric Treatment*. Washington, DC: American Psychiatric Press.

Gill, M. M. (1984). Psychoanalysis and psychotherapy: A revision. *International Review of Psycho-Analysis*, 11: 161–179.

Gray, P. 1994. *The Ego and Analysis of Defense*. Hillsdale, NJ: Jason Aronson.

Green, A. 1995. Has sexuality anything to do with psychoanalysis? *International Journal of Psychoanalysis*, 76(5): 871–883.

Greenberg, J. R., & Mitchell, S. A. (1983). *Object Relations in Psychoanalytic Theory*. Cambridge, MA: Harvard University Press.

Greenson, R. R. (1965). The working alliance and the transference neurosis. *Psychoanalytic Quarterly*, 34(1): 155–181.

Greenson, R. R. (1967) *The Technique and Practice of Psychoanalysis*, Vol. I. New York: International Universities Press.

Hartmann, H. (1939). *Ego Psychology and the Problem of Adaptation*. New York: International Universities Press.

Hoffman, I. Z. (1983). The patient as interpreter of the analyst's experience. *Contemporary Psychoanalysis*, 19(3): 389–422.

Horgan, J. (1996). Why Freud isn't dead. *Scientific American*, 275(6): 106–111.

Hurvich, M. S. (1989). Traumatic moment, basic dangers and annihilation anxiety. *Psychoanalytic Psychology*, 6(3): 309–323.

Jacobs, T. (2013). *The Possible Profession: The Analytic Process of Change*. New York: Routledge.

Jacobson, E. (1964). *The Self and the Object World*. New York: Basic Books.

Katz, G. A. (1998). Where the action is: The enacted dimension of analytic process. *Journal of the American Psychoanalytic Association*, 46(4): 1129–1167.

Kernberg, O. F. (1966). Structural derivatives of object relations. *International Journal of Psychoanalysis*, 47(2): 236–253.

Kernberg, O. F. (1984). *Severe Personality Disorders: Psychotherapeutic Strategies*. New Haven, CT: Yale University Press.

Kernberg, O. F. (1996). Thirty methods to destroy the creativity of psychoanalytic candidates. *International Journal of Psychoanalysis*, 77(5): 1031–1040.

Kernberg, O. F. (1999). Psychoanalysis, psychoanalytic psychotherapy and supportive psychotherapy. *International Journal of Psychoanalysis*, 80(6): 1075–1091.

Knafo, D. (2009). Freud's memory erased. *Psychoanalytic Psychology*, 26(2): 171–190.

Knafo, D. (2012). Dancing with the unconscious: The art of psychoanalysis. *Psychoanalytic Inquiry*, 32(3): 275–291.

Knafo, D. (2013). Alone together: Solitude and relatedness in the creative process. In A. K. Richards, L. Spira & A. Lynch (Eds.), *Encounters with Loneliness: Only the Lonely*, 2nd Edn., pp. 17–36. New York: International Psychoanalytic Books.

Knafo, D. (2016). Going blind to see: The psychoanalytic treatment of trauma, regression and psychosis. *American Journal of Psychotherapy*, 70(1): 79–100.

Knafo, D., & Feiner, K. (2006a). *Unconscious Fantasies and the Relational World*. Hillsdale, NJ: Analytic Press.

Knafo, D., & Feiner, K. (2006b). Castration fantasies, sexual difference, and mind–body matters. In *Unconscious Fantasies and the Relational World*, pp. 125–142. Hillsdale, NJ: Analytic Press.

Knafo, D., & Moscovitz, S. (2006). Psychoanalytic treatment of anger and aggression. In E. L. Feindler (Ed.), *Anger-Related Disorders: A Practitioner's Guide to Comparative Treatments*, pp. 97–114. New York: Springer.

LaFarge, L. (2012). The screen memory and the act of remembering. *International Journal of Psychoanalysis*, 93(5): 1249–1265.

Lemma, A., & Lynch, P. E. (Eds.) (2015). *Sexualities: Contemporary Psychoanalytic Perspectives*. London: Routledge.

Lewin, B. D. (1933). The body as phallus. *Psychoanalytic Quarterly*, 2(1): 24–47.

Loewald, H. W. (1960). On the therapeutic action of psychoanalysis. *International Journal of Psychoanalysis*, 41(1): 16–33.

Loewald, H. W. (1962). Internalization, separation, mourning, and the super-ego. *Psychoanalytic Quarterly*, 31(4): 483–504.

Loewald, H. W. (1970). Psychoanalytic theory and the psychoanalytic process. *Psychoanalytic Study of the Child*, 25(1): 45–68.

Loewald, H. W. (1976 [1980]). Perspectives on memory. In *Papers on Psychoanalysis*, pp. 148–173. New Haven, CT: Yale University Press.

Lorand, S. (1939). Contribution to the problem of vaginal orgasm. *International Journal of Psychoanalysis*, 20(3/4): 432–438.

Mahler, M., Pine, F., & Bergman, A. (1975). *The Psychological Birth of the Human Infant: Symbiosis and Individuation*. New York: Basic Books.

Mancia, M. (2004 [2007]). *Feeling the Words: Neuropsychoanalytic Understanding of Memory* (J. Baggott, Trans.). Hove, UK: Routledge.

Moscovitz, S. (2014). Hans Loewald's "On the therapeutic action of psychoanalysis": Initial reception and later influence. *Psychoanalytic Psychology*, 31(4): 575–587.

Ogden, T. H. (1994). The analytic third: Working with intersubjective clinical facts. *International Journal of Psychoanalysis*, 75(1): 3–20.

Ogden, T. H. (1989). The initial analytic meeting. In *The Primitive Edge of Experience*, pp. 169–194. Northvale, NJ: Jason Aronson.

Pine, F. (1984). The interpretive moment. *Bulletin of the Menninger Clinic*, 48(1): 54–71.

Pine, F. (1989). Motivation, personality organization, and the four psychologies of psychoanalysis. *Journal of the American Psychoanalytic Association*, 37(1): 31–64.

Pine, F. (1992). Some refinements of the separation-individuation concept in light of research on infants. *Psychoanalytic Study of the Child*, 47(1): 103–116.

Porder, M. S. (1987). Projective identification: An alternative hypothesis. *Psychoanalytic Quarterly*, 56(3): 431–451.

Rapaport, D., & Gill, M. M. (1959). The points of view and assumptions of metapsychology. *International Journal of Psychoanalysis*, 40(2): 153–162.

Reik, T. (1965). *Listening with the Third Ear: The Inner Experience of a Psychoanalyst*, 2nd Edn. New York: Pyramid Publications.

Renik, O. (1993). Analytic interaction: Conceptualizing technique in light of the analyst's irreducible subjectivity. *Psychoanalytic Quarterly*, 62(4): 553–571.

Roland, A. (1996). *Cultural Pluralism and Psychoanalysis: The Asian and North American Experience*. New York: Routledge.

Sandler, J. (1976). Countertransference and role-responsiveness. *International Review of Psycho-Analysis*, 3: 43–47.

Schafer, R. (1968). *Aspects of Internalization*. New York: International Universities Press.

Schafer, R. (1973). The idea of resistance. *International Journal of Psychoanalysis*, 54(3): 259–285.

Solms, M. (2007). Freud returns. In F. Bloom (Ed.), *Best of Brain: Mind, Matter, and Tomorrow's Brain*, pp. 35–43. New York: Dana Press.

Stern, D. N. (1985). *The Interpersonal World of the Infant: A View from Psychoanalysis and Developmental Psychology*. New York: Basic Books.

Stolorow, R. D., & Atwood, G. E. (1992). *Contexts of Being: The Intersubjective Foundations of Psychological Life*. Hillsdale, NJ: Analytic Press.

Stone, L. (1954). The widening scope of indications for psychoanalysis. *Journal of the American Psychoanalytic Association*, 2(4): 567–594.

Tyson, R., & Sandler, J. (1971). Problems in the selection of patients for psychoanalysis: Comments on the application of the concepts of "indication", "suitability", and "analysability". *British Journal of Medical Psychology*, 44(3): 211–228.

Vaillant, G. (1992). *Ego Mechanisms of Defense: A Guide for Clinicians and Researchers*. Washington, DC: American Psychiatric Press.

Van der Kolk, B. (2014). *The Body Keeps the Score: Brain, Mind, and Body in the Healing of Trauma*. New York: Viking.

Waelder, R. (1936). The principle of multiple function: Observations on over-determination. *Psychoanalytic Quarterly*, 5(1): 45–62.

Westen, D. (1999). The scientific status of unconscious processes: Is Freud really dead? *Journal of the American Psychoanalytic Association*, 47(4): 1061–1106.

Winnicott, D. W. (1971). *Playing and Reality*. London: Tavistock Publications.

2

JUNGIAN APPROACHES TO PSYCHOTHERAPY

Lionel Corbett

Introduction: Jung's attitude to psychotherapy

Carl Jung believed that the personality of the therapist, and his or her level of psychological development, are more important than any type of technique. In Jung's words: "Every psychotherapist not only has his own method – he himself is that method... The great healing factor in psychotherapy is the doctor's personality... theories are to be avoided, except as mere auxiliaries" (Jung, 1966, p. 88). Even though the analyst inevitably has a theoretical model in the back of his or her mind, during the process of psychotherapy theoretical ideas are to be avoided as much as possible, because Jung believed that every patient needs his or her own theory. The therapist's work has to be individual; as Jung (1973, p. 405) noted in a letter: "I can only hope and wish that no one becomes 'Jungian'... I proclaim no cut-and-dried doctrine and I abhor 'blind adherents.'" Therefore, "[t]he therapist must abandon all his preconceptions and techniques and confine himself to a purely dialectical procedure, adopting the attitude that shuns all methods" (Jung, 1966, p. 8). Jung maintained that psychotherapy is like a chemical reaction, in that, if either person is going to change, both must change; the analyst is in the analysis as much as the patient. Jung believed that it is futile for the therapist to shield him- or herself from the influence of the patient: "By doing so he only deprives himself of a highly important organ of information" (1966, p. 71). As he put it: "In any effective psychological treatment the doctor is bound to influence the patient; but this influence can only take place if the patient has a reciprocal influence on the doctor. You can exert no influence if you are not susceptible to influence" (p. 71). This mutual influence approach is an early field theory, but, unlike contemporary intersubjective approaches, Jung added that the therapeutic field is also affected by the transpersonal Self (*vide infra*), which is a superordinate field in which both participants are contained.

Jung did not use a couch, because he believed it is the analyst's "duty to accept the emotions of the patient and to mirror them… I put my patients in front of me and I talk to them as one natural human being to another" (Jung, 1977, p. 139). He preferred to think of treatment as a conversation between two people who meet on equal terms. He also rejected Freud's insistence on abstinence and neutrality, because the analyst is not a "superior wise man" but "a fellow participant who finds himself involved in the dialectical process just as deeply as the so-called patient" (Jung, 1966, p. 8). This attitude is strikingly similar to the approach of contemporary relational theorists (Giannoni, 2009). Although Jung's therapeutic method was dialectical, so that he did not remain neutral during the therapeutic process but contributed his own ideas about the patient's situation, he always believed that the patient's unconscious was the final authority.

Jung was quite clear that patients can "read the analyst's character intuitively" (Jung, 1961, p. 260) and that "nothing is finer than the empathy of a neurotic" (p. 277). Jung had not heard of the notion of projective identification; instead, he described his theory of the countertransference metaphorically, likening it to a kind of infection, as if the sufferer can transmit his disease to a healthy person, who must then deal with it, albeit at the risk of his own well-being (Jung, 1966, p. 72). Thus he wrote: "The doctor, by voluntarily and consciously taking over the psychic sufferings of the patient, exposes himself to the overpowering contents of the unconscious and hence also to their inductive action… The patient, by bringing an activated unconscious content to bear upon the doctor, constellates the corresponding unconscious material in him, owing to the inductive effect which always emanates from projections" (p. 176). Even though the effects of psychotherapy are reciprocal, and the patient is usually more affected by the work than the analyst, it is also true that with some individuals the analyst may be profoundly affected. Jung believed that exposure to the inductive effect of the patient's material is part of the destiny of those who do this work. In his words: "The confrontation of the two positions generates a tension charged with energy and creates a living, third thing" (Jung, 1969a, p. 90). This third thing, which is reminiscent of Ogden's (2004) "analytic third," becomes a third presence, which "flits about from patient to doctor and, as the third party in the alliance [, is] sometimes impish and teasing, sometimes really diabolical" (Jung, 1966, p. 188). This "third party," for Jung, is the unconscious.

Very traditional Jungian analysts are mostly concerned with the individual's relationship to the unconscious. However, many contemporary Jungians have been strongly influenced by the relational turn in psychoanalysis, though Jung himself did not develop his own ideas about the therapeutic relationship much further than the dialectical approach mentioned above. Instead, he became engrossed in the development of his theory of the Self and the collective levels of the unconscious, described later in this chapter. Accordingly, in order to understand the complexities of the transference and other relational material, contemporary Jungians often turn to other theorists, turning back to Jung when working with archetypal material.

Most Jungian analysts do not focus on a detailed reconstruction of childhood, though these memories naturally emerge. Jung noted that we cannot free ourselves from childhood through intellectual knowledge alone: what is effective is "a remembering that is also a re-experiencing" (Jung, 1968, p. 62). However, Jung believed that we should avoid setting any kind of exact goal for the process of analysis; he believed that the analyst cannot know better than the patient's own nature and that "mysterious unconscious factors" are more important than "conscious will and well-meaning reasonableness... [T]here is no universal recipe for living" (Jung, 1996, p. 41). There are only individual solutions. In Jung's words: "My aim is to bring about a psychic state in which my patient begins to experiment with his own nature – a state of fluidity, change, and growth where nothing is eternally fixed and hopelessly petrified" (p. 46).

The Freud–Jung break

The disruption of the Freud–Jung relationship in 1912 was the result of their disagreements about the nature of libido, the meaning of incest fantasies, the nature of the unconscious, the nature of religion and Jung's rejection of Freud's drive theory. For Jung, libido is not purely sexual, as Freud insisted, but a kind of neutral life energy, quantitative rather than qualitative, which may express itself as will, interest, emotional investment or attention flowing into any life pursuit. Jung believed that certain symbols, such as those found in mythological imagery or dreams, were not simply images of repressed libido, as Freud suggested, but were symbols of the psyche's capacity for transformation. They have an energizing effect, which allows the psyche to move on with its development. Whereas Freud saw in the desire for incest a boy's literal wish for sexual relations with his mother, Jung wanted to de-literalize these fantasies, and saw them as symbolic. For him, the incest desire represents the yearning to return to a regressive state of merger with mother, or a wish for rebirth or for unconsciousness free of any responsibility, for which the womb is a good symbol (Jung, 1967a). When these fantasies appeared during psychotherapy, Jung interpreted them as a form of resistance to dealing with a current challenge in the patient's life. Jung rejected drive theory for two reasons. One was that he thought it was too limited a view of the unconscious; he could not see sexuality as involved in the etiology of all neurosis (Jung, 1961). Furthermore, he felt that Freud overvalued the instinctual processes of the body, whereas Jung preferred to "start with the sovereignty of the psyche" (Jung, 1971, p. 547). Jung also saw a spiritual component to the psyche, a view that Freud believed was merely an avoidance of the reality of unconscious conflicts.

The sad irony is that, although these theoretical differences with Freud led to Jung's expulsion from the psychoanalytic fold, so that he was ignored by subsequent generations of Freudian psychoanalysts, few contemporary clinicians are concerned about issues such as the nature of libido, and many would also agree that the origin of emotional disorder cannot be reduced to sexuality. Nevertheless, until quite recently Jungian approaches to analysis were systematically excluded from psychoanalytic texts, except for passing criticisms based on Freud's rejection of Jung's contributions. This situation began to change in 1996, when *The Psychoanalytic*

36 Lionel Corbett

Review published a symposium on post-Jungian thought. Since then interactions between Freudians and Jungians have become more common (Beebe, Cambray & Kirsch, 2001).

Key Jungian concepts: the structure and dynamics of the psyche

The unconscious and its archetypal processes

For Jung, the unconscious is an unknown, ontologically real dimension of the psyche, and the psyche is a domain in its own right, as real as the material world and not entirely reducible to brain functioning. He insisted that we have no idea of the nature of the unconscious, which is only something we posit, not an entity whose metaphysical or ontological essence we understand. The unconscious "designates only my *unknowing*" (Jung, 1973, p. 411, emphasis in original). "The concept of the unconscious is an assumption for the sake of convenience" (Jung, 1970, p. 39). Jung saw the unconscious as a kind of consciousness in its own right; he noted that perception, thinking, feeling, volition and intention go on in the unconscious as though a subject were present (Jung, 1969a). The unconscious cannot be hypostasized; it contains many centers of consciousness, and it should not be thought of as "an encapsulated personal system" (Jung, 1969b, p. 22).

Jung's view of the unconscious differed radically from the classical Freudian view. For Jung, the unconscious certainly contains the repressed contents of childhood, but it is also the source of new material that has never been conscious and that is gradually emerging (Jung, 1969a). The unconscious also has a transpersonal dimension; the deeper layer of the unconscious, referred to as the collective unconscious or the objective or autonomous psyche, is represented in mythological, religious and folkloric imagery. These symbolic systems reveal recognizably consistent, archetypal patterns that are found across diverse cultures and historical periods. This archetypal level of the psyche also appears in dream imagery and in the productions of psychotic people. The notion of intrinsic organizing principles in the psyche is found in Freud's work in the form of what he called "archaic remnants" or as universal mythic imagery, such as the Oedipus story. However, Jung's theory of archetypal patterns in the psyche radically expands the number of these mythic, collective psychological motifs. Thus, the Narcissus myth or any of many such recurrent themes may be relevant to certain individuals. These archetypal forms are considered to represent innate processes within the psyche, somewhat analogous to the laws of physics, which describe how the material world works. Just as the physical world is ordered, so the psyche has its own intrinsic structures and dynamics, which appear in myths and religions in the form of typical archetypal imagery.

Importantly, although the concept of the archetype has been criticized as a Lamarckian idea, in fact Jung stresses that the archetype-as-such is a pure form with no specific content until it emerges symbolically, using imagery derived from personal and cultural sources. The archetypes provide the *potentials* or predispositions for typically human types of experience; the human content of the experience is given by the individual and the local culture. Thus, at the personal level, a baby expects to experience a mother, because of the presence in the psyche of the Mother archetype; mothering is universal but the details or the style of mothering are culturally colored, and are a function of the human being who brings this potential into personal time and space. At the collective level, in mythological and religious traditions, some version of the Mother archetype is typically referred to as a goddess, as the feminine aspects of the divine, the Great Mother or the Queen of Heaven. Local cultures give her a particular name, such as the Blessed Virgin Mary, Sophia, Kuanyin, Kali or Demeter – but these are all cultural instantiations of a deep structure in the psyche. Similarly, Zeus, Jupiter, Yahweh and Odin are mythic images of the Sky Father archetype. In other words, what the ancients referred to as gods and goddesses can be thought of as local names for archetypal processes in the psyche, projected outwards as if they were divinities. It is important to note that the archetype is always ambivalent; like the divinities of antiquity, the archetype can be positive or negative. Thus, mythic images of the Great Mother archetype can be nurturing and life-giving or death-dealing and devouring.

For many Jungians, the archetypal levels of the unconscious are synonymous with what the religious traditions refer to as the spiritual dimension. Jung believed that direct contact with the archetypal level of the psyche, which may occur in the form of a dream, produces an experience that is synonymous with traditional descriptions of religious experience. This identical quality is important to Jung's approach to spirituality and religion, discussed below.

In his early writing, Jung suggested that the archetypal ground of the psyche is genetically inherited (Jung, 1977). However, later he realized that this was too reductive an approach, so that in his later work (Jung, 1964) he said that the origin of the archetypes is unknown and the question of how they originated is an unanswerable metaphysical problem; they appear with the appearance of the psyche, whose origin is a mystery. Like the psyche, the archetypes enter into the picture "with life itself" (Jung, 1970, p. 149).

There is a growing opinion from a range of disciplines that the mind has innate structures within it, for example in the notion of innate affects found cross-culturally. In contemporary thinking, the notion of the archetype has been compared to the "strange attractors" of chaos theory, to the innate potential for language acquisition, to the innate releasing mechanisms described by ethologists and to the perceptual motor schemata described by Jean Piaget. Some Jungians regard Melanie Klein's notion of unconscious phantasy as closely related to Jung's concept of the archetype; so also Lacan's notion that the unconscious is structured like a language, not to mention Freud's suggestion in his 1916 *Introductory Lectures on Psycho-Analysis* (see Freud, 1916a, 1916b) that primal fantasies are a phylogenetic endowment. Wilfred Bion's "preconceptions" or inborn rudimentary dispositions or states of expectations also come to mind. That is, within Jungian theory, the individual is by no means a *tabula rasa*; each personality is considered to have a unique archetypal endowment, which helps to explain particular talents, such as musicality, that are not attributed solely to the individual's developmental history.

38 Lionel Corbett

Archetypal imagery is commonly found in contemporary literature and film. An example is the heroic Luke Skywalker in *Star Wars*, who undergoes a rite of passage to free himself from his mother and confront his father's power. Darth Vader represents archetypal evil or the negative aspect of the father archetype, while Obi-Wan Kenobi is an archetypal mentor or wise old man figure.

The theory of archetypes has been criticized on several grounds, not least because Jung made several contradictory statements about the idea during the 40 years he wrote about it. Sometimes he failed to make his own distinction between archetypes-as-such and their symbolic expression. The notion of archetypes is essentialist, in a sense, and is reminiscent of Platonic idealism, though Plato's ideas are cosmic and not psychological. The concept is difficult to pin down, because archetypal images are found across an enormous range of phenomena, such that they are difficult to demarcate in a systematic manner, and the theory is impossible to falsify. Jungians are often accused of stripping mythic imagery from its unique historical and cultural setting, ignoring the specificity of individual cultures in the service of a theoretical abstraction. The similarity of mythic themes found across cultures has been said to be simply due to the diffusion of ideas and the result of the similarity of life experiences in different cultures. Jung is often accused of being too subjectivist in his approach, and his view of archetypes as spiritual principles seems too mystical to many people. Clinically, a potential drawback of the theory of archetypes is that it may be used defensively to avoid personal material or even personal responsibility – but it is also true that one may focus exclusively on personal material and ignore the important archetypal aspects of a situation.

The theory of archetypes is most helpful in a variety of situations. Sometimes there is no personal or developmental explanation for a clinical phenomenon but the situation can be understood in terms of its archetypal characteristics. In addition, archetypal theory allows us to locate the individual's situation within the larger stories of humanity and allows us to discover a universal story within the individual, which may have a helpful effect. The notion of a common human heritage in the psyche has a potentially unifying effect, showing what we have in common with other cultures. Furthermore, the archetypal dimension of the psyche is considered to be the realm of spirit or the transpersonal dimension, which is important to many people. The identification of an archetypal background to a human dilemma suggests a background intelligence or ordering principle to the situation, however that is conceived. Archetypal theory allows for a spiritual approach to the psyche and a theory of its numinous imagery that is not easily explained in other schools of thought without recourse to theology. Overall, therefore, in clinical practice Jungians find the idea of great value.

The Jungian approach adds an archetypal dimension to the traditional understanding of the transference, which is considered to have archetypal as well as personal dimensions. Thus, a patient who sees the therapist through the lens of a mother transference may attribute qualities to the therapist that do not belong to the patient's actual mother but, rather, are characteristic of the archetype of the mythic Great Mother. Accordingly, even when the patient's personal mother was negative, the therapeutic situation may activate the latent positive potentials of the Mother archetype. This may result, for example, in an idealizing transference, so that the therapist is seen as a nurturing Great Mother, somewhat larger than life. In some borderline or psychotic individuals the transference may take on overtly negative archetypal characteristics, as in a delusional transference in which the therapist is seen as terrifyingly witch-like or demonic.

The following is a description of some important archetypal structures and processes.

The Self

The transpersonal Self is the central organizing principle of the personality, a kind of center of gravity (Jung, 1969c). The Self is also seen as the totality of the psyche, the sum of all its contents and processes. For Jung, the Self is a priori, not the result of the accretion of experiences, as is the personal self or the ego. In the English-language literature, the Self is usually capitalized to distinguish it from the personal self, because the Self is thought to be an *imago dei*, an image of the divine within the personality, analogous to the Atman of the Upanishads. The Self is projected onto local images of God, such as Christ, Zeus, Yahweh or any mythological divinity, but whether the Self corresponds to the transcendent divine of the theistic traditions is not knowable. The Self manifests itself symbolically; collectively it appears as the local God-image, while individually it appears in dreams in the form of symbols of wholeness and totality, such as a mandala, the Sanskrit term for a circle. In Eastern religious traditions these highly symmetrical forms, usually a combination of circles and squares with religious imagery superimposed, are used as aids to meditation. They tend to occur in dreams when the dreamer's life feels chaotic, apparently in an attempt to restore a sense of order.

Jung's notion that the Self is an intrapsychic image of the divine has led to major disputes with Jewish and Christian theologians, who believe that Jung reduces the transcendent divine to "nothing but" an intrapsychic image. Jung's response to this criticism is, first, that the psyche is real, so its God-images are real; and, second, that images and experiences of the Self are empirically demonstrable. One of the difficulties faced by patients in Jungian therapy who are committed to a specific God-image, such as Christ, is that they cannot accept Jung's idea that the Self can appear in any other form (Corbett, 2007).

The ego

For Jung, the ego is the center of the field of consciousness and the conscious agent of the personality. Anything conscious, by definition, is part of the ego. Jung believed that the ego arises in infancy like a number of islands of awareness emerging out of an a priori Self. These islands of consciousness gradually coalesce as the personality develops, due to the interaction of the child with the outer world. The notion of an unfolding nuclear self is found in theorists such as Heinz Kohut and

Donald Winnicott; what is unique to Jung is the notion of a transpersonal Self that provides a ground plan or matrix for the development of the personal self. The personality therefore has an essence to it that unfolds during the course of life. That is, for Jung, development arises under the influence of both the environment and the a priori Self. Jung wrote that "the ego stands to the self as the moved to the mover" (Jung 1970, p. 259) or "like a part to the whole" (Jung, 1969c, p. 5). Their dialogical relationship is referred to as the ego–Self axis. One example of this axis is found in our attention to dreams; the Self is thought to be the maker of dreams, to which the ego responds.

The shadow

The shadow is an intrapsychic structure with two aspects. In its negative form it consists of aspects of the personality of which the individual is unconscious or would prefer to repudiate, such as envy, hatred or other unacceptable, disavowed or repressed material (Jung, 1969c). In its positive aspect, the shadow consists of the individual's undeveloped talents and potentials. Typically, the shadow is projected onto others when it is unconscious; shadow projection contributes to racism and the devaluing of other cultures. The negative shadow manifests itself either in overtly problematic behavior or when the individual is intoxicated, or it appears in dreams in the form of the dreamer or another same-sex figure behaving in a disreputable manner. For example, a surgeon in analysis often dreams of mercenary soldiers, suggesting that he sublimates his aggression or greed in his work. Ideally, therapeutic work leads to the integration of shadow material, so that aggression becomes assertiveness or vulnerability becomes sensitivity to others. If the shadow cannot be integrated, it has to be contained. The limitation of Jung's notion of the shadow is that it is a very broad concept and the details of its specific internal dynamics for a given individual have to be understood using developmental theory.

Not just the individual but also societies have shadow aspects; Nazi Germany is an example of an entire society falling prey to its collective shadow. The shadow of societies and organizations leads to a kind of unconscious mass-mindedness in which individual discrimination is lost, often resulting in evil.

Anima and animus

Jung believed that there are opposite-sex qualities within every personality, which appear in the form of contra-sexual figures in dreams (Jung, 1967b). The feminine aspects of a man are referred to as the anima, while the masculine components of a woman are known as the animus. For the full development of the personality it is important to integrate or become conscious of these qualities within oneself, becoming somewhat psychologically androgynous. Jung believed that qualities such as receptivity, relatedness and nurturing are archetypally feminine, while those such as assertiveness, structure and power are masculine. Many people now believe that these attributes are merely social stereotypes, imposed by patriarchal consciousness, and the content of masculine and feminine behavior is culturally determined. But the notion of an opposite-sex component to the personality persists and is a useful contribution, because opposite-sex figures do occur in dreams. By understanding the qualities they represent within the dreamer, one gains access to deeper levels of the unconscious. We are fascinated by people onto whom we can project the anima or animus; when we fall in love, the beloved embodies qualities within our own unconscious to which we are drawn.

The puer/puella aeternus

This phrase, Latin for the eternal boy or girl, describes an archetypal pattern found in individuals who refuse to grow up emotionally; like Peter Pan, they wish to remain eternal adolescents, and no matter their age their emotional life never seems to mature beyond this stage (von Franz, 2000). They are reluctant to make long-term commitments because they are afraid of being caught in a situation from which they might not be able to escape. They are often imaginative and creative but they have no concern for the future, they dislike ordinary limits and boundaries and they feel rather special. They need the kind of excitement found in stunt flying, mountaineering and other dangerous sports. Many are charming but they often refuse to work, living on money wheedled from others. The other pole of this archetype is the *senex*, a personality that is overly controlled, rule-bound and rational. The therapeutic task when dealing with these personalities is to achieve a balance between these polarities.

The persona

The persona is a mask, the demeanor we adopt in order to adapt to the world in an acceptable way (Jung, 1967b). Its content varies with the situation in which we find ourselves, so that we have a different persona with friends and family from the one we have in professional situations. The persona is usually a compromise between the demands of the environment and our own feelings, and it is often used to mask the shadow. In dreams the persona appears when clothing is stressed, or occasionally when the dreamer is naked and exposed, suggesting an inadequate persona. The main problem with the persona occurs when people over-identify with it, as if it were their real identity. A marine sergeant who trains recruits at boot camp traumatizes his children if he cannot relinquish his persona when he is at home.

Individuation

Jung's work on development in childhood was minimal. He largely left this work to his followers and to other schools of analytic thought. His interest was mainly in psychological development during the second half of life, a process that he referred to as individuation, meaning that the individual forms a unique personality that differentiates him or her from collective psychology. Individuation for Jung (in contrast to the use of this word by other theorists) means the fullest possible development of the personality and the realization of the Self (Jung, 1967b). This process occurs naturally, but our awareness of the need for it is often triggered by an emotional crisis that brings a person into therapy. Then, as the presenting problem resolves, the individual may become interested in continuing to pay attention to the manifestations of the unconscious for the sake of ongoing development, at which point individuation becomes the central goal of Jungian psychotherapy. Individuation occurs as the non-ego contents of the psyche, such as the shadow and the contra-sexual components, are gradually assimilated into consciousness as we pay attention to dreams, symptoms, fantasies and other manifestations of the unconscious. This gradual expansion of consciousness is considered to be of great value but complete individuation is a theoretical goal that can never be fully achieved. The process leads to increasing wholeness and individuality but not to individualism; individuation makes one unique but also better able to fulfill one's collective responsibilities. Ideally, the individuation process also leads to improved relationships, for example because we become aware of what we have been projecting onto others. The Self acts as a "transpersonal control point" (1967b, p. 134) or guiding function for this development, which can be facilitated by psychotherapy. It is as if each personality has its own lawfulness, which moves it in a particular direction, toward a goal (Jung, 1967b). Teleological views of development are currently not popular, since they seem to imply that the future is pulling us toward it, but the notion that each personality has its own unique destiny is an important theme in Jung's work. For example, for Jung (1954), one's true vocation in life is given by the Self; it is not an accident.

Dreams

Because of the primary importance of the unconscious for Jung, analytic work with dreams is central to the Jungian approach to psychotherapy. Although Jung (1974) did not think we could develop a comprehensive theory of dreams, he made several basic assumptions. For him, dreams express the structure and dynamic processes of the unconscious, both personal and archetypal, so they are always meaningful. Dreams either compensate for a conscious attitude that is too one-sided or they complement or modify one's conscious attitude when it is appropriate, because the psyche is self-regulating in a way that is analogous to the body's attempt to maintain a stable internal environment. Most importantly, dreams are purposive, fostering the individuation process of the dreamer, sometimes pointing to its future developments. The dream reveals either the intrapsychic situation of the dreamer or his or her relational dynamics, in symbolic form, and the therapeutic task is to decode the dream text and its metaphors. Dream figures other than the dream ego often personify qualities of the dreamer that are projected onto others. A dream figure that is currently important in the dreamer's life may refer to that person himself, or the figure may personify a subjective quality of the dreamer. Dream animals often represent instinctual forces.

The initial dream in an analytic process is often considered to presage the type of work that will be done. For example, a patient dreamed that he and I were climbing a hill together and we had to walk gently because, otherwise, wherever we placed our feet the grass underfoot became singed or burned. This suggested to me that we would have to tread very lightly, which proved to be the case. Dreams are particularly helpful when considered in a series in which a particular theme is developed over time. For example, at the beginning of therapy a man has a frightening dream of an unknown figure chasing him, but he is too afraid to look back. A year later he again dreams that he is being chased, but now he is able to look behind him, and he discovers that a bear is after him. After further therapeutic work he dreams he is being chased by a malevolent female figure who reminds him of his mother.

Occasionally dreams seem to point to developmental possibilities or they suggest a way out of the dreamer's current dilemma. A remarkable if uncommon type of dream recognized by Jungians is the prospective or pre-cognitive dream, in which a future event is foretold; one example is that a death is imminent, and it subsequently takes place. Needless to say, this type of dream is discernible only in retrospect. Depending on the therapist's metaphysical commitments, such a dream could be dismissed as a coincidence. A related type of dream is the synchronistic form (see below), in which a dream image such as a plane crash coincides in time with an actual plane crash. Of course, a plane crash in a dream could simply have symbolic meaning for the dreamer's life, but occasionally such a dream corresponds in a meaningful if mysterious and acausal way with a physical event – an offense to materialist critics of Jung. He would simply respond that these things happen even if we cannot explain them.

Jung did not distinguish between the dream's latent and manifest content, and he did not believe that dreams mainly consist of forbidden wishes. He did not think that dreams were disguises; instead, he thought of dreams as a natural product of the psyche and preferred to think of the difficulty in understanding dreams as a problem of translation, as if they were a text in an unknown language. For this purpose Jung used the dreamer's associations, but only to the extent that these bear upon the dream; he did not encourage the dreamer to continue free-associating into areas of the psyche unrelated to the dream. Rather, he advised "circumambulating" the dream, or walking around and around its imagery, looking at it from all sides until its meaning becomes clear.

When the patient has exhausted his or her personal associations, Jung would further amplify the dream's imagery using associations to it from world mythology, anthropology, folklore and religions, always looking for an association that has emotional resonance for the dreamer. Amplification means that we try to find the way a particular image has been used within these other symbol systems in order to better understand the image in the individual's dream. This is a method derived from philology, in which a text in an unknown language is compared to a similar text in a known language. Thus, if the dreamer is lost in a deep forest, to which he or she has no personal associations, at first glance the dream may seem to refer to the dreamer's feeling psychologically lost with no path in sight. In addition, to deepen one's understanding of this image, one might appeal to the use of forest imagery in mythology and folklore, so that the archetypal setting of the dream might be the Earth Mother. Or the forest might refer to a place of initiation and trials far from the dreamer's ordinary urban life. This kind of mythic association, which can be supplied by the therapist when the patient has exhausted his or her own associations, may spark renewed ideas in the dreamer, and even a tiny fragment of such a dream may lead to an important sense of meaning. Yet the method of amplification can be a mixed blessing; sometimes it expands the patient's understanding of his or her dream by linking it to the cultural history of humanity, but at other times the use of mythological imagery acts as a defense against looking at the patient's personal life or it avoids the relational dynamics in the therapy or it fosters an overly idealized transference.

Most importantly, no dream symbol has a fixed meaning in the Jungian approach. One cannot simply equate tunnels or church steeples with male or female genitalia. Even overt sexuality in a dream may not represent literal sex; it may depict the need to unite with whatever quality is depicted by the sexual partner in the dream. A dream symbol for Jung is the best possible expression of an important unconscious content that is trying to bridge into consciousness. A dream snake, for instance, may have personal associations to the dreamer but the snake also has a range of symbolic meanings in world mythology and folklore; the therapeutic task is to discern which of these is relevant to the dreamer. The snake may represent renewal, because it sheds its old skin: it may represent evil or temptation, as in the Garden of Eden; healing, as part of the physician's caduceus; or poison, guile and cunning. In antiquity the snake was sacred to the goddesses of various traditions. The snake is a chthonic or subterranean animal, and so may represent earthiness, the underworld or the unconscious, or our primordial, instinctual nature, such as the primitive nervous system – and this list only scratches the surface of the meaning of this complex symbol. To reduce the meaning of a dream snake to a penis would be to commit a cardinal Jungian sin, which is to reduce the symbol to a sign with just one meaning. The same symbol in the dreams of different people may have very different meanings. Only by looking for the dreamer's emotional resonance with a possible mythic amplification of the symbol can one discover which amplification is relevant – but this is a tricky problem, because of the influence of the transference on the dreamer's responses to the analyst's suggestions.

After working on a dream, the dreamer may be asked "Dream the dream onward" in his or her imagination. This process, known as active imagination, involves a waking dialog with a dream figure, in which the figure is allowed to speak spontaneously as if the ego is having a conversation with it. This can be carried out as an internal dialog in the mind's eye, or through painting, dancing or sculpting the image, leading to a greater appreciation of it. This process of interacting with dream figures can be a lifelong form of continuing self-analysis or dialog with the unconscious, after the individual has ended personal therapy. A related nonverbal method favored by some Jungians is the use of a sand tray that contains miniature figures of many types, which allows the individual to produce a three-dimensional image representing an intrapsychic situation (Kalff, 1980).

Alchemy

The ancient tradition of alchemy is typically understood only as a historical precursor to modern chemistry. However, Jung realized that the alchemists were in fact projecting their unconscious intrapsychic processes onto the material operations of their laboratories. Images they believed they were seeing in their retorts were actually going on in their minds, so that alchemical imagery is a rich source of psychological information about the dynamics of the psyche. For example, the "gold" that the alchemists were attempting to produce out of lead was actually the experience of the Self, trying to emerge from the initial heavy darkness of the alchemist's mind. To describe chemical combinations, given no knowledge of the actual chemistry involved, the alchemists used imagery such as the union of a king and queen or the sun and moon into a unified figure. They referred to this process as a *coniunctio*, which can be thought of as an early, mythic prefiguration of the intrapsychic union of the therapeutic couple. Using a series of dreams of one of his patients (the physicist Wolfgang Pauli), Jung (1968) showed how ancient alchemical symbols appear in the psyche of a modern man. He believed that this imagery is part of the reservoir of mythopoetic imagery found in the objective psyche, confirming his notion that the psyche has a collective level, producing imagery that is not the result of introjection or learning. The Jungian literature has subsequently described many analogues between psychological and psychotherapeutic processes and the operations of medieval alchemical laboratories (Edinger, 1991).

Psychological types

Jung developed a theory of psychological types in order to try to understand the conflicts and theoretical differences that arose between himself and Freud or between Freud and Alfred Adler. Jung believed that some of these disagreements were attributable to differences in temperament, leading to different ways of viewing the world. He described two attitudes of consciousness; the extraverted attitude is habitually and preferentially oriented toward the outer world, to people and events, while the introvert prefers to relate to his or her inner world. Extraverts typically adjust in a direct way to outer situations, while introverts are often less concerned with outer events themselves than with their subjective reactions to them. There are four types of psychological functions; two ways of perceiving the world and two ways of judging one's perceptions. We may perceive through the senses directly or through the unconscious; these are known, respectively, as the sensation and the intuitive functions. The sensation function deals with immediate facts, the intuitive function with possibilities or what might happen. We may then judge our perceptions either with thinking, which deals with the true–false distinction and with planning, logic and order, or by means of feeling, which deals with values, desirability, likes and dislikes, indicating the degree of emotional importance of an object. Each of these functions may be either extraverted or introverted, depending on whether it is directed to the outer or the inner world, so the system becomes quite complicated (Sharp, 1987).

Jung believed that one of these functions is dominant within the ego, while its opposite function remains relatively undeveloped and undifferentiated, so that in a thinking type the feeling function is relatively primitive, while in a feeling type thinking is undeveloped, and so on. The full development of the personality (individuation) requires that we try to develop all these functions. His typology has been widely adopted in the form of the Myers–Briggs Type Indicator, but this kind of static approach does not do justice to that aspect of the theory that makes the development of the inferior function part of the individuation process.

The fourth or inferior function is often our Achilles heel; it becomes a source of emotional difficulties. For example, a man who is a feeling type with undeveloped thinking may have superior overall intelligence but have difficulty coping with abstract subjects such as mathematics. As a child he may not do well in such academically oriented subjects and may grow up thinking of himself as unintelligent, especially if his family members are all strong thinking types who cannot understand the child's emotional sensitivity or his enjoyment of a subject such as art. These kinds of situations tend to produce psychological problems.

Typology has a variety of implications for the practice of psychotherapy. In work with couples we often find that people are attracted to their typological opposite, but eventually their type difference can lead to serious conflict in the relationship. An explanation of their different ways of experiencing the world may lead to forgiveness and understanding. Significant typological mismatch between therapist and patient makes their relational dynamics more problematic. For example, a therapist whose feeling function is very introverted and private may experience the vivid emotional displays of a very extraverted feeling type as somewhat overwhelming, while such a patient may mistakenly experience the therapist as cold and unresponsive because his or her feelings are not visibly expressed.

Jung's theory of psychopathology and complexes

Jung viewed symptoms such as anxiety and depression as signals from the unconscious that something needs attention; he always looked for meaning in our emotional difficulties. He believed that emotional problems cannot be understood purely developmentally; they also represent unsuccessful attempts to cope with a current existential problem. The past is important but the symptom also points to the future, taking the person in a direction that he or she might not otherwise take. This is Jung's prospective or synthetic view of symptoms: they have a purpose for the future direction of the personality. Symptoms indicate that some new growth is necessary. Growth toward wholeness is the major goal of treatment and is often more important than the relief of symptoms.

Jung (1969a) used the term "complex" to mean an intrapsychic structure consisting of a group of related thoughts, associations, beliefs, images and memories that have an important emotional charge. Adler identified the inferiority complex and Freud the Oedipus complex but for Jung the psyche may contain many other types of complex. One can have complexes around money, self-esteem, power or compulsive behaviors. A Medea complex might describe the hatred of a mother for her children, or a Don Juan complex a man's need for repeated, superficial sexual conquests of women with no capacity for real relationship. A messiah or redeemer complex is seen in clergy who see themselves as having a mission to save others. Broadly speaking, Jungians refer to a mother or father complex in a way that roughly corresponds to the notion of an internal object and its associated self-representation, which may be positive or negative. However, because Jung was not a drive theorist, he would describe the internal dynamics of such a complex without reference to terms such as "id" or "superego." Complexes are like splinter psyches within the overall personality and their point of view may be more or less in harmony with the larger personality. Complexes tend to be autonomous, acting like internal subjects that may color perception and behavior. They typically become the central issue discussed in therapy and they radically affect the transference/countertransference when the analyst is seen through the lens of a complex.

A complex can be positive or negative in its emotional tone; a positively toned father complex may allow the individual to be a good mentor for younger men, while a negative father complex may lead to constant struggles with authority figures or hierarchies. A positive mother complex gives the capacity for emotional bonding, while the negative form may lead to features such as abandonment depression. A hero complex may lead to either adventurousness or to foolhardy bravado. Negatively toned complexes manifest themselves in minor ways as parapraxes, over-reactions or forgetfulness, or – more seriously – as shame, grandiosity, self-hatred or fear of intimacy or any other manifestation of emotional vulnerability. A complex may suddenly become active in response to a particular situation, in which case we may become transiently "possessed" by it, so that the reality ego is temporarily swept aside and we behave in ways not consistent with our usual personality. When a complex is split off from the totality of consciousness, it acts like a sub-personality dissociated from the rest of the personality; in the extreme, this may produce a multiple personality, each alter representing a particular complex.

An important feature of Jung's approach is the idea that at the center of a complex lies an archetype, such as the Mother, Father, hero or child archetype, which helps to account for the gripping power and emotional intensity of the complex, since the archetype is always affectively laden. This means that the complex has a transpersonal core surrounded by a shell of personal material based on the individual's life experience and early attachments. Consequently, the therapist has to be aware of both levels, working with personal material as it arises but also cognizant of a deeper level, which is occasionally seen in dreams or fantasies. For example, a patient dreams that her mother's head is chasing her, and instead of hair the head is covered in snakes. The dreamer is terrified but unable to escape. This is an obvious allusion to the mythic Medusa or Gorgon, whose appearance turned people to stone, which tellingly illustrates the effect the dreamer's mother had on her. Such a negatively toned mother complex can be addressed at the personal level in the ordinary way, but the mythic image adds a sense of depth and emotional intensity to the situation that may not be reached by only focusing on the personal level of the dreamer's mother. In Freud's 1922 text "Das Medusenhaupt" ("The Medusa's head"), he suggests that this is an image of castration and maternal sexuality, since the snakes represent multiple phalluses and the observer's turning to stone represents an erection. However, for most Jungians this would be too experience-distant an interpretation of the dream image, and it ignores the other possible meanings of the image, which can be fully appreciated only by looking at other aspects of the myth. To name just a few: according to the myth, the head could be safely looked at only as a reflected image, suggesting that this patient's mother problem could not be approached too directly. Medusa was herself dehumanized by the goddess Athena, the masculinized, intellectual goddess of thought, perhaps indicating tension between the instinctual body and the mind, either in the dreamer or in her mother. In antiquity, young women used the image of Medusa's head as a way of warding off male lust. In other words, there can be no single meaning to this mythic image, and the therapist's task is to discover which meaning is relevant to the dreamer rather than imposing a theoretical point of view.

Psychotherapeutic work with complexes leads to a gradual increase in the patient's consciousness of them and a degree of integration of their contents; for example, the need to dominate others might be transformed into leadership potential. As a result of therapeutic work, the structure of the complex often remains unchanged but its emotional intensity is softened and it becomes less troublesome. Because all archetypes are ambivalent, with both positive and negative poles, even when an individual has suffered from a very negative personal mother or father the potential for the experience of the positive side of the archetype is always present, and may be activated in the form of a reparative transference during psychotherapy. The positive experience of the therapist (such as a positive selfobject experience) fosters the emergence of a latent archetypal possibility. The result often appears in dreams in the form of symbolic material that casts new light on the patient's difficulty, for example as a dream image of a radiant newborn baby – an archetypal representation of the Self as a mythological divine child, suggesting the dreamer's potentials for the future. The analytic task is then to assimilate the possibilities presented by the dream. Therefore, in Jung's model, the benefits of psychotherapy are not only the result of the therapist's behavior; psychotherapy activates an unconscious healing potential within the patient.

One's complexes might determine one's vocation. The wounded healer is a mythic image of the centaur Chiron, a teacher of healing in Greek mythology who suffered from an incurable wound. This archetypal image is important to many psychotherapists, if only unconsciously; it refers to the individual who is able to help others as a result of his or her own wounds. Such a complex may radically affect the course of a life. Eleanor Roosevelt grew up feeling unattractive, insecure and rejected; out of this complex emerged her lifelong commitment to helping people who suffer from poverty and discrimination.

A major limitation of the theory of complexes is that the term is very general and covers a wide variety of emotional difficulties. Therefore, apart from understanding the archetypal core of the complex, Jungians must often apply other theoretical approaches (such as psychoanalytic self psychology or object relations theory) in order to clarify its internal dynamics and developmental sources.

Synchronicity

A synchronistic event is an occurrence in the physical world that coincides in time and in a meaningful way with an individual's psychological state. Even though the mental state and the physical event are simultaneous, they do not cause each other. Jung came to this idea when he was working with a woman who was proving to be difficult because of her excessive intellectualizing. She had brought in a dream about a piece of jewelry in the form of a scarab beetle, and while she was telling the dream a beetle of a similar species tapped at the window of the consulting room; Jung opened the window, caught the beetle and showed it to her. This was a deeply meaningful, acausal connection between the dream image and the actual insect, which had a profound effect on the patient's overly rational defenses (Jung, 1969a). A skeptic might protest that it is not surprising that a beetle might bump against a window and that such events are simply coincidences with no larger meaning – the apparent detection of a pattern in random events. However, Jung developed this idea in collaboration with the physicist Wolfgang Pauli, and the theory of synchronicity is sometimes thought to link depth psychology with quantum theory. Both disciplines suggest that the reality that seems to consist of isolated events is actually a manifestation of a deep level of unity between consciousness and the physical world. In therapeutic practice, synchronistic events have a "meant to be" or fateful quality about them, and they often produce the sense of a background order that patients and therapists find quite impressive. However, at the moment we know of no mechanism or processes that might explain these events, which partly accounts for the skeptic's wariness about taking the idea of synchronicity as anything other than the result of pure chance. Joseph Cambray (2012) argues that synchronicity can be seen as an emergent property of complex adaptive systems such as the psyche.

Jung on religion and spirituality

Religion was one of the sources of the Freud–Jung break. For Freud, religion was illusory; for Jung, religion was an essential and ineradicable function of the psyche, even an instinct, and he believed that the absence of any form of spirituality or sense of meaning and purpose is a cause of suffering. But Jung was mainly interested in direct religious experience, not speculative theology or belief, which he thought was too easily affected by circumstances.

50 Lionel Corbett

As well as the usual range of individuals who seek psychotherapy, there is a certain type of person who is particularly likely to consult a Jungian therapist. He or she is an individual in the second half of life, often successful in the sense of being well adapted to the world and not suffering from any specific disorder, but for whom life has lost its meaning. Such a person often has no faith in traditional religions. Jung (1970) believed that the solution to this dilemma is a religious attitude but not necessarily in the sense of adherence to a specific creed. Rather, it is important to develop an individual spirituality, which can be fostered by paying attention to the numinous manifestations of the psyche and to the discovery of meaning in life. The term "numinous" refers to an experience with a special emotional quality, which the theologian Rudolph Otto (1917) believed to be the distinctive characteristic of an experience of the holy. According to Otto, this type of experience is mysterious, tremendous and fascinating, often ineffable, producing feelings such as awe, dread and the sense that one is in touch with something completely other than the usual sphere of experience. Biblical examples are those of Moses hearing God's voice at the burning bush and Saul on the road to Damascus hearing the voice of Jesus. Our religious traditions are founded on these kinds of experiences, but Jung believed that these experiences are not confined to special people within religious traditions, because experiences with this quality can occur to anyone. Jung did not think the content of the experience has to conform to the Judeo-Christian God-image to be authentic; only its emotional quality matters. Whereas, for Otto, these are experiences of the Judeo-Christian God, Jung believed that such an experience is an encounter with the Self or with the archetypal level of the psyche. He pointed out that numinous experiences are psychological facts, indisputable and self-authenticating to the subject even though they are not reproducible. They are best understood using a phenomenological-hermeneutic approach. They occur in dreams, in waking visions, in the natural world and sometimes at important moments such as birth and death. They often have a particularly helpful effect, since they typically address a central psychological issue of the subject. For example, during a period during which the subject felt alienated and desperately alone, she experienced the following:

> Everything stood still, and it was as if time didn't exist because I was time, and I knew I was connected to everything in and around me. I could feel the wind on every inch of my body, and I could hear everything in my surroundings as if it were all living within me. Everything was alive, and in that moment I was the wind, the waves, the sand, the sky. I have never felt so open in my entire life. Tears streamed down my face and I knew I had experienced oneness with the divine.

It would be easy to reduce this kind of experience, known to the mystics of all religious traditions, to either an overheated imagination, temporal lobe epilepsy or some kind of brief psychotic episode. However, this woman had no evidence of psychosis, no thought disorder and no other perceptual changes. The experience was transient, and when it ended she was able to function normally within consensual reality. Jungians would consider this to be an experience of the transpersonal Self and that it can be taken at face value. I suspect that these types of experiences are not especially rare but that they are rarely reported, because of a fear that the subject will not be taken seriously. They may not be discussed with the therapist if the patient senses that the therapist will not be receptive or might dismiss the experience reductively – as a regression, for example. This potential problem arises when the therapist's metaphysical commitments are at variance with the patient's experience. I have discussed a psychotherapeutic approach to numinous experiences elsewhere (Corbett, 1996, 2007, 2011, 2013), and there is a large Jungian literature on the subject. Fortunately, spirituality is no longer taboo among psychotherapists, and the importance of spiritual experience is increasingly discussed by psychoanalytic writers such as Michael Eigen (1998).

For Jung, attention to the inner life, for example by working with dreams, allows increasing consciousness of the Self and fosters the individuation process, which is a spiritual practice in its own right. This is important throughout life, but it becomes particularly important in the second half of life as we approach death.

References

Beebe, J., Cambray, J., & Kirsch, T. B. (2001). What Freudians can learn from Jung. *Psychoanalytic Psychology*, 18(2): 213–242.

Cambray, J. (2012). *Synchronicity: Nature and Psyche in an Interconnected Universe*. College Station, TX: Texas A&M University Press.

Corbett, L. (1996). *The Religious Function of the Psyche*. New York: Routledge.

Corbett, L. (2007). *Psyche and the Sacred: Spirituality beyond Religion*. New Orleans: Spring Journal.

Corbett, L. (2011). *The Sacred Cauldron: Psychotherapy as a Spiritual Practice*. Wilmette, IL: Chiron Publications.

Corbett, L. (2013). Jung's approach to spirituality and religion. In E. Shafranske & K. Pargament (Eds.), *APA Handbook of Psychology and Religion*, pp. 147–167. Washington, DC: APA Publications.

Edinger, E. (1991). *Anatomy of the Psyche: Alchemical Symbolism in Psychotherapy*. Peru, IL: Open Court Publishing.

Eigen, M. (1998). *The Psychoanalytic Mystic*. London: Free Association Books.

Freud, S. (1916a [1963]). Introductory lectures on psycho-analysis (parts I and II). In J. Strachey (Ed. & Trans.), *The Standard Edition of the Complete Psychological Works of Sigmund Freud*, Vol. XV, pp. 15–242. London: Hogarth Press.

Freud, S. (1916b [1963]). Introductory lectures on psycho-analysis (part III). In J. Strachey (Ed. & Trans.), *The Standard Edition of the Complete Psychological Works of Sigmund Freud*, Vol. XVI, pp. 243–463. London: Hogarth Press.

Giannoni, M. (2009). The session of the two dreams. *Journal of Analytical Psychology*, 54(1): 103–115.

Jung, C. G. (1954). *The Development of Personality*, Vol. XVII, *The Collected Works of C. G. Jung* (G. Adler & R. F. C. Hull, Eds. & Trans.). Princeton, NJ: Princeton University Press.

Jung, C. G. (1961). *Freud and Psychoanalysis*, Vol. IV, *The Collected Works of C. G. Jung* (G. Adler & R. F. C. Hull, Eds. & Trans.). Princeton, NJ: Princeton University Press.

Jung, C. G. (1964). *Man and His Symbols*. New York: Doubleday.

Jung, C. G. (1966). *Practice of Psychotherapy*, Vol. XVI, *The Collected Works of C. G. Jung* (G. Adler & R. F. C. Hull, Eds. & Trans.). Princeton, NJ: Princeton University Press.

Jung, C. G. (1967a). *Symbols of Transformation*, Vol. V, *The Collected Works of C. G. Jung* (G. Adler & R. F. C. Hull, Eds. & Trans.). Princeton, NJ: Princeton University Press.

Jung, C. G. (1967b). *Two Essays on Analytical Psychology*, Vol. VII, *The Collected Works of C. G. Jung* (G. Adler & R. F. C. Hull, Eds. & Trans.). Princeton, NJ: Princeton University Press.

Jung, C. G. (1968). *Psychology and Alchemy*, Vol. XII, *The Collected Works of C. G. Jung* (G. Adler & R. F. C. Hull, Eds. & Trans.). Princeton, NJ: Princeton University Press.

Jung, C. G. (1969a). *The Structure and Dynamics of the Psyche*, Vol. VIII, *The Collected Works of C. G. Jung* (G. Adler & R. F. C. Hull, Eds. & Trans.). Princeton, NJ: Princeton University Press.

Jung, C. G. (1969b). *The Archetypes and the Collective Unconscious*, Vol. IX, Part i, *The Collected Works of C. G. Jung* (G. Adler & R. F. C. Hull, Eds. & Trans.). Princeton, NJ: Princeton University Press.

Jung, C. G. (1969c). *Aion: Researches into the Phenomenology of the Self*, Vol. IX, Part ii, *The Collected Works of C. G. Jung* (G. Adler & R. F. C. Hull, Eds. & Trans.). Princeton, NJ: Princeton University Press.

Jung, C. G. (1970). *Psychology and Religion: West and East*, Vol. XI, *The Collected Works of C. G. Jung* (G. Adler & R. F. C. Hull, Eds. & Trans.). Princeton, NJ: Princeton University Press.

Jung, C. G. (1971). *Psychological Types*, Vol. VI, *The Collected Works of C. G. Jung* (G. Adler & R. F. C. Hull, Eds. & Trans.). Princeton, NJ: Princeton University Press.

Jung, C. G. (1973). *Letters*, Vol. I, *1906–1950* (G. Adler & A. Jaffé, Eds.; R. F. C. Hull, Trans.). Princeton, NJ: Princeton University Press.

Jung, C. G. (1974). *Dreams*. Princeton, NJ: Princeton University Press.

Jung, C. G. (1977). *The Symbolic Life: Miscellaneous Writings*, Vol. XVIII, *The Collected Works of C. G. Jung* (G. Adler & R. F. C. Hull, Eds. & Trans.). Princeton, NJ: Princeton University Press.

Kalff, D. V. (1980). *Sandplay: A Psychotherapeutic Approach to the Psyche*. Boston: Sigo Press.

Ogden, T. H. (2004). The analytic third: Implications for psychoanalytic theory and technique. *Psychoanalytic Quarterly*, 73(1): 167–195.

Otto, R. (1917 [1958]). *The Idea of the Holy*. New York: Oxford University Press.

Sharp, D. (1987). *Personality Types: Jung's Model of Typology*. Toronto: Inner City Books.

Von Franz, M.-L. (2000). *The Problem of the Puer Aeternus*. Toronto: Inner City Books.

3

LACAN AND THE EVOLUTION OF HERMES

David Lichtenstein

Introduction

Hermes is a young god in the Greek pantheon, son of Zeus, the father god, and of Maia, a mountain nymph associated with growth, nurturance and maternity. He had numerous roles, many of them associated with the function of boundaries; with both marking real property boundaries, as in the English word "herm" (a stone marker), and crossing textual boundaries, as in the act of interpretation we call hermeneutics. Hermes is the god who moved most easily between the realms of the divine and the mortal. He became the messenger between these realms and is described as having a cunning and mutable character, useful for moving across the boundaries between metaphysical categories. The Romans called him Mercury, another word for quicksilver, the liquid metal, and the source of our word "mercurial." Cunning, shifting, living on the borders, Hermes is the spirit of multiple meaning: both creating multiple meaning and interpreting it. The link between interpreting and creating is the province of Hermes.

Hermes has been credited with inventing the lyre, the instrument that accompanies song, though Apollo, Hermes' older and more established brother, is also given this credit (Brown, 1947). Hermes is associated with craft in the productive sense but he is also called crafty in the sense of deception. In being associated with boundaries, he is also associated with the thieves who cross them. He knows how to invent and to fabricate and thus how to create both truths and falsehoods. That there is an inescapable interplay between invention and deception is essential to the character of Hermes.

The role of the Greek gods often evolved as their characters took on different functions in different times and places in the culture (Brown, 1947). In Hermes' case, the evolution reveals various aspects of his basic character as the marker of

54 David Lichtenstein

boundaries, and thus it reveals dimensions of the boundary as a concept and what it means to work with, observe and cross boundaries.

"Fiction" derives from the Latin root *fingere*, meaning "to form" (something), and it may be used to convey both truth and falsehood. Thus, we speak of *a fiction* as a falsehood but a *work of fiction*, such as *Don Quixote*, as something that conveys truths. The character of Hermes reflects this same dualism of creation and deception. He reflects the duality of representation and alteration inherent in both interpretation and translation. There is neither interpretation nor translation that is not simultaneously a loss and a creation of meaning. No message can ever be delivered unaltered. Even if the contents are sealed, the act of delivery itself affects the meaning that is received. The messenger always affects the message, and the evolution of Hermes records the various dimensions that people have come to recognize in this truth.

At its root, to interpret also means to negotiate – that is, not only to set a meaning but also to set a value. Hermes also became the god of exchange and commerce, as the commerce between people is one way that they reckon with each other in terms of what they value and desire.

Hermes was sent among the mortals by Zeus to help them to get along and to communicate better – apparently an unfinished project. The hermeneutic arts derive from this facility with borders and the messages that cross borders, with pursuit of the truth but also with mystery and deception. Some call psychoanalysis a hermeneutic art.

Much of the character of Hermes, his dual nature as hidden and revealed, his focus on representation, seeker of truth and maker of tales, a master of boundaries and skilled at crossing them, is fundamental to the psychoanalytic craft as well. It is difficult to pin down the character of Hermes. It is likewise difficult to define the interpretive or hermeneutic functions of psychoanalysis. In fact, to call psychoanalysis hermeneutic raises more questions than it answers, because psychoanalysis introduces a new sense to what messages are and how they work. Psychoanalysis differs from all prior forms of interpretation since the act of interpretation itself is seen as part of the message. Hermes is the god of both invention and interpretation, and psychoanalysis is likewise engaged in both.

From its inception, psychoanalysis put representation and interpretation at the center of its therapeutic art and science. Freud's first psychoanalytic books – *The Interpretation of Dreams* (1900), *The Psychopathology of Everyday Life* (1901) and *Jokes and Their Relationship to the Unconscious* (1905) – were about the mechanisms of *representation* and *interpretation* in realms in which those mechanisms were hidden or in doubt. The absurdity of the dream, the meaningless character of the slip and the trivial aspect of the joke are all ways that the message is disguised and the receiver deceived. It was Freud channeling Hermes who demonstrated how these deceptive representations were formed and therefore how they could be recognized and translated.

Jacques Lacan, the French psychoanalyst who led an important and influential bi-weekly seminar in Paris from the early 1950s until his death in 1980, was interested as well in the psychic processes of representation and interpretation and in the therapeutic work on the boundaries associated with them. He called his teaching a "return to Freud" largely because he thought that the Freudian interest in the mechanisms of representation was not sufficiently appreciated by contemporary psychoanalysts at the time, not in a manner that took account of the rich and complex semiotic processes involved. Developments in linguistics, cultural anthropology and philosophy that were occurring contemporaneously with the discovery of psychoanalysis allow a fuller understanding of psychoanalytic processes and especially their symbolic and representational functions.

Lacan was attentive to these parallel developments in the human sciences and was also appreciative of the early Freudian texts cited above, and of Freud's analysis of the symbolic function of disguised messages. It may be helpful, therefore, to think of Hermes in approaching the work of Lacan. Like Hermes, Lacan was interested in the exchange of messages, both between speakers and between the different registers of human experience – i.e. between "gods and mortals." And, like Hermes, Lacan recognized that interpreting a message is never a simple communicative act but, rather, an event that has the potential to transform both the listener and the speaker. Psychoanalysis as the "talking cure" is quite simply the discovery that interpreting the message may be a transformative act, not simply a communication of meaning but the creation of new possibilities in being.

Many of the debates in psychoanalysis and the different psychoanalytic schools or traditions that have developed over the past 100 years or so can be looked at in terms of their approach to the interpretive function. What the analyst chooses to interpret, how much of the material to be interpreted is created in the relationship between the two participants, the choice of patterns of development and/or psychic structures to provide templates for interpretation, etc. are some of the debates that have animated the field since its inception and are still active today. Lacan addressed many of these different psychoanalytic approaches and their implications in his seminars, and he did so through a rigorous study of representation, the exchange of messages and the functions of meaning and interpretation in the psychoanalytic setting.

Messages from the Other

Although the gods and their divine Olympian realm are no longer present for psychoanalysis, Lacan proposed in their place the figure of the Other (*l'Autre*, in French). An important concept in Lacan's work, and one through which we can begin to see his approach to psychoanalytic interpretation and the goals of treatment, this term is derived in part from Freud's use of the concept (*das Andere*, in German) to describe unconscious functions in general (Laplanche, 1992). For Freud, the alterity, or otherness, of the unconscious had multiple meanings. It was another scene – i.e., a place where thoughts and emotions operated apart from the conscious mind. However, to the extent that the unconscious expresses itself, it does so as though it is another and a subject apart from the self. We know that a dream is our own yet it always seems as though it is created by another mind.

Unconscious messages come to us as though from a place other than our conscious mind. That other place is experienced as though it is another mind altogether, like that of the gods: another realm in which all is known and the truth resides. The *Other* in this sense is not the same as the *other* in the sense of another person – i.e., the social other. The Other is a virtual figure implicit in our discourse but not encountered as a real being. However, the relationship between the Other and the other is an important one in Lacanian thought, since we do often experience messages from others as though they are from the Other, and vice versa. The Other is a point of reference where all is known and the truth resides. While this point of reference functions to establish discourse, the Other does not actually exist in the world as a real being.

Lacan's seminar in the fall of 1968 was titled *From an Other to the other* (*D'un Autre à l'autre*; 1968) and it begins with Lacan writing the following statement on the blackboard: "The essence of psychoanalytic theory is a discourse without words" (*"L'essence de la théorie psychanalytique est un discours sans parole"*) (p. 1). I will say more below about what this might mean, but for now it is enough to recognize that Lacan viewed psychoanalysis as a project that went to the core of human discourse and discovered something new there, something deeply related to the very nature of human expression itself and to its interpretation by another subject; something that has forever changed our idea of the human subject.

A *discourse without words* is a paradox, since discourse relies on speech. Lacan was suggesting that there is something paradoxical at the heart of human speech, something other than words and their usual meanings. Freud believed that the discovery of psychoanalysis fundamentally changed our idea of the human subject. Lacan shared this view and elaborated it in terms of our discursive being.

The psychoanalyst and the Other

That this encounter with a structural alterity (the Other) is always virtually present in human discourse is related to the essential mechanism of transference in psychoanalytic work. By "virtually present," I mean that the Other is always implicitly there, but not necessarily in a way that is noticed. In fact, one of the effects of the psychoanalytic situation, the fundamental rule, the silent attention of the analyst, etc. is that the effects of the Other become more apparent. And it is especially through transference that the effects of the Other come to be seen. The analyst's remarks, or even the analyst's silence, may be heard as expressions from the Other, someone who knows all and dwells in that other place where all is known.

While we think of transference as related to the earlier significant figures in the subject's life, it is also true that those figures were significant not only as sources of love, nurturance and authority. They were also the source and locus of all meaning,

Lacan and the evolution of Hermes **57**

where we learn our "mother tongue." Initially parents may stand in the place of the Other, the necessary counterpoint for the speaker. In time, a subject comes to recognize, more or less, that these figures who represent a transcendental authority are in truth just other people, like oneself, and that this status of the Other where all is known is a symbolic status that doesn't really exist in the form of real people. Something similar is repeated in the process of analysis. The analyst's knowledge initially has a transcendent power that gradually disappears. Thus, once again, like Hermes, the analyst is the one whose very presence carries messages across the boundaries between the other and the Other, between the realm of Olympus and that of the mortals.

For Lacan, the existence of the Other is rooted in the very structure of language and the function of speech, a function that is not merely a developmental add-on to our essential being but in fact essential to the nature of that being. The clinical process of psychoanalysis rests on this intersection of speech and the function of the Other as the locus of the unconscious. Of course, we also communicate nonverbally, by gesture and physical expression, or by visual art, dance and music. And, of course, there are those who live fully social lives without speech. Yet all these instances of nonverbal expression occur in the context of a cultural matrix that presumes speech and language as its essential medium. In 1972 Lacan coined the word *parlêtre* ("speakbeing"; Lacan 1975) to indicate that our human being is always that of a linguistically grounded being and to reinforce the idea that our unconscious lives are a consequence of this ground. It is the *parlêtre*, the "speakbeing," who enters psychoanalytic treatment.

The linguistic grounding of distinctly human being is relevant to the contemporary psychoanalytic idea that the human subject is inherently relational rather than monadic. In fact, this is a view that has had a long history in psychoanalysis, and it was present in some of the early debates in the field. Lacan proposed a particular framework for this relationality. He argued that the relational foundation of human being is neither the biological conditions of dependency nor the early object relational matrix of nurturance and attachment alone but, rather, the complex and profound fact that we speak to one another, and that in so doing we represent ourselves to one another in language. According to Lacan's view, it is within the matrix of linguistic representation that the distinctly discursive (or relational) human being emerges. Conditions of dependency and our earliest intimate relationships come to be represented in our discourse and there take on their full human meaning. That they may come to be represented in the gaps of speech, in what may be impossible to say, in slips and in symptoms is entirely consistent with the idea that we are subjects of discourse provided we recognize that discourse is never seamless and complete, never in words alone, but often fractured and incomprehensible; that it is always an occasion for interpretation and the arts of Hermes. Jean Laplanche, who initially studied with Lacan, developed the idea of the *enigmatic signifier* to refer to a discourse that functions precisely by not being understood. The function that he linked to this early encounter with language was nothing less than the origins of infantile psychosexuality (Laplanche, 2006). Note that the linguistic origins

58 David Lichtenstein

of the word *enigma* are related to the Greek word *ainos*, which means a fable, proverb or riddle – that is, a message to be interpreted.

The idea that signifiers function as enigmatic vehicles between the unconscious and conscious thought has great importance in Lacan's view of the clinical process of psychoanalysis at work. The concept of the signifier and its role in psychoanalysis is an idea that Lacan worked on continually over the course of his teaching, in rich and complex ways. To begin with the simplest and perhaps clearest definition, the signifier is that part of a sign that is perceptible, as opposed to that part of the sign that is conceptual. Thus, in the verbal sign, the spoken word, the sound of the word is the signifier while the meaning of the word is the signified. There is a somewhat loose and unfixed connection between signifiers and signified. They are linked in a way that also allows them to be taken apart from one another. Consider, for example, the word *grand*. Its signified meaning can be represented by synonyms such as *outstanding*, *impressive*, *imposing*, *majestic*, etc. They are all linked to the signified aspect of the word *grand*. However, as a signifier, *grand* also functions in the word *grandfather*, which simply means "the father of a father." It is the same signifier but is linked to a different signified. It doesn't signify a "magnificent father" but, rather, a particular family member. This ambiguity in language is quite familiar and is often at work in the disguised messages that cross from unconscious to conscious thought, as Freud noted in his earliest psychoanalytic writings. It is one of the ways that messages both disguise and reveal their unconscious truths. The signifiers in speech inherently generate riddles to be interpreted – enigmas – since they are not tied inextricably to their meanings.

In his first seminar, which took place in 1953–4 and was entitled *Freud's Papers on Technique* (Lacan, 1954), Lacan began his exploration of these linguistic mechanisms and their significance for clinical practice. At one point in this seminar, he took up a case reported by Ernst Kris in an article published in 1951 entitled "Ego psychology and interpretation in psychoanalytic therapy" (Kris, 1951). In this case, Kris reported on a patient who was inhibited in his intellectual work by the belief that he could never be original but was always instead stealing others' ideas. This made it hard for him to complete his work and get it out in the world, but also, if he were able to do so, it would plague him with guilt when he thought of the plagiarism he had committed. On one occasion, Kris actually verified outside the treatment setting that no actual plagiarism had occurred regarding this patient's recent work, and pointed this out to the patient to demonstrate that he was distorting reality. The analyst then added that in falsely believing that he was stealing from another he was giving that other more credit than was warranted. An interpretation then followed that this belief repeated a family drama in which the patient's father had been less accomplished than his *grand*father, and the patient was always looking for ways to bolster his father and to make him appear more *grand*. The idea about stealing others' work was an expression of a wish to bolster them, to attribute more to them than was warranted; a wish displaced from the wish to similarly bolster his father. If the patient always felt he was stealing, then the other must have something

Lacan and the evolution of Hermes 59

worth stealing. We can see how this belief might be not merely about certain others but about the Other, in the Lacanian sense. We might say that the patient believed he always stole from the Other because he could not accept the notion that the Other might be lacking.

Returning to the unconscious functions of the signifier, Kris illustrated the interpretation by saying to the patient that he was always trying to make his father into a *grand* father – that is, more impressive, like his grandfather. This play on words based upon the ambiguous function of the signifier "grand" was noted by Lacan as an example of a successful interpretation and an illustration of how the unconscious works and how clinical psychoanalysis can base technique on such a process.

However, Lacan subsequently returned to this case in 1958, in a paper he delivered at the Royaumont Colloquium entitled "The direction of the treatment and the principles of its power" (in Lacan, 1966). In this discussion, while still appreciating Kris's attention to the play on the signifier "grand," he suggested that ultimately Kris was wrong in telling the patient that he did not steal anything from the other author. Recall that Kris said this to the patient to correct the patient's distortion of reality, leading to the interpretation as to why he would distort things that way. Lacan in this second discussion suggested that, instead of telling the patient that he did not steal, a more effective intervention might have been to point out that "he steals *nothing*" (1966, p. 502, emphasis in original). Thus Lacan, in admiring Kris's use of the signifier "grand," criticized Kris for missing another element of the enigmatic message conveyed by the patient's symptom. To steal *nothing* is a peculiar and paradoxical transgressive act. The subject is simultaneously guilty and not guilty since a theft took place but nothing was stolen. Lacan was suggesting that the patient's symptom is a message that can be interpreted as representing this sort of paradoxical act. This leads the analysis to new questions, such as: Why would someone be interested in stealing nothing?

This subtle question gives us a chance to see how Lacan thought about the clinical process and the role of the message. The message to be interpreted is the patient's conviction that he is a thief. This is his symptom. It comes to the patient from the "Other," as a truth that he can't dispel. Kris in effect tried to dispel the message as a distortion of reality by pointing to the facts: in reality he is not a plagiarist. Lacan instead suggested that the message should not be dispelled but, rather, should be appreciated as saying something more than it appears at first. To dispel the message too quickly in an effort to encourage adjustment to reality has the cost of losing some of its truth. Indeed, the message is true: the patient is a thief, though what he steals is nothing. This is not trivial. It leads Lacan to another place in understanding the case, namely: What does it mean for the patient to believe in this nothing that is worth stealing? The reason Lacan gave is that the patient's desire is not only to support his father but also to deflate the *grand*iosity of the grandfather. By the desire for nothing, the patient seeks to separate himself from the whole complex problem of the grandfather/grand father. Rather than just making the father more grand, his desire is to be free of the whole discourse of grandiosity. The *nothing* is thus an antidote to the *grand*.

Lacan suggested that this effort to separate is akin to anorexia nervosa, whereby the subject desires to eat the nothing so as to separate oral desire from the *too much* that food has come to signify. However, for Kris's patient, rather than food, it is a discourse that surrounds intellectual production; a discourse that involves the patient, his not so grand father, his grandfather and the other from whom he steals nothing. This is initially a "discourse without words," since the patient does not yet know nor speak about it, yet it "speaks" wordlessly through him in the form of guilt and the idea of plagiarism. In truth, the subject is guilty of stealing, and hence the persistent guilt, but he is not guilty of stealing ideas. What he is guilty of stealing – the nothing – carries an important message regarding the discourse of his life and subjective being.

"Discourse" is another word for this matrix of representation between and among "speakbeings." Our relational being is a discursive being. Being a discursive being doesn't mean that the only way we can relate to one another is by speaking. On the contrary, nonverbal communication is also a fundamental character of discourse. Nevertheless, any nonverbal communication that is human communication per se assumes a linguistically formed subject, a subject for whom speech is present as a real possibility. The matrix of discourse in which we relate to one another is one in which speech is possible. That speech may also be impossible – that is, that there are times when we don't know what to say or how to say what we want to say, that at times we are speechless or struck dumb – is essential to the psychoanalytic truth about discourse. What is important is what is said but also what has not yet been said, or what seems as if it cannot be said, what is as yet beyond speech. This is why, from Lacan's point of view, it was important to sustain the symptom/message in the case that Kris was discussing. To refer to reality so as to point out the distorted nature of the symptom may seem like a helpful therapeutic intervention. However, it carries the risk of shutting down the exploration of the message. It fails to carry the process to the further point of what may be beyond what is said. In this instance it forecloses the encounter with "the nothing."

Lacan's interest in the structural linguistics of Ferdinand de Saussure (1916) and Roman Jakobson (1990), as well as the anthropology of Claude Lévi-Strauss (1949) and the philosophy of Martin Heidegger (1927), was connected to his view of the human subject as a linguistically formed and symbolically grounded being. That the work of these thinkers was directly relevant to psychoanalysis was rarely appreciated before Lacan, and the links to their theories rarely studied aside from Lacan and his students. The matrix of representation and its linguistic, anthropological and philosophical elaboration is the domain in which Lacan reinterpreted the psychoanalytic endeavor. However, as Lacan worked with these other disciplines, he also articulated repeatedly and increasingly over the course of his teaching how psychoanalysis and psychoanalytic treatment brings new questions to those of linguistics, anthropology and philosophy.

The formation of the subject

This mutual interaction between the linguistic and anthropological perspectives on subjectivity and the more individual and personal dynamics of the psychoanalytic perspective results in the distinct approach found in Lacan's work. In considering the importance, say, of mother–infant dynamics in the formation of the young subject, Lacan did not start from the observable and manifest relationship. Instead, he viewed the mother as a culturally embedded subject defined by her linguistic community, her personal fantasies, the structure of her unconscious desires, etc. Into this representational matrix arrives a baby who is already anticipated, named, spoken about. Indeed, the baby has something of a subjective being well before he or she is actually born. And the parents both consciously and unconsciously create that subjective being who is the baby to be. How the actual baby encounters and interacts with the symbolic and imaginary baby that was in the process of being created alongside the organic gestation becomes part of the child's history, and, indeed, part of the unconscious subjectivity of the person who emerges.

This happens through very real exchanges involving the parent's fantasies and modes of responding, even if no one thinks about it very much if at all. It is here that modes of attachment and the manifest relational determinants in infancy take on meaning. They are part of the protolinguistic framework that forms the young subject *as a subject of discourse*. Relationships, character and identity develop in this way due to the fact that the players in this story are all themselves subjects in a representational matrix. Thus, in the Lacanian framework, development is never an independent biological and/or psychological process but always a structural emergence, an articulation of possibilities within a system of largely unconscious fantasies and expectations, a system that is structured like a language in its representational character.

Among these unconscious fantasies are those that represent the desires of the parents. The mother's desire, for example, in having a baby is never a straightforward dyadic interplay between her and the baby, in spite of how much it might look that way at times from the outside, or, indeed, in her own conscious self-reflection. There are always other registers in her experience, and in the baby's as well. The mother's desire for a baby in relation to her partner's desire, in relation to her own parents' desire, in relation to siblings and/or figures of the extended family all play a part in constructing the meaning and the enigma of this particular child at this particular time.

That the infant in his or her helplessness is dependent on a mother who is herself, as a subject, also oriented in her own particular way to the desire of others means that, for this baby, there is an inevitable encounter not only with a structure of meaning but also with a profound and puzzling threat, namely the mother's turning away, the enigma of separation, her emotional, psychic and/or real absences due to the complex structure of other desires that form her as a subject. Thus, the state of being incomplete, that state of being that is reflected by the fact that the mother desires, is a profound and formative loss for the infant. It introduces the

62 David Lichtenstein

principle that the mother, like all desiring subjects, lacks something, as evidenced by her expressed desire, and that it is something that the baby cannot sufficiently provide, since she turns away to find it elsewhere. It is thus a double lack. It is a lack in the mother's being for which the baby is insufficient. Mother–infant attunement can never be more than partial except as a delusion. Its incompleteness presents an enigma that defines the new subject.

Delusions of perfect attunement do exist, and can indeed be tragic obstacles to the formation of the subject. Donald Winnicott (1971), the child analyst, who wrote so much about the emergence of subjectivity in infancy, also addressed in his writings this important break in the ideal and complete connection to the mother. For Lacan as for Winnicott, although in different ways, this break in the idealized connection is not an avoidable failure of attunement and/or parenting but a formative gap that allows a new human subject to emerge.

Lacan linked this structuring loss to what Freud identified as castration anxiety. This link to the Freudian idea of castration is not as salient for Winnicott nor for those who work from within the broadly conceived object relations framework (see Benjamin, 1998), and asserting it has been a controversial element regarding Lacan's thought. For many contemporary psychoanalytic theorists, retaining the importance of castration fantasies and/or castration anxiety in the psychoanalytic theory of gender and sexuality is seen as a carryover from Freud's earlier biological bias. For those critics, it also implies a failure on Lacan's part to appreciate the primacy of the mother–infant relation and the development of the socially embedded subject on their own terms. Concerns about the presence or absence of the male organ are thus seen as reflecting a patriarchal or phallocentric ideology that many contemporary psychoanalysts reject. This rejection has extended therefore to Lacanian theory in general. Since the notion of symbolic castration is indeed an important principle in Lacan's thought, and since Lacan thought that it retains its importance as a fundamental principle in the psychoanalytic theory of the subject, it is important to clarify the concept in relation to these objections.

Symbolic castration

Lacan's conception of castration is not rooted in either a biological or a masculinist bias. It was instead an effort to recuperate the Freudian concept on a new plane, one that is concerned not with the male organ per se but with its representational function. The human subject emerges inevitably as a gendered subject not because of biological imperatives but because of the linguistic-cultural organization of the world that is itself so ordered. A baby must take its place as either a *he* or a *she* in the culture, and thus in the family relationships that themselves are culturally embedded. The *he-ness* and *she-ness* differ in varying cultural milieus but every culture is so ordered. Even bisexuality and fluid, multifaceted gender identifications derive from this binary structure even as they play upon it. Likewise, contemporary gender and psychoanalytic theories that question what it may mean to move beyond the binary must engage this structure even as they work to open it up.

If, with Lacan, we accept Freud's idea that there is a time in infancy prior to this distinction between the sexes, then, at that time, the mother is understood by the child to be the complete embodiment of all human possibility. Lacan then suggested that the infant's encounter with incompleteness in the mother, an incompleteness that is the inevitable fate of all subjects, initiates the encounter with sexual difference. The mother is not everything, and is in fact only one sex out of two. There is another gender, one perhaps associated with fathers, but in any case not that of mothers. This division of the sexes, together with the fact that, as a subject, it seems that one must take up a place on one side of this division or the other, is related to the loss described above. It is the loss of a narcissistic completeness in the subject accompanying a disillusion with the idealized power of the mother, and it is a loss that accompanies the recognition of gender as a division, a split, that means no one can be all nor complete as a "speakbeing." Thus, for Lacan, this structure of insufficiency at the formation of the human subject regardless of gender is the context for that which is defined as castration in psychoanalytic thought.

At the same time, this realization of gender division and process by which the subject takes a place in the cultural order as a gendered being is accompanied by a reflection upon the body and upon the physical distinctions between the sexes. Sexual difference on the physical level is a way to represent the truth of the gendered subject. We know quite well that the subject does not necessarily assume the subject gender of his or her own physical body. The contrary identification can be made, but, nevertheless, the available representation for the subjective gender is the physical body. Transgender subjects are rarely indifferent to their bodies; on the contrary. We may jettison aspects of the Freudian elaboration of sexual difference as reflecting Viennese culture at the time he wrote without giving up the fundamental truth that the body, and especially the genitals as markers of sexual difference, takes on a signifying function, a function of representation rather than a biological givenness.

The concept of castration in Lacanian thought stands for the entire complex process of representing the loss of narcissistic completeness and coming to recognize the structures of sexual difference. It is a representational process that employs the male organ as a symbol – i.e., the phallus rather than the penis – for the complex and difficult acceptance of sexual incompleteness and division. Lacan's interest in structural linguistics, anthropology and the logic of representational systems allowed him to elaborate this concept in rich and surprising ways. "On the signification of the phallus," an essay written in 1958 and published in his collected *Écrits* (1966), is an instance of his early development of these ideas. Seminar XX, which was given in 1972–3 and which was entitled *On Feminine Sexuality: The Limits of Love and Knowledge* (1975), was a later development and one in which Lacan addressed the idea of symbolic castration for the feminine subject. The challenge for the contemporary reader of Lacan is whether his efforts to retain and recuperate the idea of symbolic castration successfully address the complexity of

64 David Lichtenstein

gender roles as lived in contemporary society. Juliet Mitchell and Jacqueline Rose have written important essays (Mitchell & Rose, 1982) that address this seminar of Lacan in relation to feminist thought. The more recent work of Judith Butler, for instance, who both credits Lacan and critiques aspects of his thought, is also relevant to this question; see, for example, Butler (2006).

For Lacan, castration represents the encounter with the idea of not being sufficient in relation to the desire of the mother. Both boy and girl babies encounter this insufficiency. That they interpret it differently due to their awareness of sexual difference is why it is linked to the presence/absence of a penis. The idea is that the penis is put to service in the fantasy life of children as the representative of lack and insufficiency. As a fantasy, the castration involved is an imaginary one. In treating psychoanalysis as a field organized around representation and symbolization and around the problem of how an embodied being assumes a subjective place in this representational matrix, Lacan shifted the role of the body from that of a biological ground to a signifying element. The body and fantasies about the body, including fantasies of castration, may take on symbolic functions.

Messages from and about the body are no less in need of interpretation and translation than any other. This implies that the body creates messages that may potentially be deciphered, that the body speaks. The body speaks, but not always in words nor conveying messages that are explicit and comprehensible. The discourse of the body can be obscure and troubling, and certain critical periods in the development of the subject are characterized by encounters with this discourse.

Hermes and Oedipus

In the Middle Ages a quasi-mythical figure known as Hermes Trismegistus (the "thrice great Hermes") was associated with the occult and alchemical arts. He was thought to be an ancient priest of magic and the source of secret hidden knowledge – i.e., the hermetic. That he was named after the god who is charged with delivering messages and facilitating exchange suggests that Hermes also became the god of a secret and closed world of knowledge. To know the mechanisms of exchange is also to know the mechanisms of occultation. Likewise, the psychoanalyst hears both the expressed unconscious message and the mechanisms of repression that occult it. To recognize the hidden character of a message is to listen at the border between sense and nonsense, between the present and the absent.

The psychoanalyst is concerned with how fantasies, partly conscious but largely unconscious, are conveyed by signs. Those signs may then operate according to their own linguistic character, substituting for one another through mechanisms of displacement, condensation and the associated processes of representation. Inherent in the function of signs is the interplay of revelation and occultation.

While we might be inclined to dismiss mythical and magical representations from an earlier time, we can recognize that what was being represented in the evolution of the figure of Hermes, for instance, is the elaboration of a certain set of significant human functions that operate in an interrelated way. The vehicle of myth was a way to convey the recognition that something important is represented by this combination of functions.

Representing them as the attributes of a god or legendary priest is one way to convey their complex coordination and interrelation. It is a function of mythical thinking to bring together related but sometimes contradictory qualities and functions and organize them as the attributes of a superhuman character (Calasso, 1993). While we may no longer represent these functions as the attributes of a god, we may still learn a great deal about those functions by studying the evolution of the myth (Brown, 1947), just as it is the myth of Hermes and the evolution of his complex and contradictory qualities that may tell us about the structure of psychoanalysis.

It was similar, of course, regarding Freud's interest in Oedipus. The myth of Oedipus was the basis for Sophocles' plays but it already had a life of its own as myth in its representation of certain critical functions of the family and the origins of subjectivity. The idea that the infant subject is cast out of the original family and left in the wild to die conveys an important truth about the origins of subjectivity that appears in many myths.

This truth is found in the story of Moses set out on the river and raised by strangers, or of Perseus similarly cast adrift as an infant. That Moses and Perseus go on to found civilizations and establish the law of those civilizations is part of their myth and linked in significant ways to the crisis of their origin. We can therefore identify the story as the myth of Oedipus/Moses/Perseus, for, indeed, when we discover these common principles among myths it becomes possible to see them all as versions of the same myth (Calasso, 1993). It is a myth regarding how the crisis between the generations gives rise to a subject who creates a new order. Viewed this way, it is clearer why Freud thought it might be central to the psychoanalytic endeavor. Reduced to its structural core, it is a myth that says that, despite the conflictual and indeed murderous impulses in the family, a subject may emerge to create something new. Indeed, this myth may even be read as saying that, because we are cast out, and indeed only insofar as we experience exile, we may emerge as heroic creators.

The psychoanalytic truth that reflects the sense of the Oedipal myth is that there must be an equivalent of a casting out, some rupture or break between the parent and the child, in order for the creative subject to emerge. There is an idea here, obviously a very ancient one, that the human subject is not ideally shaped only by harmony and attunement but also by something else, something that appears more troubling, something involving a break or rejection and the possibility of restoration. This idea appears in many different psychoanalytic formulations, and it was central for Lacan. This was another significance of Lacan's return to Freud: the idea that the Oedipal myth or structure contains a robust theory of the subject and of human development and should not be discarded, as some post-Freudian approaches seem eager to do.

In Lacan's view, the moment of the *casting out* is the moment in infancy (even calling it a moment is resorting to myth) when the infant experiences the mother (or primary caregiver) as in some way insufficient. In that moment, the infant, like

66 David Lichtenstein

the infant Moses on the Nile or Oedipus left exposed on the mountainside, is at the mercy of fate. This break defines the infant's destiny. Likewise, for Lacan, encountering the mother's lack or insufficiency is the defining event in a subjective destiny as well.

It is possible to shift our framework from that of myth to that of unconscious fantasy. The infant's idea of the mother as the complete source of being is understandable given the circumstances of infantile dependence; as an idea, though, it is unconscious rather than a conscious thought. Indeed, it is hard to imagine what form of conscious thought it could be. However, it does make sense to conceive of it as an unconscious fantasy, an implicit belief or framework of truth that influences the subject without any conscious awareness. In this it is like a myth, somewhat occluded and appearing only in partial revelations.

This returns us to Hermes and to his facility with the message, both revealed and hidden. What appears and what remains unseen, the dialectic of presence and absence and the subject's reworking of that dialectic in the matrix of representation are at the heart of the psychoanalytic endeavor.

It is as a consequence of absence, some lack, that the subjective is constituted as an expressive and desiring being. To represent absence, and to make it simultaneously present and yet still lacking, is the distinctly human act that links speech and language to the mechanisms of the drives and desire.

Freud noted this dilemma in *Beyond the Pleasure Principle* (1920), in which he told of his infant grandson representing his mother's departure through his game of *Fort-Da*. This passage in Freud is one of the strongest links to Lacan's endeavor to ground psychoanalysis in a theory of representation, and indeed to then ground that theory of representation in an appreciation of the unconscious fantasy that constitutes the material to be represented. The dialectic of representation and the unconscious message to be represented lie at the core of the psychoanalytic theory of the subject for Lacan. However, since the very nature of representation is that its presence conveys an absence by substitution, there is an inherent link between the message and its means of conveyance. In this sense, the very existence of the message *is* the message. That there is a message means that there is a boundary to be crossed, that there is something unknown on the other side, and that is the content of the message as well.

Freud's grandson uttered two phonemes: a sort of "ooo" and a sort of "ah." The adults who knew the child, and especially his mother, recognized that these phonemes were linked to the German words *fort* ["gone"] and *da* ["there"]. However, it is a basic principle in structural linguistics (Saussure, Jakobson, etc.) that the smallest recognizable difference between phonemes is sufficient to establish their representational function – that is to say, that language works by a system of differences or phonetic oppositions, in this case "ooo-ah." Thus, the discovery and the significance of the event for Freud's grandson were not only that a message about his mother's departure and return could be represented but that the message itself could be conveyed by a simple phonetic opposition. The creation of the message was accompanied by the game that the child was simultaneously playing, of throwing a spool out of his crib and hauling it back by its thread. The creation of the message is linked to play and to a game – indeed, a language game (Wittgenstein, 1953). Freud related his grandson's game to what he called "the child's great cultural achievement" (Freud, 1922, p. 15) in allowing his mother to leave; however, it is the representation that supports that achievement, and indeed embodies it.

Winnicott (1971) developed a similar idea with his transitional object and transitional phenomena, which occupy a space in which questions of reality and fantasy, and thus questions of presence and absence, are temporarily suspended. The representation and the thing it represents are considered to be the same. Lacan called this thing that can be represented, and yet still be absent, the "cause of desire." He recognized his debt to both Freud and Winnicott, and developed this virtual object into a central feature of his psychoanalytic theory.

The object "a," as Lacan called it, is neither wholly real, nor imaginary nor symbolic, but exists in a paradoxical space as all three. It is the lost object that causes desire to come into being. The paradox is that it is represented only as something lost, and isn't lost until it is represented that way. Desire comes into being as pursuit of this lost object, circumscribes the place where it is missing and gives it a presence even in its absence.

Hermeneutics in general, as the art and science of interpretation, is concerned with understanding; however, especially in the psychoanalytic hermeneutic, that object, like the missing object that causes desire, is always over the horizon. It is always across the border, an object of pursuit but never found once and for all time. There is never a full understanding of what the lost object is, since it exists only as lost. Thus, moments of understanding in psychoanalysis are fleeting and invariably lead to a new enigma. They are mercurial. Psychoanalysis is a hermeneutic of suspicion (Ricoeur, 1981), but a suspicion that is never laid to rest in an answer. Why this is so, why in this sense psychoanalysis is not a hermeneutic science at all but a process that only appears hermeneutic, only appears to be interested in interpretation with some other goal in mind, adds to the mercurial aspect of character. Lacan's idea of psychoanalysis involves the limits of understanding, the limits of meaning and the boundary with something beyond. But this too is in keeping with the character of Hermes. He is not simply interested in decoding the message but in recognizing what the message is meant to do, not just knowing what the message means but knowing what is at stake in its delivery.

In 1955 Lacan wrote an important essay on E. A. Poe's short story "The purloined letter" (1966). Recall that, in the story, a letter involved in a blackmail plot is hidden in plain sight, and for this reason the police cannot find it. As the plot develops, the location of the letter becomes more important than its content. In his analysis of this story Lacan concludes: "[T]he letter was able to have its effects on the inside – on the tale's actors, including the narrator – just as much on the outside – on us, its readers, and also on the author – without anyone ever having had to worry about what it meant" (p. 43).

68 David Lichtenstein

The message in its material form is what is at stake: the letter itself as an object rather than its content. That the message was disguised as something trivial and left out in plain sight is what needs to be interpreted more than what is said in its text. So it may be that the psychoanalyst will be less concerned with the meaning of what is being said than with how and where it is said, and who may recognize it as a message. Thus it is also the cunning nature of Hermes to recognize when interpretation may in fact miss the meaning of the message.

Having a facility with borders and messages, like Hermes, psychoanalysis is concerned with these both within the mind and between minds. If I misplace an object and then want later to understand what that act of misplacement may have meant, do I consider what I lost, or do I consider where I lost it, or, indeed, what I was doing when I lost it? It is not enough to know that the act might be a message; it is also necessary to know how that message was meant to function.

It is often said about Lacan's contributions to psychoanalysis that he focused on language. It is true that he often addressed the function of speech in psychoanalysis and recognized that it was important to know how speech operated in relation to the structure of language. However, he was interested in speech and language in order to see how the exchange of messages, what we call discourse, forms the human subject. Ultimately, it is the effects of discourse – that is, the very acts of saying and listening – that make a difference in psychoanalysis more than an understanding of what is said.

It is the very conditions of the message and in the cultural framework that allows for the exchange of messages, a framework we now call discourse, that these terms come about. It is part of the Hermes legend that, as a baby, he stole Apollo's cattle because he craved the meat and cleverly hid the theft by reversing the hooves on the cattle, thereby leaving a deceptive trace. When Apollo figured out what had happened, accused Hermes of the crime and asked for justice from Zeus, their father, the puckish Hermes so artfully defended himself that he was forgiven his crime as a reward for his artistry. By his actions, Zeus affirmed that the crime of sibling rivalry as an expression of desire is forgivable once it is brought into the play of discourse.

This linkage between discourse, desire and an original crime is also at the heart of psychoanalysis. Freud, of course, linked the formative crime to Oedipus rather than to Hermes, but Oedipus, like Hermes, had the gift of interpretation; he solved the riddle of the sphinx, as well as the debt and destiny of an original crime, both what was done to him when he was abandoned as an infant and what he subsequently did while trying to escape his fate. Before Oedipus was born, there was the prophecy that the baby would eventually slay his father. The birth itself presaged the tragedy. The myth is built on the idea that the birth of a child is not a blank slate, but the vehicle for a story already being told. As Lacan might put it, the unconscious is the discourse of the Other. Oedipus represents the fate of the human subject, to be born into a discourse prefiguring one's fate, and yet, as a subject of desire, to fabricate something new.

Psychoanalysis has long struggled with the meaning and importance of its own mythic resonance. In the 1950s, as the dominant psychiatric ideology in the United States, and only beginning to lose its preeminence to the burgeoning biological and pharmaceutical approach that soon took over, psychoanalysis presented itself not as the legacy of Hermes, the cunning trickster, but primarily as a secure repository of authority and knowledge about social adaptation and emotional well-being. If it was an interpretive endeavor, those interpretations tended to rest upon the already known, rather than the possibility of discovery. Psychoanalysis in those years was often represented as a predictive stage theory of psychosexual development, and its interpretive clinical focus was on recognizing particular deviations from the normal progression of stages. This view not only narrowed the interpretive range but also minimized reflection on the mechanisms of representation per se. Too much weight rested upon the already known.

There were notable exceptions. Herbert Marcuse (1955) and Norman Brown (1959) both published books that suggested that there was something still capable of generating surprise and discovery in the psychoanalytic endeavor. The texts of Freud, as well, read mostly either in philosophy classes or on one's own rather than a part of academic psychology, still conveyed a level of inquiry, uncertainty and the roots of something enigmatic to support the view that something had gone missing in mainstream psychoanalysis, something of its mythopoeic possibilities. In the midst of this crisis regarding the vitality of psychoanalytic thought, Lacan's work appeared, and opened possibilities for reflection and reconsideration that are still generating new work.

Jacques Lacan, trained in psychiatry and psychoanalysis in the 1920s and 1930s, began developing his ideas about the structure of discourse and the mythic resonance of unconscious desire in the 1940s and 1950s. However, it wasn't until the late 1960s, with the publication of *The Language of the Self*, translated by Anthony Wilden (Lacan, 1956), that the English-speaking world could begin to get a sense of his work. Translations appeared only gradually at first. It is now possible to read a great deal of Lacan's work in English, and the translations continue to improve. There is now a vast secondary literature available in English as well, and the full scope and import of his ideas are being addressed.

There has been a historical tension within the field of psychoanalysis between those who view it as a prescribed clinical discipline, with well-established rules and procedures, and those who see it as a humanistic inquiry open to creative possibilities in both theory and practice. Lacan took a slightly different view from both of these and asserted that there is a distinctly human science called psychoanalysis that follows neither the principles of natural science nor those of a more literary or philosophical hermeneutics. Psychoanalysis is a clinical treatment and thus concerned about its effects in a way that is not the concern of philosophy or literary criticism. Thus psychoanalysis, for Lacan, is neither a branch of the humanities nor of the natural sciences, governed as they are by principles of replicability and observable,

70 David Lichtenstein

operational variables. It is a unique clinical discipline, a human science that stands on innovative principles of truth and meaning.

Ultimately, these questions about psychoanalytic theory are important because they affect how we conduct our clinical practice. In the view that we have been considering here, the clinical process of psychoanalysis entails helping the analysand encounter the cause of his or her desire. In the case above, reported by Kris, the patient who was caught by the idea that he was an inescapable plagiarist, Lacan suggested that the cause of his desire is *the nothing* that he steals in order to get free of the family drama surrounding the status of his grandfather and his father. His symptom is listened to as a message, but an enigmatic message that must be deciphered in order to reveal the cause of desire. The analyst's task is to stay focused on that process of deciphering, translating and interpreting. As the one who does so, the analyst becomes implicated in the exchange; however, that implication and the relational dynamics that ensue are not the focus per se. They too become clues as to the function and sense of the message and the cause of desire that is at its heart. The message and its effects are ultimately experienced by the analysand, not given by the analyst.

Lacan's approach to psychoanalysis faces objections from at least two sides. From the side of classical psychoanalysis, ego psychology and modern conflict theory, Lacan's ideas take psychoanalysis too far from its biological roots. The drives, viewed by Freud as phenomena on the border of the biological and the psychic, would thus seem to require that we maintain more of an anchoring in the former than Lacan's turn to language and discourse seems to allow.

From the side of relational theorists (Benjamin, 1998), Lacan's approach is not sufficiently attuned to the importance of real relationships both in the development of the self and in the clinical process. Lacan's notion that social relations should be viewed as discursive structures may be responsible for this sense that he fails to appreciate the affective, interpersonal realities, and their role in the development of psychic structures.

There are, no doubt, important elements of truth in both these objections; however, the work of Lacan is nothing if not highly complex and extensive in its scope and implications. How he does indeed maintain places in his teaching both for the biological roots of the drives and for the real experience of affective interchanges is beyond the scope of this discussion. Perhaps the fairest judgment on these points is that, if he has done so, it is in ways that are either too obscure or marginal to have received the attention they deserve.

Lacan once said that the objective of analysis is "that the subject should come to recognize and to name his desire" (Lacan, 1966). To recognize desire requires an encounter with that desire in a form that can be recognized. This is where the analyst comes in, as the one who can represent back to the analysand that which is to be recognized in the discourse of the analysand. To name desire is a creative act, like all naming, that marks something new coming into the world. Thus, to recognize and name is to simultaneously see something that has been there and then, by an act of naming, establish it as something new. In this sense, the knowledge that comes from a psychoanalytic treatment has both always been there and also is created anew in the analytic work, created finally by the analysand, or perhaps by the analysis itself.

The idea of a unique human science based on principles of knowledge that alter our idea of how we know things, on principles of behavior that alter our definition of an action and how it can be observed, on principles of expression that alter our idea of what it means to be a discursive being – this is the sort of science that Lacan proposed psychoanalysis to be. He maintained that this upheaval in knowledge was the full implication of Freud's discovery. We are left to consider whether he may have been correct in this assessment.

References

Benjamin, J. (1998). *Shadow of the Other: Intersubjectivity and Gender in Psychoanalysis.* New York: Routledge.

Brown, N. O. (1947). *Hermes the Thief: The Evolution of a Myth.* Madison, WI: University of Wisconsin Press.

Brown, N. O. (1959). *Life against Death: The Psychoanalytical Meaning of History.* Middletown, CT: Wesleyan University Press.

Butler, J. (2006). *Gender Trouble: Feminism and the Subversion of Identity.* New York: Routledge.

Calasso, R. (1993). *The Marriage of Cadmus and Harmony.* New York: Alfred A. Knopf.

De Saussure, F. (1916 [1986]). *Course in General Linguistics* (R. Harris, Ed. and Trans.). Chicago: Open Court Publications.

Freud, S. (1900 [1953]). The interpretation of dreams. In J. Strachey (Ed. & Trans.), *The Standard Edition of the Complete Psychological Works of Sigmund Freud,* Vol. IV, pp. 1–338. London: Hogarth Press.

Freud, S. (1901 [1960]). The psychopathology of everyday life. In J. Strachey (Ed. & Trans.), *The Standard Edition of the Complete Psychological Works of Sigmund Freud,* Vol. VI, pp. 1–280. London: Hogarth Press.

Freud, S. (1905 [1960]). Jokes and their relation to the unconscious. In J. Strachey (Ed. & Trans.), *The Standard Edition of the Complete Psychological Works of Sigmund Freud,* Vol. VIII, pp. 9–238. London: Hogarth Press.

Freud, S. (1920 [1955]). Beyond the pleasure principle. In J. Strachey (Ed. & Trans.), *The Standard Edition of the Complete Psychological Works of Sigmund Freud,* Vol. XVIII, pp. 7–64. London: Hogarth Press.

Heidegger, M. (1927 [2008]). *Being and Time* (J. MacQuarrie & E. Robinson, Trans.). New York: HarperCollins.

Jakobson, R. (1990). *On Language* (L.R. Waugh & M. Monville-Burston, Eds.). Cambridge, MA: Harvard University Press.

Kris, E. (1951). Ego psychology and interpretation in psychoanalytic therapy. *Psychoanalytic Quarterly,* 20(1): 15–30.

Lacan, J. (1954 [1974]). *Le Séminaire,* Book I, *Les Écrits techniques de Freud.* Paris: Seuil.

Lacan, J. (1956 [1968]). *The Language of the Self* (A. Wilden, Trans.). Baltimore: Johns Hopkins University Press.

Lacan, J. (1966 [2006]). *Écrits: The First Complete Edition in English* (B. Fink, Trans.). New York: W.W. Norton.

Lacan, J. (1968 [2006]). *Le Séminaire,* Book XVI, *D'un Autre à l'autre.* Paris: Seuil.

Lacan, J. (1975 [1998]). *On Feminine Sexuality: The Limits of Love and Knowledge* (B. Fink, Trans.). New York: W.W. Norton.

Laplanche, J. (1992 [1999]). *Essays on Otherness* (J. Fletcher, Ed.; L. Thurston, Trans.). Abingdon, UK: Routledge.

Laplanche, J. (2006 [2011]). *Freud and the Sexual* (J. Fletcher, J. House & N. Ray, Trans.). New York: International Psychoanalytic Books.

Lévi-Strauss, C. (1949 [1969]). *The Elementary Structures of Kinship* (R. Needham, Ed.; J. Hark, Trans.). Boston: Beacon Press.

Marcuse, H. (1955). *Eros and Civilization: A Philosophical Inquiry into Freud*. Boston: Beacon Press.

Mitchell, J., & Rose, J. (Eds.) (1982). *Feminine Sexuality: Jacques Lacan and the école freudienne* (J. Rose, Trans.). New York: W.W. Norton.

Ricoeur, P. (1981). *Hermeneutics and the Human Sciences: Essays on Language, Action and Interpretation* (J. Thompson, Trans.). Cambridge: Cambridge University Press.

Winnicott, D.W. (1971). *Playing and Reality*. London: Tavistock Publications.

Wittgenstein, L. (1953 [2009]). *Philosophical Investigations* (G. E. M. Anscombe, P. M. S. Hacker & J. Schulte, Trans.). Chichester, UK: Wiley-Blackwell.

PART II
Object relations

4

A CONTEMPORARY KLEINIAN/ BIONIAN PERSPECTIVE

Marilyn Charles

Introduction

Melanie Klein was writing at a time when psychoanalytic theory was drawn largely from work with adult patients, the focus on verbal language and Oedipal development. Klein's work with young, traumatized children whose development had been foreclosed offered a useful perspective on pre-Oedipal development and nonverbal meanings. Her conceptualizations opened up profound territory for psychoanalytic exploration, pivotal to have in mind in our work with more fragile patients. With those with no secure grounding in self-development, it is essential to be able to ground ourselves in a coherent theoretical understanding at just those times when rational understanding is least accessible within the process itself. That grounding can help us to remain empathically present and available even under strain and to keep our thinking more closely in relation to the experience of the patient.

Wilfred Bion was an independent thinker who greatly extended Klein's ideas through his own explorations. In many ways, Bion was beyond his time, a fact affirmed by the relatively recent "discovery" of his work in the broader psychoanalytic community in the United States. I always appreciated Bion because he was such a right-brained thinker who doggedly found his way to the heart and soul of the human mind and being, affirming the importance of *learning from our own experience,* beyond any received knowledge we might take in from others (Bion, 1977). Bion recognized early on how profoundly moved we are by those around us, noting ways in which group experience moves toward resolution of tension and away from mindful or reflective thought (Bion, 1961). The heart of Bion's contributions can be found in the collection of his early papers, in which he thought through his work with psychotic individuals, and then looked back on that work to show the reader how his own reflective capacities had developed over time (Bion, 1967a).

Bion recognized the ubiquity of psychotic experience and the internal tensions between the more primitive types of thinking highlighted by Klein versus the conscious, rational thought that might seem reassuring while also missing important elements of the situation. Notably, Bion contended that our most important processing occurs through the unconscious. Psychoanalysis, then, becomes an important means of gaining greater access to and facility with the unconscious. To help the clinician to recognize that our actions might belie our conscious intentions, Bion helped to better illuminate the psychoanalytic field by tracking the complexity of the thought *and also* the uses to which the thought is being put (see Charles, 2002a, for an explication of Bion's grid).

The legacy of Klein's and Bion's work can be found in contemporary Kleinian and Bionian studies in which the countertransference experiences of the analyst are the primary source of data for insights into the mind, heart and being of the patient. In this chapter, I will highlight ideas from that tradition that I have found particularly useful and will offer very brief clinical vignettes so that we can anchor the theory and technical considerations in personal experience. I will also provide a brief introduction to some salient aspects of Bion's work, which will be referred to later in the chapter on field theory. Finally, I will note some of the limits I come to in working with Kleinian ideas, along with conceptualizations that help me to move beyond those constraints.

Kleinian theory

Kleinian theory is deeply embedded in classical Freudian technique, with a profound respect for the importance of the frame in bounding the treatment (Segal, 1967). Keeping a strict frame enables the analyst to note deviations and invite reflections upon them. As Hanna Segal puts it: "The role of the analyst is confined to interpreting the patient's material, and all criticism, advice, encouragement, reassurance, and the like, is rigorously avoided. The interpretations are centered on the transference situation, impartially taking up manifestations of positive and negative transference as they appear" (p. 3). The Kleinian perspective is *interpersonal*, part of the object relations tradition, recognizing that all relationships are filtered through the internal figures that make up the individual's inner world. The focus, however, is *intrapsychic*. The analyst reflects on what is going on inside the patient – the internal *object world* – using the analyst's ideas and experiences to make hypotheses about what the patient is working at and then noting the impact of those interpretations on the process itself in order to obtain evidence regarding the relative accuracy of the working hypotheses.

Many people come to us suffering from early and unintegrated assaults and deprivations that have left them with no secure foundation. Because identity is formulated in the context of an evolving life narrative, deficits in early relationships between child and caregiver impede both self- and relational development and, with these, the capacity to translate experience into words. In work with individuals whose development has been obstructed, and who therefore speak primarily through feelings rather than words, the lens of Kleinian theory and technique can be particularly useful.

Klein's work evolved in relation to her attempts to discern the unconscious phantasies that underlay her young patients' behaviors. Her working principle was that, in providing access to unconscious phantasy, psychoanalysis affords a means by which those phantasies might be relived and remodeled. Kleinians use *phantasy* to denote unconscious material versus the conscious *fantasy* of daydreams and other imaginings that may, as Donald Winnicott (1971) notes, be more routinized and have less depth or creative potential.

Kleinian language can be off-putting, inviting the reader of even the contemporary Kleinians to think "I could never imagine saying that!" The power of what the Kleinians offer to us as clinicians, however, is not so much in the precise form of their interventions but, rather, in the attention to process, nuance and emotional meanings as they develop and play out in the transference. The term *total transference* marks how the experience of the moment illuminates the patient's internal objects, including experiential, relational and situational elements (Joseph, 1985). To understand the other's object world, we need to be willing to participate in it, to experience the "transference as a living relationship in which there is constant movement and change" (p. 453).

The transference/countertransference matrix, for the Kleinians, is much more than the particular relational dynamic and the feelings associated with it. There is also attention to the larger patterns of meaning that are communicated through the prosodies of affective tensions as they play out within the consulting room. The Kleinian willingness to be present in the moment and to engage deeply with phantasy and primary experience give their work a potency and vitality that help to link meaning and experience, encouraging a confrontation with the difficulties needing to be faced, including the internal signals to our own ambivalence as we encounter them in a given moment. Bion's (1992) notions of *dreaming the session* invite the analyst to take seriously ways in which his or her unconscious relates to the unconscious of the patient, adding another "voice" to the conversation.

To help acquaint you with the strengths of the Kleinian/Bionian perspective, I will offer a few of the conceptualizations that I have found most useful, including *projective identification*, the *paranoid-schizoid position* and *defensive organizations*. I will also say a little about Kleinian views of transference and countertransference, and the importance of recognizing aggression and envy, and of paying attention to the effects of one's interpretations upon the work. I use the term *interpretation* broadly to refer to the analyst's statements, which are inevitably hypotheses about what is going on in the moment. For Kleinians, the present moment matters, and there is an attempt to stay with the experience as it emerges in the transference/countertransference engagements in the consulting room, to find what Bion (1977) terms the *passion* that leads us *toward* the point of difficulty rather than away.

From that vantage point, Bion (1977) highlights the constant tensions between *growth* and *evasion* that challenge us all. Part of the analyst's job is to track these tensions within the work and to recognize ways in which resistance can be a defense against insight. Bion enlarges our view of the Oedipal dilemma from a focus on the primal scene, as such, to recognize the more general tendency to *turn a blind eye* to whatever is too difficult to bear. Unconscious phantasy helps turn our attention back toward whatever we are resisting knowing. Phantasy provides a window into the defenses by recognizing ways in which defended material emerges in the consulting room as the unconscious anxiety softens.

The emergence of such material may be essential to understanding not only the defenses but also ways in which the character of the individual has been shaped and structured. According to Segal (1967, p. 8), "The fact that structure is partly determined by unconscious phantasy is of paramount importance from the therapeutic point of view, since we have access to these phantasies in the analytic situation and, through mobilizing them and helping the patient to relive and remodel them in the process of analytic treatment, we can affect the structure of the patient's personality." However concrete a statement might be, the analyst is always considering how unconscious phantasy may be coloring the remark. Even a comment about the weather, for example, can also be considered in relation to a comment on the analyst's demeanor, his or her warmth or coldness, etc. One then can look for confirmation or disconfirmation of one's musings as more material emerges.

Klein certainly seemed fearless in her own clinical engagements. One wonders if part of her clinical efficacy lay in being so daring that there was nothing off-limits in terms of what might be thought or spoken about.

Perhaps Klein's greatest contributions to technique were informed by her attempts to understand the factors that move us in our earliest years and in the deepest recesses of our beings. Klein's work brings us into the heart of our most basic needs, desires and fears. Her conceptions help us find our way through the primal terrors we experience when taxed to our utmost resources. Through it all, she maintained an appreciation of the ambivalence at the heart of all human relationships. In Klein's view, the process of learning to acknowledge the good and the bad – the hostility and the care that can intermingle and obscure one another – helps to heal the splits that arise under extreme pressure. Kleinian interpretations are aimed at the level at which the anxiety is most active in that moment, so as to lessen the anxiety sufficiently to facilitate knowledge and communication.

Pre-Oedipal development

Klein (1930) builds on Freud's drive theory, linking early anxieties to an excess of sadism that is expelled/projected (because it is ego-dystonic and therefore unknowable) but then becomes dangerous (because of the potential for retaliation). Always, in Klein's work, there is the affirmation that experience not explicitly known is still held within the individual at some level of awareness, carried in the less conscious regions through what Klein (1957) has called *memories in feeling*, the *language of the body* (Charles, 2002b). These feelings *mark the spot* (Charles, 2004) of the distress, holding the place of what ultimately must be recognized if we are to master the anxiety sufficiently to thrive.

Contemporary Kleinian/Bionian perspective **79**

This type of difficulty is prevalent in individuals whose early lives do not give them sufficient grounding for development to proceed unimpeded, resulting in tensions between understanding and not understanding. Betty Joseph (1997a) emphasizes how conflicted the desire for understanding can be, inviting us to look and listen more closely to the ways in which patients both hide and reveal, pointing to the trouble while also covering it over. This process of titrating distressing meanings has been described by Bion (1977) in terms of relationships between *container* and *contained*, in which meanings must first be held and recognized, and then broken into so that growth can continue.

The parent is the first container of excessive affect, standing between the child and the "too much" of daily existence. Lack of containment in early childhood is experienced as traumatic because the child is thrust into overload without the resources to recover. Such individuals get caught between their dependency needs and the impossibility of depending on anyone. The analyst must be able to tolerate being experienced as the insufficient object in the transference, while also working to hold the meanings in mind *as they evolve in the relational matrix*, in the reciprocal process of knowing and not knowing that allows those meanings to transform. That process requires the analyst's ability to recognize her own resistances and try to work with them as they arise, so that whatever is unresolved in her is not blindly obstructing the development of the patient.

Both Bion and Winnicott (1971) use maternal metaphors to describe this crucial *containing* or *holding* function, achieved in part through the analyst's *reverie*, her ability to absorb and metabolize the material as it emerges and to engage in phantasies in relation to it. Meeting our patients where they are, through our own affective attunement, helps them to tolerate the present moment sufficiently to provide grounding for further growth. That attunement can provide the essential ground through which we can find our way through work with individuals whose development has been severely impeded by trauma and/or neglect (Charles, 2006).

The attachment literature shows how unresolved mourning can leave even good parents at times inaccessible and therefore unable to provide these crucial holding, soothing and metabolizing functions (Liotti, 2004). When the parent has been unreliably present, relying on others invites ambivalence or even counterdependent rejection. In such moments, tolerating being the bad object is an important, albeit difficult, challenge.

That challenge mirrors the task of the parent of the young child, to tolerate one's own needs and feelings in times of strain and attend to the needs of the child. If this can happen sufficiently, the child learns to internalize the soothing functions offered by the parent and, over time, is better able to tolerate frustration. This tolerance, however, must be learned. Insufficient or inappropriate responsiveness can result in boundless moments of seeming annihilation, whether through the parent's angry attempts at control, submersion in his own distress, or failures in attention. If we think of what we know about mirror neurons and embodied simulation (Gallese, 2009), we can recognize that, as we work toward softening our own

80 Marilyn Charles

distress and invoking once again our capacity for reflective thought, we are inviting the other person to engage in those same processes.

Kleinian and Bionian theories rest on the assumption that primary experiences must be metabolized in order to be useful as symbols through which the experiences can be managed and mastered. When the child's attempts to master overwhelming anxiety have not been effective, relational needs can be experienced as impossibly tantalizing, leading to splits between the desire for a good object and situations in which people seem impossibly bad because they are not good enough.

Symbolization and dreaming

Over time, as primary experience is titrated and metabolized, the early prosodies of nonverbal meanings are translated and elaborated into verbal form. Bion (1977) termed the bits of primary experience *beta elements*, contending that thinking translates these bits into *alpha elements*, data that can be stored in verbal memory, repressed, processed and worked through. As the parent makes meaning from the child's experience and gives language to it, the child learns to recognize and name his feelings and develops a way of narrativizing his own life story. These are the symbolization processes through which reflective function and identity develop.

Alpha elements are the stuff of which symbolization, phantasy and dream thoughts are made. Bion (1977) explicitly linked symbolization to the capacity to dream, which, in turn, depends on the ability to use symbols. For Bion, dreaming is an ongoing function of the unconscious at work. The free associations of psychoanalysis help strengthen our access to that dream-work. Whereas psychotic dreams tend to be concrete, residing in the realm of metonymy rather than metaphor, most dreams lend themselves to the type of creative, reflective thinking through which meanings can be considered and played with. Encouraging the patient to associate to the dream elements takes a stand regarding the possibility – and inherent value – of making meaning for oneself from one's internal phantasies. Bion's contention that thoughts precede meaning, that *thoughts await the thinker*, is in line with current conceptions regarding the analytic field, as will be discussed more fully in Chapter 7.

Segal (1967) notes that the form and function of the dream are often more important than the actual content, particularly when dreams become concrete or evacuative. Dreams are often lived out in the transference so that, if we can attend to the form and function, we are more likely to recognize these enactments and speak to them as they occur (Joseph, 1985). The function of a communication can be much more important than the words themselves. Bion's (1977) metaphor of the tennis net (noting the importance of recognizing the holes along with the ways in which those holes are structured in relation to one another) highlights ways in which the structure of meaning can be hidden because of how our lens is focused. He suggested that, "instead of trying to bring a brilliant, intelligent, knowledgeable light to bear on obscure problems," we should, instead, "turn down the light, turn off the brilliant intuition, and see these holes, including the fact that they are knitted, or netted together" (Bion, 1990, pp. 20–21). This insight is similar to Jacques Lacan's (1973) *gap*, which signals that something important is missing from the conversation, awaiting symbolic representation.

The paranoid-schizoid and depressive positions

For Klein, a primary task of early childhood is to integrate good and bad experiences with the parent into a coherent whole. She called the point at which one can mourn the loss of the all-good object – the recognition of the inevitability of *lack* – the *depressive position*. In contrast, Klein conceptualized the *paranoid-schizoid position* as both a phase in development – before good and bad can be tolerated and integrated – and also a state characterized by excessive affective arousal that impedes the ability to invoke rational thought. Thinking may be too painful at times and may be hated and attacked because it limits the omnipotence of fantasy (Segal, 1978). There may also be a resistance to knowing that the analyst can think thoughts of her own, as such knowledge can invoke painful self-consciousness and humiliation by marking the limits of omnipotence (Feldman, 1997a).

The paranoid-schizoid position is the realm of feeling, in which reality is configured primarily by sensory and emotional elements. Clinically, we encounter this position in the individual who becomes not merely distressed by what we say but, rather, so hurt or angry that our previous benign or empathic presence has disappeared. This type of disjunctive reality is a hallmark of so-called *borderline* dynamics, characterized by a lack of ego or object permanency that lends itself to splitting and to *projective identification*.

Take as an example Val, a very bright young woman who comes to a standstill in her late teens because of her inability to continue to thrive in the face of massive losses. Her object world is split between the devalued mother, who is ostensibly available but emotionally remote and does not understand her intense emotionality, and the idealized father, who is rarely present but can become affectively engaged. The daughter's solution is to be like the father and unlike the mother. Neither parent, however, is sufficiently emotionally engageable to be useful as an object with whom to test herself and to grow.

Val's identification with her contemptuous father leaves her critical and deprecating toward the very emotions in which she becomes caught. Her attempts to have no needs and no emotions have failed. She finds herself sufficiently at a standstill that she works diligently to try to learn about what she is missing rather than disdainfully rejecting what she is offered. In the transference, however, I easily become the "stupid mother" who is distraught and immobilized in relation to Val's contempt. To meet her, I must tolerate the countertransference experience of being the deprecated other and insist that, even though I may be all of those things she finds in me, I also am more than that. I potentially have something useful to offer if she can listen without rejecting all my words out of hand. That stance can be extremely difficult to sustain.

82 Marilyn Charles

When I can manage to keep my bearings, at times Val becomes angry and reactive at what she experiences as *my* contempt and lack of empathy. At other times, however, she is relieved by her inability to utterly destroy and immobilize me, and we are able to refind one another and continue our work together. We can see in this latter engagement the work toward object usage described by Winnicott (1971), which helps us to recognize how early the developmental impasse must have occurred for this young woman. Having a sense of where development has gone awry can help the clinician respectfully engage with adults who have missed important milestones and need to catch up with themselves in order to make use of their capacities more fully.

Whereas Freud (1917) posited the loss of a (whole) loved object as the fundamental cause of despair, for Klein (1935) the early losses or deprivations associated with part objects are far more insidious, because they impede the integration of good and bad that mourning requires. When maternal containment, or reverie, has been insufficient, the lack of integration of good and bad aspects into a coherent whole lends itself to impoverished relations with self and others: *as-if* relationships that do not evolve, develop, enrich or grow. This is the type of constricted, imprisoning cocoon in which Val finds herself when her anxieties begin to supersede her desires for relationship. From this perspective, the self is experienced as inevitably bad and wanting, and the other appears to be in danger from this deprecated self. The *defensive organization* (described later) may be seen as an attempt to escape from the humiliation of finding oneself in this position, whereas resolution of this conflict comes in the form of a drive to accept limits and make reparation, a function of the *depressive position*.

Confronting such difficulties can be extremely intense, as the analyst weighs out the relative risks of remaining silent (and thus leaving the impasse to play out once again) versus speaking up (and thereby overriding the patient's defenses). In such moments (when we find ourselves inevitably caught up in enactments as the affective intensities play themselves out), speaking to the dynamic being played out, as best we can, asserts our role as analyst in spite of whatever else is occurring. Interpretations that integrate details of the regressive situation help to mark the functional elements of the problematic interchanges. Although such interpretations can lead to reactivity, anger or depression in the short term, they can also lead to greater integration and tolerance of the recursive phases of fragmentation and integration that occur across the lifespan.

Klein's metaphors help us to position ourselves in these odd engagements in which a battle is being played out for psychic survival and the sides can change quite rapidly. She links persecutory anxiety to fears of psychic annihilation, and depressive anxiety to guilt in relation to injury of the good object (Klein, 1948). Whereas persecutory anxieties provide a means for avoiding guilt and despair, the reparative tendency is a more adaptive function of the sense of guilt. Notably, however, as with Val, what may appear to be guilt can represent an attempt to bypass the shame experienced in relation to failures in omnipotence. From this framework, progress is presaged by Val's growing awareness that she is not merely a helpless victim or an omnipotent savior but, rather, a complicit actor, playing out a role in the drama in which she feels imprisoned.

This growing awareness helps to bring Val out of the dichotomized experience of self versus other, which gives us a bit more room for reflection, rather than being so overwhelmed by the affect of the moment. Being able to be present with our diverse thoughts and feelings helps us to better understand the transference, including "the fluctuations between objects, loved and hated, external and internal [and] the interconnections between positive and negative transferences" (Klein, 1952a, p. 53). To truly understand the transference, Klein suggests, we must be able to "explore the early interplay between love and hate, and the vicious circle of aggression, anxieties, feelings of guilt and increased aggression, as well as the various aspects of objects towards whom these conflicting emotions and anxieties are directed" (p. 53).

This task is easier said than done. Recognition of the splitting helps us to tolerate moments of extreme dysregulation so that we might more constructively illuminate the patterns, not only of relationships or characteristics but also of modes of being and of defense, reactivity and adaptation that are being repeated. At times the analyst's best move may be to recognize, out loud, that a pattern is being replayed, in this way insisting that it is something that can and should be looked at together. Words such as these help to break into the direness of whatever affective meanings are in place, so that we can move back toward the ability to know and to link, to recognize patterns and make use of that knowledge.

Our ability to confront and engage with the world facilitates development. "The continued experience of facing psychic reality, implied in the working through of the depressive position, increases the…understanding of the external world" (Klein, 1952b, p. 74), thereby reducing distortion, enhancing reality-testing and reducing anxiety. Being able to differentiate between internal and external sources of danger and disequilibrium helps to reinforce more adaptive ways of coping, which reduces both aggression and guilt, and aids in effective sublimation of these. Real successes and new achievements are reparative, strengthening object relations as well as the ego.

Projective identification

In the preceding example, we see the force of *projective identification* at work. Projective identification describes the situation in which the individual locates an aspect of self in another person. Feelings that are ego-dystonic become dislocated, experienced as external forces that threaten one's equilibrium. Val's contempt for the caring part of herself makes her virulently and contemptuously reactive to the caring part of me. Recovering my own reflective function sufficiently to be able to be caring without being mindlessly insufficient and in need of Val to save me becomes an important counter to the projective impasse. In turn, I need to be able to recognize the angry part of me so that she is not left alone, once again, as the angry "monster," the role in which she is too often cast in her family.

In projective identification, difficult feelings such as anger or contempt that cannot be recognized inside oneself seem to be coming from outside. Such dislocation can be disorienting for the analyst, who is being treated as though he or she is the source. Our own reactivity to finding feelings being pushed inside us further confuses the issue, and it may be difficult to regain sufficient reflective capacity to think through why we might be feeling such extreme emotion at that particular point in time. In such moments, having a conceptualization that outlines this projective process can help us to reorient ourselves and invoke our thinking functions, so that we can begin to reflect on what is being denied and displaced, and why (Feldman, 1997b; Joseph, 1997b).

Projective identification makes itself known through the countertransference, as we begin to recognize in ourselves a thought or emotion that does not quite fit. At times it is the intensity of the affect or the one-sidedness that alerts us that something is being split off. Although projective identification is most often thought of in terms of the projection of "bad" parts of the self into others, good parts of the self may also be projected (Klein, 1946). It may be more difficult to notice an idealization being imposed on us than deprecation, inviting us to become complicit in supporting the splitting.

Another example of this type of splitting process is when we find ourselves overly invested in a patient's well-being, trying to be helpful or provide reassurance. Michael Feldman (1997a) notes that such reassurance may seem comforting in the moment but ultimately it is not helpful because of the dishonesty at the heart of the engagement. Encountering an analyst who can hold steady in times of strain and empathize with the patient's feelings without providing false reassurance can be profoundly containing. It is in these moments that I am most grateful for having spent time in my own analysis, which makes me familiar with my own patterns of denial and avoidance so that I can better distinguish between my own defenses and those of the patient, and recognize ways in which they might intertwine, evoke or mask one another. Such perspective invites me to formulate the pattern being played out and speak to it rather than merely reenacting it.

Transference/countertransference

As we can see from the previous examples, meanings emerge in the countertransference, our feelings providing crucial pieces of information. Emotional meanings are particularly important in our work with individuals dealing with traumatic experience or early disruptions or lacks, who may not consciously *know* what they are contending with. If we can track these meanings rather than merely reacting to them, we can develop ideas about the person's defenses and also about the ways in which that individual tends to interact with and make use of others in her life. From the Kleinian perspective, the analyst's role is to interpret – to put ideas into words – as a way of saying back to the patient whatever sense we are making of the situation. Our job is not to make anything better but, rather, to put into words whatever meanings we are making in ways we hope might be useful to the patient

Contemporary Kleinian/Bionian perspective **85**

in developing her own capacities for meaning-making. This stance is similar to the Lacanian respect for the primacy of the patient as the *subject*, rather than the *object*, of the conversation.

Psychoanalysis is a process in which the capacities for reflective function are built and enhanced. Klein recognized the function of the analyst in helping the patient to affirm and acknowledge unknown meanings. In this way, we mark the feelings (and their relative absence) that characterize the patient's presentations and also the process between us, so that we begin to recognize patterns and delineate both the dilemma and the path toward resolving it.

Recognizing the value and validity of inchoate or bodily feeling-memories is pivotal in our work with traumatized individuals, who may have no other way of communicating even to themselves what they are contending with. Our determined respect for the work being done by the patient to make sense of whatever is nascent and coming into being provides the space through which we might catch hold of the meanings, put them into words and begin to develop a coherent narrative. The language of trauma can be off-putting, and the clinician must guard against whatever defenses in herself might push away from the language of trauma and define it as psychotic or meaningless. Instead, we must often fight against our own resistance and allow ourselves to be drawn into the language as the person can grab hold of it, and thereby pull it toward greater coherence, rather than leaving the patient floundering, further alone.

Symbol formation

Klein (1930) linked the primal fear of knowing – Bion's *blind eye* – to tensions between annihilation anxiety and the creation of the symbols through which these anxieties might be softened and mastered. In this way, she points to the desperate struggle to hold on to meaning in adverse circumstances. The ability to create meaning is a crucial step toward building relationships between two separate beings. Initially, however, the beings are not entirely separate, nor are the symbols.

According to Klein (1930), early symbols take the form of *symbolic equations*, a type of proto-symbol in which no distinction is made between the object and the representation. Symbolization processes offer a means of relief from these untenable equations, providing respite from the intensity of the affective charge. Through the creation of the symbol proper, an object can be internally represented and more explicitly thought about, and thereby used more freely in the service of meaning-making and communication (Segal, 1957). Alan Bass (1997) suggests that concreteness can be a way of avoiding an encounter with difference, the difference that demands recognition of the ultimate separateness of the other's mind and being (Joseph, 1997a).

Symbols give us conceptual anchors. They provide relief from anxiety by linking objects while also obscuring problematic aspects of reality so that we can keep the dilemma in mind with sufficient distance to be able to think about it more freely. In this way, the internal object is protected by virtue of the very forces that keep it

86 Marilyn Charles

at peril. If we are aware of the representative nature of the internal object, we have some way of thinking about it and thereby taming its more terrible aspects. This transformation entails also coming to terms with the ultimate separateness of self and other (Grotstein, 1982–3), something that some patients may actively oppose (Feldman, 1997a).

In psychosis, for example, there is a concreteness of meanings such that it is difficult to reflectively consider possibilities. If we see such concreteness as a way of maintaining equilibrium in spite of a very shaky foundation, then we are in a better position to help provide firmer ground on which the person might stand. In such moments, if we try to meet the person where he is, we might be able to see the sense in what initially appears to be nonsense and thereby find some ground on which to stand together. Taking seriously the idea that symptoms both *arise from* and *speak to* a central difficulty helps us to look for the meanings as they are offered, rather than insisting that our patients translate those meanings into *our* language. I worked with one young woman, for example, whose speech could devolve into sequences of numbers under strain but, when I searched diligently for a meaning to those numbers and found one, her anxiety was relieved and our discourse facilitated (see Charles, 2012).

The process of differentiation of good and bad, self and other, requires our ability to note similarities and differences while keeping the boundaries sufficiently permeable *and* separate to make real contact, without the symmetrization of self and other that occurs when primary process thinking holds sway (see Matte-Blanco, 1975). Generalization helps us to link similar objects, which helps organize our world, but it can impede development if insufficient discriminations are made. Severe anxiety (fear) impedes symbolization, so that we can fail to make the critical distinctions between dangerous versus non-dangerous aspects of others that are so essential to the capacity to ground our observations in consensual reality.

Recognizing the essential relationship between meaning and feeling, Bion (1977) placed emotion at the heart of meaning, highlighting an essential underpinning of psychoanalytic work (see Meltzer, 1981). He termed this quality *passion*, to denote the quality of feeling that marks the essential truth of an experience. Valuing the feelings that arise with patients helps us to mark these essential truths, so that we can attend to them more carefully and perhaps come to understand them better over time (Charles, 2002b).

Klein's ability to track emotional realities seems to have been quite profound. She linked anxiety to the experience of dependence, noting the delicate balance between the need to rely on others versus the terrible vacuum that results from insufficient responsivity to the child's experienced needs. When there is a lack of fit between the child's needs and the mother's capacities, the excess of dependency needs can feel like an open chasm. The ensuing rage then loops back into the relationship, further toxifying need, self and other. For some people, acknowledging relational needs is so dangerous that they must be denied, at times resulting in obsessive symptoms that become addictive precisely because they cannot fill the void.

Words must be linked to feelings in order to be meaningful. The desire to have no needs can manifest as a desire to have no words, no way in which to symbolize – and thereby make more palpable – thoughts that seem too distressing to think about. Words then may stand in the way of communication rather than enhancing it. Bion's (1967a) term *attacks on linking* marks the virulence with which connecting links can be denied when the anxiety is too extreme. His emphasis on *passion* invites clinicians to take more seriously our countertransference experience and helps us to focus on the process – the moment-by-moment affective engagement – and notice what is missing as well as what is present. This willingness to engage directly in the moment is a hallmark of Kleinian clinical practice, encouraging active engagement in the analysand as well. "Instead of being about the patient's intrapsychic dynamics, interpretations should be about the *interaction* of patient and analyst *at an intrapsychic level*" (O'Shaughnessy, 1996, p. 139, emphasis in original).

For Kleinians, interpretations titrate anxiety by allowing for a redistribution and reconstruction of elements in a way that is more tolerable to the self. Making the conflict explicit helps to illuminate unconscious fears and phantasies in ways that facilitate the working through. Interpretation serves as a mode of implicit education that puts forward an alternative way of thinking, an alternative way of being, that is more readily integrated than explicit, rational instruction.

Defensive organizations

The inability to acknowledge internal realities can result in avoidance of contact with others as a way of providing a *psychic retreat*, a refuge from overwhelming anxiety (Steiner, 2004). This state of siege has been characterized variously by contemporary Kleinian theorists in terms of *narcissistic* (Rosenfeld, 1971), *defensive* (O'Shaughnessy, 1981) or *pathological* organizations (Steiner, 1990). These terms characterize an interim state in which the individual is caught between the fragility of the ego and the intensity of the anxieties, resulting in oscillations between exposure and restriction. A pathological organization may provide respite from the paranoid anxieties associated with the paranoid-schizoid position or, alternatively, from the loss, guilt and relinquishment of control associated with the depressive position (Steiner, 1997). Edna O'Shaughnessy (1988) describes the defensive organization in terms of "an overall pathological formation, a fixation of object relations when progress is impossible" (p. 309) that provides relief from anxiety but can also foreclose growth or more adaptive resolution of the distress.

This is an inherently narcissistic position in which objects are controlled through projective identification. The nature of the defenses, themselves, may vary according to the character of the individual, from obsessive to histrionic, having elements that may be manic, perverse or even psychotic (Steiner, 1997). This type of no-man's-land may offer respite from the fragmentation and confusion of the paranoid-schizoid position, and from the anxiety and anguish of the depressive position (Steiner, 1997). Although the defensive organization may represent an entrenched avoidance of growth or development, paradoxically, it may also diminish anxiety, potentially strengthening the ego by providing respite from nonproductive oscillations between exposure and restriction, and thereby affording the ego sufficient respite within the analytic frame that growth is eventually possible (O'Shaughnessy, 1981, 1988). This possibility can help the clinician to tolerate the hours of silence that can ensue in work with individuals for whom relational engagement has been fraught with danger.

The defensive organization arises in relation to the abject terror experienced when faced with impossible realities. "One of the earliest methods of defence against the dread of persecutors...is that of scotomization, the *denial of psychic reality*; this may result in a considerable restriction of the mechanisms of introjection and projection and in the denial of external reality" (Klein, 1930, p. 262, emphasis in original). Bion's (1967a) term *attacks on linking* recognizes the extreme level of denial that can result in the circling around so typical of a defensive organization. Recognizing that very circling as a sign that something important cannot be metabolized can help the analyst to tolerate holding alone whatever cannot be held together. It can be confusing for the clinician to be confronted with that type of gap, an empty space in which some mutual understanding had been. That dilemma was prominent in my work with a severely traumatized young woman I will call "Emma."

Emma came to an impasse in relation to a story that needed to but could not be told, first accusing her parents for failing her but then accusing herself for not having been up to the task of saving herself or her sisters. Her unworthiness even to have a life was a matter of certainty, something she came up against most notably when anything good happened. At those times, it was as though something relentless and virulent in her took over, anything good became bad and any possibility was defeated. It was after our richest and deepest engagements that Emma was most likely to return the following day utterly shut down, certain that nothing good could come from our conversations. Knowing this pattern did not make her experience of it any less dire or deadly, leaving me feeling as though we were in the movie *Groundhog Day*, in which the main character lives through each day only to find himself back at the beginning once again. The concept of the defensive organization helped me to tolerate what otherwise felt useless and hopeless, trusting that Emma was building something with me that ultimately would help her to shift from this pattern toward an engagement that might afford us greater traction.

In the *narcissistic* organization, the destructive aspects of narcissism are linked with envy, which aligns with the powerful parts of the destructive other as a means for psychic survival (Rosenfeld, 1971). This characterization helps us better understand one aspect of Emma's dilemma: her alliance with her pain that seemed to keep her from straying too far from its sources. At this level, pain and pleasure can become so intermingled that we must be able to discern whatever has become "home" for that individual (see Novick & Novick, 1996). My recognition of the very different meaning of "home" for Emma helped us to tolerate this interim period of building sufficient safety within the consulting room to allow meanings to endure from one day to the next.

Greed, envy and gratitude

Kleinian theory highlights difficulties in locating oneself in relation to others. Primary feelings of need and unmet desire easily turn into aggressive and even sadistic attacks on those who might thwart those desires or who possess what is out of reach, as desire turns to envy. For Klein, the depressive position represents the ability to come to terms with limits and be grateful for what we have, to tolerate limits and derive pleasure from what can be obtained. This developmental challenge requires a mourning process through which the desire for an all-perfect other is relinquished such that the ego is strengthened and the good enough object is more securely established.

For Klein, greed is a primary emotion that "aims at possession of all the goodness that can be extracted from the object, regardless of consequences" (Segal, 1967). At that level, greed is more important than the relationship, and ruthless destruction and spoiling of the object help to relieve the envious feelings. Development is forestalled because there is no good object to whom to turn. We can see this type of ruthless spoiling in our work with narcissistic individuals who are too distressed by encountering something they had not known to take it in but, rather, overlook or spoil what is offered.

Because of the essential humiliation built into seeking assistance, inviting narcissistic individuals to tolerate not knowing sufficiently to be curious is an ongoing challenge. For example, take a man in his early fifties who is caught between his sense that I know something of importance about him that he can't quite grasp and his fear of being seen as the pathetic person he believes himself to be. "Nikolai" goes to great lengths to impress me and keep me at bay, and spends the better part of each session complaining or philosophizing. When I remark on his tendency to already have the answers such that he seems to have very little interest in anything I might add to the conversation, he listens with apparent interest but often merely is waiting for me to finish speaking so that he can bury my words under a rash of his own. Any difference becomes a sign of my not understanding, resulting in further attempts to explicate his position. If I persist in saying something to him about what I see, he is either entirely dismissive or tolerates the intrusion but then returns with renewed grievances regarding my failures in understanding or in offering him relief from his distress.

In the transference, I am the impossible mother who overrides his sensibilities and denies his manhood, putting him in the position of the impotent father. Taking a Kleinian perspective, I use my feelings in the countertransference as a frame through which to interpret my ideas about his dilemma in being confronted with the limits of what he knows and the need to learn from another. Shamed as a child for whatever he did not know and could not understand, Nikolai now pulls out of relationships with others as a way of not having to face humiliation but then finds himself utterly and terribly alone. He is so certain of his deficiency that being seen is itself shameful. So, then, he talks about wanting intimacy but fends off real engagement instinctively, vehemently and virulently.

90 Marilyn Charles

Although viewing his dilemma from another perspective is humiliating, if he can bear to see it, he can repair some of the shame he encounters in being the object of scrutiny. In Lacanian terms, he recovers himself as the subject of the conversation, even though he is also the object. As a small child, Nikolai turned to solving puzzles as a way of hiding from repeated humiliations at the hands of peers and family. He always kept his toys to himself so that he would be the holder of the prize rather than the person left behind.

Nikolai's envious desire to be the holder of the prize leaves him hiding his troubles, such that he comes to me seeking not the understanding he claims but, rather, to have a misperception affirmed. We find ourselves in the territory of truth and lies marked by Bion (1977), in which statements can be used for very different purposes (Charles, 2002a, 2002b). For Nikolai, there are truths that must become lies and lies that must become truths, making it very difficult at times to have any ground between us on which to stand. I tell him that I think he has the idea that, if he could just "say it right," then I would understand and things would change. So he keeps trying to tell me what he has already told me, hoping that this time it will stick. But, I tell him, I don't think that his problems will be fixed by a more accurate description. Rather, I think that I am hearing what he is saying but have a different perspective, that it is likely what he cannot see and therefore can't describe to me that he needs to learn something about.

We get caught in a terrible dilemma in which he is desperately trying to maintain the grandiose façade he has erected and I am hoping to invite the person behind the mask into being. He wards off opportunities to learn something more because of his envy and shame, which invite him to fend off potentially useful information rather than taking it in.

Weaknesses and limitations

Although Kleinian theory helps me to conceptualize the difficulties my patients encounter and to make sense of my feelings as they arise in the consulting room, at times it is not sufficient to direct my actions. I appreciate the emphasis on psychic reality and the avoidance of becoming overly ensconced in pragmatics or in "support" that may be reassuring at the surface but works against moving toward greater depth (Feldman, 1997a). Weaknesses of the Kleinian perspective, however, include the emphasis on only interpreting the transference rather than recognizing other possible functions the analyst might hold.

A more fundamental weakness is positioning the analyst as the authority. On this issue, I prefer to take a Lacanian perspective, to avoid being caricatured as the "one who knows" so that I might invite the patient to become the Subject of the inquiry. This stance can be quite different from the more traditional Kleinian analyst, who does tend to position himself as the one who knows. For me, that is an inherently untenable position to take in relation to the individual who comes into my consulting room precisely because she cannot take up her own authority and legitimize her needs, feelings and desires. Bion (1967b) seems

Contemporary Kleinian/Bionian perspective **91**

to have come to a similar stance in his admonition that the analyst should seek to avoid memory or desire but, rather, determine to be open to the present moment.

Many people come to us with little sense of internal desire or agency, a dilemma that is most salient in the schizoid patient. For example, "Greg," a young man in his mid-twenties, had come to an impasse in his life. Klein (1946) helped me to understand his schizoid withdrawal in relation to his parents' utter inability to acknowledge needs or feelings. Even ideas that he could recognize as potentially valuable seemed remote and difficult to engage. Technically, however, it was Lacan's (1973) idea of the *Subject caught by the desire of the Other* that enabled us to move beyond the impasse (see Charles, 2014). In Lacan's formulation, we arrive in a world in which ideas about us precede our entry. We internalize the world as it is given, accommodating to these demands while also rebelling against them, and become lost in relation to that desire of the Other that holds the possibility of an unlimited *jouissance* (Lacan, 1973). The challenge is to de-idealize – de-authorize – the other, to accept the inevitability of lack – of limit – and to recognize and articulate our own particular desire.

Greg's social inhibition had become so severe that it was difficult for him to even earn a living. Our conversations tended to circle around in crazy ways, as I became the voice of possibility in relation to his stance of utter hopelessness. Where, then, might be a place where we could stand together? I took the position that I had no way of working with him unless there was something that he wanted to work on. For some time there seemed to be nothing he wanted – no place where he could locate a desire – until one day, when he was talking about wanting to leave treatment, and I recognized in this a desire that was truly his own.

Working together toward that goal enabled Greg to think about what else he might like to achieve, and to inquire into the lacks and limits that were keeping him from discovering a life worth living. Being able to recognize a lack and also be able to reflect on it were huge challenges, given the terrible shame that engulfed him, leaving him unable to make use of his considerable cognitive resources. Navigating this territory with one another required exhaustive attention and sensitivity to meanings as Greg experienced them, so that he might learn to track his own relative safety and ability to take in information in a given moment.

In contrast to the Kleinian focus on the here and now of the transference and avoidance of giving information, I find that people at times are in need of information, particularly information about development, so that they can better recognize ways in which their own development has been waylaid. This type of information can help an adult to better tolerate some of the regressive feelings and desires that are evoked as the work proceeds. Having in mind developmental tasks, including the development of reflective function, can be crucial as we try to invite an interest in and ideas about feelings and ideas as they occur.

For example, when I tracked with Greg his experiences in narrative form, and made sense of them in a developmental context, I became a new object who might have his needs and feelings in mind. My conjectures about what it must have been like for him at various stages of his early life, given the context and characters he

92 Marilyn Charles

described, helped us to build a narrative in which we could locate a child with needs that were not being recognized, and developmental milestones that were not being achieved. In this process, Greg began to have a sense of himself, not as impossibly flawed but, rather, in need of maturation and further development. Unlike Nikolai, that recognition helped Greg to tolerate the narcissistic injury because of the potential for growth.

Particularly important was the moment when I tracked for him the experience of shame, in Silvan Tomkins' (1982) terms, as a cut breaking into a moment of pleasure or interest. This conceptualization related directly to his own experience, inviting him to be curious about shame *as an experience-near phenomenon*. Being able to see his problems in context broke into Greg's concrete and universal presumptions of meaning. Rather than merely signs of danger, internal cues became useful signals, the ground on which reflective function and resilience are built (Lysaker et al., 2011).

Although Kleinians recognize dreams as opportunities to explore unconscious fears and phantasies, Lacanians show how crucial dream work can be for those who are cut off from their internal experience. For such individuals, the dream can be pivotal because it can be recognized as *one's own production* in ways that the symptom cannot (Apollon, Bergeron & Cantin, 2002). Dreams help us to recognize the *structures* of meanings and relationships, including transference elements that may not be yet available for conscious thought (Charles, 2010, 2015). With Greg, for example, I had to be able to recognize myself as the well-intentioned but dangerous other of his dreams in order to have ideas about the terrain he needed to learn to navigate.

Dreams have also been important in my work with "John," initially the only way he could tell me about the frightening urges and impulses that seemed too dark even to consider (Charles, in press). John quickly noticed that dreams provided a vantage point he could not obtain in any other way and assiduously reported his dreams throughout the treatment. In that way, the dreams provided a secondary narrative through which we could watch him evolve over time, a *binocular perspective* that helped us better understand issues as they arose in his waking life (Bion, 1977).

Although our patients often expect us to be *the one who knows*, we depend on our patients to show us the way. With individuals such as Greg and John, who come to us with little capacity for reflective function, it is in our struggle to make sense of their experience that they can begin to take in what it means to be with and think with another person. At the most primary level, through our deep and honest and respectful engagements with our patients, they are learning something about the actuality and integrity of such an encounter through processes of embodied simulation (Gallese, Eagle & Migone, 2007) and the development of reflective function that we can see, in Kleinian language, in terms of a movement toward the depressive position, from which place limits can be recognized without overwhelming shame or terror.

Conclusion

The Kleinian frame helps the clinician to recognize both the experienced and the potential self, perhaps an essential precondition for any real work to take place.

Contemporary Kleinian/Bionian perspective **93**

There is a recognition of how fundamentally the transference/countertransference experience of patient and analyst is tied to constructive working through in the analysis. Irma Brenman Pick (1997, p. 352) writes: "I wonder whether the issue of truly deep versus superficial interpretation resides not so much in terms of which level has been addressed but to what extent the analyst has worked the process through internally in the act of giving the interpretation."

Our ability to track the other's affect and patterns of meaning grounds our recognition in ways that enable greater tolerance of both distress and enjoyment, so that the person can struggle with tensions rather than being overwhelmed. One of our roles is to become *the one who knows* while also recognizing the need to defer and refer back to the patient, who ultimately must know for him- or herself in order for the work to be meaningful.

The Kleinians help us to respect ways in which we build, through our interaction at both verbal and nonverbal levels, an understanding of the experience of the other. For Klein (1946), the most useful interpretation is one that binds past to present, highlighting the functional aspects of the dilemma while also anchoring our awareness in the affective cadence of the lived moment and titrating the affect sufficiently to maintain our capacity for reflection.

This process is facilitated by our ability to use symbols, which enable us to *mark the spot* (Charles, 2004) of important meanings, while also titrating the exposure. Until this titration process becomes internalized, the analyst's ability to carry the words, images, sensations and metaphors – along with their potential meanings in light of the patient's history – enables her to meet people where they are and also implicitly to confront them with the challenge of coming to know more explicitly what has been segmented off, denied or projected.

Work with individuals functioning at this level can be extremely difficult and taxing. In the dark and dire moments when there is no hope in the room, only silence and darkness, having a sense of these Kleinian and Bionian ideas offers me a conceptual map through which to find my way. These conceptualizations help me to locate myself in psychic space as I struggle through the long and at times torturous hours spent together. This conceptual map is an essential ally in my ability to tolerate being in these dark and terrible spaces together, and is also an important guide in working together toward a place where these dangers become less imminent and healing more possible.

References

Apollon, W., Bergeron, D., & Cantin, L. (2002). *After Lacan: Clinical Practice and the Subject of the Unconscious* (R. Hughes & K. R. Malone, Eds.). Albany, NY: SUNY Press.
Bass, A. (1997). The problem of "concreteness." *Psychoanalytic Quarterly*, 66(4): 642–682.
Bion, W. R. (1961). *Experiences in Groups and Other Papers*. London: Routledge.
Bion, W. R. (1967a). *Second Thoughts: Selected Papers on Psycho-Analysis*. Northvale, NJ: Jason Aronson.
Bion, W. R. (1967b). Notes on memory and desire. *Psychoanalytic Forum*, 2(3): 271–280.
Bion, W. R. (1977). *Seven Servants*. New York: Jason Aronson.

Bion, W. R. (1990). *Brazilian Lectures: 1973 São Paulo, 1974 Rio de Janeiro/São Paulo.* London: Karnac Books.

Bion, W. R. (1992). *Cogitations* (F. Bion, Ed.). London: Karnac Books.

Charles, M. (2002a). Bion's grid: A tool for transformation. *Journal of the American Academy of Psychoanalysis*, 30(3): 429–445.

Charles, M. (2002b). *Patterns: Building Blocks of Experience.* Hillsdale, NJ: Analytic Press.

Charles, M. (2004). *Learning from Experience: A Guidebook for Clinicians.* Hillsdale, NJ: Analytic Press.

Charles, M. (2006). Precious illusions: Re-constructing realities. In J. Mills (Ed.), *Other Banalities: Melanie Klein Revisited*, pp. 77–104. Hove, UK: Routledge.

Charles, M. (2010). When cultures collide: Myth, meaning, and configural space. *Modern Psychoanalysis*, 34(1): 26–47.

Charles, M. (2012). *Working with Trauma: Lessons from Bion and Lacan.* Lanham, MD: Jason Aronson.

Charles, M. (2014). Klein and Lacan meet 21st century schizoid man: fairy stories for the modern era. *American Journal of Psychoanalysis*, 74(3): 215–232.

Charles, M. (2015). *Psychoanalysis and Literature: The Stories We Live.* Lanham, MD: Rowman & Littlefield.

Charles, M. (in press). The dream and the image: Creative transformations in psychoanalytic space. *American Journal of Psychoanalysis.*

Feldman, M. (1997a). The dynamics of reassurance. In R. Schafer (Ed.), *The Contemporary Kleinians of London*, pp. 321–343. Madison, WI: International Universities Press.

Feldman, M. (1997b). Splitting and projective identification. In R. Schafer (Ed.), *The Contemporary Kleinians of London*, pp. 119–139. Madison, WI: International Universities Press.

Freud, S. (1917 [1957]). Mourning and melancholia. In J. Strachey (Ed. & Trans.), *The Standard Edition of the Complete Psychological Works of Sigmund Freud*, Vol. XIV, pp. 243–258. London: Hogarth Press.

Gallese, V. (2009). Mirror neurons, embodied simulation, and the neural basis of social identification. *Psychoanalytic Dialogues*, 19(5): 519–536.

Gallese, V., Eagle, M. N., & Migone, P. (2007). Intentional attunement: Mirror neurons and the neural underpinnings of interpersonal relations. *Journal of the American Psychoanalytic Association*, 55(1): 131–175.

Grotstein, J. S. (1982). The significance of Kleinian contributions to psychoanalysis III: The Kleinian theory of ego psychology and object relations. *International Journal of Psychoanalytic Psychotherapy*, 9(4): 487–510.

Joseph, B. (1985). Transference: The total situation. *International Journal of Psychoanalysis*, 66(4): 447–454.

Joseph, B. (1997a). On understanding and not understanding. In R. Schafer (Ed.), *The Contemporary Kleinians of London*, pp. 299–315. Madison, WI: International Universities Press.

Joseph, B. (1997b). Projective identification: Some clinical aspects. In R. Schafer (Ed.), *The Contemporary Kleinians of London*, pp. 100–116. Madison, WI: International Universities Press.

Klein, M. (1930 [1975]). The importance of symbol-formation in the development of the ego. In *Love, Guilt, Reparation and Other Works, 1921–1945*, pp. 219–232. London: Hogarth Press.

Klein, M. (1935 [1975]). A contribution to the psychogenesis of manic-depressive states. In *Love, Guilt, Reparation and Other Works, 1921–1945*, pp. 262–289. London: Hogarth Press.

Klein, M. (1946 [1975]). Notes on some schizoid mechanisms. In *Envy and Gratitude and Other Works, 1946–1963*, pp. 1–24. London: Hogarth Press.

Klein, M. (1948 [1975]). On the theory of anxiety and guilt. In *Envy and Gratitude and Other Works, 1946–1963*, pp. 25–42. London: Hogarth Press.

Klein, M. (1952a [1975]). The origins of transference. In *Envy and Gratitude and Other Works, 1946–1963*, pp. 48–56. London: Hogarth Press.

Klein, M. (1952b [1975]). Some theoretical conclusions regarding the emotional life of the infant. In *Envy and Gratitude and Other Works, 1946–1963*, pp. 61–93. London: Hogarth Press.

Klein, M. (1957 [1975]). Envy and gratitude. In *Envy and Gratitude and Other Works, 1946–1963*, pp. 176–234. London: Hogarth Press.

Lacan, J. (1973 [1978]). The partial drive and its circuit. In *The Four Fundamental Concepts of Psycho-Analysis* (A. Sheridan, Trans.), pp. 174–186. New York: W. W. Norton.

Liotti, G. (2004). Trauma, dissociation, and disorganized attachment: Three strands of a single braid. *Psychotherapy: Theory, Research, Practice, Training*, 41(4): 472–486.

Lysaker, P. H., Erickson, M., Ringer, J., Buck, K. D., Semerari, A., Carcione, A., & Dimaggio, G. (2011). Metacognition in schizophrenia: The relationship of mastery to coping, insight, self-esteem, social anxiety, and various facets of neurocognition. *British Journal of Clinical Psychology*, 50(4): 412–424.

Matte-Blanco, I. (1975). *The Unconscious as Infinite Sets: An Essay in Bi-Logic*. London: Duckworth.

Meltzer, D. (1981). The Kleinian expansion of Freud's metapsychology. *International Journal of Psychoanalysis*, 62(2): 177–185.

Novick, J., and Novick, K. K. (1996). *Fearful Symmetry: The Development and Treatment of Sadomasochism*. Northvale, NJ: Jason Aronson.

O'Shaughnessy, E. (1981). A clinical study of a defensive organization. *International Journal of Psychoanalysis*, 62(3): 359–369.

O'Shaughnessy, E. (1988). A clinical study of a defensive organization. In E. B. Spillius (Ed.), *Melanie Klein Today: Developments in Theory and Practice*, Vol. I, *Mainly Theory*, pp. 293–310. Hove, UK: Routledge.

O'Shaughnessy, E. (1996). Words and working through (1983). In E. B. Spillius (Ed.), *Melanie Klein Today: Developments in Theory and Practice*, Vol. II, *Mainly Practice*, pp. 138–151. London: Routledge.

Pick, I. B. (1997). Working through in the countertransference. In R. Schafer (Ed.), *The Contemporary Kleinians of London*, pp. 348–367. Madison, WI: International Universities Press.

Rosenfeld, H. (1971). A clinical approach to the psychoanalytic theory of the life and death instinct: An investigation into the aggressive aspects of narcissism. *International Journal of Psychoanalysis*, 52(2): 169–178.

Segal, H. (1957). Notes on symbol formation. *International Journal of Psychoanalysis*, 38(3): 391–397.

Segal, H. (1967 [1981]). Melanie Klein's technique. In *The Work of Hanna Segal: A Kleinian Approach to Clinical Practice*, pp. 3–24. New York: Jason Aronson.

Segal, H. (1978 [1981]). Psychoanalysis and freedom of thought. In *The Work of Hanna Segal: A Kleinian Approach to Clinical Practice*, pp. 217–227. New York: Jason Aronson.

Steiner, J. (1990). Pathological organizations as obstacles to mourning: The role of unbearable guilt. *International Journal of Psychoanalysis*, 71(1): 87–94.

Steiner, J. (1997). The interplay between pathological organizations and the paranoid-schizoid and depressive positions. In R. Schafer (Ed.), *The Contemporary Kleinians of London*, pp. 195–219. Madison, WI: International Universities Press.

Steiner, J. (2004). *Psychic Retreats: Pathological Organizations in Psychotic, Neurotic and Borderline Patients*. New York: Taylor & Francis.

Tomkins, S. S. (1982). Affect theory. In P. Ekman, W. V. Friesen & P. Ellsworth (Eds.), *Emotion in the Human Face*, 2nd Edn., pp. 353–305. Cambridge: Cambridge University Press.

Winnicott, D. W. (1971). *Playing and Reality*. London: Tavistock Publications.

5

D. W. WINNICOTT

Holding, playing and moving toward mutuality

Joyce Slochower

Introduction: analytic ideals and the ideal analyst

The clinical work we each do is rooted in the professional ideal we embrace – a vision of the kind of therapist we want to be. Our ideal embodies our wish – and often also our need – to heal, to change, to engage, to do something useful. Contained therein are ideas about what will help our patients (e.g., insight, empathy, relational engagement, confrontation) and how we should (and shouldn't) function in the consulting room. It's a vision that guides and inspires us.

We don't form our ideal in an interpersonal vacuum; along with the psychoanalytic theories we read about, we absorb and react to the orientations of our teachers, supervisors, analysts or therapists. We may embrace some perspectives and reject others, attempt to bridge clashing perspectives or move in a third, different direction.

It's not surprising, therefore, that our analytic ideal has strong personal resonances. Implicitly, it embodies the hopes and fantasies that shape us as human beings. Often enough, we aim to become the kind of analyst we want(ed) for ourselves. We needed (or need) a reparative maternal or paternal presence, someone who calls a spade a spade, someone non-intrusive and containing, someone who can see through and into us, or (and) someone who can engage with us on a deeply intimate level.

It takes time and training for us to formulate that ideal and far more time for aspects of it to become assimilated, appropriated and recreated so that it represents a very personal professional idiom. Across our career, our idiom may shift or even transform, but, whatever its particulars, it represents a potentially stabilizing and orienting backdrop within the clinical hour (Slochower, 2006b, 2014c).

However, unless we are pigheaded and unthinking, things don't stop there. Our clinical work is also shaped by the particular patient we encounter moment to moment. Her needs, issues and life circumstances influence and intersect with our own, yielding a pattern of mutual influence too complex to fully unpack. I think this is true no matter what theory we espouse and no matter how rigidly we use that theory to define our clinical practice.

More, perhaps, than any other psychoanalytic theorist, Winnicott spoke to our belief in the possibility of maternal repair in the consulting room. His work is widely admired, often idealized and sometimes misunderstood. This chapter examines his particular idiom and its implications for – and applications to – clinical work. It's decidedly *not* a review of his entire theoretical contribution. That project would require a book of its own, and there are many good ones out there.

I have a narrower aim: to focus on those elements of Winnicott's thinking that altered the way clinicians practiced then and practice now. After describing what I view as Winnicott's most important clinical contributions, I discuss their potential weaknesses. Finally, I review my own effort to create a relational bridge to the Winnicottian perspective.

The bulk of this chapter aims to offer you an objective reading of Winnicott. But this is impossible. Winnicott's writing is lyrical more than concrete, replete with metaphors that don't always make clear what he actually *did* – or thought – moment to moment. I have been teaching Winnicott for decades, yet I find that I say "I don't know" in response to a student's question (or my own) at least once in every class. I think this is because Winnicott invited creative engagement rather than the integration of facts. Inevitably, you will be reading *my* interpretation of Winnicott and what *I* view as his central clinical contribution. Other Winnicott scholars might offer a somewhat different take. And they would be no less right – or wrong – than I. Rather than leaving you frustrated or confused, I hope that, as you read this chapter (and all the chapters in this volume), you will feel your way into this material from the inside out. I hope you will locate its fit – and collision – with your own professional idiom and perhaps rewrite the material in your own words.

Winnicott: personal influences

Like most of us, Winnicott brought himself – his early history, wishes and needs (particularly, perhaps, the wish for a reparative, emotionally present maternal figure) – along with his professional trajectory to the field (he was a pediatrician before he became a psychoanalyst). Winnicott saw first-hand what happened in the lives of children who were exposed to ongoing impingements and whose needs went unmet; he carried that awareness into the consulting room. For him, psychoanalysis represented an opportunity to mend the patient in ways not unlike those required by troubled children.

In part, this perspective was born out of Winnicott's professional experiences; in part, he was probably reacting to what had been missing in his own childhood (see Anderson, 2014, 2015a, 2015b) and later (as he himself articulated in his analyses with a Freudian – James Strachey – and a Kleinian – Joan Riviere).

Winnicott pushed back hard against theories that seemed – from his point of entry – to privilege drive over experience. His thinking clashed sharply with that of many of his British Psychoanalytical Society contemporaries. Whereas Freudians emphasized the interpretation of unconscious, Oedipal conflict, Winnicott – with Melanie Klein – turned to the baby's earlier pre-Oedipal beginnings. But Winnicott (e.g., 1960) de-emphasized notions of drive gratification. He argued instead for the centrality of a protective maternal holding environment that would facilitate the baby's experience of "going on being" in a setting protected from excessive impingements.

Winnicott (1962) increasingly moved away from the motivational centrality of drives in general and the death instinct in particular. In rejecting Kleinian and Freudian darker views of human nature as deeply conflicted, Winnicott created a different kind of child (and mother) for the psychoanalyst to contemplate. His perspective emphasized the child's inherent potential rather than its unconscious conflicts and drives.

Winnicott's was a benign and hopeful perspective. He renamed and redefined the Kleinian depressive position as the "stage of concern" (1963a), for example. In so doing, he replaced a baby struggling with its own ambivalence with one who, given a facilitating environment, had an inherent potential to care *about* the (m) other.

And it wasn't just the baby who had these positive capacities. Winnicott also underscored parents' (mainly mothers') ability to meet the child's spontaneous gesture and mend what had gone wrong. He was convinced that the "ordinary devoted mother" (1949, 1953) could meet her child's needs and facilitate a positive developmental trajectory. The concept of *good enough* made room for human error in the context of an overarching belief in the mother's benign intention and loving capacity.

Yet Winnicott's was not a romantic view. He noted that the mother has many reasons to hate her baby, and detailed them carefully (1947), but added that

> mothers who are not distorted by ill-health or by present-day environmental stress do tend on the whole to know accurately enough what their infants need, and further, they like to provide what is needed. This is the essence of maternal care.
>
> *(Winnicott, 1960, p. 54)*

Winnicott's 1965 book *The Maturational Processes and the Facilitating Environment* articulates this perspective so well that, had I merely five minutes to teach his work, I'd just talk about this title. Far more than most of his contemporaries, Winnicott believed in each child's positive inherent potential in the context of a benign parental environment that held and met need. It's the parent's (and, by extension, the analyst's) task to *allow what's naturally there to emerge* rather than to inculcate values or love *into* the child.

100 Joyce Slochower

In Winnicott's view, then, the child is not impelled toward destruction and hate. Anger is reactive rather than instinctual, a response to trauma and a not-good-enough environment. Goodness, morality and forward movement don't have to be taught; the child's own aliveness – spontaneous gesture – is *there*, waiting to be found and met.

The psychoanalytic set situation

Winnicott's writings on child development anticipated his psychoanalytic perspective. In fact, nearly everything he said about mothers and their children would find its way into his understanding of the psychoanalytic situation. His work is embedded in what Stephen Mitchell (1988) would later call (and critique for) its developmental tilt: Winnicott engaged a maternal metaphor to describe the psychoanalytic setup. Emphasizing the analyst's reparative capacity in work with more vulnerable patients, he invoked notions of parental holding and repair as they apply to the analytic setting.

In a wonderful early paper (1941), Winnicott described the behavior of infants whom he observed in a "set situation," a quasi-experimental paradigm that introduced the baby to a shiny, appealing object that he called a "spatula" (what Americans think of as a metal tongue depressor). As the mother held her baby on her lap, Winnicott offered the spatula to the baby; he both observed and theorized the baby's responses in minute detail.

Winnicott delineated a three-phase process. After a period of hesitation during which the baby eyes the spatula but doesn't dare take it, the baby takes a chance. Tentatively picking it up, the baby mouths and cautiously plays with it. As mother and Winnicott watch but don't interfere, the baby's hesitancy falls away and she appropriates the spatula with increasing pleasure and abandon. Eventually, the spatula is dropped, perhaps accidentally. But a new game soon ensues as the spatula is returned, only to be deliberately tossed away again and again. That game continues as the baby flings the spatula away with increasing gusto, until eventually she loses interest in the spatula altogether and throws it determinedly away.

Winnicott had many things to say in this paper about babies and development, but there is one thing I want to emphasize. The set situation represented an early version of what would become Winnicott's core clinical conviction: a central therapeutic element is inherent *not* in what the mother or analyst *does* but simply in the baby or patient having the opportunity to live through "the full course of an experience" (1941, p. 246) in the presence of a benign and facilitative other.

Like Winnicott's set situation, the analytic setting is "set." The consulting room is constant: the patient arrives and leaves at a predictable hour; the analyst is present and available to the patient, who initiates the conversation in her own way. The patient (like the baby) responds to the analyst's interpretations (shiny spatulas) by hesitating, playing with, making over or throwing away (rejecting) the analyst's offerings.

Certainly, nearly all analysts invite the patient to set the pace and tone of the session and make plenty of room for the patient's experience to unfold. *But Winnicott* gave new therapeutic meaning to this dimension of the process: analytic space was not primarily designed to facilitate the patient's free association and thus invite the analyst's interpretations. The session's set elements themselves had *intrinsic therapeutic potential – as an opportunity for whole (uninterrupted) experience.* Here is an analytic paradigm organized *not around what the analyst does* but around the establishment of a protected space, within which the patient's process is allowed to unfold with minimal disruption/interruption by the analyst.

Inserted in the "set situation" paper is a whole paragraph in parentheses, as if no more than an aside. It underscores Winnicott's reluctance to take an authoritative analytic position:

> (I have frequently made the experiment of trying to get the spatula to the infant's mouth during the stage of hesitation. Whether the hesitation corresponds to my normal or differs from it in degree or quality, I find that it is impossible during this stage to get the spatula to the child's mouth apart from the exercise of brute strength. In certain cases where the condition is acute any effort on my part that results in the spatula being moved towards the child produces screaming, mental distress or actual colic.)
>
> *(Winnicott, 1941, p. 231)*

An interpretation (like the shiny spatula) can be offered, but never forced. The patient, like the baby, needs to examine, play with and perhaps make over the analyst's interpretation in the patient's own way and time if it is to be of therapeutic use. Inherent here is enormous respect for the capacity of the patient to sort out what's useful from what's not and to encompass the former in her own way and in her own time.

Of course, there are differences between the set situation and the analytic setting. We analysts end the session when it's time to end; our patient may or may not be ready to leave. We try to put words and meaning to what we hear and understand; in this sense, we're far more actively and interactively engaged with our patient than in the set situation. Still, this paper expressed Winnicott's belief in the inherent therapeutic potential of the analytic frame and in our capacity to offer a consistent, engaged but non-intrusive environment that is inherently curative.

The limits of interpretation

While Winnicott viewed interpretations as clinically essential in the 1940s (provided they were encompassed by the patient), he became increasingly disillusioned with their mutative potential over the course of his career. Thirty years after the set situation was published, he offered a more radical perspective (1971, p. 86):

> [I]t is only in recent years that I have become able to wait and wait for the natural evolution of the transference arising out of the patient's growing trust in the psychoanalytic technique and setting, and to avoid breaking up this natural

process by making interpretations. It will be noticed that I am talking about the making of interpretations and not about interpretations as such. It appals me to think how much deep change I have prevented or delayed in patients *in a certain classification category* by my personal need to interpret. If only we can wait, the patient arrives at understanding creatively and with immense joy, and I now enjoy this joy more than I used to enjoy the sense of having been clever.

Here, Winnicott emphasized the patient's capacity to know herself and reminded us that the analyst's knowledge can be harmful to therapeutic process. This was a radical clinical/theoretical reformulation: *the analyst is not – and should not be – the knower*. In work with very ill patients, interpretations actually may *prevent* deep change. This perspective reduced the asymmetry embedded in a belief in the analyst's superior wisdom. It simultaneously underscored the patient's capacity to know herself.

Hate in the countertransference

In an era when analytic neutrality was assumed to be therapeutically central (and in an era when mothers were expected to love their children with purity of feeling), countertransference was viewed as the analyst's personal (neurotic) response to the patient. The analyst was expected to address her countertransference feelings privately (or in her own treatment) with the aim of returning to an emotionally neutral position vis-à-vis the patient. But, pushing back once again, Winnicott (1947) boldly declared that *countertransference hate is inevitable both for mothers and for analysts*. Separating neurotic (subjective) countertransference hate from what was evoked by the baby because of its demandingness *and* by the patient because of her "actual personality and behaviour" (p. 70), Winnicott blew up the myth of the neutral analyst. Rather than suggesting that the analyst who feels hatred toward the patient had a countertransference problem and needed more analysis, he said:

> It seems to me doubtful whether a human child as he develops is capable of tolerating the full extent of his own hate in a sentimental environment. He needs hate to hate. If this is true, a psychotic patient in analysis cannot be expected to tolerate his hate of the analyst unless the analyst can hate him.
>
> *(Winnicott, 1947, p. 74)*

Here was a dramatic shift toward a dyadic vision of psychoanalytic work. Analytic hate is inevitable and may even be therapeutically necessary.

Winnicott's perspective opened the door to an exploration of analytic subjectivity. But he was very cautious about the active use of the countertransference and remained convinced that a protected holding environment was most often clinically necessary. Both mothers and analysts, he maintained, can and must keep their hate latent (i.e., to themselves), because it's in the best interest of the baby and patient to do so. Winnicott also reminded us that mothers have ways of expressing hate indirectly – e.g., in the nursery rhymes they sing – while analysts express hate, for example, in the ending of the hour.

Still, alongside his caution were some radical ideas. While the analyst should contain her hate most of the time, it was sometimes essential for that hate to be communicated.

> If all this is accepted there remains for discussion the question of the interpretation of the analyst's hate to the patient. This is obviously a matter fraught with danger, and it needs the most careful timing. But I believe an analysis is incomplete if even towards the end it has not been possible for the analyst to tell the patient what he, the analyst, did unbeknown for the patient whilst he was ill, in the early stages. Until the interpretation is made the patient is kept to some extent in the position of infant, one who cannot understand what he owes to his mother.
>
> *(Winnicott, 1947, p. 74)*

Here was a bold statement that shattered the myth of the neutral analyst and complicated Winnicott's own ideal of a "holding" analyst who consistently contains her hate. Winnicott pushed the therapeutic trajectory in the direction of intersubjective dialogue by suggesting that the treatment experience isn't complete without mutual engagement. The patient sometimes needs the analyst to be "real," open and emotionally direct, even about her hate. Indeed, the treatment experience won't be complete until this happens. And, although Winnicott viewed this kind of expressiveness as an "interpretation" lodged in the "reality" of the patient's hate, I'd call it the beginning of a clinical revolution.

Holding, false self defenses and regression to dependence

The bulk of Winnicott's clinical writing focused on the treatment of schizoid and psychotic patients. While standard interpretive technique could help healthier (neurotic) patients, schizoid and psychotic patients – many of whom we would now call trauma patients – needed something different. They brought very early, unmetabolized experiences of parental failure into the therapeutic situation. They needed a regression to dependence.

> There is a vast difference between those patients who have had satisfactory early experiences which can be discovered in the transference, and those whose very early experiences have been so deficient or distorted that the analyst has to be the first in the patient's life to supply certain environmental essentials… [T]his provision and maintenance of an ordinary environment can be in itself a vitally important thing in the analysis of a psychotic, in fact it can be, at times, even more important than the verbal interpretations which also have to be given.
>
> *(Winnicott, 1947, p. 72)*

104 Joyce Slochower

By establishing a therapeutic holding environment, the analyst creates an antidote to the experience of ongoing impingements (trauma) that had characterized the patient's infancy. Those impingements foreclosed the possibility of true self expression, of the spontaneous gesture received. The true self (a sense of vitality and aliveness) progressively withdrew and allowed the false self to take over. The false self was a protector self: pseudo-maturity and pseudo-independence replaced parental absence *and* covered over need.

The false self exists on a continuum: in health, it represents a layer of social appropriateness, what the French call *politesse*. It keeps relationships functioning smoothly while allowing the individual to remain in contact with a sense of authenticity. But when the false self – a form of protection against the unbearable – takes over and the true self retreats altogether, contact is lost with what lies beneath. Only when the true self can safely be accessed will the schizoid patient find the aliveness that had gone into hiding in childhood (Winnicott, 1955). This will require the establishment of a protective analytic holding environment. The analyst

> must deal with the early stages of emotional development before and up to the establishment of the personality as an entity, before the achievement of space-time unit status. The personal structure is not yet securely founded. In regard to this third grouping, the accent is more surely on management, and sometimes over long periods with these patients ordinary analytic work has to be in abeyance, management being the whole thing.
>
> *(Winnicott, 1955, p. 17)*

Winnicott may have doubted the therapeutic efficacy of the analyst's interpretations, but he passionately believed in the analyst's reparative potential – a potential lodged in her capacity to hold the patient through a regression to dependence. This therapeutic holding environment, characterized by the analyst's resonant, empathic responsivity, would allow the patient to relive and repair early trauma in the presence of a symbolic maternal figure.

Arguing forcefully against the analytic ideal of abstinence, Winnicott met his patient where she was. His idea of holding was both symbolic – reflected in his consistent empathic resonance – and concrete. For example, Winnicott thought it unfortunate that analysts were afraid to touch patients, and did so when he felt it necessary. With one patient he made milk and cookies (biscuits) part of the fixed therapeutic setting. He made a point of opening his front door before one patient rang the bell (symbolically allowing her to "create" the analytic object). These are dramatic (and concrete) examples of what he meant by "holding."

In more ordinary treatment situations, however, holding is symbolic. The holding analyst is responsive, empathic and reparative. She minimizes therapeutic disruptions and receives the patient's experience (spontaneous gesture). This highly protective setting will allow the patient to turn over false self functioning to the analyst, and contact and express true self experience, especially early trauma. That trauma, now re-experienced in the analytic setting, will be fully remembered and then repaired, allowing the maturational processes to proceed (Winnicott, 1960, 1969).

This idea of analytic holding was lodged in a parental metaphor, a vision of a new, improved mother/father. It generated a powerful response. If the analyst symbolically can become the mother, the possibility of reworking early trauma is enormously increased; what cannot be remembered can be re-experienced and then repaired. The patient can, in fact, be a baby again, but with a better, more responsive mother.

Winnicott dramatically changed the clinical landscape by moving analytic work away from a focus on sexual and aggressive conflict (the repeated relationship) and toward the needed one (S. Stern, 1994). Maternal metaphors gave a name and shape to something that had remained largely unspoken: the clinical value of empathic responsivity. Now it was theorized: dependence was not defensive; it was real, and needed real repair.[1]

But Winnicott did not advocate regression for all. Dividing psychiatric illness into three rough categories, he linked each to a different therapeutic model. Whereas classical technique (organized around interpretation) was appropriate for neurotic patients, Kleinian patients (those in need of work around the depressive position) needed both interpretation and management (holding).[2] (Incidentally, Winnicott was well aware that the more troubled the patient, the more countertransference hate would likely be aroused in the analyst. More about that shortly.)

Illusion: transitionality, play and paradox

Had Winnicott's therapeutic vision been organized solely around the notion of parental repair, we would have been left with a rather one-dimensional version of analytic process. But his clinical perspective was far more layered than this; it was lodged in ideas about transitionality, paradox and illusion.

Holding a regression to dependence involves all these elements. If a regression is to function therapeutically, the analytic couple must imaginatively *recreate* the patient-as-baby (and analyst-as-parent) while simultaneously retaining awareness of the paradoxical, playful element inherent in this construction: the patient both *is* and *isn't* a baby; the analyst *is and isn't* the mother. The analytic couple plays at recreating the early environment without explicitly acknowledging the "as if" element inherent in that recreation or challenging the "truth" of the holding moment. Here's an illustration from my own practice:

> *A patient who moved in and out of dependent states in her treatment came in one day carrying an aromatic bag of bagels, still warm from the (then) best bagel bakery in New York. Holding up the bag and smiling, she said: "Bagels" (this was obvious, and she knew it). I smiled and responded, "They smell great." She: "Want one?" I: "Sure." She laughed and lay down on the couch. I laughed too.*

106 Joyce Slochower

No bagels were exchanged as a result of this exchange, and we both knew they wouldn't be. This was analytic play, but it was enormously important play. My patient played at feeding me and I agreed to be fed – symbolically. Embedded in that enactment were all kinds of wishes *and* a symbolic repair. My patient both expressed and reversed her desire to be fed while letting me know something about her gratitude toward me. She also communicated her wish to reciprocate – to "feed me back" – and expected (hoped) that I would accept and appreciate her own potential feeding (maternal) capacity. After all, she had the bagels, not I. Embedded in this exchange was an implicit acknowledgment of sameness (we both liked those particular bagels). We played at breaking boundaries and enjoyed the illusion that we were. But we didn't break them.

It's also important to note that I was able to engage in this playful way *because I knew that I wasn't going to be confronted with an actual bagel* (something I neither would have been comfortable eating nor wanted just then).[3]

Holding and the shift to object usage

A superficial reading of Winnicott's clinical approach would stop here. In holding, the analyst symbolically becomes the parent and the patient regresses, re-finds and re-experiences early trauma in the presence of a reliable, maternal analyst who repairs by virtue of her capacity for empathy and nurturance. The analyst, like the mother, contains her countertransference and bears its strain without letting the patient know about it. Even when the analyst plays, she remains empathic and resonant with the patient's needs.

Standing alone, this is a narrow clinical perspective. It leaves patient and analyst completely lodged in a positive transference paradigm. There's no room for negative transference or countertransference, no room for working through the anger that inevitably accompanies trauma.

This is a misreading of Winnicott's view, however. Regression to dependence *begins, but does not complete, the process of therapeutic repair*. The analyst's capacity to function within a holding space allows the patient to turn over false self defenses to the analyst and regress to the point of the original failure. That failure, now relived rather than remembered, will be found (created) within the analytic setting. But Winnicott added something more, something that vastly enriched and usefully complicated his clinical perspective: *holding allows the patient to get angry at the analyst for the original failure.*

> But even so, the corrective provision is never enough. What is it that may be enough for some of our patients to get well? In the end the patient uses the analyst's failures, often quite small ones, perhaps manoeuvred by the patient, or the patient produces delusional transference elements…and we have to put up with being in a limited context misunderstood. The operative factor is that the patient now hates the analyst for the failure that originally came as

an environmental factor, outside the infant's area of omnipotent control, but that is *now* staged in the transference.

(Winnicott, 1963b, p. 258, emphasis in original)

There is enormous therapeutic potential inherent in the analyst's failure. If the analyst can tolerate the patient's attacks without retaliating or withdrawing (not always easy to do), a crucial therapeutic shift takes place. The analyst becomes *other*, someone with a separate existence, someone who resides outside the resonant arena of the patient's need. So analytic failure *sets the stage for anger – even hate – to enter the analytic discourse and be worked through, often for the first time.*

It's the analyst's failures that facilitate a shift out of a holding frame and toward work around anger and survival. One of Winnicott's last and most important papers theorized this transition as a developmental progression from *object relating to object usage* (1969). In this sequence, Winnicott envisioned object usage as a development endpoint that reflected *a more mature capacity to recognize the object* than did object relating.

Winnicott's language is counterintuitive. We think colloquially of "relating" as a positive capacity to be in a relationship and "usage" as meaning treating the other as an object rather than a person. But Winnicott – unfortunately, I think – inverted the terms' ordinary implications: he invoked the term "object relating" to describe the baby's *unawareness* of the (m)other's separate existence. In the phase of object relating, the mother exists as the baby's creation; she isn't experienced as a separate other. It's not until object usage is achieved that the baby can sort out the mother *as created* from the mother who exists *out there in the world.*

Holding involves object relating: the analyst is a subjective object, created by the patient, not seen for herself. Not until the patient can get angry at the analyst for her failures *and discovers that the analyst survives (without retaliating)* will there be a transition to object usage – a recognition of the analyst's separateness. This recognition opens the door to mutual engagement and a more mature way of being with the other.

The shift to object usage is joyous. It locates the other (mother or analyst) in a world of others rather than in a world that is the baby's/patient's own creation. Essential in this trajectory is the mother's (analyst's) capacity to survive the baby's (patient's) destruction of it (in fantasy).

> This change (from relating to use) means that the subject destroys the object… After "subject relates to object" comes "subject destroys object" (as it becomes external); and then may come "*object survives* destruction by the subject"… The subject says to the object: "I destroyed you", and the object is there to receive the communication. From now on the subject says: "Hullo object!" "I destroyed you." "I love you." "You have value for me because of your survival of my destruction of you." […] The subject can now *use* the object that has survived…
>
> *(Winnicott, 1969, p. 173, emphasis in original)*

It's the shift away from the holding illusion that will allow the patient to *see* the analyst and move in the direction of mutuality. Here is a recent illustration from my own practice:

> *Jane, in her fifth year of a treatment, became uncharacteristically furious when I (unusually) began her session a few minutes late. Accusing me of putting her last, Jane freely expressed anger at me for the first time. Having harbored a mostly unconscious fantasy that she was my only patient (itself a fantasy that reversed her feeling of being utterly forgettable), Jane now confronted my failure to repair. Her sense of being forgotten had a very long history but, until now, I had been the one who remembered her. In this session I ruptured her illusion of attunement. My lateness precipitated a disturbing yet exciting awareness on Jane's part: we were not as much the same as Jane had thought. She now looked me over and discovered that I was myself – not her creation.*

Confronted with the reality of my existence as a separate entity outside the realm of her control, Jane felt thrown – hurt and angry. I did my best to contain (bracket) my own bad feelings (worry, guilt and defensiveness) about what I had done. I didn't explain or defend myself, but accepted her anger without trying to quell it and – crucially – without either counterattacking or defensively withdrawing. In Winnicottian terms, I survived. Jane moved from object relating toward object usage because I began to exist outside the realm of her fantasies about me (i.e., as a subjective object). Now I was an other with a separate existence – an other who could be seen, loved and hated.

Winnicott's work on object usage extended his earlier ideas about the potential therapeutic impact of the analyst's communicated hate by defining recognition of the other as a psychoanalytic goal. Pushing the boundaries of contemporary practice by inviting mutuality into it, Winnicott identified the patient's capacity to *see* the analyst as a person (rather than using her as a transference figure) as a clinical aim. No longer was the analyst purely an objective observer who would – and should – remain a subjective (transference) object.

Winnicott: contemporary retrospectives

Winnicott's therapeutic perspective was not universally embraced. His notions of true and false self clashed with contemporary relational ideas about self states as fluid and shifting rather than fixed. The idea that there is *a* true and *a* false self is based on a Cartesian model. It implies that the self is "findable" and "definable" outside the moment and outside the interpersonal context, that one is real and the other a cover. For interpersonal and social constructivist writers, this model is far too concrete and linear; the self is moveable and shifting. It's not possible to locate the "true" and "false" self because no fixed "self" is to be found; what's experienced as "me" shifts from moment to moment as the individual encounters and reacts to the other (e.g., D.B. Stern, 2007).

Another area of critique organized around the gratification implicit in ideas of regression to dependence. Winnicott's focus on analyst-as-reparative-mother seemed to ignore the role of sexual and aggressive drives as well as the repetition compulsion. It implied that repair could replace the analysis of conflict. Where were the dynamics of aggression and envy – of attachment to bad objects – in this model? Wasn't holding a way of gratifying rather than analyzing? And what about regression's problematic underbelly – what Michael Balint (1968) has called malignant regression? Winnicott seemed to ignore the possibility that the patient could get stuck in a regression rather than using it to further growth.

Social constructivist thinking added other critiques of the Winnicottian model. Historical truth is contextual rather than absolute. We can never really know what occurs outside the relational moment. Analyst and patient can, at best, create a shared narrative that feels like a "best fit" description. But this narrative is one that lacks certainty or truth. If it's not possible to reconstruct a patient's history or "find" what went wrong, we cannot assume a reparative therapeutic posture vis-à-vis a patient's early trauma. Who's to say that the analyst knows what the patient needs? Doesn't that vision leave the patient more or less at the mercy of the analyst's "good enough" efforts to repair and empty the analyst of her own non-maternal subjectivity?

Also problematic were the implicit superiority and omniscience attributed to Winnicott: his developmental tilt seemed to idealize the analyst-as-mother and render the patient both unknowing and infantilized. Didn't it empty the patient of her own capacities? After all, the patient is an adult, capable of seeing the analyst and knowing things about her. What *was* no longer *is*; the patient brings her non-baby self – with all its attendant conflicts and complex ways of experiencing things – to the consulting room.

Interpersonal writers especially critiqued Winnicott's "developmental tilt." They argued that, when enacted, developmental illusions created an as-if therapeutic situation that locked the patient into a position of helpless dependence while encouraging the analyst's grandiosity (e.g., Mitchell, 1984, 1988, 1993; Hoffman, 1991; Stern, 1992; Aron, 1992). This vision of patient-as-baby sidestepped the omnipresence of the analyst's subjectivity by implying that she was capable of holding a patient from a position outside the relational matrix – i.e., that it's possible to contain and de-center from one's own countertransference experience.

Adding to this critique were voices rooted in feminist thinking. Beginning in the 1960s, feminists challenged both the idealization of motherhood and its associated demand for maternal self-abnegation, noting that traditional views of motherhood obliterated the father and located all the child's pathology in the maternal lap. Those views foreclosed the idea, no matter the experience, of mother-as-person.

Picking up and elaborating this argument as it applied to the consulting room, feminist psychoanalysts including Dinnerstein (1976), Chodorow (1978), Fast (1984), Benjamin (1986, 1988, 1995) and many others have critiqued dichotomized depictions of gender implicit in notions of analytic repair. Visions of what Grand (2000) calls maternal bounty, of analyst-as-Earth-Mother,

110 Joyce Slochower

negate the irreducible nature of analytic subjectivity (Renik, 1993) and ignore the pre-Oedipal father.

While Winnicott explicitly acknowledged the inevitability of the analyst's hate, he also expected that both analyst and mother could and would set themselves aside in the best interest of their patient/baby. But isn't it possible that the mother or analyst might hate – or have another problematic feeling – toward the baby/patient at just the *wrong* moment (see Kraemer, 1996)? And what about the patient's (and baby's) subliminal awareness of what's *not* acknowledged by the analyst? Might that kind of analytic silence feel gaslighting to the patient?

On one level, Winnicott made the analyst a real object for the patient: she was someone who existed "out there," someone whose existence was of therapeutic value. Winnicott's bold ideas about object usage turned our attention to the baby's (and patient's) awareness of the mother/analyst as *other*. But Winnicott's mother is idealized, as is the analyst's reparative capacity. This idealization obscures the therapeutic potential inherent in the patient's acknowledgment of the analyst's subjectivity (vulnerability, hate, conflict, and so on). Might the analyst's explicit acknowledgment and exploration of her countertransference be therapeutic *across* the treatment relationship rather than merely at its termination?

A relational Winnicottian response

Beginning in the 1990s, I, influenced by both Winnicott and the relational critique, proposed several clinical/theoretical alterations to the Winnicottian position that accounted for the analyst's subjectivity and retheorized the holding experience as one that's created dyadically. In a series of essays and two books (Slochower, 1991, 1992, 1993, 1994, 1996a, 1996b, 1996c, 1999, 2006a, 2006b, 2008a, 2008b, 2011a, 2011b, 2012, 2013a, 2013b, 2014a, 2014b, 2014c), I explored and elaborated Winnicott's ideas about holding, regression, idealization, object usage and collisions between the ideal and actual analyst. I then considered their clash with a relational clinical perspective and proposed a formulation that would resolve this clash.

I had three overall aims: first, to expand Winnicott's conception of holding and explore how it might emerge in work with patients struggling with a range of disturbing affect states other than dependence; second, to integrate the Winnicottian sensibility within an overarching relational framework that took account of the intersubjective element inherent *within* the holding moment; and, third, to theorize the analyst's experience during work within the holding trope.

In *Holding and Psychoanalysis: A Relational Perspective* (1996a, 2014b), I made a plea for the therapeutic value of empathic responsivity, reconceived to account for the relational and feminist critiques and expanded to encompass a developmental trajectory that extends beyond the nursery. Here's a brief summary: there are limits to the clinical value of intersubjective exchange. Some especially vulnerable patients cannot tolerate the analyst's otherness without prolonged derailment that shuts down, rather than opens up, therapeutic process. The Winnicottian holding metaphor permits a blurring of the permeable boundary between patient and analyst. It buffers the impact of her otherness and opens up therapeutic process. I suggested that we can engage this metaphor without negating the omnipresence of the analyst's subjectivity.

In my view, holding means paying particularly close attention to my patient's emotional responses to evidence of my "otherness" – that is, my separate thoughts, reactions or ideas. I'm not referring to whether or not my patient accepts what I say. A loud "No damn way, you're wrong" can be the opener for a rich and useful interchange. But when my patient consistently shuts down at these times, when she is unable to accept and work with *or* reject my perspective while sustaining her own, I sit up, therapeutically speaking. I ask myself whether I might be off-base emotionally or dynamically, whether we're involved in a potentially useful – or very problematic – reenactment. Is my patient reacting to my being too much like old objects or too different from them? I do all this while working hard to track my own subjectivity, my own reactions to the clinical moment.

When I'm trying to hold, however, I don't explicitly introduce my otherness into the consulting room. Instead, I aim to help my patient feel seen, not from the outside in but from the inside out (Bromberg, 1991). This way of working helps my patient to make fuller contact with acutely painful feelings; at others, it helps her to down-regulate and move out of a flooded emotional state.

Winnicott linked holding to patients who needed a regression to dependence. But other kinds of affect states (and other kinds of patients) sometimes need holding. When, for example, rage or contempt cannot be examined and worked with, I try to hold – though certainly not from an idealized parental position. I hold by accepting being the perpetrator (Davies & Frawley, 1994; Grand, 2000, 2009), by struggling to survive and not retaliate (Winnicott, 1971). This kind of holding may communicate, via interpretive action (Ogden, 1994), that I recognize and accept my patient's difficult feelings along with a double communication: I am affected but not destroyed by you.

From a relational perspective, it's impossible to do this because, inevitably, our subjectivity seeps into the clinical moment. It seeps in by virtue of what we say (and don't) and how we say it. It's also reflected in when we try to hold and when we don't. For all these reasons, if we are to hold our patient, we need to do something with those aspects of our separate subjectivity that would excessively disrupt the holding illusion.

I invoked the idea of *bracketing subjectivity* to capture that process. When we're holding, it's essential that we remain aware of what we're feeling and thinking even as we do our best to contain rather than express it. The concept of bracketing alludes to the doubleness of the holding experience, the "there but not there" quality of our subjectivity. I may well feel stressed, tired, impatient, even furious with my patient in ways that would be disturbing, anxiety-arousing or otherwise deeply upsetting to her. In these moments, I bracket by privately noting, struggling with but trying to set aside my reaction – crucially – without disavowing it.

But, no matter how self-aware we are and no matter how well we hold, some of the time I (we all) fail when we try to hold. There will be moments when we think we know what's needed but don't; moments when we're in the throes of an enactment, selfobject failure or other kind of misattunement. And, of course, there are clear limits to what we can hold and what we can bracket, because we can't bracket what we don't know we're feeling. Additionally, many of our patients are pretty perceptive (sometimes more than we'd like), and may well pick up aspects of our reactions despite our attempts at bracketing.

So bracketing takes two; when our patient needs not to know something about us, she does as much bracketing as we do – or even more – by shielding herself from those aspects of our otherness (our variability, reactivity, and so on) that would disrupt or shatter the sense of resonance on which she relies.

From my relational, Winnicottian perspective, the holding space can be maintained *only if it's co-constructed*. We don't bracket alone; our patient also brackets those aspects of our presence that would disrupt the holding illusion on which she relies. In this sense, the holding experience is established *jointly* by the dyad. The concept of mutual bracketing moves holding out of the analyst's corner and into dyadic space, reversing the asymmetry associated with the holding metaphor.

A most dramatic example of this kind of bracketing harkens back to my days as a young analyst, very pregnant with my third child. At eight months I was enormous. Feeling that I could no longer wait for my patient, Jonathan, who was neither very ill nor especially dissociative, to address the obvious, I said: "There's something we need to talk about." Fully expecting Jonathan to acknowledge that he hadn't wanted to bring my pregnancy up but of course had noticed, I didn't anticipate that he would do a double-take and virtually fall back into the chair, stunned.

Jonathan's need to see us as a couple within this protected space had utterly obfuscated my pregnancy, a most concrete indication of my otherness. He had excluded it and what it represented (the prospect of a symbolic sibling, not to mention my shadow husband – the unseen sexual partner who had fathered this child). In so doing, Jonathan sustained an essential experience of togetherness with me, the first such experience he could recall. Ours wasn't a holding space reminiscent of the nursery, though. Jonathan felt me to be more of a peer/older sister who was identified with his needs and was able to be together with him in them. An element of twinship merged with maternal longings to render me "a woman, but just like him." Hence, not pregnant. And, as much as I consciously wanted to be seen in my expectant state, perhaps on another level I unconsciously supported this bracketing via my wish to protect our relationship (and my baby) by leaving the latter outside therapeutic space.

Eventually Jonathan and I talked about this, about what he had needed to miss and why. Our conversations filled in and thickened the therapeutic dialogue, but I'm pretty sure that they couldn't have taken place had I insistently introduced my pregnancy early on. And it's worth noting that I never told Jonathan that I had been bothered by his oblivion to my pregnancy. I chose not to because I sensed that this kind of disclosure would have been intensely shaming to this sensitive, shy man.

It's difficult to describe all this without making it sound deliberate, even choreographed. But, in my view, shifts in and out of a holding metaphor are anything but: they are multiply determined, at once conscious, intentional and not. In part, I move toward holding based on my clinical/theoretical point of entry. In part, this shift is procedural, a spontaneous reaction to aspects of my own experience that I don't even know I'm perceiving. In part, it's enacted, responsive to pulls and pushes from my patient that are at once responsive to the pulls and pushes that come from me.

Whatever its particular shape, the Winnicottian holding metaphor pulls us to partially set aside the parental/analytic protest ("Hey, wait a minute; I'm a person too"). So holding requires a lot of self-holding on the analyst's part. And, despite what some critics think, holding patients usually isn't gratifying; it can feel oppressive and limiting, and can leave us thinking that we're not doing enough work or as if we're constantly holding our breath, staying too still, tracking our patient too closely. Holding hate and contempt is even more difficult. As Davies (2004), Epstein (1987) and others remind us, when we're bad objects to our patient, we're also bad objects to ourselves. It's not only our patients who need holding.

The take away

Winnicott's use of the baby metaphor expressed the phenomenological reality of these baby states while temporarily ignoring the other actuality – that of patient-as-adult. I think we can, finally, take both for granted. Certainly, it was never merely babies who needed holding; older children – and we adults – sometimes need it too, sometimes from within a much younger self state, sometimes from a very adult but very vulnerable one.

Winnicottian developmental metaphors have been critiqued for their idealization of both the analytic and the therapeutic function. But it seems to me that, even when we formulate therapeutic process outside the idea of holding – whether we think about patients' need for confrontation, authenticity, mutuality, selfobject experiences or recognition – we idealize something. Our personhood limits our capacity to meet that ideal and confronts us with what I've called a *psychoanalytic collision* (Slochower, 2006a, 2014c). Collisions emerge, independent of our theoretical allegiance, out of the space between the professional ideal to which we aspire and the actuality of our human fallibility.

If there's a problem with the use of concepts such as *regression to dependence* and *holding* today, it's not that they idealize the analyst more than other theories; it's that they have been overused and sometimes misused. Indeed, the concepts have bled so far beyond their original edges that I hear them invoked to describe almost everything we analysts do other than confront or piercingly interpret. It's too easy to use concepts such as regression to categorize what we're doing and why. Both withholding *and* impulsive gratification can be justified as holding. We need to pause before assuming that our patient needs holding in just the same way that we need to pause before assuming that she needs to hear about our subjectivity.

114 Joyce Slochower

Holding's therapeutic function

What does holding do, dynamically speaking? What's the impact of privileging our patient's perspective on herself and allowing it to unfold, received but not altered? Certainly, holding creates a protected space and facilitates emotional expression. But I think it does more than this.

When we hold, we bear witness to our patient's experience without challenging it, and in so doing we help create a particularly effective buffer against shame states. Holding buffers shame because it softens the impact of the analyst's otherness and creates an illusion of emotional attunement between analyst and patient.

The experience of affective attunement – however it's configured – establishes a shield against the sense of exposure to an outside eye. My patient and I feel what he or she feels *together*, and so she comes to feel *with* me rather than feel seen *by* me. So holding helps us create a shield against shame. Over time, a scaffolding that protects against humiliation and allows self-experience to coalesce will allow patient and analyst to enter the arena of shame. Together.

Any good psychoanalytic treatment – including a Winnicottian one – does way more than holding, and the rest of what we do counts a lot. Whether we identify the holding dimension as figure or as ground depends on our theory. But the experience of early need remains an alive layer of human experience, and this is where the shadow holding element comes in; it guides us on a procedural level with regard to when and how we enter the clinical dialogue, how directly and how deeply.

So, to get back to our Winnicottian beginning: there's no simple baby – or adult – in the consulting room, because both members of the dyad move from moment to moment, imperceptibly and unconsciously, toward and away from relating to the other as a collaborative subject. In this process, patient and analyst contact, enact and perhaps meet the needs of these baby and child self states, for better and for worse.

We don't have to abandon Winnicott's idea of a psychoanalytic baby because it can, in fact, swim in contemporary psychoanalytic bathwater – bathwater that includes an analyst who holds and who fails to hold, who is mostly (but not always) capable of being a reflective professional who has access to her own baby self states and sometimes mixes it up with her patient. The developmental trajectory, such as it is, has so many bumps and reversals that it would be absurd to call it linear. Still, the notion of progression from a world dominated by the experience of a single subject to one characterized by interpenetrating subjectivities and the possibility of mutuality – itself a shifting rather than linear progression – remains appealing. En route to that aim, we engage a range of Winnicottian metaphors that enrich and deepen our understanding of analytic process. And help our patient.

Notes

1 In some respects, Winnicott's ideas about holding and analytic repair mirror the self psychology model of selfobject rupture and repair. But there are differences too: Winnicott identified analytic holding as a *phase* that would be followed by a shift toward object usage rather than as intrinsically mutative on its own.

2 I have always wondered whether this division represented Winnicott's genuine take on clinical work, or whether it represented an attempt to placate his mentors by carving out a separate area (patients in need of a regression) that was *his*, and leaving untouched the perspective of his Freudian and Kleinian colleagues.
3 The power of this play was such that I didn't "translate" or interpret it, but let it stand as it was.

References

Anderson, J. W. (2014). How D. W. Winnicott conducted psychoanalysis. *Psychoanalytic Psychology*, 31(3): 375–395.

Anderson, J. W. (2015a). D. W. Winnicott's constant search for the life that feels real. In M. B. Spelman & F. Thomson-Salo (Eds.), *The Winnicott Tradition: Lines of Development: Evolution of Theory and Practice over the Decades*, pp. 19–38. London: Karnac Books.

Anderson, J. W. (2015b). Winnicott's search for the life that feels real. Paper presented at the 35th annual spring meeting of the Division of Psychoanalysis of the American Psychological Association, San Francisco, April 24.

Aron, L. (1992). Interpretation as expression of the analyst's subjectivity. *Psychoanalytic Dialogues*, 2(4): 475–508.

Balint, M. (1968). *The Basic Fault: Therapeutic Aspects of Regression*. London: Tavistock Publications.

Benjamin, J. (1986). A desire of one's own: Psychoanalytic feminism and intersubjective space. In T. de Lauretis (Ed.), *Feminist Studies/Critical Studies*, pp. 78–101. Bloomington, IN: Indiana University Press.

Benjamin, J. (1988). *The Bonds of Love: Psychoanalysis, Feminism and the Problem of Domination*. New York: Pantheon Books.

Benjamin, J. (1995). *Like Subjects, Love Objects: Essays on Recognition and Sexual Difference*. New Haven, CT: Yale University Press.

Bromberg, P. M. (1991). On knowing one's patient inside out: The aesthetics of unconscious communication. *Psychoanalytic Dialogues*, 1(4): 399–422.

Chodorow, N. J. (1978). *The Reproduction of Mothering: Psychoanalysis and the Sociology of Gender*. Berkeley, CA: University of California Press.

Davies, J. M. (2004). Whose bad objects are we anyway? Repetition and our elusive love affair with evil. *Psychoanalytic Dialogues*, 14(6): 711–732.

Davies, J. M., & Frawley, M. G. (1994). *Treating the Adult Survivor of Childhood Sexual Abuse: A Psychoanalytical Perspective*. New York: Basic Books.

Dinnerstein, D. (1976). *The Mermaid and the Minotaur*. New York: Harper & Row.

Epstein, L. (1987). The problem of the bad-analyst-feeling. *Modern Psychoanalysis*, 12(1): 35–45.

Fast, I. (1984). *Gender Identity: A Differentiation Model*. Hillsdale, NJ: Analytic Press.

Grand, S. (2000). *The Reproduction of Evil: A Clinical and Cultural Perspective*. Hillsdale, NJ: Analytic Press.

Grand, S. (2009). *The Hero in the Mirror: From Fear to Fortitude*. New York: Routledge.

Hoffman, I. Z. (1991). Discussion: Toward a social-constructivist view of the psychoanalytic situation. *Psychoanalytic Dialogues*, 1(1): 74-105.

Kraemer, S. B. (1996). "Betwixt the dark and the daylight" of maternal subjectivity: Meditations on the threshold. *Psychoanalytic Dialogues*, 6(6): 765–791.

Mitchell, S. A. (1984). Object relations theories and the developmental tilt. *Contemporary Psychoanalysis*, 20(4): 473–499.

Mitchell, S. A. (1988). *Relational Concepts in Psychoanalysis: An Integration*. Cambridge, MA: Harvard University Press.

Mitchell, S. A. (1993). *Hope and Dread in Psychoanalysis*. New York: Basic Books.

Ogden, T. H. (1994). *Subjects of Analysis*. New York: Jason Aronson.

Renik, O. (1993). Analytic interaction: Conceptualizing technique in light of the analyst's irreducible subjectivity. *Psychoanalytic Quarterly*, 62(4): 553–571.

Slochower, J. (1991). Variations in the analytic holding environment. *International Journal of Psychoanalysis*, 72(4): 709–718.

Slochower, J. (1992). A hateful borderline patient and the holding environment. *Contemporary Psychoanalysis*, 28(1): 72–88.

Slochower, J. (1993). Mourning and the holding function of shiva. *Contemporary Psychoanalysis*, 29(3): 352–367.

Slochower, J. (1994). The evolution of object usage and the holding environment. *Contemporary Psychoanalysis*, 30(1): 135–151.

Slochower, J. (1996a). *Holding and Psychoanalysis: A Relational Perspective*. Hillsdale, NJ: Analytic Press.

Slochower, J. (1996b). Holding and the evolving maternal metaphor. *Psychoanalytic Review*, 83(2): 195–218.

Slochower, J. (1996c). The holding environment and the fate of the analyst's subjectivity. *Psychoanalytic Dialogues*, 6(3): 323–353.

Slochower, J. (1999). Interior experience in analytic process. *Psychoanalytic Dialogues*, 9(6): 789–809.

Slochower, J. (2006a). *Psychoanalytic Collisions*. Hillsdale, NJ: Analytic Press.

Slochower, J. (2006b). Holding: Something old and something new. In L. Aron & A. Harris (Eds.), *Relational Psychoanalysis*, Vol. 2, *Innovation and Expansion*, pp. 29–50. Hillsdale, NJ: Analytic Press.

Slochower, J. (2008a). Un uso intersoggettivo del sogno. *Ricerca Psicoanalitica*, 19(3): 355–376.

Slochower, J. (2008b). Del sostén a la colaboración: Una perspectiva relacional. In *Winnicott Hoy: Su Presencia en la Clínica Actual*, pp. 361–383. Madrid: Psimática.

Slochower, J. (2011a). Holding, collaborating, colliding: A cross theoretical conversation. *Psychoanalytic Inquiry*, 31(5): 501–512.

Slochower, J. (2011b). Analytic idealizations and the disavowed: Winnicott, his patients, and us. *Psychoanalytic Dialogues*, 21(1): 3–21.

Slochower, J. (2012). L'idealizzazione nel rapporto con pazienti e allievi. *Ricerca Psicoanalitica*, 2(2): 101–126.

Slochower, J. (2013a). Using Winnicott today: A relational perspective. *Revue Roumaine de Psychanalyse*, 2(1): 13–41.

Slochower, J. (2013b). Psychoanalytic mommies and psychoanalytic babies: A long view. *Contemporary Psychoanalysis*, 49(4): 606–628.

Slochower, J. (2014a). Idéalizations analytiques et le désavoué: Winnicott, ses patients, et nous. *Revue Française de Psychanalyse*, 78(4): 1136–1149.

Slochower, J. (2014b). *Holding and Psychoanalysis: A Relational Perspective*, 2nd Edn. New York: Routledge.

Slochower, J. (2014c). *Psychoanalytic Collisions*, 2nd Edn. Hillsdale, NJ: Analytic Press.

Stern, D. B. (1992). Commentary on constructivism in clinical psychoanalysis. *Psychoanalytic Dialogues*, 2(3): 331–364.

Stern, D. B. (2007). Opening what has been closed, relaxing what has been clenched: Dissociation and enactment over time in committed relationships. *Psychoanalytic Dialogues*, 16(6): 747–761.

Stern, S. (1994). Needed relationships and repeated relationships: An integrated relational perspective. *Psychoanalytic Dialogues*, 4(3): 317–346.

Winnicott, D. W. (1941). The observation of infants in a set situation. *International Journal of Psychoanalysis*, 22(2): 229–249.

Winnicott, D. W. (1947 [1958]). Hate in the countertransference. In *Through Paediatrics to Psycho-Analysis: Collected Papers*, pp. 194–203. London: Tavistock Publications.

Winnicott, D. W. (1949 [1957]). The ordinary devoted mother and her baby. In *The Child and the Family*, pp. 15–102. London: Tavistock Publications.

Winnicott, D. W. (1953). Transitional objects and transitional phenomena: A study of the first not-me possession. *International Journal of Psychoanalysis*, 34(2): 89–97.

Winnicott, D. W. (1955). Metapsychological and clinical aspects of regression within the psycho-analytical set-up. *International Journal of Psychoanalysis*, 36(1): 16–26.

Winnicott, D. W. (1960 [1965]). Ego distortions in terms of true and false self. In *The Maturational Processes and the Facilitating Environment: Studies in the Theory of Emotional Development*, pp. 140–152. London: Hogarth Press.

Winnicott, D. W. (1962 [1965]). A personal view of the Kleinian contribution. In *The Maturational Processes and the Facilitating Environment: Studies in the Theory of Emotional Development*, pp. 171–178. London: Hogarth Press.

Winnicott, D. W. (1963a [1965]). The development of a capacity for concern. In *The Maturational Processes and the Facilitating Environment: Studies in the Theory of Emotional Development*, pp. 73–82. London: Hogarth Press.

Winnicott, D. W. (1963b [1965]). Dependence in infant-care, child-care, and in the psycho-analytic setting. In *The Maturational Processes and the Facilitating Environment: Studies in the Theory of Emotional Development*, pp. 249–259. London: Hogarth Press.

Winnicott, D. W. (1965). *The Maturational Processes and the Facilitating Environment: Studies in the Theory of Emotional Development*. London: Hogarth Press.

Winnicott, D. W. (1969). The use of an object. *International Journal of Psychoanalysis*, 50(4): 711–716.

Winnicott, D. W. (1971). The use of an object and relating through identifications. In *Playing and Reality*, pp. 86–94. London: Tavistock Publications.

PART III
Building bridges

6

TOWARD A NEW MIDDLE GROUP

Lacan and Winnicott for beginners

Deborah Luepnitz

Introduction

In order to understand the work of Lacan and Winnicott in contemporary theory and practice, one must begin by reflecting on the relationship of both to Sigmund Freud. When teaching, I often ask students to identify the following quotations:

> My discoveries are not primarily a heal-all. My discoveries are a basis for a very grave philosophy. There are very few who understand this, *there are very few who are capable of understanding this.*
>
> *(H.D., 1956, p. 18, emphasis in original)*

> If [your son] is unhappy, neurotic, torn by conflicts, inhibited in his social life, psychoanalysis may bring him harmony, peace of mind, full efficiency…
>
> *(Freud, 1961, p. 423)*

Few correctly associate them with the founder of psychoanalysis. The first is something Freud said to a patient of his, Hilda Doolittle – the American poet known as H.D. – as reported in her memoir, *Tribute to Freud.* The second comes from a letter he wrote in response to a mother who had asked if psychoanalysis could cure her son, who apparently was not interested in women.

Although Freud made the two statements around the same time – the response to H.D. in 1934, and the letter a year later – they bespeak remarkably different perspectives. In the first quotation, we see the Freud who observed that there is something intrinsic to the sexual drive in humans that makes full satisfaction impossible, and who insisted on the importance of the death drive. For him, psychoanalysis is not primarily a method of healing but the basis of a *grave philosophy* – perhaps, in

122 Deborah Luepnitz

part, a philosophy of the grave. Here we have the patrician intellectual who believed that very few could even comprehend his ideas.

In the letter to a worried mother, in contrast, we encounter Freud the humanist, the Enlightenment thinker interested in the relief of suffering. This is the Freud who wrote the *Introductory Lectures on Psycho-Analysis* (Freud, 1916a, 1916b) so that his ideas would be widely accessible. He took time to reply to an anxious parent and, while stating that her son probably did not need psychoanalytic treatment, promised a great deal for those who do: *harmony, peace of mind, full efficiency.* This is the Freud who advocated treatment at no cost, and was immensely proud that, in his lifetime, ten free clinics sprang up in seven European countries (Danto, 2005).

Which is the real Freud: the compassionate physician or the radical truth teller, optimist or skeptic, humanist or post-humanist?

The answer, of course, is that both are the real Freud. To paraphrase Walt Whitman, he was vast and contained multitudes. One might say that the analysts following him have been drawn to either one stream of thought or the other, expanding the field accordingly. In my view, Donald Winnicott developed the humanist strand in Freud. Winnicott was a meliorist; he believed that happy families are possible and that mankind is changing for the better. Reading Winnicott reassures us that, even absent a wholesome environment in early childhood, a good enough analyst can help the individual grow to *wholeness* and experience *mature intimacy*.

Jacques Lacan encountered a different Freud. He did not see psychoanalysis as something that could make broken human beings whole. "Have you ever encountered whole beings? I've never seen any. I'm not whole, neither are you" (Lacan, 1978, p. 243). He never used the term "self" but wrote instead of the "divided subject," because, for him, the human subject is always divided by the unconscious. His famous teachings include "Life does not want to be healed" (Lacan, 1978, p. 233) and "[T]here is no sexual relation" (Lacan, 1975, p. 170). Of humanism, he said explicitly: "As for us, we consider ourselves to be at the *end of the vein* of humanist thought" (Lacan, 1986, p. 273, emphasis in original).

Winnicott and Lacan were contemporaries. They knew each other professionally, exchanged several letters and maintained a cordial (if strained) relationship. Whereas Winnicott would become president of the venerable British Psychoanalytic Society, Lacan was the subject of an IPA (International Psychoanalytic Association) investigation for his clinical methods, and claimed to be "excommunicated" by the establishment (Roudinesco, 1986). Both men experimented with analytic time. Winnicott often extended the session to provide a better *holding environment*. One patient, Margaret Little, wrote that, during a period of therapeutic regression, her sessions lasted for hours, as Winnicott held her head in his hands. She was charged only for the first hour, and they always ended with coffee and biscuits (Little, 1990). Typically, Winnicott's holding was not hands-on but, rather, an atmosphere of emotional safety and trust.

Lacan was known for the *variable-length session*, still used by contemporary Lacanians. Some of his sessions were long, but others lasted only minutes – and sometimes mere seconds. This is consistent with his teaching that finding the truth of one's desire requires an unsettling of the ego, which he regarded as "the human symptom *par excellence* – the mental illness of man" (Lacan, 1975, p. 16). Not surprisingly, nearly every former patient who has written about working with Lacan compares him (appropriately or not) to a Zen master (e.g., Haddad, 2002; Rey, 1989; Schneiderman, 1983; Godin, 1990).

It is important to keep in mind that Freud never insisted on a rigidly fixed hour. In fact, in his essay "On beginning the treatment" (Freud, 1913) he explicitly mentions the need to offer more time when a patient is slow to engage. Moreover, in the case of the Wolfman (Freud, 1918) we learn that the patient, who used to enjoy sick days in childhood because they won his mother's attention, may have enjoyed Freud's couch for the same reason. "The first years of the treatment produced scarcely any change," wrote Freud (p. 156). Freud did not put pressure on the patient for quite a while. "I had to wait until his attachment to myself had become strong enough…" (p. 157). At that point, Freud set a fixed and firm date for the end of the analysis, and in that final, short span of time "the illness gave way" (p. 157). Here, again, we see Freud setting the stage for what Winnicott would call a *holding environment*, and also for what Lacan would do to interrupt the fantasy of perfect holding. In fact, it is precisely in the context of discussing the Wolfman that Lacan launched a memorable commentary on "the length of the session" (Lacan, 1966, p. 257).

It is not only because of his experimentation with analytic time that Lacan was associated with scandal (Roudinesco, 1986). Later, many boundary violations were alleged, and at least one patient, Sonia Schoonejans (2008), claims that they engaged in a physical fight. Winnicott, in contrast, is typically considered to be a thoroughly benign figure, the last person one would associate with such behavior. Linda Hopkins (2006), in her biography of Masud Khan, makes it clear, however, that Winnicott was aware of the abuse of patients perpetrated by Khan – his colleague and protégé – but did little or nothing to stop him. I have noticed in both camps a tendency to minimize or sidestep the bad behavior of their respective hero. Wallowing in scandal is not illuminating but, without confronting the legacy head-on, one wonders how its replication can be avoided. This is a question not only for the devotees of the two analysts featured here, but also of Carl Jung, Sándor Ferenczi, Wilhelm Reich, Karen Horney, Harry Stack Sullivan and Freud himself. "Unhappy the land that needs heroes," says Bertolt Brecht. The challenge remains of learning from great thinkers without negatively hallucinating their failings, contradictions and destructiveness. (For further exploration of the alleged transgressions of Lacan, see Roudinesco, 1986; Roustang, 1990; of Winnicott, see Godley, 2001; Hopkins, 2006.)

The writings of Winnicott and Lacan have had enormous impact on the psychoanalytic worlds they left behind, and their influence continues to grow. The year 2015 saw both the publication of Winnicott's collected works for the first time and

124 Deborah Luepnitz

the first congress of IWA, the International Winnicott Association. Winnicott is one of the main inspirational figures for the extremely popular movement known as *relational psychoanalysis* (Mitchell, 1988). As for Lacan, the perception of him on the part of anglophone analysts – as an obscurantist philosopher whose followers form a fringe movement – is changing. More readers now understand that Lacan himself practiced full-time for 40 years and that, by some estimates, over half the world's analysts identify as Lacanian (Fink, 2007). Whereas Lacanians once practiced mainly in Europe and Latin America, they are growing in number in Australia, the United States and Canada, as new translations and training programs emerge. English-speaking clinicians tend to prefer Winnicott's relatively straightforward prose to the non-linear, allusive style of Lacan, whose texts yield but grudgingly to the reader. One cannot master them or quickly get their gist, as students raised on textbooks – as opposed to primary sources – expect to do. Lacan noted that Freud's writings – which tend to be clear and straightforward – were easily bowdlerized. Anglophone analysts, for example, felt that they knew just what Freud was saying, though many of his central concepts were distorted in translation. They felt confident enough of his "message" that they could popularize it, and purge it of unpalatable items such as the death drive. Lacan let the energy of the unconscious run through his *Écrits* (Lacan, 1966). It is much more difficult to sanitize his ideas, since they were written to resist the person in a hurry. He criticized American ego psychologists for turning Freud's radical project into a conformist psychology bent on helping patients adapt to bourgeois social and sexual codes rather than allowing the unconscious to speak. A danger all clinicians face is distorting the patient's history by making too much sense of it; Lacan was always underscoring that danger.

Before describing the ways that I endeavor to think with both Lacan and Winnicott, I will provide an introduction to some basic concepts. Note that it is customary to speak of Lacan's work in several phases. The concepts I discuss come from the early and middle phases, when his ideas formed the sharpest contrast with those of Winnicott. This is a purely personal preference; others working with Lacan and Winnicott highlight different constructs (Vanier & Vanier, 2010; Kirshner, 2011) and have different goals from mine. It should also be noted that, while some believe that an author's later works represent the fruition of his or her ideas, supplanting the early work, I do not subscribe to that kind of developmental reading. Some of Freud's earlier writings, such as *The Three Essays on the Theory of Sexuality* (Freud, 1905), are more mature (in the sense of complex), as well as more radical, than his later essays on femininity.

Selected concepts from the work of Winnicott and Lacan

Winnicott

Toward the end of his life Freud glimpsed the importance of the mother and the pre-Oedipal period for children's development and hoped that analysts of the future would build on his foundation. Both Melanie Klein and Anna Freud answered the call, with Klein focused on infants' *phantasies* and Anna Freud on the actual role of the mother in the child's developing ego. The rivalry between the two women over what was more important – phantasy or reality – festered and threatened to derail the British Psychoanalytic Society. The person whom both women trusted was Donald Winnicott, who saw that each had much to offer. He didn't set out to form a third, non-aligned group, but that is essentially what happened. He is associated with what is still called the *British Middle Group* or the *Independent tradition*.

Not only did Winnicott write about the importance of mothers, he spoke *to* mothers about child development. His postwar BBC broadcasts aimed first and foremost to give credit to what he called "the ordinary devoted mother." He felt that, if fathers could support mothers, and experts could stay out of the way, mothers would follow their natural tendencies and all would be well. His contrasting the concept of the *true self* with the *false* or *compliant self* represented his respect for nonconformity and the self-as-creative (Winnicott, 1971). He did not reject the drives – oral, anal and genital – but he felt they were more or less secondary in importance to the drive to *relate.* His patient, the analyst Harry Guntrip, recalls Winnicott saying: "We differ from Freud. He was for curing symptoms. We are concerned with living persons, whole living and loving" (Guntrip, 1975, p. 462). Winnicott's oeuvre is appreciated by many as a counter-force against an increasingly dehumanized world.

Lacan

The work of Jacques Lacan can be understood, in no small measure, as a life-long challenge to the psychoanalytic establishment, which he saw as destroying Freud's radical project. Following are three examples of what Freud himself called "an attempt at [the] repression" of psychoanalysis by American analysts and others (Freud, 1927, p. 258).

(1) Whereas Freud had said that the worst possible training for an analyst would be medical school (Freud, 1927), the Americans decided that *only* physicians could train as analysts. This egregious reversal of his teaching was mitigated by the training of lay analysts after 1948 through the NPAP (National Psychological Association for Psychoanalysis). A fuller correction came only in 1986, when psychologists – and, later, social workers – were accepted to the medicalized institutes (Welch *v* American Psychoanalytic Association, 1986). There was a split on this issue in France, and Lacan – firmly opposed to a "physicians only" stance – ended up resigning from the Société Psychanalytique de Paris (Roudinesco, 1986). The United Kingdom, to its credit, never gave up on lay analysts.

(2) Whereas Freud had worked hard to depathologize the non-normative, homosexuality was repathologized in the United States. It was ultimately taken out of the *DSM* in 1971, but not before many gay and lesbian analysands had been made to feel damaged or perverse (Glassgold & Iasenza, 1995). Lacan's "return to Freud" reminds us that Freudian theory insists on the bisexuality of every individual – and

126 Deborah Luepnitz

of every object of the drive as well. The attempt to use psychoanalysis to make individuals conform to bourgeois norms was anathema to Lacan.

(3) Lacan opposed what he saw as an obsession with the mother, the pre-Oedipal and affect in the British school. He mocked those "nurse analysts" who had lost sight of the importance of language, signification and dream interpretation. When Lacan said famously that "the unconscious has the radical structure of language" (Lacan, 1966, p. 496) he was urging us to remember what Freud had taught about the importance of words and letters. How could one interpret a dream without grasping the unstoppable wordplay of the unconscious, using tropes such as metaphor and metonymy? For Lacan, the analyst occupies not the position of the mother but the *Other* – a place of radical alterity some associate with death, or the unconscious itself.

While both Winnicott and Lacan were great originals who made daring advances in the field that earned them both enemies and friends, they had different political sympathies. Winnicott was conservative, a defender of the British monarchy. While Lacan was not a leftist, he took seriously the radical students of 1968, and reportedly even helped one of their leaders, "Danny the Red," escape to Switzerland. In a letter to Winnicott (Lacan, 1960) he wrote of the deep worry and profound pride he and his wife took over the political resistance and the arrest of their daughter (as well as a nephew), sentenced to prison for protesting the French–Algerian war. Lacan is not associated with the work of the free psychoanalytic clinics (Danto, 2005) but he was an outspoken critic of capitalism (Lacan, 1974).

Both Winnicott and Lacan developed a feminist following. Anglophone analysts such as Nancy Chodorow (1978) and Jessica Benjamin (1988) found Winnicott's work valuable, in part because, unlike Freud or Klein, he understood the profound importance of the actual mother's role. Moreover, by framing the analyst's position as "good enough mother," he was affirming the very qualities – relational attunement, intuition, playfulness – that had been socially devalued within patriarchy over centuries. Luise Eichenbaum and Susie Orbach (1983) agreed, but pointed out that what was still not elaborated in Winnicott's work was a notion of the mother's *subjectivity*. I would add that it is ironic and unfortunate that, although Winnicott expressed gratitude for the "multiple mothers" he himself had in childhood (Kahr, 1996, p. 5), he went on to write about "*the* mother" as though a single female caretaker were optimal. This has opened the door for blaming "*the* mother" for every problem of childhood and adulthood (Luepnitz, 1992).

What some feminists have appreciated about Lacan is the fact that he does not over-implicate mothers as the cause of psychopathology (Luepnitz, 2003). Others, however (e.g., Flax, 1990), argue that the central place Lacan gives to the phallus and castration – even defining clinical structures in terms of how the subject approaches castration – marks him as misogynist. Juliet Mitchell (1974), in her classic *Psychoanalysis and Feminism*, concludes that, of all the great analytic thinkers to date, the one whose work is most compatible with feminism is Jacques Lacan, in part because he redefined the phallus as a function, not an organ like the penis. Lacan's Seminar XX, of 1975, is understood as a response to feminist criticism – a sign of taking the women's movement seriously (Mitchell & Rose, 1982). Many felt Lacan's tone there was one of condescension, but he never wrote anything as explicitly anti-feminist as Winnicott did in a 1964 essay titled "This feminism" (Winnicott, 1964).

The mirror stage in Winnicott and Lacan

In the *Project for a Scientific Psychology*, Freud (1895) made reference to the help-lessness of the human infant, in contrast to newborns of other species. Whereas most animals are, within hours or days of birth, able to run from predators and for-age for food, the human infant, without a caretaker, will simply perish. Moreover, whereas the newborn dog or raccoon can cling to its mother's fur or tough skin, the human baby's ability to hold on is more tenuous. Human babies are thus des-tined to experience more anxiety than other babies. Most animals seem to know *fear* of something, but humans are also prone to free-floating *anxiety*, rooted in the fear of abandonment. Lacan refers to this as the "specific prematurity of birth" in our species (Lacan, 1966, p. 78), and its importance may be one thing on which all psychoanalysts actually agree. The infant body flails about and, even as it gains strength, experiences things (e.g., urine and feces) as falling away or out of the body. In *Les Complexes Familiaux*, Lacan (1938) hypothesized that, even before the infant can experience loss of the breast in weaning, it has already been separated from its first "other," the placenta.

Some relief comes in what he called the *stade du miroir* – usually translated as the "mirror stage." In a paper originally delivered in 1936, Lacan (1966) described a developmental moment between six and eighteen months of age, when the baby comes to recognize its image in the mirror. Given its lack of coordination and mus-cle control, how would the infant – until that moment – even know its body was a single thing, easily locatable in space? Lacan described the instant when the baby makes the connection as the mother or caretaker typically says something such as: "Look – that's you!" Lacan observed the infant showing a jubilant expression at this recognition. He hypothesized that there is a kind of relief that must come as the little one is able to see itself as coherent, intact, in the mirror. While this is a neces-sary developmental stage, without which there would be no ego formation, it also portends something unfortunate. From the mirror stage on, we are captivated by images, and look outside rather than inward to pose questions about who we are and how we are. We look at actual mirrors on the wall and at reflections in the eyes of others to decide if we are attractive, intelligent, successful enough. The mirror stage thus sets up a condition of alienation. The patient will come to analysis hop-ing to find the perfect mirror in the analyst, and must ultimately learn that there is nonesuch.

Winnicott also wrote a paper on the mirror stage, some 30 years later. He made reference to Lacan's article, and said in fact that it "has certainly influenced me" (1971, p. 111). He said no more about that influence and took the developmen-tal scheme in a wholly different direction. The important mirror for the infant,

128   Deborah Luepnitz

according to Winnicott, is the maternal gaze. "In other words, the mother is look-ing at the baby and *what she looks like is related to what she sees there*" (1971, p. 112, emphasis in original). If the mother is good enough, she will reflect a recognition that her infant is both separate from and connected to her. When the infant cries, she will say with a look, "I know something's not going right; let's figure it out." If all goes well, the infant will learn that it is safe to look, to see and be seen, and thus come to feel that it exists. From this beginning, the true self can emerge and grow. But if the mother is depressed or psychotic, the infant's gaze will not be recipro-cated. In that case, the baby comes to study the mother's face as we do the weather, said Winnicott. Is it safe to go out and take a look? The true self of such infants may never develop, or – he also suggested – may go into hiding. In its place comes the false self, also called a *caretaker self*. In essence, the baby or child becomes the mother's mother. The ability to express a need, to make a spontaneous gesture, to feel real: these are jeopardized. Clinically, this state can be seen as the precursor to personality disorders and addictions. Someone with an eating disorder, for example, typically ignores physical cues of hunger, and eats instead according to social pres-sures or superego demands.

The three registers

One of Lacan's signature constructs is the three registers: Imaginary, Symbolic and Real – often depicted as three interlocking circles. The *Imaginary* is the register of emotions, perceptions, feelings, affects. The *Symbolic* is the register of language, cul-ture, signification. The *Real* is the most difficult to grasp, because it is often confused with the English word "reality." The Real, for Lacan, is what can neither be emo-tionally experienced nor represented in words. *The three registers are of equal impor-tance.* Unfortunately, beginners assume that Lacan privileged the Symbolic, perhaps because he saw his fellow analysts eliding it – becoming lost in the Imaginary. The latter Lacan called attention to the Real, as he took up the work of James Joyce and *le sinthome*.

In teaching, I ask students to which register *the body* belongs. Some will answer that the body belongs to the Symbolic, because we weigh and measure it and give it a host of cultural values. Others will place the body in the Imaginary, citing the example of the anorectic, who views an emaciated body as "fat." Still others will maintain that the body exists in the Real, because, regardless of how we measure it or feel about it, it ages and dies. All three answers are correct. Indeed, *everything* exists in all three registers.

Another way to approach this construct is to begin with the memory of a shared event. It's probably true that anyone reading this book remembers September 11, 2001. Some of us heard a news report or read something online; others looked up at the sky and saw a plane explode into the World Trade Center. In the moments that followed, we began to operate in the Symbolic register. That is, we used language to ask questions: "What just happened?" Could it be an accident?" Of course, before mobilizing words, we couldn't help but feel things: panic, dread, curiosity, disgust.

Lacan would say that, anterior even to having feelings, there was an *encounter*: the image of a plane, or words in a news report, hit retinas and ear drums. That is, the event occurred in the Real prior to its being felt in the Imaginary or verbalized in the Symbolic. Many years have passed since that day, and we have had time to talk, read and write about it. We have also had time to feel rather than deny our emotions. For most of us, much of the impact of what happened in the Real that day has been parsed into the Symbolic and Imaginary. According to Lacan, however, that parsing can never be complete; there is always a remainder. Survivors of the attack and families of the victims, in particular, may find it impossible – even after decades – to feel all their feelings or put the experience into language. The word we use for this – when an event remains lodged to a great degree in the Real without giving way to Symbolic expression or the felt Imaginary – is *trauma*. This is why Lacanians conceive of analysis as a cure of the Real by the Symbolic. It is, after all, a "talking cure." (The Winnicottian in me wants to say that it's a cure of the Real by both the Symbolic *and* the Imaginary.)

Although it takes some time to become accustomed to these categories, their value in working with patients is great. I find the three registers extremely useful in thinking about cases of sexual abuse, for example. Research tells us that rates of sexual molestation in the United States are extremely high, and that victims are often not believed (Herman, 1992). Knowing the statistics does not solve the problem of working with the countless patients who wrestle with the question "Was I, as a young child, forced to have sex, or have I imagined it?" Every experienced analyst has witnessed the torment of analysands who say: "My memory of this thing is so vague. Sometimes I'm sure it happened and sometimes I think I've made it up. Which is it: real or imagined?"

Example

Margaret was a patient who suffered from a number of disabling gynecological symptoms that had no medical explanation, despite years of work-ups. She enjoyed pursuing men, and was very frustrated by the impediment caused by her dysfunctional bleeding and discharges. Clearly, the body was talking – but about what? A previous therapist asked if she had ever been sexually abused. She recalled an inappropriate conversation with her uncle in adolescence, and pictured him initiating sexual behavior. Had it occurred once, more often or not at all? There were no witnesses or hospital records, and the suspected perpetrator was deceased. She entered treatment with me, tormented by the question "Was it real or imagined?" In an early session, she said: "It's easy for someone else to say: 'You must simply accept never knowing.' Who in this world could be so indifferent?" At one point during our work, the patient's mother confided to her that she herself had been sexually victimized as an adolescent. The realization that there had indeed been a violation of female flesh, though not necessarily her *own*, broke through the obsessional, either/or thinking. It was a way of understanding how the abuse could seem both very real and very imagined. Parents who have been subjected to sexual assault cannot *not* pass this trauma on to their children, even if – or especially if – the younger generation is never told about it. In this case, a representation of the female body as vulnerable, easy prey for male sadism was communicated through the Symbolic mechanisms of the unconscious. Of course, no person can prove that they were not sexually abused, and it is still possible that Margaret was molested by her uncle – and/or by another person or persons. This shift in thinking enabled her to stop her all-day ruminations, however, and it revived her relationship with her mother. Only at this point did the patient reflect on the fact that she had been named for a maiden aunt – someone who had kept herself cut off from male sexuality. There is no call in this theory to blame victimized parents; it is simply a matter of acknowledging the work of the unconscious. And, in fact, every instance of molestation must be understood in all three registers, since the same act will be felt and represented differently depending on the individual.

The family atè

In his work on Antigone, Lacan (1986) used the Greek word *atè*, which he rendered, slightly idiosyncratically, as the family's *madness* or *curse*. Antigone, in the Theban plays of Sophocles, is the daughter of Oedipus and Jocasta. When Oedipus discovers that he has indeed fulfilled the oracle that predicted he would kill his father and marry his mother, he blinds himself and goes into self-exile with his daughters. His sons take up arms against each other in battle, and, when Antigone discovers that her brother's body has been left unburied by order of King Creon, who considers him a traitor, she defies the law and buries him. Sophocles makes it clear that, while she almost certainly could have gotten away with this transgression, she acts in a way that ensures she will be caught. Why? For centuries scholars have commented on her deed, typically seeing her as a pure and noble figure who wants to demonstrate that divine law supersedes that of mortal rulers. Lacan found those readings sentimental and argued that Antigone's desire was simply to die. When we consider the horrors of her life – incest and patricide uncovered, a mother who then hangs herself with her bridal dress, and a father/brother who gouges out his eyes – we can take Antigone at her word: that her desire is simply to die. Via suicide, Antigone repeats the behavior of her *mother*, hanging herself with her own dress. Lacan did not make that repetition explicit; perhaps it is too obvious. What he did assert, however, is that everyone has a family saga that includes its share of pain and madness. Furthermore, in his discussion of three generations of a family portrayed by the playwright Paul Claudel, Lacan showed that we cannot make sense of the present without knowing the family *atè* – meaning what has occurred not just in the previous generation but in those that preceded it (Lacan, 1991). It is possible that no individual – indeed, no symptom – can be understood without recourse to at least three generations, not just two.

Of course, all Lacanians don't work exactly the same way, and some place more emphasis than others on three generations, depending on the patient. In general, however, this material can be elicited in the preliminary sessions, which are conducted face to face. The family *atè* provides a context for all that the analysand will express in following the fundamental rule: "Say everything that comes to mind..."

I find the *atè* extremely useful in analysis, which otherwise can degenerate into a "blame your parents" sport. This is not to say that parents are never to blame, or that it isn't cathartic to describe our brokenness in terms of their toxicity or empathic failures. Nevertheless, people who have spent years filled with shame – blaming *themselves* for their own suffering – and then switch to blaming bad parents eventually feel just as ashamed to have had bad parents. When the focus moves to the family *atè* – i.e., to generations of deprivation, neglect, geographical displacement, poverty, madness, genocide or slavery – what follows is a different understanding of desire. Ultimately, we must come to grips not only with the harm done to us and the losses we invariably face but also with what Lacan calls our "castration": the fact that none of us is whole (Lacan 1975). As neurotics, we defend against this fundamental lack through various postures of having or being the phallus, but lack cannot be avoided, except in psychosis.

The term "intergenerational transmission" is something that has appeared in some therapeutic/analytic circles for several decades. I emphasize it here to make the historical point that Lacan was already describing it in 1953 (Lacan, 1953), and later in his seminars on the transference and on the ethics of psychoanalysis (Seminars VII and VIII; Lacan, 1986, 1991, respectively). It is not clear whence Lacan drew this multi-generational insight, though it is certainly implicit in Freud. It was Freud who chose the Sophoclean plays to formulate the cornerstone of his theory, and Freud, of course, would have assumed that his readers knew the myth in full. (Laius, the father of Oedipus, and son of Labdacus, abducted and molested a young boy.) Moreover, in the case of the Rat Man, Freud (1909) showed that the patient's troubles had begun in the generations preceding him. Some, though not all, American family therapists have used the technique of drawing a "genogram" in sessions to give a context for the family's presenting problem. Without a commitment to the unconscious, however, there is the danger of simply mapping a family tree that cannot easily explain the apples that fall far away – and at bizarre and obtuse angles.

These insights connect with Lacan's teaching about the *goals* of treatment. Simply put, the goal is for the patient to discover the truth of his or her desire. This is extremely difficult, given that desire is defined by Lacan as always "the desire of the Other" (Lacan, 1975, p. 222). This means that what we want is always mediated by culture, language, family and/or our understanding of God or fate. Some people from a young age believe they were put on this earth to suffer, to avenge a death or to replace a dead sibling. Where do those beliefs come from, and how can they be claimed, satisfied, shaped or refused? It is certainly true that, before we speak, we have been spoken about. Some individuals know much more than others of their history, however. One place to begin is with the patient's names.

There are many ways that names subtly shape subjectivity – as well as social opportunities. Some research suggests that, when the same résumé is sent out to

132 Deborah Luepnitz

employers with an African-American-sounding name, such as "Tyree" or "Jamal," fewer calls for interviews result than when it is sent by a "Greg" or a "Miles" (Levitt & Dubner, 2005). A study using thousands of death certificates (Christenfeld, Phillips & Glynn, 1999) showed that people with "good" initials such as "J.O.Y" or "A.C.E." actually lived several years longer than those with "bad" initials such as "R.A.T" or "D.U.D." Those with "neutral" initials such as "T.R.H." had lifespans that fell in between the two. Lacan was no empiricist, and never would have bothered to conduct research such as this. It's not even clear if these results, though published, were ever reproduced. The authors' reasoning is evocative, however: "You get teased at school, wonder what your parents thought of you – maybe fate is out to get you – but at every stage, it's a little tiny depressant to be called PIG or a little tiny boost to be called ACE or WOW" (McConnaughey, 1998). A Taiwanese student, on reading this research, told me he had just spent several hundred dollars for the services of a professional "baby-namer" for his newborn daughter. What could be more important, he said, than giving one's child an auspicious name?

Winnicott

Psychoanalysis, according to Winnicott, is about two people playing together, and if the patient doesn't know how to play then the goal of the work is to foster that capacity. No one has written more brilliantly about the Imaginary, particularly with regard to young children. It was on the basis of his work with young children that he developed his notion of the transitional object. Others had noted that many toddlers come to carry around a piece of cloth or blanket that becomes hypercathected. That item was generally assumed to symbolize the mother, however. Winnicott pointed out that, if that special object (which he called the first "not-me possession") is left behind at the neighbor's house, the child might sob desperately even if mother were there, at hand. Thus, the blanket has to stand for something besides mother. The transitional object, he said, is neither something internal nor external, but exists in the space between. (For a comparison of the transitional object with Lacan's very important concept of the *objet a*, see Bernstein, 2007). He maintained that it is the prototype for other methods of self-soothing in life: art, music, literature, sports. Although some mothers appear embarrassed that their children have such objects, because of the addictive quality that characterizes the relationship (Applegate, 1989), Winnicott argued that this was a good thing, a creative act, to be encouraged. For example, the transitional object should never be washed or changed – except by the child. He had enormous faith in "ordinary devoted mothers" and their babies to trust their instincts. To pay this much attention to what actual mothers did and thought and worried over was something new. Moreover, Winnicott (1947) thought about the "good enough mother" in an exceptionally useful way: as one capable of having a straightforward love–hate relationship with an infant. He has been correctly criticized for ignoring the role of the father, but contemporary followers have found that his definition works as well for male parents. Many of us believe that it doesn't matter who changes diapers or helps with math homework. A good enough father is one capable of a straightforward love–hate relationship with a child (Samuels, 1993). This seems compatible with the term "the decent Daddy," as described by sociologist Elijah Anderson (1999) in his writing about contemporary African-American families.

Klein had discussed the hatred that the infant feels toward the mother or the bad breast. In "Hate in the countertransference," Winnicott (1947) listed 18 reasons the good enough mother has to hate the baby. The list is blunt, witty and anything but sentimental. The final reason is: "He excites her, but frustrates – she mustn't eat him or trade in sex with him" (1947, p. 201). By extension, the good enough analyst provides a holding environment through weathering the crashing surf of love, hate, appetite, confusion and boredom that arises in the consulting room. Freud (1915) had noted that "the unconscious of one human being can react upon that of another without passing through the conscious" (p. 194) but used the term "countertransference" to mean what I would call *countertransference that is out of control*. Winnicott used the term differently: to refer to an inevitable set of experiences and information source. It was apparently first used as such by his colleague, Paula Heimann (1950), but Winnicott elaborated the idea, and it is he who is credited with its important place in contemporary psychoanalysis. (With regard to the borrowing of ideas, Winnicott, to his credit, acknowledged taking the term "facilitating environment" from Phyllis Greenacre, and "the nursing couple" from Merell Middlemore, according to Thompson, 2015.) Often overlooked is the influence of Clare Winnicott on her husband's theories (see Kanter, 2004).

Just as parents or teachers who can recognize their own aggressive fantasies are less likely to act out than those who deny them, so too will analysts trained to observe their own subjective states during the hour be less likely to act out. There were times when Winnicott actually reported those feelings to the patient (Little, 1990). He was careful not to do so, however, when it might cause what he called an *impingement*. His approach should not be confused with Ferenczi's "mutual analysis," in which the analyst took his turn, inviting the patient to analyze *him*.

Another one of Winnicott's most valuable papers is titled "Fear of breakdown" (1963). Over the years he encountered many patients who lived in fear of being emotionally annihilated – falling apart permanently. The question for such individuals is not *if* but *when*. Winnicott noticed that, with many of these patients, the breakdown had already occurred in infancy or childhood but had not been experienced. How does one grieve something that has not yet happened? It is projected into the future, and defended against, not as a memory but as something lurking around the corner. There is much to be said for this notion that what we fear most has already happened. One can say that it leans on Freud's concept of *nachträglichkeit* (Laplanche & Pontalis, 1967), as it points to the absence of time in the unconscious. Hopefully, the "breakdown" will be recreated in the transference, where it can be experienced and worked through.

Example

A middle-aged patient insisted for years that, despite a stable marriage and professional success, her sanity was precarious, and that someday she would be found in her room, sobbing uncontrollably. Something I asked in response to a dream caused exactly this kind of emotional reaction, and she recalled a long hospital stay for a pulmonary infection at age five, when she felt abandoned by her parents. This was an era when parents were not permitted to visit hospitalized children. During the course of her psychotherapy she was able to make use of this Winnicottian idea about the most feared outcome being behind her, rather than ahead of her.

Thinking in the space between the French and British traditions

I first read Jacques Lacan and Donald Winnicott in a graduate class in Buffalo with Professor Murray Schwartz in the 1970s. This course was offered in the English department, not in psychology, where psychoanalysis was often reduced to illiterate quips about Freud. Professor Schwartz assigned the two mirror stage papers, and many of us found those obverse points of view equally compelling. In the 1980s Lacan developed a following among anglophone academics, and articles began to appear comparing the French and British traditions. Most authors who took up this task did so tendentiously. That is, some inveighed against the familiar humanism of Winnicott and the Middle Group, preferring the iconoclastic Frenchman, whom one author described as "[t]he most important thinker in France since René Descartes" (Ragland-Sullivan, 1986, p. ix; see also Finlay, 1989; Mitchell, 1974; Moi, 1985). Others campaigned for the delightfully imaginative, environment-sensitive Winnicott over Lacan, the "narcissist" who rejected the mothering role of the analyst and overvalued the phallic function, and whose writing style seemed designed to frustrate the reader (Flax, 1990; Rudnytsky, 1991; Rustin, 1991).

Perhaps the first major thinker whose work reflects a deep appreciation of both Winnicott and Lacan was André Green. Green was a colleague of Lacan early on, but broke ranks because he felt the latter was becoming intolerant of new ideas. He turned his attention to the British Middle Group and found a home there. In contrast to some francophone analysts, who dismissed Winnicott as intellectually soft – a kind of analytic teddy bear – Green wrote: "I consider *Playing and Reality* to be one of the fundamental works of contemporary psychoanalysis" (1986, p. 10). For Green, concepts such as the pre-Oedipal period, attention to countertransference and the borderline diagnosis – all anathema in Lacan's school – were integrated into clinical practice. He continued to distance himself from Lacan, and in later interviews (e.g., Benvenuto, 1995) condemned the latter's ethical violations. Nonetheless, Green felt the need to state: "I am not an unconditional Winnicottian... [A]n analyst who really wants to think about practice cannot dispense with a reflection on language, a reflection that is absent in Winnicott" (Green, 1986, p. 124). To me, Green exemplifies those analysts who eschew the thralldom of undivided loyalty to one man or one school of thought, taking inspiration from the Freudian/Lacanian reflection on language, while making full use of British Middle Group constructs.

Over the past several decades a striking number of writers – seemingly independent of each other – have found themselves thinking creatively with both Lacan and Winnicott in mind. The work of these writers fills two published volumes, one in French (Vanier & Vanier, 2010) and another in English (Kirshner, 2011). Some of them set out merely to compare and contrast the theories of Lacan and Winnicott; others see them as complementary and mutually limiting. For example, Jeanne Wolf Bernstein (1999), while appreciative of the Winnicottian use of countertransference, asks if American relational practitioners haven't taken it too far. She points to a paper given by a well-known analyst of which two-thirds were devoted to the analyst's feelings and only one-third to what was going on with the patient. She asks if we have made countertransference into our new "royal road to the unconscious." As someone well acquainted with Lacanian theory, Bernstein critiques this tendency as a matter of being trapped in the glass cabinets of the Imaginary – ignoring the Symbolic. Thus, she uses Lacan as a corrective to one aspect of Winnicott-inspired practice. Freud, of course, said the "royal road" to the unconscious was the interpretation of dreams, which requires facility with linguistic wordplay, cultural symbols and myth. Bernstein is right to point out that it's far easier to discuss a patient by saying "I felt annoyed with him, and realized he looks like my ex." I agree with her, although, in discussing cases with Lacanian colleagues, I have encountered the obverse problem. That is, a focus on the Symbolic can obscure attention to the Imaginary – including that of the *analyst*. True, the position of the Lacanian analyst is not mother, but *Other*. Perfect neutrality is not possible, however, and even experienced clinicians must contend with feelings and fantasies that arise during the hour. Some followers of Lacan argue that he addressed this with the concept of "the analyst's desire." As Bruce Fink (1997) points out, however, this is not to be confused with the concept of countertransference, grounded in projective identification. Nearly all Lacanians think of countertransference as something to *free oneself from*. It is not clear, however, how one frees oneself from something one is not monitoring. In my opinion, this is a consistent weakness in the French tradition, just as inattention to language is a weakness in British object relations and American relational practice. It does no good to point out that Winnicott himself said "A word like 'self' naturally knows more than we do: it uses us and can command us" (1960, p. 158). It's true, and he may have believed it, but there are few, if any, examples of him elaborating on an etymology, or reflecting on a patient's name or word choice. In 2016, I had the opportunity of interviewing the woman who was Winnicott's child patient, known as "the Piggle" (Winnicott, 1977). She became intrigued by our exploration of her names, as well as three generations of family history, neither of which had been touched on by Winnicott (Luepnitz, 2017).

Some analysts now borrow so creatively from both traditions that one can say they use them in supplementary, if not complementary, ways. The work of Mardy Ireland is a case in point. Depending on the needs of the patient, she assumes the position of good enough mother and, at other times, the Lacanian Other. She pays

136 Deborah Luepnitz

close attention to the patient's signifiers, as well as to her countertransference. She asks some patients to *draw* as a way of cutting into the Real (as Winnicott did with the famous Squiggle game). Ireland (2003) invokes the analogy of the wave/particle theory of light in contemporary physics. She argues that Winnicott's thinking

> ...can be depicted more by the metaphor of psyche... as... dispersed particles, and treatment as what enables their organization... The Lacanian field is better represented by the metaphor of the psyche as embedded within preexisting wave patterns (setting degrees of freedom concerning love, desire, thought, etc.) within which each individual must find/create a place. (p. 6).

Ireland describes her analytic project as "a Squiggle game" between the figures of Winnicott and Lacan. It is not surprising that Green enthusiastically endorsed her book, *The Art of the Subject: Between Necessary Illusion and Speakable Desire in the Analytic Encounter.*

Example

"William Carey" was a surgeon who suffered from chronic anxiety. Although not attracted to men, he ruminated about being gay, and reported dreams of being imprisoned for unknown crimes. In one of our first sessions he said, "I'm afraid that this strange feeling of doom is something I will carry all my life." In the early sessions I did something Winnicott did not do; I took a history, going back several generations. I also asked about his names and learned that his parents, hoping for a daughter, had picked out only a girl's name. After our preliminary sessions, the patient decided to continue sitting up, stating that lying down on the couch was terrifying. He remembered times when his overwhelmed mother had threatened to run away from home, locking herself in the bathroom. The youngest of five boys, he felt utterly helpless, and remembered knocking with his fists, arms and head on the bathroom door, begging to see her. It was important to provide a holding environment for this patient that included his being able to see me, and at times involved scheduling an extra hour. During this time I was the good, slightly idealized mother in the transference. My countertransference included the occasional experience of being disproportionately "overwhelmed" by him, which I assume was an unconscious communication about his early environment.

Although Winnicott was essential to this treatment, Lacan's idea of the family *atè* was key. When Will's grandfather had become old and sick, decades earlier, none of the seven children had wanted to take him in, and he was sent to live with a brother he hated. The plane crashed and burned, leaving no survivors. Will's father entered an abyss of shame and guilt, and "walked around our house like a zombie." Only now did Will associate his own guilty sense of doom with the horrific death of his grandfather. He had never even connected his career as a surgeon specializing in *burn victims* to this event. It was transformative for him to realize how the family *atè* – the family curse – had not only influenced his life's work but was also written into his name. "This doom is something I will carry" equals "I, Will Carey." He had felt his anxiety to be a cruel punishment from a God he didn't believe in; it meant he could never fully enjoy even simple pleasures, such as a real vacation or sex with his wife. In the transference, I was sometimes the zombie father, answering his questions with silence. At one point the patient slipped and said, "Since my parents had only *daughters…*" instead of "sons." He imagined me then as the disappointed mother who wanted him to be a girl and couldn't see his masculine body. The insight that the guilt tormenting him was his father's guilt, and that he could free himself of that burden, reckoning with his own desire, was liberating. His dreams of being charged with a crime shifted to dreams of helping the police solve a crime. Yet, as Will began to glimpse the possibility of leaving his dread behind, he was frightened anew. Who would he be without it? Lacan's notion of the *jouissance* of the symptom is important. We loathe our symptoms, but are also attached to them, as Freud taught. The pain they cause us is a tie – sometimes the only tie – to our objects. (Samuel Beckett, an analysand of Bion, sounds Lacanian when he writes: "[H]ow lost I would be, bereft of my incapacitation" (Beckett, 1935, p. 250). This patient was eventually able to live with far less anxiety than before treatment, and without the need for medication. The fantasy that he could avoid human vulnerability by working non-stop, and become whole by being heroic, was traversed.

The risk of working with Lacan and Winnicott

Some have argued that Winnicott and Lacan are utterly incompatible – convergent in no significant way – and that interested clinicians must choose one or the other (Fink, 2007). It is precisely their incompatibility that draws some of us to this work, however. The risk of eclecticism is not trivial, but there are also serious risks that come from working only with Winnicott *or* Lacan, as I have suggested throughout.

I am not advocating for the formation of a new Middle Group so much as I mean to point out that such a thing *seems already in process* – as contemporary analysts consider forgoing the perks of being "true believers" in one school or another. Otto Kernberg (2001) has cautiously predicted a "convergence" not only within anglophone schools of psychoanalysis but also between the English and French traditions, as "previously hotly defended differences" continue to be modified (p. 543).

With regard to training, however, it should be emphasized that reading secondary sources such as the present volume, or integrative works of any kind, is no substitute for reading the works of great analysts, at least in translation, if not in their original language.

Furthermore, if secondary sources are consulted, one should be aware of very different possible readings of these two thinkers – particularly of Lacan. Bruce Fink, a Lacanian psychoanalyst trained in Paris and entrusted with the first and only translation into English of the complete *Écrits*, points out, for example, that there are over a dozen *Lacanian* schools in the world that may disagree with each other and, moreover, that "not even a small fraction of them would agree with" his own writing about Lacan! (Fink, 2007, p. xii).

In conclusion

It was Arthur Schopenhauer who observed that many new ideas go through three phases. First they are ridiculed, then they are violently opposed, then they are shrugged off as common sense. Perhaps it will be so for a new Middle Group.[1]

The most important thing to remember is something that great clinicians of many schools have pointed out – namely, that psychoanalysis must be reinvented for each patient.

Note

1 Following is a history of the term "new Middle Group." In the late 1980s I returned to an earlier interest in Winnicott and Lacan, and began speaking to colleagues about an analytic orientation that was "between" the two, just as the original Middle Group was formed to include the ideas of Klein and Anna Freud. When I first mentioned the phrase "new Middle Group" to Freud and Winnicott scholar Peter Rudnytsky, he suggested instead the "new Independents" (personal communication, 1991) because, while harking back to the Middle Group of the 1940s, it also suggests something more contemporary and inclusive. At the 2002 meeting of the Association for Psychoanalysis, Culture and Society, I suggested that many of us were moving toward a third way in psychoanalysis, a new independent tradition or even a new Middle Group. This raised no obvious objections. In 2005, at the APA Division 39 meeting, I again brought up the question of a new Middle Group, and this time two discussants questioned the term, saying the last thing needed was a new analytic faction. They felt it best to go on working with Winnicott and Lacan, without reifying it with a label that might only suggest a new orthodoxy. I found their argument persuasive, and, in a 2009 article in *The International Journal of Psychoanalysis* (Luepnitz, 2009), removed my intended subtitle: "Towards a new Middle Group." When that article, slightly revised, was reprinted in Kirshner's (2011) edited collection, I went so far as to say: "There is no reason to consider the contributors to this volume as anything but a group of analysts interested in Winnicott and Lacan" (Luepnitz, 2011, p. 4). Ironically, Paul Verhaege, a widely respected Lacanian analyst, endorsed Kirshner's book enthusiastically, writing: "A new middle group is in the making, and thanks to the efforts of Lewis Kirshner, we can participate in its first steps." The term is mentioned by Ireland (2011, p. 65) and later by Kirshner himself (2015, p. 93).

Acknowledgement

The author thanks Dr. Mardy Ireland for her encouragement and for reading an earlier draft of this chapter.

References

Anderson, E. (1999). *Code of the Street: Decency, Violence, and the Moral Life of the Inner City*. New York: W. W. Norton.

Applegate, J. S. (1989). The transitional object reconsidered: Some sociocultural variations. *Child and Adolescent Social Work*, 6(1): 38–51.

Toward a new Middle Group **139**

Beckett, S. (1935 [2009]). Letter to Thomas McGreevy, February 14, 1935. In M. D. Fehsenfeld & L. M. Overbeck (Eds.), *The Letters of Samuel Beckett*, Vol. I, *1929–1940*, p. 250. Cambridge: Cambridge University Press.

Benjamin, J. (1988). *The Bonds of Love: Psychoanalysis, Feminism and the Problem of Domination.* New York: Pantheon Books.

Benvenuto, S. (1995). Against Lacanism: A conversation of André Green with Sergio Benvenuto. *Journal of European Psychoanalysis*, 2(1): 1–17.

Bernstein, J. W. (1999). Countertransference: Our new royal road to the unconscious? *Psychoanalytic Dialogues*, 9(3): 275–299.

Bernstein, J. W. (2007). Love, desire, and jouissance: Two out of three ain't bad. *Psychoanalytic Dialogues*, 16(6): 711–724.

Chodorow, N. J. (1978). *The Reproduction of Mothering: Psychoanalysis and the Sociology of Gender.* Berkeley, CA: University of California Press.

Christenfeld, N., Phillips, D. P., & Glynn, L. M. (1999). What's in a name? Mortality and the power of symbols. *Journal of Psychosomatic Research*, 47(3): 241–254.

Danto, E. (2005). *Freud's Free Clinics: Psychoanalysis and Social Justice 1918–1938.* New York: Columbia University Press.

Eichenbaum, L., & Orbach, S. (1983). *What Do Women Want? Exploding the Myth of Dependency.* London: Michael Joseph.

Fink, B. (1997). *A Clinical Introduction to Lacanian Psychoanalysis: Theory and Technique.* Cambridge, MA: Harvard University Press.

Fink, B. (2007). *Fundamentals of Psychoanalytic Technique: A Lacanian Approach for Practitioners.* New York: W. W. Norton.

Finlay, M. (1989). Post-modernizing psychoanalysis/psychoanalyzing postmodernity. *Free Associations*, 16(1): 43–80.

Flax, J. (1990). *Thinking Fragments: Psychoanalysis, Feminism, and Postmodernism in the Contemporary West.* Berkeley, CA: University of California Press.

Freud, E. L. (Ed.) (1961). *Letters of Sigmund Freud 1873–1939* (T. Stern & J. Stern, Trans.). London: Hogarth Press.

Freud, S. (1895 [1966]). Project for a scientific psychology. In J. Strachey (Ed. & Trans.), *The Standard Edition of the Complete Psychological Works of Sigmund Freud*, Vol. I, pp. 295–387. London: Hogarth Press.

Freud, S. (1905 [1953]). Three essays on the theory of sexuality. In J. Strachey (Ed. & Trans.), *The Standard Edition of the Complete Psychological Works of Sigmund Freud*, Vol. VII, pp. 135–243. London: Hogarth Press.

Freud, S. (1909 [1955]). Notes upon a case of obsessional neurosis. In J. Strachey (Ed. & Trans.), *The Standard Edition of the Complete Psychological Works of Sigmund Freud*, Vol. X, pp. 155–250. London: Hogarth Press.

Freud, S. (1913 [1958]). On beginning the treatment. In J. Strachey (Ed. & Trans.), *The Standard Edition of the Complete Psychological Works of Sigmund Freud*, Vol. XII, pp. 121–144. London: Hogarth Press.

Freud, S. (1915 [1957]). The unconscious: Communication between the two systems. In J. Strachey (Ed. & Trans.), *The Standard Edition of the Complete Psychological Works of Sigmund Freud*, Vol. XIV, pp. 190–195. London: Hogarth Press.

Freud, S. (1916a [1963]). Introductory lectures on psycho-analysis (parts I and II). In J. Strachey (Ed. & Trans.), *The Standard Edition of the Complete Psychological Works of Sigmund Freud*, Vol. XV, pp. 15–242. London: Hogarth Press.

Freud, S. (1916b [1963]). Introductory lectures on psycho-analysis (part III). In J. Strachey (Ed. & Trans.), *The Standard Edition of the Complete Psychological Works of Sigmund Freud*, Vol. XVI, pp. 243–463. London: Hogarth Press.

Freud, S. (1918 [1955]). From the history of an infantile neurosis. In J. Strachey (Ed. & Trans.), *The Standard Edition of the Complete Psychological Works of Sigmund Freud*, Vol. XVII, pp. 7–122. London: Hogarth Press.

Freud, S. (1926 [1959]). The question of lay analysis. In J. Strachey (Ed. & Trans.), *The Standard Edition of the Complete Psychological Works of Sigmund Freud*, Vol. XX, pp. 183–250. London: Hogarth Press.

Freud, S. (1927 [1959]). Postscript to the question of lay analysis. In J. Strachey (Ed. & Trans.), *The Standard Edition of the Complete Psychological Works of Sigmund Freud*, Vol. XX, pp. 251–258. London: Hogarth Press.

Glassgold, J., & Iasenza, S. (1995). *Lesbians and Psychoanalysis: Revolutions in Theory and Practice*. New York: Free Press.

Godin, J. (1990). *Jacques Lacan, 5 rue de Lille*. Paris: Seuil.

Godley, W. (2001). My lost hours on the couch. *The Times*, February 23: 2–5.

Green, A. (1986). *On Private Madness*. Madison, CT: International Universities Press.

Guntrip, H. (1975). My experience of analysis with Fairbairn and Winnicott: How complete a result does psycho-analytic therapy achieve? *International Review of Psycho-Analysis*, 2: 145–156.

Haddad, G. (2002). *Le jour où Lacan m'a adopté: Mon analyse avec Lacan*. Paris: B. Grasset.

H.D. [Hilda Doolittle] (1956 [1974]). *Tribute to Freud*. New York: New Directions.

Heimann, P. (1950). On counter-transference. *International Journal of Psychoanalysis*, 31(6): 81–84.

Herman, J. (1992). *Trauma and Recovery: The Aftermath of Violence – from Domestic Abuse to Political Terror*. New York: Basic Books.

Hopkins, L. (2006). *False Self: The Life of Masud Khan*. New York: Other Press.

Ireland, M. (2003). *The Art of the Subject: Between Necessary Illusion and Speakable Desire in the Analytic Encounter*. New York: Other Press.

Ireland, M. (2011). Vicissitudes of the real: Working between Winnicott and Lacan. In L. A. Kirshner (Ed.), *Between Winnicott and Lacan: A Clinical Engagement*, pp. 65–80. New York: Routledge.

Kahr, B. (1996). *D. W. Winnicott: A Biographical Portrait*. London: Karnac Books.

Kanter, J. (2004). "Let's never ask him what to do": Clare Britton's transformative impact on Donald Winnicott. *American Imago*, 61(4): 457–481.

Kernberg, O. F. (2001). Recent developments in the technical approaches of English-language psychoanalytic schools. *Psychoanalytic Quarterly*, 70(3): 519–547.

Kirshner, L. A. (Ed.) (2011). *Between Winnicott and Lacan: A Clinical Engagement*. New York: Routledge.

Kirshner, L. A. (2015). Between Winnicott and Lacan. In M. B. Spelman & F. Thomson-Salo (Eds.), *The Winnicott Tradition: Lines of Development: Evolution of Theory and Practice over the Decades*, pp. 85–96. London: Karnac Books.

Lacan, J. (1938 [2001]). Les complexes familiaux dans la formation de l'individu: Essai d'analyse d'une fonction en psychologie. In *Autres écrits*, pp. 23–84. Paris: Seuil.

Lacan, J. (1953 [1979]). The neurotic's individual myth (M. Evans, Trans.). *Psychoanalytic Quarterly*, 48(3): 405–425.

Lacan, J. (1960 [1985]). Lettre à Winnicott. *Ornicar?*, 33: 7–10.

Lacan, J. (1966 [2006]). *Écrits: The First Complete Edition in English* (B. Fink, Trans.). New York: W. W. Norton.

Lacan, J. (1974 [1990]). *Television: A Challenge to the Psychoanalytic Establishment* (J. Mehlman, Trans.). New York: W. W. Norton.

Lacan, J. (1975 [1982]). Seminar of 21 January 1975. In J. Mitchell & J. Rose (Eds.), *Feminine Sexuality: Jacques Lacan and the* école freudienne (J. Rose, Trans.), pp. 162–171. New York: W. W. Norton.

Lacan, J. (1975 [1988]). *The Seminar of Jacques Lacan*, Book I, *Freud's Papers on Technique: 1953–1954* (J.-A. Miller, Ed.; J. Forrester, Trans.). New York: W. W. Norton.

Lacan, J. (1978 [1988]). *The Seminar of Jacques Lacan*, Book II, *The Ego in Freud's Theory and in the Technique of Psychoanalysis: 1954–1955* (J.-A. Miller, Ed.; S. Tomaselli, Trans.). New York: W. W. Norton.

Lacan, J. (1986 [1992]). *The Seminar of Jacques Lacan*, Book VII, *The Ethics of Psychoanalysis: 1959–1960* (J.-A. Miller, Ed.; D. Porter, Trans.). New York: W. W. Norton.

Lacan, J. (1991 [2015]). *The Seminar of Jacques Lacan*, Book VIII, *Transference: 1960–1961* (J.-A. Miller, Ed.; B. Fink, Trans.). Cambridge: Polity Press.

Levitt, S. D., & Dubner, S. J. (2005). *Freakonomics: A Rogue Economist Explores the Hidden Side of Everything*. New York: Morrow.

Little, M. (1990). *Psychotic Anxieties and Containment: A Personal Record of an Analysis with Winnicott*. Northvale, NJ: Jason Aronson.

Luepnitz, D. (1992). *The Family Interpreted: Psychoanalysis, Feminism, and Family Therapy*. New York: Basic Books.

Luepnitz, D. (2003). Beyond the phallus: Lacan and feminism. In J. M. Rabaté (Ed.), *The Cambridge Companion to Lacan*, pp. 221–237. Cambridge: Cambridge University Press.

Luepnitz, D. (2009). Thinking in the space between Winnicott and Lacan. *International Journal of Psychoanalysis*, 90(5): 957–981.

Luepnitz, D. (2011). Thinking in the space between Winnicott and Lacan. In L. A. Kirshner (Ed.), *Between Winnicott and Lacan: A Clinical Engagement*, pp. 1–28. New York: Routledge.

Luepnitz, D. (2017). The name of the Piggle: Reconsidering Winnicott's classic case in light of some conversations with the adult "Gabrielle." *International Journal of Psychoanalysis*, 98(2): 343–370.

McConnaughey, J. (1998). San Diego researchers make much of initial findings. *Los Angeles Times*, March 29: 3; http://articles.latimes.com/1998/mar/29/news/mn-33836.

Mitchell, J. (1974). *Psychoanalysis and Feminism: A Radical Reassessment of Freudian Psychoanalysis*. London: Allen Lane.

Mitchell, J., & Rose, J. (Eds.) (1982). *Feminine Sexuality: Jacques Lacan and the école freudienne* (J. Rose, Trans.). New York: W. W. Norton.

Mitchell, S. A. (1988). *Relational Concepts in Psychoanalysis: An Integration*. Cambridge, MA: Harvard University Press.

Moi, T. (1985). *Sexual/Textual Politics: Feminist Literary Theory*. New York: Methuen.

Ragland-Sullivan, E. (1986). *Jacques Lacan and the Philosophy of Psychoanalysis*. Champaign, IL: University of Illinois Press.

Rey, P. (1989). *Une saison chez Lacan*. Paris: R. Laffont.

Roudinesco, E. (1986 [1990]). *Jacques Lacan & Co.: A History of Psychoanalysis in France, 1925–1985* (J. Mehlman, Trans.). Chicago: University of Chicago Press.

Roustang, F. (1990). *The Lacanian Delusion* (G. Sims, Trans.). Paris: Odeon.

Rudnytsky, P. L. (1991). *The Psychoanalytic Vocation: Rank, Winnicott, and the Legacy of Freud*. New Haven, CT: Yale University Press.

Rustin, M. (1991). *The Good Society and the Inner World: Psychoanalysis, Politics, and Culture*. London: Verso.

Samuels, A. (1993). *The Political Psyche*. London: Routledge.

Schneiderman, S. (1983). *Jacques Lacan: The Death of an Intellectual Hero*. Cambridge, MA: Harvard University Press.

Schoonejans, S. (2008). *Le Geste de Lacan: Chronique des années 1970*. Brussels: Luc Pire.

Spelman, M. B., & Thomson-Salo, F. (Eds.) (2015). *The Winnicott Tradition: Lines of Development: Evolution of Theory and Practice over the Decades*. London: Karnac Books.

Thompson, N. (2015). A measure of agreement: An exploration of the relationship of Winnicott and Phyllis Greenacre. In M. B. Spelman & F. Thomson-Salo (Eds.), *The Winnicott Tradition: Lines of Development: Evolution of Theory and Practice over the Decades*, pp. 97–116. London: Karnac Books.

Vanier, A., & Vanier, C. (Eds.) (2010). *Winnicott avec Lacan*. Paris: Hermann.

Voruz, V., & Wolf, B. (Eds.) (2007). *The Later Lacan: An Introduction*. New York: SUNY Press.

Welch v American Psychoanalytic Association, no. 85, civ. 1651 (JFK), 1986 U.S. Dist. Lexis 27182 (S.D.N.Y., April 14, 1986).

Winnicott, D. W. (1947 [1958]). Hate in the countertransference. In *Through Paediatrics to Psychoanalysis: Collected Papers*, pp. 194–203. London: Tavistock Publications.

Winnicott, D. W. (1960 [1965]). Counter-transference. In *The Maturational Processes and the Facilitating Environment: Studies in the Theory of Emotional Development*, pp. 158–165. London: Hogarth Press.

Winnicott, D. W. (1963 [1989]). Fear of breakdown. In C. Winnicott, R. Shepherd & M. Davis (Eds.), *Psycho-Analytic Explorations*, pp. 87–95. Cambridge, MA: Harvard University Press.

Winnicott, D. W. (1964 [1986]). This feminism. In C. Winnicott, R. Shepherd & M. Davis (Eds.), *Home Is Where We Start From*, pp. 183–194. New York: W. W. Norton.

Winnicott, D. W. (1971). Mirror role of mother and family in child development. In *Playing and Reality*, pp. 111–118. London: Tavistock Publications.

Winnicott, D. W. (1977). *The Piggle: An Account of the Psychoanalytic Treatment of a Little Girl*. London: Penguin Books.

PART IV
Field theories

7

PSYCHOANALYTIC FIELD THEORY

Montana Katz

Introduction

Psychoanalytic field theory refers to a family of related bi-personal theories and clinical techniques. Field theory developed beginning in the 1960s in South America and North America and by the 1980s in Europe, primarily in Italy. In this chapter I will describe some of the context for the developments of the three principal forms of field theory and their distinct models and clinical techniques. I will also briefly explore some of the similarities and differences of the models.

It is difficult to recapture the full extent of the excitement and innovation involved in the initial development of field theories and bi-personal psychoanalysis in general. This is because most psychoanalytic perspectives have moved in this direction, including modern conflict theory. It is unthinkable today, for example, to not consider countertransference a useful clinical tool. In earlier periods the emergence of countertransference in sessions was thought to be something to be eliminated. The old intrapsychic models that include a version of the blank screen analyst no longer exist. Interestingly, the movement toward explicit bi-personal dimensions in psychoanalytic theory and technique took place across three continents roughly concurrently. This was part of a larger Western trend toward context-sensitive and holistic formulations across disciplines in the sciences, the humanities and the arts. It was an extended period of ferment, change and questioning of fundamental assumptions and beliefs.

In the period preceding the development of psychoanalytic field theory, in the first half of the twentieth century, research in the physical and social sciences afforded an emerging understanding of the effects of interaction and that no thing or person can be considered in isolation. The act of measurement, it was discovered, has an impact on what is measured; the act of observation has an impact on what is observed. The emerging discoveries can be described as recognizing the salience of context and the inevitability of interaction. Social psychologist Kurt Lewin's creation of the concept of the *psychological field*, in which an individual is understood as immersed in a constellation and in interaction with his or her environment, catalyzed changes in psychoanalytic formulations of theory and technique (Lewin, 1938, 1943).

These changes involved the questioning of intrapsychic models of the mind and of clinical technique. In this period Freud's structural model was increasingly straining under the weight not only of problems of substance; it was also beleaguered by problems arising from having been described in the outdated language of old scientific and philosophical paradigms. Radical departures from the idea of human motivation as drive-based began to locate motivation as emerging within environments. Interest in the changing context gave rise to an understanding of the individual and of human motivation as emerging within and integral to context and situations. This opened up new vistas for theories of mental functioning, of human nature and of technique.

In Argentina, for Madeleine and Willy Baranger (1961, 1961, 1964), the structural model was a point of departure upon which to build a psychoanalytic field theory. In a different manner and with different interests, the trends in North America also launched from – but then moved significantly away from – the version of the structural model that resulted in American ego psychology. The motivation in North America was to provide alternatives to drive theory and to the perceived "mechanical" clinical approach of the structural model. In Italy, Antonino Ferro, influenced by Baranger and Baranger, developed a field theory based on the work of Wilfred Bion. The resulting three field theory models will now be described in succession.

The psychoanalytic field theory of Baranger and Baranger

In South America, a psychoanalytic field theory was developed primarily by Madeleine and Willy Baranger. Their seminal paper, "The analytic situation as a dynamic field" (see Baranger & Baranger, 1961), was first published in 1961 in Spanish (Baranger & Baranger, 1961). This model was influenced by Gestalt psychology and the work of Lewin. Placing Lewin's field concept at the basis of their psychoanalytic theory, together with Melanie Klein's work on projective identification and Maurice Merleau-Ponty's philosophical reflections on psychological concepts, Baranger and Baranger offered what may be viewed as a bi-personal reformulation of the structural model. The concepts of projective identification and countertransference contributed to Baranger and Baranger's development of a field concept to describe what unfolds in an analytic process. They emphasized the interdependence of the co-participants in the process. The impetus for Baranger and Baranger's work can be understood as a fresh approach to thinking through psychoanalytic concepts and principles as bi-personal and their consequences for clinical work.

Psychoanalytic field theory **147**

They retained much of the structural model of psychoanalysis, including the objectives of analytic process, the concept of the frame, free association and interpretation. The objective of a therapeutic process that uses the analytic field theory of Baranger and Baranger is for the analysand to gain insight. They described the goals of psychoanalytic process in traditional terms as the resolution of the analysand's conflicts through the fundamental rule and accompanying interpretation. Striking new ground, Baranger and Baranger described the relationship of the analytic couple as bi-personal. They saw that developments in the analytic process cannot be exclusively ascribed to either one of the participants. Baranger and Baranger further understood unconscious processes and fantasies as bi-personal and as belonging to the field. They viewed the psychoanalyst as a full participant in the analytic process. The roles of the two participants are asymmetrical in this model, however, and the psychoanalyst's observing ego is considered always active.

For Baranger and Baranger, the factor of the bi-personality of the field is the foundation of the model. In keeping with the heuristics of this field model, movement and development in the analytic process are understood as belonging to the field. In the model of Baranger and Baranger, the principal object of interest and observation within a therapeutic process is the analytic field and not the analysand, as in older models. This shift in analytic attention away from the analysand as a discrete individual object of study goes to the heart of all bi-personal models. It constitutes a major departure for the psychoanalysis of the middle of the last century. Because the field is the object of study, while there are two individuals involved in an analytic process, each participant is understood as also constituted by the process within the field. Neither member of the analytic couple can be understood without the other. Both are immersed in and emerge from the process of the field.

In the model of Baranger and Baranger, the field itself has its own unconscious process. The unconscious process of the field is described as a unique creative product of the analytic process. It is the unconscious process of the field – not of the analysand – that is the focus of a therapeutic process in Baranger and Baranger's model. In their exploration of the bi-personal analytic field, Baranger and Baranger offered fresh insight into the details and consequences of psychoanalytic processes and concepts. They developed new terms with which to pursue what is involved in basic psychoanalytic ideas, such as analytic listening, the multi-valence of emotional communication and the creative emergence of something new in therapeutic processes. In elaborating their modifications to and divergences from the structural model, Baranger and Baranger devised new technical terms. Some of these new terms are *the psychoanalytic field*, *the point of urgency*, *essential ambiguity*, *bastion* and *second look*.

The psychoanalytic situation from which fields emerge in the Baranger and Baranger model has three principal components. The first is the *spatial component*, which consists of the configuration of the consulting room and its surround, including the relative placement of furniture. Baranger and Baranger noted that the experience of the room will be different depending upon such placement – for example, whether the couch is placed alongside a wall or in the center of the room.

By extension, the office entrance and the waiting area – how public they are, for example – and other considerations relating to physical space are also factors in the participants' experience of and in the sessions.

The second component of the Baranger and Baranger field is the *temporal structure*. This includes the duration of sessions, their frequency, and planned and unplanned breaks in sessions over time. Each of these elements also contributes to the participants' experience of and in the sessions.

The third component of the Baranger and Baranger field is the *functional configuration*. This includes the initial agreement about the relative roles of each of the participants. One participant, the analysand, agrees to pay an agreed-upon amount at an agreed-upon frequency, and agrees to cooperate in the process and to communicate and follow the fundamental rule. The other participant, the psychoanalyst, agrees to try to understand the analysand and to help her resolve conflicts through interpretation, promises confidentiality and agrees not to interfere with the analysand's life outside the sessions.

Time in this model is conceived of as a spiral process. The spiral nature of time indicates that, through the analytic process, emotional experiences are revisited and worked through, arriving at constructions rather than straightforward repetitions. This means that analytic work is focused on and grounded in the present, including present conceptions of the past and of the future. All thought is filtered through the present and affords constructions of the past. All three field theory models emphasize the interactions in the therapeutic process as grounded in the present.

Additionally significant in this model is the understanding of the three components of the analytic situation as infused with what Baranger and Baranger called the *essential ambiguity*. This concept is another point in which the Baranger and Baranger model can be seen to be exploring the implications of the core psychoanalytic principles in an innovative way. Without this essential ambiguity, there is no transference – and, furthermore, as Baranger and Baranger noted, there is no analysis. Baranger and Baranger uncovered the meaning and relevance of the concept of the essential ambiguity for this model, and this concept led them to understand the quality of sessions as dream material. The manner in which Baranger and Baranger pursued working with sessions as taking place within a dreamlike situation was at the same time novel and an elaboration of fundamental psychoanalytic principles of technique. The pervasive use made of this oneiric quality of sessions by Baranger and Baranger impacted future developments of field theory in significant ways.

Baranger and Baranger understood the essential ambiguity of the session as consisting in the altered temporality of the analytic process – a temporality similar to that of fairy tales or dreams. The time of and in the session spirals through past, present and future simultaneously. Ambiguity in the analytic situation for Baranger and Baranger takes on what they called a *mythopoeic* quality. This concept elaborates and articulates an aspect of unconscious processes and the multiple affective experiences involved in each moment. It is here that their emphasis on Freud's metaphor of psychoanalytic process as being like a chess game, rather than like an archeology expedition, takes on specific importance.

Psychoanalytic field theory **149**

A session thus has two participants who engage in a structured, creative process similar to a game of chess. The meanings of the moves in the session, the communications between the participants, are understood as mythopoeic, indicating the essential ambiguity feature. Within the analytic process communications reveal their poetic and mythic meaning. In so doing there is an oneiric quality to sessions. The quality of the experience of the sessions is that of a dream space, in which every element of the field is at the same time something else. The analyst listens to the communications of the analysand as if listening to a story. Baranger and Baranger called this the *mythopoetic circuit* of the analytic process. This form of analytic listening and bi-personal interaction attends to all communications as infused with metaphoric and fantasy elements. The Baranger and Baranger field is a dreamscape asymmetrically constructed by the participants. It is the job of the analyst to determine the salient unconscious fantasy, the nodal fantasy, of a session or sessions and to interpret. The fantasies that emerge in the field belong to the field and not to either participant separately.

A result of the emergence of fantasies of the field is the creation of the unconscious process belonging to the field. This is also different from the unconscious processes of the participants and is not a sum or any other kind of direct combination of their two unconscious processes. The unconscious of the field is a creative product of the psychoanalytic process. The fantasies and unconscious processes of the field are fundamentally different from those of either participant. The unconscious processes of the field could not have been predicted prior to their moment-by-moment unfolding in the analytic process. According to Baranger and Baranger, it is the unconscious process and fantasies of the field that are the specific objects of interest in a therapeutic process, rather than those of the analysand understood as a separate individual.

The pair of terms, *bastion* and *second look*, was introduced to describe blockages or impasses in therapeutic work and their dissolution. A *bastion* evolves in the field through the unconscious collusion of the participants. When the analyst recognizes this block to the analytic work, she must step back and try to evaluate the situation, taking what Baranger and Baranger called *a second look*. By means of interpretation, it is the job of the analyst to extricate both participants from pathological processes that emerge in the field.

The following is an example of clinical work with the concepts of the bastion and the second look:

> A seriously psychopathic patient. The analyst is terrified, fearing the analysand's physical, homicidal aggression without being able either to suspend the treatment or to carry it forward. The nodular fantasy of this bastion is the patient's as torturer in a concentration camp, and the analyst's as tortured, powerless victim. With the conscious formulation of this maneuver, the analyst's terror disappears. The two individual histories converge in the creation of this pathological field.
>
> *(Baranger & Baranger, 1964)*

150 Montana Katz

The work of Baranger and Baranger can be understood as raising the grain of what is at the essence of psychoanalysis. They provided a new depth of understanding to unconscious processes by describing them as fundamentally bi-personal and mythopoeic.

The psychoanalytic field theory based on psychoanalytic perspectives developed in North America

The field theories that evolved in North America take several different forms. All of them were distinct from the model developed in South America. Unlike the motivations for the development of the Baranger and Baranger model, the field theories that developed in North America were a reaction to perceived problems with American ego psychology. Instead of a focus on the psychoanalytic field, these models explore and emphasize the analytic relationship. This focus remains unique to North American psychoanalysis. It has yielded new thinking about psychoanalytic theory and technique.

Objections to drive theory and Freudian concepts of drive were a major force in the development of field theories in North America. Other related motivations derived from the rethinking of psychoanalytic concepts of neutrality, the interchangeability of the analyst, the role of the analyst and countertransference. The trend of questioning basic concepts of psychoanalysis led to several different ways of replacing the intrapsychic and genetic models. This resulted in new models that involve a psychoanalytic field that includes the analytic couple as a unit. Field theories in North America were also influenced by postmodernism and hermeneutics, in addition to Lewin's work. This meant that an emphasis on language, meaning and narrative infused the new North American models.

There are different strands of field theories in North America. These include a dominant strand from Harry Stack Sullivan through Edgar Levenson (1987, 2001, 2005; Levenson, Hirsch & Iannuzzi, 2005) and on to Irwin Hirsch (2015) and Donnel Stern (1997, 2015). Another runs from British object relations through Stephen Mitchell and from Heinz Kohut to George Atwood and Robert Stolorow (Atwood & Stolorow, 2014; Stolorow, 1995, 2013). Yet another makes use of systems theories, primarily in the work of Joseph Lichtenberg (1989, 2001, 2013) and Lichtenberg, Frank Lachmann and James Fosshage (2011; Fosshage, 1997, 2002). The result has been different forms of psychoanalytic field theories, called *interpersonal, intersubjective, relational psychoanalysis* and *motivational systems* theories. While distinct, these field theories have more in common than not. The common core includes emphases on human development and language, as well as the analytic goal of freeing the analysand from ossified experiential structures (Katz, 2013, 2017; Katz, Cassorla & Civitarese, 2016).

In the movement away from American ego psychology and drive-based intrapsychic models in general there was a relative de-emphasis on psychoanalytic theory and increased attention to therapeutic process. Increasing importance was given to the implications of the recognition that there are two persons involved

Psychoanalytic field theory **151**

in a therapeutic process. As a consequence, there are two unconscious processes involved. In what was a revolutionary position, countertransference came to be viewed as a necessary part of analytic process and a useful tool. It also was increasingly noted that, as a result of the two subjectivities involved in the therapeutic process, there are points of contact outside the awareness of each of the participants. Such nodal points could lead to the formation of emotionally laden interactions that held information about each of the participants' filtered ways of experiencing the other. This was recognized as holding for the analyst and not only for the analysand. In particular, such interactions, when understood and reflected on by the analytic couple, could afford understanding aspects of the analysand's difficulties.

A fresh understanding of the meaning of the exchange between two persons in an analytic process led to another trend of this period: an emphasis on language. The work of Harry Stack Sullivan, beginning in the early part of the last century, especially stands out in this regard (see Sullivan, 1953). Sullivan understood all relationships between two persons — and the therapeutic relationship in particular — as embedded in an interpersonal field. He described the therapist as a participant-observer in therapeutic processes, and he took a developmental approach to human experience.

For Sullivan, attending to communication was essential in a therapeutic process. The close study of patterns and problems in communication was his focus. He described therapeutic change as arising out of a kind of unconscious creation by the therapist and the patient together. These were considered *enactments* between therapist and patient, and they reflected the patient's patterns of living. Change emerged from the subsequent exploration of an enactment. From a psychoanalytic perspective, Edgar Levenson was influenced by and expanded the work of Sullivan. Levenson's elaboration of the interpersonal approach led to additional new ways of practicing psychoanalysis.

Levenson has emphasized attention to language, and he was the first psychoanalyst in the United States to demonstrate the importance of making use of postmodern concepts in psychoanalysis. In this regard, he stressed narrative description over objective truth. Levenson's work has deepened the understanding of the importance of a psychoanalytic emphasis on the present. The past is understood as reflected through an understanding of and in the present; indeed, the past is considered a construct in the present, without independent or objective existence in and of itself. The analytic process, then, centers on live interactions between the psychoanalyst and analysand in the present.

Patterns that emerge in the interpersonal analytic relationship emanate from the participation of both participants with a weighting that tends toward the analysand's experiential patterns. In Levenson's work, the concept of mind is articulated in a radical way as a field phenomenon. He writes, "Brain is individual but mind is a field phenomenon... À la Winnicott, there is no such thing as a mind" (Levenson, 2001, p. 250).

Levenson locates analytic cure as arising within and from the present situation in which the psychoanalyst and analysand find themselves together. Ultimately, they explore and come to understand their interactional patterns and situations. Embedded in the patterns that emerge in their dialogue will be some of what Levenson calls the *personal myths* of the analysand. According to Levenson, the interpersonal field contracts the analysand's "disease," which consists of lived, recursively generated patterns of experience. The psychoanalyst becomes involved in and a part of the problem to be understood. It is the job of the psychoanalyst to recognize the experiential configuration that the analytic couple has constructed.

The psychoanalyst's task is to first understand her own involvement. Following this, she may engage the analysand in coming to a joint understanding of a response to Levenson's clinical question "What is going on around here?" In this exploration, the objective is to extricate the analytic couple out of the diseased field. The goal of an analytic process is to progressively bring the elements of the analysand's personal myths to light in the interpersonal field. A way that this is approached is by means of what is called a *detailed inquiry* into the emerging personal myths of the analysand. The objective is to deconstruct these myths and resulting patterns to open up new possibilities for the analysand. From this deconstructive process the analysand may be afforded greater freedom from the constrictions of her personal myths. In this process, the psychoanalyst is immersed in the field and participates in it. It is the psychoanalyst's job to be an observer of her experience in the field in real time.

The following is an example of Levenson's way of working (Levenson, 2005, pp. 65ff.):

> A woman [patient]…is at a major crisis point in her life, concerning work and marital relationship. A crucial paradigmatic memory in therapy, an iconic memory (not arrived at in the therapy), is of a period in her childhood from age eleven to thirteen when, every Sunday, her mother would leave the house with her youngest sister and she would remain with her father. He was an opera buff and would insist that she lie down on the bed with him and listen to the radio opera. She would acquiesce; according to her reports, would lie rigidly next to him without any snuggling or holding until he would doze off, usually in an hour or so. At that point, she would slip away with a feeling of great relief. Neither he nor she would mention her having left. She apparently never told him in so many words that she hated to be there and that she felt constrained, tied down, which is her present representation of the event…
>
> Suppose…that when she tells the story one thinks, "So what? What does she want from me? Why am I interested in revising her perception of the story? I've moved from the historical inquiry to a transaction with her around the material, that transaction being a transformation of the material, because she wouldn't have told me, to begin with, except as a transaction; that is, she is saying, "I'm telling you this so you will react to it and participate with me around it." … She is talking to me (qua therapist) about something that happened to her. The question then becomes not what really happened to

Psychoanalytic field theory **153**

her or what her symbolic distortion of the real event is, but what is she doing with me now and how am I participating?

The obvious implication is that we shall recapitulate the relationship with her father. She will lie stiffly next to me, never indicate her resistance but never relent, and she will sneak away at the first opportunity. My experience is that I pursue this issue with great good will, patience and commitment. Why? Why, like the father, doesn't the therapist hear that she is in a rage, by her own description, and doesn't want to be here? The question then becomes to examine this bind we have in reality recapitulated.

Hans Loewald was also influential in North American developments in psychoanalysis. He took a somewhat different approach with different points of emphasis. Loewald understood the intrapsychic mind as developing from the beginning of life within an interpsychic field. An individual's instinctual drives and the resulting conflicts arise from the individual's experience from birth onwards, originally within the mother–child matrix. Loewald emphasized transference and countertransference within therapeutic processes. The analyst was characterized as a participant in the process and as embedded in the interpsychic field formed by the analyst and analysand throughout the process.

Another significant thread of the new psychoanalytic thought of this period was developed by Heinz Kohut, who pioneered the conceptual model and technique of self psychology. Development is viewed as a crucial factor in this model. Attending to individual developmental trajectories and the analysand's developmental arrests are crucial to the role of the psychoanalyst. In proceeding along these lines, the psychoanalyst engages the analysand in various forms of the therapeutic field called *self object matrices*. Kohut's model led to the development of the intersubjective approach and contributed to forms of psychoanalytic systems theories.

Intersubjective psychoanalysis was developed by Robert Stolorow and George Atwood. Intersubjectivity theory was influenced by structuralism, phenomenology, existentialism and hermeneutics, in addition to self psychology. In this model, developmental structures are emphasized. A focus of the therapeutic process is to discern the analysand's developmental patterns and structures as they emerge in the intersubjective interaction between psychoanalyst and analysand. The organizing principles and structures are understood as evolving out of early and ongoing intersubjective interactions with caregivers and others. Psychoanalytic process is described as proceeding in an intersubjective field.

Another psychoanalytic conceptualization, motivational systems theory, was developed by Joseph Lichtenberg and by Lichtenberg in collaboration with Frank Lachmann and James Fosshage. Motivational systems theory was informed principally by infant research. In this theory, human motivation arises from intersubjective experience. The motivational systems approach of Lichtenberg and of Lichtenberg, Lachmann and Fosshage is a developmental model emphasizing intrapsychic experience within an intersubjective context. Seven motivational systems are seen as operative in each person from the beginning of life. Each system consists of a need, evolves over the life of an individual and can be either more or less salient relative to the other six motivational systems at any given moment in the individual's experience. Motives are understood as the basic elements of human experience.

Each motivational system operates within the immediate context of all seven systems in the individual, who in turn operates within the larger context of interaction with the motivational systems of others. Together, the psychoanalyst and analysand form an interactive system. The empathic mode of the psychoanalyst is described as situating the psychoanalyst within the analysand's experience. In an analytic process, psychoanalyst and analysand construct and are immersed in model scenes that capture and organize the analysand's experience and developmental structures. In so doing, the analytic couple develop an understanding of the relative roles of the motivational systems in the model scenes and the embedded metaphors therein.

Another development of field theories in North America is the relational theory of Stephen Mitchell (1984, 1986, 1988a, 1988b, 1991a, 1991b, 2000). Relational psychoanalysis is a two-person developmental model. Relational psychoanalysis was influenced by object relations theory – especially Ronald Fairbairn's – and by the interpersonal model. According to relational theory, clinical work takes place in a relational field from which the understanding of the analysand is constructed as a result of the analytic process. The relational analytic process seeks to make use of history and genetics understood as idiosyncratic developmental structures that arose for the analysand relationally. This approach uses object relations to model early experience and development. The understanding of these elements is contextual. The relational field is called an *interactive matrix* and is considered unique to the analytic couple. It is here in the matrix that communication and embedded threads of experiential sequences in the analytic process assume meaning.

Meaning is constructed in the interactive field and is not something preexisting, to be discovered or uncovered. The field also has embedded historical relational content. The object of interest in a therapeutic process in relational psychoanalysis is the interactional relational field. The individual – and, in particular, the analysand – is described as arising out of the field. The concept of mind is described as consisting of the patterns and structures derived from the relational field. The goals of a relational therapeutic process are for the analysand's relational patterns and structures to emerge between the analytic couple, and to be explored and understood. As a result, the analysand becomes capable of building new relationships.

The following is an abbreviated example of the clinical use of relational theory (Mitchell, 1991b, pp. 165–168):

> Shortly after a young architectural student began treatment on a twice-a-week basis, he brought up the possibility of a third session, which seemed desirable to both of us, although he felt it was out of reach in terms of his finances. He asked about the possibility of my reducing the fee somewhat. We agreed that if he came three times a week, I would reduce the fee for all three sessions by $5...

Psychoanalytic field theory **155**

> In his associations to the dream he recalled several scenes from his child-
> hood involving "sweet" moments between himself and his father, the lat-
> ter's returning home from work with special presents for him, both of them
> overjoyed at seeing each other again. ... As the son grew to manhood, the
> father was constantly trying to give him money, both larger amounts and
> also subway tokens, which he would try to smuggle into his son's pockets
> when his son wasn't looking. The son sometimes refused his aid, sometimes
> accepted it. He sensed that to finally and definitively turn down his father's
> money would have been to somehow shatter their relationship; his saintly
> father would never be able to understand, and there would not be much else
> between them. ...
>
> The relevance of [a] dream to the underside of his relationship to his father
> was clear; although it would have been tempting to stay with the past, what
> seemed more important now was its relevance to his feelings about him and
> me. The lowered fee felt to him like his father's tokens, in some way mean-
> ingless, yet a powerful, two-sided symbolic statement both about my protec-
> tiveness toward him and my efforts to cripple him with my kindness. A major
> theme in the transference had been his tendency to split his experience of
> me; there had been a largely idealized, somewhat formal image of me as help-
> ful, successful, somewhat guru-like, as well as various circumscribed, split-off
> images of me as ruthless, sleazy, teetering on the edge of decompensation.
> He felt a powerful need to "keep things sweet here." It became clear that the
> reduced fee had been laden with meaning for him all along. It had made him
> feel special and cared for, yet also reduced and infantilized. ...
>
> My own experience during these sessions fluctuated back and forth
> between various countertransferential positions. I began to wonder why I
> had been so quick to tell him I wouldn't raise the fee. How invested was I in
> being his saintly protector? Was it at my own expense? Did I really not need
> the extra money? ... We seemed trapped in the closed world of these two
> relational configurations in which he was either cruelly deprived or lovingly
> crippled. This was, in my view, precisely the sort of trap in which we needed
> to be caught.

All approaches in the United States from this period reject the concept of
instinctual drives. In the place of drives, each perspective offers a concept of motivation. These new lines of thinking broke new ground in the idea that motivation
is idiosyncratic and not universal. Moreover, an individual's motivation is described
as evolving out of ongoing bi-personal experience. In the words of Donnel Stern
(1997, p. xii): "[T]he interpersonal field is the smallest meaningful unit of human
living."

Field theory models from this period also rely on and make significant use of
research in and the concepts of human development. All reject postulates involving
universal and fixed developmental stages and complexes. All agree that the individual's experience of the world is informed by idiosyncratic personal patterns and

structures that develop within unique bi-personal experience from the beginning of life onwards. Part of the objective of therapeutic processes in these models is for the psychoanalyst and analysand to discern and explore these structures as they emerge in the analytic engagement during sessions.

With regard to clinical technique, the North American theories agree that the analytic couple are working in and about the present moment of the session. Clinical work is experience-near and in the here and now. Understanding the analysand and the analysand's experience as shaped by developmentally evolving organizing structures is considered a central analytic task. A core common focus of the models is to discern patterns and structures in the analytic relationship that arise from the analysand's experience in the present and of the past, including fossilized narratives of the self. Once this is discerned, the possibility emerges to deconstruct the rigidified patterns and personal narratives of the analysand within the psychoanalytic relationship. This is understood in the models as opening the potential for the analysand to have new self-, other and relational experiences.

Levenson understood therapeutic work as consisting of deconstructing and modifying the metaphors of the analysand. Once these metaphors are discerned, the possibility emerges to deconstruct the analysand's rigidified patterns and personal narratives within the psychoanalytic relationship. As he noted, to change a person's metaphors is to change his or her self system. These concepts come together under the category of *unconscious metaphoric processes*. This model grounds unconscious mental processes with the concept of metaphoric processes.

The mind in this model includes and operates by means of its organizing principles, templates or interactive configurations. These organizing principles are formed in an individual from early on and evolve and are repeated in experiences with others. These experiences are internalized and form an idiosyncratic structure. In turn, the individual's experience is the result of what is shaped by the filters of the organizing principles operative in the mind. Mental processes, according to this field theory, consist of the activation, ongoing modification and development of the individual's organizing principles in interaction with others. Although each individual's organizing principles are unique, they hold the potential of sharing aspects of similar developmental patterns with others. Patterns of human development, rather than rigid developmental stages, are emphasized in this model of mental processes.

The bi-personal psychoanalytic field models of this period in North America rely on a core of commonly held themes. These common themes include the essential use of a bi-personal field in analytic process and in understanding human experience generally. They also include essential use of the research concerning human development and a focus on developmental structures and patterns, which are understood as having evolved within bi-personal experience. Another common theme is the replacement of Freudian drives with conceptions of motivation that are developmentally created. There is also an understanding in all these field theories that the goals of psychoanalytic therapeutic processes include the exploration of the analysand's structures and patterns as they emerge in the analytic exchange. Finally, there is also a core interest in the nature of the language and communication

Psychoanalytic field theory **157**

of psychoanalytic process. These common themes, taken together, form a model of a psychoanalytic field theory that is distinctly North American.

North American field theory has uniquely investigated the analytic relationship. It has also been the only form of field theory to emphasize the central and essential role of the analytic relationship to the therapeutic process and analytic change.

The psychoanalytic field theory of Ferro

Primarily in Italy, another field theory developed, under the influence of Baranger and Baranger but also strongly influenced by Bion. This model has been developed by Antonino Ferro (2002a, 2002b, 2006, 2007, 2009; Ferro & Basile, 2009), joined by Giuseppe Civitarese (2008, 2013, 2013; Civitarese & Ferro, 2013). This kind of field theory boldly pushes the limits of the consequences of the oneiric quality of sessions. In this model, techniques suggested by Bion are sharpened and strengthened. It is the field theory developed by Ferro that affords the greatest involvement of the analyst in the therapeutic process.

This form of field theory makes use of Bion's model of mental functioning. The model posits that the objective of psychoanalytic process is to mobilize and develop the alpha function of the field and, ultimately, that of the analysand. This is alternatively formulated as expanding the analysand's thinking, dreaming and feeling.

Bion's notion of *waking dream thought* is used in this model to expand upon the dream quality of sessions seen in Baranger and Baranger's model. Here the oneiric quality of sessions is made use of to analyze all communications between analysand and analyst as a dream in and about the field. This leads to differences not only in theory but centrally in technique. One difference is a greater emphasis on reverie.

Ferro's model adopts and accentuates the oneiric quality of the field seen in the model of Baranger and Baranger. The psychoanalytic fields of Ferro's model are dreamscapes in which the oneiric quality of the sessions is essential and omnipresent. Ferro describes the psychoanalyst as listening to all communications from the analysand as communications in and also about the dream of the field. This kind of analytic field has its own co-created and independent unconscious process. The field – its movements, stagnations and perturbations – is the object of interest in the analytic process.

Waking dream thought is emphasized in this field theory model as a way of describing ongoing aspects of mental processes. Bi-personal interaction in the analytic process is seen as including the evacuation and projection of the analysand's beta elements. Beta elements, the unmetabolized protosensory elements, are idiosyncratic. An individual's alpha function, which transforms the beta elements into pictograms, is also unique.

The beta elements of the analysand are processed by the alpha function of the psychoanalyst. The resulting alpha elements may then be projected back to the analysand for metabolization and use in waking dream thought. In accordance with Bion, Ferro's clinical objectives are for the psychoanalyst to remain open to the reception of the analysand's beta elements – those aspects of the analysand's experience that are not usable, yet create anxiety. Ferro places emphasis on the psychoanalytic field that emerges and is created in the sessions of an analytic process. An evacuated beta element of the analysand can be experienced as a vortex in the field.

The transformation into alpha elements affords waking dream thoughts and thinking. A principal aspect of the role of the psychoanalyst in this model is to lend his or her somewhat stronger alpha function to the field. The field then uses the psychoanalyst's alpha function to create the alpha function of the field. The alpha function of the field catalyzes the analysand's capacity for thinking. Progressively, the analysand's alpha function develops and grows stronger in this process. In this model, aspects of clinical process are thought of in terms of an ongoing interplay between projective identification and reverie. In this field theory model, a principal objective of psychoanalytic processes is to mobilize the alpha function of the field, and ultimately that of the analysand. In this way, the goals of an analytic process are to increase the capacity of the analysand to symbolize, to dream and to feel.

The medium of the field is a dreaming process in which both participants are immersed. The field itself is considered to be a living, breathing, dreaming organism. A task of the psychoanalyst is to remain sensitive to experiences in and of the field and to remain open to his or her own reverie as offering a direct way of thinking, dreaming and feeling the vortexes in the field. In this fashion, the psychoanalyst's alpha function is lent to and is also a part of the dreaming process in and of the field. The field develops an alpha function from the psychoanalyst's alpha function.

A beta element of the analysand may be made available to the field in processed and revised form. This then affords the possibility for the analysand's alpha function to make use of the processed version of the beta element. In this manner, progressively, it may be possible over time for the analysand to be able to think, feel and dream about approximations of the original beta element. More saliently, in the sequence from the analysand's beta element to the alpha function of the field, which she makes use of in thinking, dreaming and feeling, lies the analysand's progressive capacity to think, dream and feel in general. The alpha function of the analysand becomes more flexible than at the beginning of the analytic process and can make use of a greater range of the analysand's experience.

The goal of an analytic process in this field theory model is described as expanding the thinking, dreaming and feeling of the analysand. With this focus, contents and history are de-emphasized. Here the dream function of sessions is made use of to view all communications between analysand and analyst as about the field, about the dyad or about the analyst. This leads to differences from other field theory models not only in theory but also in technique.

This clinical orientation is illustrated by the following vignette (Civitarese and Ferro 2013, p. 203):

> I tell Lucio that I shall be away for a couple of weeks (for professional reasons). He begins the next session by saying that he has not had any dreams. He then tells me that he took the cat along to be neutered and that he feels

quite calm. He adds that he has met with one of the leaders of a pacifist association, who has been abandoned by his wife and weeps inconsolably. His wife cheated on him, taking up again with a female fellow student with whom she had already had a relationship.

I tell him that, if we were to look at these two communications as if they were two dreams (that is always one of my listening vertices when a patient speaks to me), we might think that he was worried that, if the cat had not been neutered, it might perhaps scratch me. What is more, who knows what might happen if the member of the pacifist organization who cried because of my cheating on him, even if the cheating was in a way "justified" (for a congress, as he tells me he has discovered on the internet), was actually the Mexican revolutionary Pancho Villa or simply the Italian national hero Garibaldi.

The influence of narratology on this field theory model shapes aspects of clinical technique. In the clinical setting, this is understood as attending to the characters introduced into the field through communications from the analysand in terms of the role they play in the story being told. A session is understood as a virtual reality, an expanding dreamscape.

Part of the role of the psychoanalyst in this model is to listen to the narrative elements of the bi-personal interactions in the field and think about them as functional holographic images. A point of emphasis is that the oneiric quality of sessions is understood as similar to that of a play – that is, the relative reality of sessions is compared with the relative reality of a play for the audience immersed in a performance. In the case of analytic sessions, the participants are at the same time both the authors of and actors in a play. The casting of characters, also a co-creation of both participants, populates the field and gives it shape.

In this model there is less of an interest in discerning the objects, structures or ongoing and historical patterns of the analysand. Emphasis is placed on opening up what is unknown in what emerges in the field. As a result, this model offers the psychoanalyst a broader range of clinical options. The analytic processes of this field theory emphasize the dream function and are less concerned with specific contents of communications or with the individual history of the analysand. In every communication from the analysand, whatever the content, it is always in the analyst's mind that the communication occurs within an analytic session and is directed toward the analyst. So, whether the analysand talks about stormy weather, or says that she has a pain in the leg after a clumsy fall, or observes how nice her friend is or relates what she ate for breakfast, all her communications are attended to as segments of the dreaming of the field. Each segment of the dreaming of the field may offer grounds for reflection about what has preceded it in the therapeutic process, either moments beforehand or in a previous session.

A salient dimension about which the field is always dreaming is the analysis, the participant's and the analyst's interventions. For example, if the analysand talks about the sound of hammering nails or hearing a screechy noise, this may be an indication to the analyst that her last interventions were too strong, and that the analysand could not tolerate them.

Transformations in dreaming constitute a therapeutic technique of this field theory that is of the essence of psychoanalysis. The technique serves to direct the analyst to what is unique about psychoanalytic listening: the listening to multiple levels at once and the emphasis on the fantasy infused in every communication, no matter how ordinary or mundane it may appear on the surface. Another technique relied upon in this model is the analyst's *reverie*. This is the analyst's waking dream activity in and out of a session. The analyst can make use of her reverie by reflecting on it – waking from it, so to speak – and formulating what elements in the field and in the analysand at that moment are reaching the analyst through the medium of reverie.

Another clinical technique used in this model is called *transformations in hallucinosis*. Transformations in hallucinosis constitute a more radical technique than transformations in dreaming. In transformations in dreaming the emphasis is on the dreams in the waking state in which the analyst may intentionally think about communications in a session as if they are dreams. The analyst uses transformations in dreaming to try to discern the unconscious communication in the field and the salient features of the field at that moment.

Transformations in hallucinosis are different from transformations in dreaming, as they are involuntary. Transformations in hallucinosis involve a momentary state of delusion. Transformations in hallucinosis provide a way of conceptualizing how the analyst's unconscious can enter into direct communion with aspects of the analysand's unconscious. In this process, the analyst becomes genuinely immersed temporarily in a delusion that resonates with something from the analysand's unconscious psychic reality. Common examples are when an analyst makes a "mistake." This may take the form, for example, of mishearing an analysand's communication, or misremembering some details about the analysand. The analyst in all such cases of transformations in hallucinosis momentarily believes the perception to be veridical. The analyst is shaken out of the hallucination by a clash with the intrusion of the introduction of a correction. The analyst can then apply the dream function to his or her momentary state of hallucinosis in order to make use of it in the session.

Ferro's model of field theory has offered an expanded set of clinical tools and techniques that go to the essence of psychoanalytic process. It has also provided a greater depth of understanding of the activity of the analyst.

Comparison of the three psychoanalytic field theory models

Each of the contemporary psychoanalytic field theory models has unique strengths and open questions. Each of the three models has introduced novel insights, concepts and technical tools to the range of psychoanalytic field theories and to psychoanalysis in general. Some of what has been offered by the work on psychoanalytic field theory has provided new ways of looking at some fundamental principles and techniques of psychoanalysis. This work has afforded a deeper understanding of the essentials of psychoanalytic thought and concepts.

In this brief comparison of the different field theories one particular contribution from each model will be noted. The field theory of Baranger and Baranger brought the psychoanalytic approach of understanding all aspects of the analytic encounter as infused with an *essential ambiguity* into fresh relief. The focus in the North American field theories on the emergence of the effects of unconscious metaphoric processes in the analytic dyad emphasizes the necessity of there being two persons who are both integrally involved in therapeutic processes. The *dream function of sessions* of Ferro's field theory highlights a fundamentally analytic way of attending to communications in therapeutic processes.

The three field theory models all offer bi-personal perspectives. And they are all three in agreement that, independent of whether mental processes are understood as dreaming, storytelling, fantasizing or metaphoric processes, mental processes are continuously ongoing, asleep and awake.

The three field theory models differ from each other in several respects. The field theory models of Baranger and Baranger and Ferro both place an emphasis on specifying which conception of the psychoanalytic field is being employed in the theoretical model and in clinical technique. Field theories in North America have not focused on an articulation of the field; rather, the emphasis in these models has been on clarification of the analytic relationship and the structures embedded there. In turn, this focus has not been emphasized in the other two models.

The fields of Ferro's model are different from those of the field theory of Baranger and Baranger. In Ferro's model, unlike in a game of chess, in which each participant makes discrete moves, the participant from whom something emerged is not always considered either ascertainable or relevant. This is also unlike the fields of the field theories in North America, in which a part of the therapeutic process is to articulate the experience of the dyad in the here and now.

Each model employs a distinct conception of mental processes. Differences in the specifications of mental processes within each model arise in three broad categories. The first of these categories is the conceptualization of unconscious processes. The field theory of Baranger and Baranger offers a modification of the conception of mind based on the structural model of Freud. While bi-personal, this model retains the tripartite structure of the mind and intrapsychic conflict. The North American field theory models offer a structural and developmental model of mental processes that integrally involves the concept of metaphoric processes. Ferro's field theory model follows Bion's model of mental functioning, which is based on the application of alpha function and the necessity of two minds for thinking.

Corollary implications to these depictions of mental processes are differing positions concerning the analyst's authority, the potential for the analyst's objectivity and the principal source of creativity in analytic processes. Each particular way of understanding the mind and mental processes also has implications for possible outcomes of therapeutic processes. The analyst's authority is approached differently in each model – from perhaps the greatest degree of authority invested in the alpha function of the analyst in Ferro's model, an intermediate position in the model of Baranger and Baranger and the least attribution of authority to the analyst in the

North American model, in which the emphasis is on the evolving relationship of the participants. All three models locate the source of creativity in the psychoanalytic field, but each understands its emergence differently.

Distinct sets of clinical objectives follow from each of the three perspectives on mental functioning. Therapeutic processes in the model of Baranger and Baranger seek to resolve the analysand's conflicts. The North American model describes therapeutic objectives as exploring, understanding, expanding and deconstructing relational patterns and structures as they emerge in the field. The therapeutic goals of Ferro's model are to expand the analysand's thinking, dreaming and feeling. Each model also holds a different view on the existence or relevance of individual and separate subjects within therapeutic processes. The model of Baranger and Baranger attends to what is created in the field with the participation of two subjectivities. The North American model explores and places significance on the contributions of separate subjectivities. Ferro's model emphasizes the concept of the *dreaming ensemble*, in which identifying the contributions of each individual is not the most salient or meaningful element.

Psychoanalytic field theory continues to evolve. The enhanced clarity of the underpinnings of each of the three principal models affords psychoanalysts from a wide range of perspectives the ability to explore what field concept is implicitly operative in their work. Psychoanalysis may be evolving into a discipline that consists of a family of interrelated psychoanalytic field theories.

References

Atwood, G. E., & Stolorow, R. D. (2014). *Structures of Subjectivity: Explorations in Psychoanalytic Phenomenonology and Contextualism*, 2nd Edn. Hove, UK: Routledge.

Baranger, M., & Baranger, W. (1961). La situación analítica como campo dinámico. *Revista Uruguaya de Psicoanálisis*, 4(1): 3–54.

Baranger, M., & Baranger, W. (1961 [2008]). The analytic situation as a dynamic field (S. Rogers & J. Churcher, Trans.). *International Journal of Psychoanalysis*, 89(4): 795–826.

Baranger, M., & Baranger, W. (1964 [2009]). *The Work of Confluence: Listening and Interpreting in the Psychoanalytic Field* (L. G. Fiorini, Ed.; H. Breyter & D. Alcorn, Trans.). London: Karnac Books.

Civitarese, G. (2008 [2010]). *The Intimate Room: Theory and Technique of the Analytic Field* (P. Slotkin, Trans.). Hove, UK: Routledge.

Civitarese, G. (2013). *The Violence of Emotions: Bion and Post-Bionian Psychoanalysis*. Hove, UK: Routledge.

Civitarese, G. (2013 [2014]). *The Necessary Dream: New Theories and Techniques of Interpretation in Psychoanalysis* (I. Harvey, Trans.). London: Karnac Books.

Civitarese, G., & Ferro, A. (2013). The meaning and use of metaphor in analytic field theory. *Psychoanalytic Inquiry*, 33(3): 190–209.

Ferro, A. (2002a). Narrative derivatives of alpha elements: Clinical implications. *International Forum of Psychoanalysis*, 11(3): 184–187.

Ferro, A. (2002b). Some implications of Bion's thought: The waking dream and narrative derivatives. *International Journal of Psychoanalysis*, 83(3): 597–607.

Ferro, A. (2006 [2009]). *Mind Works: Technique and Creativity in Psychoanalysis* (A. Ferro, Trans.). Hove, UK: Routledge.

Ferro, A. (2007 [2011]). *Avoiding Emotions, Living Emotions* (I. Harvey, Trans.). Hove, UK: Routledge.

Ferro, A. (2009). Transformations in dreaming and characters in the psychoanalytic field. *International Journal of Psychoanalysis*, 90(2): 209–230.

Ferro, A., & Basile, R. (Eds.) (2009). *The Analytic Field: A Clinical Concept*. London: Karnac Books.

Fosshage, J. L. (1997). Listening/experiencing perspectives and the quest for a facilitating responsiveness. *Progress in Self Psychology*, 13: 33–55.

Fosshage, J. L. (2002). A relational self psychological perspective. *Journal of Analytical Psychology*, 47(1): 67–82.

Hirsch, I. (2015). *The Interpersonal Tradition: The Origins of Psychoanalytic Subjectivity*. Hove, UK: Routledge.

Katz, S. M. (Ed.) (2013). *Metaphor and Fields: Common Ground, Common Language, and the Future of Psychoanalysis*. New York: Routledge.

Katz, S. M. (2017). *Contemporary Psychoanalytic Field Theory: Stories, Dreams, and Metaphor*. Abingdon, UK: Routledge.

Katz, S. M., Cassorla, R., & Civitarese, G. (Eds.) (2016). *Advances in Contemporary Psychoanalytic Field Theory: Concept and Future Development*. Abingdon, UK: Routledge.

Levenson, E. A. (1987). An interpersonal perspective. *Psychoanalytic Inquiry*, 7(2): 207–214.

Levenson, E. A. (2001). The enigma of the unconscious. *Contemporary Psychoanalysis*, 37(2): 239–252.

Levenson, E. A. (2005). *The Fallacy of Understanding and the Ambiguity of Change*. New York: Analytic Press.

Levenson, E. A., Hirsch, I., & Iannuzzi, V. (2005). Interview with Edgar A. Levenson, January 24, 2004. *Contemporary Psychoanalysis*, 41(4): 593–644.

Lewin, K. (1938). The conceptual representation and measurement of psychological forces. *Contributions to Psychological Theory*, 1(4): 1–247.

Lewin, K. (1943). Defining the "field at a given time." *Psychological Review*, 50(3): 292–310.

Lichtenberg, J. D. (1989). *Psychoanalysis and Motivation*. Hillsdale, NJ: Analytic Press.

Lichtenberg, J. D. (2001). Motivational systems and model scenes with special references to bodily experience. *Psychoanalytic Inquiry*, 21(3): 430–447.

Lichtenberg, J. D. (2013). Development and psychoanalysis: Then and now – the influence of infant studies. *Psychoanalytic Review*, 100(6): 861–880.

Lichtenberg, J. D., Lachmann, F. M., & Fosshage, J. L. (2011). *Psychoanalysis and Motivational Systems: A New Look*. New York: Routledge.

Mitchell, S. A. (1984). Object relations theories and the developmental tilt. *Contemporary Psychoanalysis*, 20(4): 473–499.

Mitchell, S. A. (1986). Roots and status. *Contemporary Psychoanalysis*, 22(3): 458–466.

Mitchell, S. A. (1988a). The intrapsychic and the interpersonal: Different theories, different domains, or historical artifacts? *Psychoanalytic Inquiry*, 8(4): 472–496.

Mitchell, S. A. (1988b). *Relational Concepts in Psychoanalysis: An Integration*. Cambridge, MA: Harvard University Press.

Mitchell, S. A. (1991a). Contemporary perspectives on self: Toward an integration. *Psychoanalytic Dialogues*, 1(2): 121–147.

Mitchell, S. A. (1991b). Wishes, needs, and interpersonal negotiations. *Psychoanalytic Inquiry*, 11(1/2): 147–170.

Mitchell, S. A. (2000). *Relationality: From Attachment to Intersubjectivity*. New York: Analytic Press.

Stern, D. B. (1997). *Unformulated Experience: From Dissociation to Imagination in Psychoanalysis*. Hillsdale, NJ: Analytic Press.

Stern, D. B. (2015). *Relational Freedom: Emergent Properties of the Interpersonal Field*. Hove, UK: Routledge.

Stolorow, R. D. (1995). An intersubjective view of self psychology. *Psychoanalytic Dialogues*, 5(3): 393–399.

Stolorow, R. D. (2013). Intersubjective-systems theory: a phenomenological-contextualist psychoanalytic perspective. *Psychoanalytic Dialogues*, 23(4): 383–389.

Sullivan, H. S. (1953). *The Interpersonal Theory of Psychiatry*. New York: W. W. Norton.

8

SELF-EXPERIENCE WITHIN INTERSUBJECTIVITY

Two clinicians' use of self psychology

Jeffrey Halpern and Sharone Ornstein

Introduction

We outline in this chapter four ways in which self psychology is useful in clinical practice. We describe introspection and vicarious introspection, or empathy, as a method of observation and understanding that builds over time. We illustrate how we use our countertransference and subjectivity to develop our empathic understanding of patients.

We examine the significance of conceptualizing narcissism as a driving force rather than as a resistance, developmental stage or disorder. The individual's original omnipotent strivings for recognition, preeminence and perfection, as well as protection, enhancement and guidance by a perfect other, are the initial constituents of healthy development. In this view, narcissism is the expression of how a self, entangled within intersubjectivity, struggles to organize experience.

This will take us to Kohut's most original contribution, his "discovery" (Cooper, 1988) of selfobject functions and selfobject transferences. Using this conceptual lens, particularly for narcissistic personality disorders, we can "see" through much of the unpromising fog of treatment to the characteristic ways an individual seeks a relationship with us in order to establish, fortify or enliven self-experience. Using this lens, we see possibilities for therapeutic action.

We explore how self psychological concepts elucidate shame and rage. We then consider the development of the self in relation to the recognition of the subjectivity of the other. Finally, we address what we think are self psychology's current strengths and limitations.

Empathy or vicarious introspection

Self psychology uses empathy in three ways. First, empathic understanding is employed as a method of psychological observation (Kohut, 1959). Introspection, as self-observation, facilitates entry into our own experience. Empathy or vicarious introspection, as observation of another, facilitates entry into another's experience. We will emphasize this use of empathy. Second, empathy creates a bond. As we discuss our empathic understanding with a patient and find experience-near explanations for what we have understood, an empathic bond develops between us (Kohut, 1984). Third, observations acquired from introspection and vicarious introspection demarcate our clinical field.

Empathy is a complex mental process composed of many parts, from instant affective resonance to painstaking reflection, centered on another's conscious and unconscious subjective experience. In ordinary speech, empathy connotes, more simply, an immediate, brief and emotional recognition of a person's plight or a fleeting identification with a person based on likeness. It arises from spontaneous imitation, unprompted thought or imaginative identification. Elements of empathy are prewired in our brains (Gallese, Eagle & Migone, 2007). Psychotherapeutic or psychoanalytic empathy includes ordinary empathy but is a more multifaceted mental process, focused on listening from within the perspective of another's self-experience *over time*. Empathic understanding goes beyond intuition to extended reflection on who the experiencing other is, and this necessitates sustained engagement in that person's experience. Empathic understanding takes labor, time and reflection.

Empathy frequently impels us, through a self-analysis of sorts, to find our way from being the target of the patient's feelings and fantasies to the perspective of the patient who has the feelings and fantasies (Schwaber, 1981). As a target, we intend not to become too charmed, excited, submissive, detached, penitent, vindictive or hurt. Yet the patient needs to know he has moved us, and that we can withstand his feelings and fantasies and reflect on them. When we are hurt or angered by a patient, or pleased or enamored, we have to reestablish an empathic understanding of ourselves, and ourselves with the patient, before we can understand our patient (Steyn, 2013). Although we may not choose to communicate this process explicitly, we communicate it implicitly in how we talk and the way we are with the patient.

We honor sustained empathic immersion – and, for that matter, free association, evenly hovering attention or technical neutrality – more in the breach than in the observance. Our inevitable breaches in our empathic immersion are as profitable as the interruptions, non-sequiturs and silences in free association and, when worked through, extend our understanding.

Empathy is not a transcendental process. It proceeds by fits and starts, by trial and error, and uses cross-sectional and longitudinal viewpoints. When we articulate what we understand to a patient and listen to his corrections, corroborations or denials, we uncertainly validate or disconfirm our empathic understanding. We evaluate whether we are engaged in predominantly disavowed, repressed or unformulated experience. We see what happens next. Are associations richer? Or is our engagement more defensive? Did we recast our relationship? The patient's responses redirect our inquiry on the model of a hermeneutic circle (Gadamer,

1975). Full empathy unfolds through engagement and dialogue in an intersubjective field (Atwood & Stolorow, 1984). As we track our patients, we track our feelings, fantasies and somatic reactions. We bring to vicarious introspection, usually nonconsciously, our knowledge of other fields, including cognitive science, neuroscience and infant research. We track how our empathy has *already* mobilized our experience, judgment, countertransference and theory. We keep our perspectives in mind as we find the patient's perspectives. When we deepen our knowledge of socioeconomics, race, ethnicity, sexuality, gender and culture we confront the ignorance and prejudice that limit our empathy.

Empathy is a method of listening and a process of understanding, not a type of intervention. Clinicians muster psychotherapeutic salves such as "It sounds like…," "So what I'm hearing…," "It seems that…" or, more firmly, "You must feel…" with a belief that they are making an empathic intervention. Echoing or mirroring what patients reveal to us is not predictably a communication of empathy. Such interventions do not substitute for the lengthy work of empathic understanding, which when articulated may take quite different forms.

A young woman, at our first meeting, told one of us (J.H.) that, as a child, her mother had "begrudged" her happiness. After a pause, she described her relationship with her boss. Feeling like an echo, I asked, "She also begrudges you?" She was curt: "No. She's not like my mother. My mother was supportive of me." As a witness to her narrative about her mother, I made what she told me unexpectedly real, possessing meanings. I did not understand, however, what it meant to her for me to see her mother as begrudging. My intervention, which prematurely exposed her disavowal *and* usefully deepened my empathic understanding, was not empathic. I was listening from my perspective – I had yet to discover hers – and she did not feel understood.

If I put myself in your shoes and imagine what I would feel if I were you, I discover an instructive ingredient of empathy; but this is not empathy. When I imaginatively project *myself* into your shoes and identify with experiences that resemble my own, it is me, in your shoes. I empathize with my feelings or with feelings we share but not with you. This is closer to sympathy. Using analogies to my experience, I infer what you are feeling and move closer to empathy.

If, unconsciously, I put myself in your shoes, we can call this projective identification. Within the theoretical framework that encompasses projective identification, if I can become conscious of the projective identification, reflect on it and metabolize it, I can use it to advance my empathic understanding of you (Brenman-Pick, 1985; LaFarge, 2015). Sometimes, when I identify with you, I lose my sense of self as separate from you and therefore lose my ability to appraise my empathic understanding of you. Or, as we talk, I am attuned to you, but my attunement is spontaneous and so bypasses the reflectiveness necessary for empathy (D.N. Stern, 1985, p. 145). Sometimes I might employ empathy for purposes untherapeutic, to procure what I desire. As I listen, I may identify with your experience, a concordant identification; I share your external view of your internal objects (Racker, 1953). Alternatively, as I listen, I may identify with one of your internal objects, a complementary identification. For example, a patient, aggrieved that his wife had again castigated him for not helping with the children, enumerated to me (J.H.) everything he did on Saturday. Everything she had stipulated, he had done, and yet she berated him. He wanted me to side with him but I felt for his wife. I imagined him reserved and compliant with the letter of her instructions but not the spirit of what his children and wife needed from him. My complementary identification offered information about his object relationships of which he was unconscious. I struggled, however, to integrate my complementary identification into a fuller empathic understanding of him; he was incensed and vindictive because she neither tended to him nor cherished the importance of doing so. We disagree that only concordant identifications correspond to an empathic position, and complementary identifications are not empathic because they converge around the experience of the (internal) object. The combined identifications bring us nearer to the total subjective experience of an individual.

Empathy may begin in attunement, projection, identification or projective identification but proceeds to discernment beyond identity and similarity. Our recognition of another's difference is essential. In sustained efforts to find the perspective of a patient's subjective experience, we collide with both the similarities and differences in our separate subjectivities.

We actively but tentatively articulate to a patient our understanding of his experience as we are making sense of it. One learns repeatedly that, as a patient feels understood, his resistances diminish; acknowledgment of defenses becomes easier; emotions, memories and fantasies become more valued; and he can participate in interpretations (P.H. Ornstein, 2011).

Narcissism as a driving force

In his first major paper, published in 1959, Heinz Kohut described empathy as a method of observation and as a perspective from which to construct psychological theories, in contrast to the extrospective perspective typically used for theory building. This paper was the foundation for his exploration of individuals with narcissistic personality disorders and for building his theory. He developed his theory in three books, *The Analysis of the Self* (1971), *The Restoration of the Self* (1977) and *How Does Analysis Cure?* (published posthumously in 1984), and in his papers, collected in four volumes entitled *The Search for the Self* (P.H. Ornstein, 1978a, 1978b, 1990, 1991). Narcissism, seen as a driving force with its own line of development, is a theoretical assumption unlike the theoretical assumptions of Freud, ego psychology and most object relational theories (Kohut, 1970). Kohut pursued ideas about narcissism as the development of a self that were hinted at by Freud (1914 p. 92) and investigated in greater depth by Ferenczi (1913), Fairbairn (1952), Balint (1968), Winnicott (1951, 1969), Loewald (1960) and others.

Kohut was part of an effort to help a *widening scope* of patients who presented as neurotic but did not manifest typical neurotic transferences (Stone, 1954). He focused on individuals with narcissistic personality disorders who relate to others

Self-experience within intersubjectivity **169**

with grandiosity, whether blithely displayed or diffidently concealed, and who possess an intractable appetite for praise, shortfalls in empathy and a keen vigilance for real and imagined slights that trigger humiliation and rage. In the office with such patients, we feel unappreciated, if not demeaned, as if we are but an echo, mirror or sounding board. Simultaneously, we may be idealized. Even "gentle" assertions of our subjectivity – a clarification, for example – may meet with fury, contempt or withdrawal, framing an impression of an individual ill equipped for relationships, transferences or working alliances indispensable for an effective treatment.

Originally narcissism signified love of oneself as opposed to love of another, expressing a defensive retreat from disappointments in love of another. Kohut, in contrast, observed that individuals with narcissistic personality disorders pursue romantic relationships and often surround themselves with friends. These relationships, moreover, can be intense. It is the *quality* of relationships (and of transference relationships), not the *absence* of relationships, that characterizes individuals with narcissistic disorders. Narcissism is defined by the characteristics of a person's investment in himself *and* others, not (as in Freud's definition) by whether the investment is in himself *or* others.

Narcissism refers to how we are driven by our ambitions and desires for recognition, led by our values and ideals, and seek a sense of belonging to communities of similar others in order to create, maintain or restore self-continuity, coherence and wellbeing. An individual with a narcissistic disorder fastens his relationships to these developmental necessities. The search for a self is, according to Kohut, "tragically" fraught with disappointments and suffered with indignity and rage. Even as healthy adults we suffer this indignity and rage although, in health, the intensity of our susceptibility, the nature of our resilience and our interpersonal costs are meaningfully different.

Seen as a driving force, narcissism is at the heart of human motivation. In health, narcissism develops from archaic to mature forms. In this view, "Mental activity is narcissistic to the degree that its function is to maintain the structural cohesiveness, temporal stability and positive affective coloring of the self-representation [or self]" (Stolorow, 1975, p. 179). Kohut described mature forms of narcissism in humor, creativity, acceptance of transience, wisdom and, notably, empathy (Kohut, 1966).

This redescription of narcissism as a driving force that creates, maintains and restores a self, rather than as a resistance or developmental phase, enabled psychoanalysts and psychotherapists to rethink their techniques with patients who did not manifest neurotic transferences or elicit typical countertransferences and were assessed as untreatable with psychoanalysis or exploratory psychotherapy. An individual's arrogance or reticence may be defensive, mobilized to protect a threatened self. The underlying narcissism is a motivated search for a recognized and stable self, however, not a defense. Our vignettes use this perspective on narcissism, which facilitated a new way to enter into and explain the subjective experiences of individuals who suffer from what Kohut came to call more broadly *disorders of the self.*

Self, selfobjects, selfobject functions and selfobject transferences

Many individuals in treatment engage us impersonally. We are theirs, engaged for their psychological functioning. Our responsiveness is oxygen for their sense of who they are, and our separate subjectivity is an impediment to their treatment. We do not revive in them coherent desires and rivalries that began in childhood. An aim more elemental and absolute animates them. They press us, imperiously or shyly, for what they feel is their right: affirmation of their sense of self. They desire us to recognize and esteem them and, when we are idealized, to enhance and restore them. When we fulfill these functions, they feel a short-lived vitality and a boosted self-esteem. When we do not, they flare with shame, rage, emptiness or feelings of fragmentation. We easily disrupt the functions we serve for them, for, as targets of their subjugating appeals, we feel disparaged, enraged or uninterested, and reveal our emotions, perhaps unwittingly, through "interpretations" that dismantle the development of distinctive transferences, described by Kohut as selfobject transferences.

(1) Kohut defined the *self* as the center of initiative and the recipient of impressions at the core of the personality (Kohut, 1977, 1979). The self organizes motivation and experience and is inseparable from its intersubjective field (Lichtenberg, 1989; Stolorow, Brandchaft & Atwood, 1987). We cannot perceive "the self" through introspection or empathy. In health, however, we have enduring inner experiences of sameness as well as distinctiveness, continuity despite life's turbulence, and a conscious sense of "I" despite the vicissitudes of self-experience. The origins of these experiences are inaccessible. In this chapter, we use "subject" and "self" interchangeably but prefer the term "subject" because, to our ears, it has less reified, isolated and spatially located connotations. Experiences of sameness, continuity and agency around a sense of "I" suggest that subjectivity has a structure. By "structure," we mean abiding and organizing patterns of perception, affect, cognition and bodily experience that develop in interaction with others (see also Rapaport & Gill, 1959; Stern, 1992; Auchincloss & Samberg, 2012).

Kohut conceptualized the self as a structure, organized at one pole around ambitions and the need to be seen and, at the other pole, around the need to feel enhanced, safe and guided by an idealized other. Between the arc of these poles are our talents and skills. Later Kohut added a third pole to the structure of the self, consisting of twinship needs to share essential likenesses and belong among similar others (Kohut, 1984).

(2) A *selfobject* is another person whose responses function in a relationship to create an experience of ourselves as (a) seen, admired and possessing a presence (mirroring selfobject), (b) enhanced, protected and emotionally regulated by another's superior qualities (idealizing selfobject) and (c) similar to others (twinship selfobject). When a person is a selfobject for us, serving a necessary psychological function, we do not experience that person as a whole object or separate subject; we feel the function the person provides as part of ourselves. The more relentless

our desire for another person to function as our selfobject, the more the selfobject's subjectivity is psychologically unimportant and unrecognized. "Selfobjects are neither self nor object; they are the subjective aspect of a function performed by a relationship" (Wolf, 1985, p. 271). Other psychoanalysts have also described, with remarkable sensitivity, selfobject-like phenomena (Winnicott, 1951; Balint, 1968; Reich, 1953; Bion, 1962; Bacal & Newman, 1990).

(3) A *selfobject function* is an act or a communication by another person that serves to enliven, stabilize or restore our self-experience. During normal development or an effective treatment, selfobject functions become part of the self and the subjectivity of the selfobject matters more. Yet, even with a consolidated and mature sense of self, our need for selfobject responses from others never ceases. Our capacity to adaptively find and specifically elicit selfobject responsiveness and to reciprocate as a selfobject to others develops throughout life.

(4) Selfobject needs correspond to the structural poles of the self and are developmental requirements to have our subjectivity and ambitions recognized, to idealize a perfect other and to feel akin to important others. In childhood, traumatically disregarded selfobject requirements arrest development, producing narcissistic disorders, or disorders of the self, in constitutionally vulnerable individuals. These unmet selfobject needs adamantly shape subsequent affective reactions, fantasies and interactions with others. Such individuals hunger for others who will provide selfobject functions. In treatment, they manifest unique transferences called selfobject transferences.

The original selfobjects are parents, who serve psychological functions for the child until the child can do so for himself. It is neither possible nor desirable for us to faultlessly meet selfobject requirements. When a child's selfobject requirements meet with optimal responsiveness (Bacal, 1985) and optimal frustration (Kohut, 1971), the child can internalize the function by symbolizing, depersonalizing and integrating it into the structure of the self in a process Kohut called transmuting internalization. A child needs to feel seen when he is looked at or he does not exist, needs to see delight in his parents' eyes when he succeeds or it did not happen, and needs to sense an easy capability in his parents' handling of him or he cannot be soothed. These are selfobject needs calling for optimal responses.

To provide selfobject functions in tune with their child's development, the parents' empathic understanding of their child's selfobject requirements has to be close enough, most of the time. Even when empathic understanding and selfobject responsiveness are good enough, parents are of necessity selective in their focus on the child's emerging sense of self. The gleam in a mother's eyes also twinkles because of her fantasies, her needs and her accent on her child's performative self. Parents evade or delight in the sexualities and genders they imagine in their child. Mismatches between who the parents are and how they parent matter. Selfobject responsiveness can be immoderate, misguided, manipulative, mercurial or more vicarious than personal to the child. As a result, aspects of the child's emerging self are repressed, split off or never formulated (D.B. Stern, 1997).

(5) As reinstated developmental needs, *selfobject transferences* (originally called narcissistic transferences by Kohut) are expressions of unconscious longings accompanied by a dread to repeat traumatic disappointments, frustrations or losses in a new relationship (A. Ornstein, 1991). To identify a selfobject transference, instead of asking which object relationship from the past I am reprising with this patient, one can begin by asking "What function am I serving for this patient?" Patients resist exposing selfobject desires or acknowledging selfobject transferences. We then have to understand and interpret resistances to the establishment of a selfobject transference. Our countertransference reactions to feeling coerced, devalued, adored or deskilled amplify a patient's resistance. When a selfobject transference operates easily for a patient, it is like the air we breathe, taken for granted. Disruptions trigger humiliation and rage. A patient's realization that we have become indispensable is another source of humiliation and resistance.

As the resumptions of developmental requirements, selfobject transferences are new experiences interwoven with old patterns. We are never only a new object for a patient. Individuals come to treatment etched with the patterns of past relationships that are now "intersubjective goals" (Stern et al., 1998). These patterns, with their intergenerational influences, continually organize new experiences by giving them old meanings. New meanings are more uncertain. When selfobject transferences are disrupted, old patterns of relating, revealing traumatic disappointments, frustrations or losses, lurch into the foreground (Stolorow, 1984). The patient's identifications with consequential others who delivered optimal or traumatic responses surface in relationship to us. Often selfobject desires, met in childhood within perverse or disorganized patterns of interactions, are replayed in treatment with us, with improvisations. We will illustrate this in our vignette about Kevin.

Mirroring and idealizing selfobject functions establish simultaneously two developmental lines for narcissism – that is, for the child's original sense of omnipotence and perfection. More selfobject functions have been defined since Kohut (Wolf, 1988; Trop & Stolorow, 1992; Lachmann, 1986; Stolorow, Brandchaft & Atwood, 1987). Clinically, the types of selfobject transferences intermingle, but one type predominates. The enlivening power of a mirror transference implies that in the background we are idealized. In an idealizing transference, the patient assumes we are affirming of him. We will focus on mirroring and idealizing transferences.

Mirror transference

The young child expresses his original sense of omnipotence through exhibitionistic desires to be seen and admired. When these desires are injuriously unmet early in life, some of the normal omnipotence of the small child is split off and some of it is repressed (Kohut, 1971, p. 185). The child feels unseen and his subjectivity tenuous. Grandiose ambitions are sequestered from actual talents and skills. The child grows up oblivious to his limitations or diffidently secretive about his undiscovered greatness. The aspirations of the grandiose self become a hunger and satisfactions overstimulating.

A mirror selfobject transference reactivates the grandiose self. Individuals struggle with their overweening and unrealized ambitions, and yearn to feel special and recognized. They seek our confirmation. Our responsiveness to this mobilization in more disturbed individuals engenders in them feelings of omnipotence and initiates the possibility for a working-through process. Our responsiveness to these desires in healthier individuals leads to more discriminating feelings of being valued and loved as well as to self-respect and to a more differentiated working-through process.

Kohut delineated three types of mirror selfobject functions and transferences: merger; alter ego or twinship; and mirror proper. He later made alter ego or twinship a separate selfobject function and line of development.

Julia: Illustration of a mirror transference

Julia was an ambitious musician in her mid-thirties. She said of herself, "I colonize people; I always need a boyfriend or a witness or else I feel invisible… I am afraid I will overestimate how good I am… I have to put myself down so as not to appear pompous."

Several years into her analysis, I (J.H.) tried to explore her feelings about my impending vacation as if she would miss me in ways that recognized my separate subjectivity. "I will miss that you will not witness the footage of my life," she clarified. I voiced curiosity, channeling my disappointment. I wanted to feel missed by her. My curiosity, which Julia did not share, hinted at my feelings and suggested criticism. Realizing this, and after some reflection and stumbling, I said, "You will miss me but you want me to know *how* you will miss me." She said, "Exactly. It's not nice of me, I feel a little badly about what it says about me, but it is true." If, in my disappointment, I had interpreted her clarification about how she would miss me as disingenuous and defensive (so as not to acknowledge me as a separate person, for example), I would have quarantined her feelings about me outside the treatment. Julia prized the mirroring function I served as her analyst; I witnessed the footage of her life, which enlivened and sanctioned the reality of her life. Later, on another occasion, Julia said, "I really care for you. You know so much about me."

In development, optimal empathic responsiveness and frustration of mirroring requirements forge grandiosity into ambitions that match our realistic talents and skills. Feelings of omnipotence develop into a sense of reality and efficacy (Ferenczi, 1913). In treatment, we may feel a responsibility to cross-examine a patient's unrealistic desires. Sometimes we must coach a patient. When improbable aspirations are prematurely fact-checked, however, patients cannot audition their fantasies and reflect upon them with us. If we can listen to grandiose fantasies, patients begin to contend with their quixotic ambitions and grieve for the loss of their imagined magnificence. As individuals begin to possess a stronger sense of self, starker confrontations with their limitations enrich experience (Loewald, 1973).

A young man, in whom a mirror transference was unfolding, noted halfway through a session how elated he was because I (J.H.) had referred to his childhood friend by name and remembered what he had told me about this friend weeks earlier. His father never remembered his friend's names. Articulating the patient's selfobject need, I said, "Feeling seen and remembered by me enlivens you." Referring to the young man's childhood friend was spontaneous, not a calculated attempt at a corrective emotional experience through selfobject responsiveness. Our task is to understand and interpret the patient's reactions to both frustration and responsiveness within the selfobject transference.

The effect of empathy, as a method of listening leading to understanding and becoming a mode of connecting, is sometimes difficult to distinguish from the effect of serving a patient's selfobject need, but the distinction is useful. Understanding is not synonymous with admiration, for example, though a patient who pursues recognition in the form of admiration may unconsciously wring praise rather than comprehension from our empathic understanding. For long stretches in a treatment, our understanding may be experienced only as being seen and affirmed by us, which are mirroring selfobject needs. Often interactions with a patient precipitate selfobject failures but not empathic failures. We may understand the patient's experiences of our selfobject failures in depth. Of course, we may fulfill our patient's selfobject desires without empathic understanding. Some individuals want to be understood but not to understand (Joseph, 1983). Others do not want to know or to be known, mortified by this spotlight on a defective self. The first vignette about Ellen, further below, illustrates this.

Kevin: Working through disruptions in a mirror transference

This clinical example illustrates disruptions in a mirror transference and its repair through interpretation. Growing up, Kevin felt he could extract recognition and admiration only through sadomasochistic clashes with his father while allying himself with his mother. He enacted an adaptation of this with me (S.O.).

Kevin began this session describing how he tactfully refereed his family over the holiday as his grandfather was dying. His father ignored Kevin's thoughtfulness. Instead, as Kevin finalized funeral arrangements, his father pressed him to read a piece in the paper about careers in finance. He praised his son's potential and reproached him again for his less lucrative choice of an academic career.

I noticed Kevin's self-possession, despite his father's belittling praise. This seemed new and related to what we were working on. I asked how he had felt when his father showed him the article. He was incensed. "Why are you focusing on this incident? You know I earn less than my friends. Why can't you ask me about how I handled my father when he canceled hospice care or refused to fill the morphine prescription? Instead, you picked this. Why do I have to work for rapport with you? I want an easy understanding." I was startled and said he was able to show his anger here. He became more incensed: "At least you could have been outraged at my father. Showing me that article was egregious. Can't you see that? You just suckerpunched me." He missed the next two sessions.

Eagerly, I had anticipated a new experience with Kevin in which I was not coaxed or commanded to applaud. Finding admiration in new ways, however, meant conceding the campaign to rectify his relationship with his father. Recognition from me in the analysis was tepid in comparison to the praise won through emotionally saturated struggles with his father. Kevin depicted his father as recurrently dissatisfied with him. Only after Kevin dramatically exposed his hurt feelings would his father offer approbation. Although Kevin commandeered selfobject provisions through this perverse pattern of relating, his father's admiration felt genuine and meaningful to Kevin. This time Kevin did sidestep this hardened sadomasochistic crusade with his father, only to explode at me. I saw too, in Kevin's entreaty for easy rapport, a plea to enact with me his alliance with his mother against his father's severity. We had been exploring this. This had the semblance of a developed Oedipal configuration but the organization of his interactions was desperately all or nothing. I was struck by how peremptory and devoid of reflection Kevin's desire to bond with me felt. In what suggested rivalry with his father, Kevin sought recognition of his subjectivity, not destruction of his competitor. His disjointed Oedipal strivings were in the service of eliciting selfobject responses that bolstered his self-organization.

When he returned, I articulated how I made sense of the selfobject disruption. I said, "You told me about your confidence when you took responsibility for the family as your grandfather was dying, even when your father belittled you, but because I did not comment on your confidence you felt I did not see it and so it lacked significance. You expected me and needed me to see it. Instead, I brought up that career article, and you felt sucker-punched." He responded, "Yes. What was important to me went unnoticed, just as it does with my father, and, when you fixated on that article, you did what he does, all over again. It sounds extreme, but that's how it felt… I appreciate you see it now, even though I was so exasperated with you." Although Kevin had again procured recognition through a sadomasochistic exchange, my recognition – and this is crucial – included my acknowledgment of his experience with his father and with me. This disruption and repair of his mirror transference led to Kevin's improved capacity for reflection and, just then, his acknowledgment of my interpretation.

In a later session, I said, "You tell me how angry you are with me by showing me how I victimize you." He agreed, saying that only after his "hostile use of victimization" would his father acknowledge admiration for him. Following these sessions, Kevin and I became aware that, when he felt unseen by me, he launched a sadomasochistic altercation between us. Gradually, we articulated how his exasperated protest that I victimized him was a "rightful" bid that I see and appreciate him.

It is not "more therapeutic" to meet selfobject requirements. I could not meet Kevin's selfobject petitions unless I joined him in a sadomasochistic relationship. When we meet a selfobject longing, our task is to interpret what our responsiveness stimulates in our patients, just as we interpret what our selfobject failure provokes. We do not decide to optimally respond or frustrate a selfobject need. I tried to understand what led me to respond to Kevin as I did. When engaged with a patient, we cannot admire if no admiration is felt, we cannot affirm if no affirmation is possible. Of course, sometimes we do admire and affirm. Meeting a selfobject need, instead of understanding and articulating the need, is often unconscious, inevitable and necessary. Consistently meeting a selfobject need engenders trouble and stagnation in a treatment.

The idealizing transference

In an idealizing transference, the patient attempts to reinstate arrested developmental requirements for protection, guidance and affect regulation through idealizations of his analyst or psychotherapist (Kohut, 1971; Stolorow & Atwood, 1996). One can encapsulate the developmental desires expressed in an archaic idealizing transference as "You are perfect. When I am part of you I become perfect. Through your knowledge and your power, I am shielded and my emotional equilibrium restored." In health, archaic desires for idealization become our engagement with admired others, internalized values and what is called wisdom. Internalized values both inspire and regulate our ambitions and desires for acclaim, and are a source of our resilience. An idealizing transference generates an agreeable glow in the room, easily extinguished. While some therapists bask in it, others feel undeserving and flustered by its rosy ambience, and still others are too stimulated by the arousal of their own grandiosity.

Idealization is a developmental necessity. Idealization is not primarily a defense, although it can be employed defensively. Many psychoanalytic models treat idealization as a defense against hostile affects that include hatred, contempt and envy. When we interpret idealization in the transference as a defense, we predictably provoke anger. When the patient hears our premature interpretations of idealization in the transference as rejections, because he is not perfect enough in our eyes, we also stimulate envy. Do interpretations of idealization as a defense reveal underlying anger or envy or are these interpretations felt as our refusals of the idealization, and consequently instigate anger or envy (Benjamin, 1988)? Based on our theoretical understanding, we see the anger or envy to our interpretations of idealization as evidence of hidden destructiveness or as reactions to prematurely thwarted developmental needs. The manifestations of destructiveness are legion but, particularly in the treatment of narcissistic personality disorders, our theoretical choices on how to understand idealization in the transference matter. We will say more about this under shame and narcissistic rage in the next section.

Anne: An archaic idealizing transference

In an archaic idealizing transference, the omnipotent attentiveness of the psychoanalyst or psychotherapist is required for the provision of safety and affect regulation. At the start of Anne's analysis, I (J.H.) mistakenly focused on what appeared to me as archaic mirroring needs. My attempts to interpret what I saw as Anne's need for my affirmation and admiration of her were seductive. I came to realize that what mattered to her was my attentive presence when it allowed her to feel protected. This vignette illustrates clinical differences between selfobject requirements for recognition of the grandiose self (mirroring) and the regulating requirements from an idealized other.

Anne was a 38-year-old recently divorced woman who had achieved professional recognition. She had a traumatic childhood. When she began analysis, Anne parsed my breathing to gauge my interest in her. When I took a deeper breath – a sigh I failed to notice until she detected it – she accused me of impatience with her and fell silent; what she was telling me became trivial. If she heard the scratch of my pen stop, she reproached me for my inattention and lost her train of thought. When I repositioned myself in my chair, she determined I was bored. She scrutinized my words similarly. She tracked my self-state more vigilantly than I did, although her sensitive attunement to me felt entirely self-referential. I felt shackled to my chair, too self-conscious to think freely or to breathe spontaneously. If I tried to discuss how I had disrupted her flow, she was derisive about my self-importance. If I was silent, she talked about the futility of the treatment. When I said to her "You feel lively when you feel my attention and panicky when you lose it," she denied a connection between her abrupt emptiness or panic and my apparent lapse in focus.

Instead, she lectured me about how this was her treatment, which entitled her to my attention. As she repeatedly experienced this with me, she began to reflect on it. Unfortunately, in helping her to elaborate, I had in mind mirroring selfobject requirements; I thought she yearned for my admiration of her. That she could be appealing and flirtatious compounded my misperception. My interpretations were not wrong but I missed what was critical. It was months before I understood that my attentiveness mattered because it meant I watched over and protected her, not because I affirmed or admired her. By tracking my attentiveness and my self-state, she was monitoring my availability for responsiveness to her idealizing selfobject needs. Once I could discuss this explicitly with her and she felt that I understood, the change in our relationship was profound. My initial emphasis on mirroring requirements felt seductive and retraumatizing to her in the context of the emotional and sexual traumas of her childhood. Ever since she was a little girl she had elicited protection by being flirtatious and clever, sometimes at a great price. She began to talk about this and connect it to what was going on between us.

Nina: a deepening idealizing transference

Nina began treatment psychologically minded. She developed an idealizing transference to me (S.O.). She had described her mother's righteous intrusiveness as intimidating but, during her mother's recent visit, she held her own without provoking her mother. She was more observant. I said I thought our work together had helped her feel sturdier in her mother's presence. She responded, "What does it mean for me to work with you? You pay attention. You take what I say and help me weave it into something. You help me hear a meaning. I can talk about things I've never thought about. It's scary. I am allowing myself to feel more." As the idealizing transference unfolded, Nina was able to experience and acknowledge feelings about

Shame and narcissistic rage

Shame is a complex mental state at the core of disrupted self-experience. It includes a spectrum of affective states from mild chagrin and painful self-consciousness to abject humiliation ending in suicide. Freud observed that shame motivates repression and resistance. He also saw shame as a reaction formation against desires to exhibit oneself (Freud, 1893, 1905, 1908, 1917). Subsequently Freud described shame as a painful diminution of self-regard when we founder before our perfectionistic ego ideals (Freud, 1914). We are ashamed when we feel too commanding a stretch between our real self and our ideal self (Sandler, Holder & Meers, 1963). In interpreting shame, clinicians generally employ versions of this last model or regard shame as a form of guilt, as did Freud after he introduced his structural theory in 1923 (Freud, 1923).

Kohut emphasized the shame aroused in us when we reveal to another person how we value ourselves and, anticipating affirmation, we encounter criticism or indifference. When the exhibitionistic desires of the grandiose self are unmet, we feel, briefly or pervasively, that we are defective (Kohut, 1971).

A graduate student, working full-time, writing her dissertation and participating in social causes, presented to her mentor a piece of writing she had worked on diligently. She offered her own harsh critique and complained how pressured she was by people in her life. He praised her work, adding that she should be less perfectionistic; we can't do it all. She knew her mentor was being supportive but she was humiliated. To her, his platitudes revealed his verdict that she did not possess deeper potential. He had "graciously" informed her that she was ordinary and would be happier relaxing her standards, but it was her omnipotence at stake, not her perfectionistic standards.

Shame often precedes rage. Kohut marked narcissistic rage as the prototype for all destructive aggression. Narcissistic rage is the most salient manifestation on a spectrum that ranges from trivial pique and varieties of envy to sadistic premeditated vengeance. Many psychoanalytic theorists see destructive aggression as a continuously running biologically based engine of motivation with its own aims, analogous to libido. Alternatively, we can see destructive aggression as a biologically based but reactively activated motivation, contingent on context. Kohut viewed aggression in this way. Narcissistic rage is a reaction to threats to the cohesiveness of the self. Like shame, it is an emergent complex mental state. Kohut wrote that underlying both shame and rage "is the uncompromising insistence on the perfection of the idealized selfobject and on the limitlessness of the power and knowledge of a grandiose self…" (Kohut, 1972, p. 643).

Melville's Captain Ahab, Dostoyevsky's Underground Man (P.H. Ornstein, 1993), Kleist's Michael Kohlhaas, Hamsun's Andreas Tangen, Shakespeare's Iago, Lear and Richard III, Homer's Achilles, Milton's Satan and, lamentably, God, as portrayed in

Self-experience within intersubjectivity **179**

countless mythologies and the Bible, are examples of the complex mental state of narcissistic rage. These protagonists seethe with the imperative quality and utterly destructive force of narcissistic rage. When driven by the injustice of real or perceived injuries to our self-esteem, our righteous demand for revenge and restitution can become limitless. We frequently applaud such rage in others as a moral, heroic and inspiring response to injustice, dishonor and humiliation. Rage can be ecstatic, shared and unifying. Our politicians – and demagogues – exploit this.

Aggression is not a unitary entity. Psychoanalytic discussions of hostile aggression become tangled because qualitatively distinct forms of aggression are not distinguished (Parens, 1979). Killing sadistically is not necessarily on the same continuum with killing to survive or commanding a battalion or performing surgery. Exploration of new worlds, even if aggressive, is not necessarily continuous with exploitation, however unerringly one follows upon another. Arguably, clinicians, regardless of their metapsychological convictions, treat hostile aggression not as a primary drive but as secondary to the contextual meaning of a patient's anger, ignited in the office with them and with roots in a past. Different theories, of course, shape dissimilar contextual details.

To view narcissistic rage as a reaction to a threatened or fragmenting self has an explicit clinical consequence; our interpretations aim to restore the structural integrity of the self. Our interpretations do not steer a patient to check, channel or sublimate rage. We elucidate the contexts for conscious, unconscious, unformulated and disavowed rage in fantasies, feelings and actions. Working through the indignation and pain of not finding recognition, or not finding an idealized other, fosters a more robust sense of self. An individual then has the possibility to competitively pursue his ambitions. As patients are able to take pleasure in their realistic ambitions, then competitiveness and anger, by degrees more circumscribed, enter the treatment. When our sense of self is sturdy we scan interactions less suspiciously and rebound from injuries to our self-esteem more agilely, but we continue to experience narcissistic rage.

Our narcissistic rage does not transform into mature aggression or self-assertion. Narcissistic rage is a reaction to threats to our self-assertion or our developmentally essential admiration of an idealized other. Self-assertion, a manifestation of narcissism as a driving force, originates from the archaic ambitions of the grandiose and exhibitionistic self. Mature self-assertion is part of our sense of agency and presence, and is the product of optimal responsiveness and frustration to mirroring requirements during development. When we assert ourselves in anger, our anger is limited, focused and adapted to circumstance. Most importantly, aggressive self-assertion, in contrast to narcissistic rage, is not founded in a sense of self that is defective or fragmenting. In narcissistic rage, our sense of self is in thrall to our rage. In narcissistic rage, the enemy is experienced "as a flaw in a narcissistically perceived reality. The enemy is a recalcitrant part of an expanded self over which the narcissistically vulnerable person had expected to exercise full control. The mere fact, in other words, that the other person is independent or different is experienced as offensive…" (Kohut, 1972, p. 644). Mature competitiveness, which includes normal Oedipal competiveness, emerges as part of the development of the ambitious strivings of the grandiose and

180 Jeffrey Halpern and Sharone Ornstein

exhibitionistic self. We may hate and attack our adversary because he thwarts our narcissistic ambitions but our adversary is experienced as a separate person.

The concept of narcissistic rage offers a new perspective on a type of masochism, classified by default as aggression turned against the self in the form of guilt and punishment. When we observe this type of individual from an external perspective, his self-sabotaging behavior is impressive. His internal experience, however, is about his inalienable right to preserve his integrity, honor and sense of justice. Although the objects of his rage are obstinately external, his unmitigated quest for retribution delivers devastation to himself. Explanations for his self-destruction are bundled with accounts of individuals who are "criminal from a sense of guilt," "wrecked by success," "or victorious through defeat." Strikingly, for this individual, the self-destructive realities of his ultimatums and conduct are not meaningful to him. Humiliation, not guilt, drives him. He is unconcerned that giving the boss uncensored hell may replicate Ahab's fate, drawing crew, whaling ship and Ahab himself to the bottom of the ocean. Or to therapy. Only the purity of his uncompromising crusade for justice and vengeance will restitute the integrity of his injured self. For many narcissistic individuals, this is a more experience-near and serviceable understanding of their masochism (Kohut, 1972; A. Ornstein, 1998).

Clinicians become uneasy that concealed behind a smoothly functioning selfobject transference lies sadistic aggression. We resent feeling controlled, devalued and fungible. We ask: Is it sadistic or pathologic for a patient to treat another human being as a psychological extension of herself (Kernberg, 2004)? The perspective from which we examine this question is decisive. As the target of an archaic selfobject transference, we feel denigrated by our patient's ruthless control of us, while our patient feels frantic to secure the vital supplies for her psychological survival. The more archaic the selfobject transference, the more implacable is our patient's siege of us, because self-esteem and preservation of the self hang upon a selfobject's response. Furthermore, in archaic selfobject transferences, we are seen as omnipotent, and therefore our errors seem calculated and sadistic to the patient. There is no shared intersubjective reality. Incensed and panicked, our patient seeks retribution. Her rage stirs a fleeting sensation of her power and will, and feels infinitely superior to her humiliation or the terror of falling apart. It is not that a patient invariably fails to mark her tyranny over others. She may take pleasure in it and feel sorry about it. These feelings are just not as meaningful to her psychological survival and wellbeing. Her plight is impossible for the people in the patient's life and onerous for her therapist.

Ellen: countertransference, empathy and the subjectivity of the other in working with shame and rage

In the following vignette, I (S.O.) tried to find my way from my engagement as the target of Ellen's demands and anger to an understanding of her subjective experience while still angry with her. This vignette illustrates the strain of facing a

Self-experience within intersubjectivity 181

patient's selfobject demands – in Ellen's case, a righteous stipulation that I admire her for how she provided *for me* and her expectation that I display my gratitude for her payments. I had to work through what I experienced as Ellen's omnipotent control of me before I was able to understand her and return to the interpretive process. We anticipate, in this clinical illustration, the next section on the recognition of the subjectivity of the other.

The overarching selfobject transference configuration in this treatment was idealizing, with archaic merger longings. There were also components of a mirror transference. Seeking certainty that she was special to me, Ellen probed me for evidence that I depended on the money she paid me every month, even though, in fact, her copay for her reduced fee was too minimal. She was frightened that, if I did not depend on her, she would cease to be special and I would abandon her. She alternated, often without awareness, between almost simultaneous feelings of superiority and shame in relation to me.

Ellen's unconscious assumption, that she was as important to me as I was to her, skirted the reality of our differences and grated on me. She venerated me. For my part, I was to keep her preeminent in my eyes and respect how she fulfilled *my* desires. She described sexual fantasies about my desires for her but my bill and her payment, which to her was not a fantasy, meant we both had "skin in the game, in reality." If I questioned this, she silenced me. In staying within a patient's experiential reality, one willingly suspends spotlighting distortions, but now I found this unworkable. Her subjugating plea that I gratefully honor her payment felt false and inhibited my empathic understanding. In this context, I had to make my experience visible to Ellen, rather than wait for her recognition of me as part of her intersubjective development (Ogden, 1994; Aron, 1996).

I was all too familiar with her vulnerability to humiliation and the ensuing contempt aimed at me. I felt able to survive her attacks although, in retrospect, I realized that, by not raising her fee, I had ducked some of her wrath. We had been analyzing her efforts to forcibly extract selfobject responses from me, often by exploring her relationships with her parents and sister. As a child, her mother's caretaking appeared, in key moments, more for herself than about Ellen. Ellen served selfobject functions for her mother in order to feel special and close to her. Her insistence on my need for her recapitulated the way she created her mother's need for her. Although we had been talking about this, I saw now how my countertransference limited my understanding.

I anticipated Ellen's disdain if her bill lacked the new codes mandated by her insurance company. I risked arriving late for another patient to revise and reprint her current bill so I could give it to her at her next session. My vigilance had become characteristic of our relationship. As I handed her the bill, I suggested that she submit this statement and I would give her the remaining revisions as soon as I could. She studied the bill and asked why I had not given her all the statements. "Why are you so lackadaisical with my bills?"

"Lackadaisical?" I repeated. After a long pause I said, "I am not sure what to say." What I could say was disparaging. I could think, but not feel, my way into Ellen's experience of me because I was too irritated with her. I said, "Maybe I understand why you see me as lackadaisical. It is important that you feel special to me. Paying me on time lets you feel that." Ellen became tearful. "Why are you making me feel so pathetic?"

I did not grasp her question. I noticed the colorless tone in my voice, which sprang from my disavowed resentment of her conviction that my deliberation with her bill verified that her payments were critical – to me. Her presumption about me around her payments seemed shameless and indicative of a disavowed or split-off self-state (Kohut, 1971; Goldberg, 1999). Her shame was mostly unconscious, easily triggered and suddenly painful. She did not want to know, nor want me to know, why she required my admiration for her timely payment. And, in my unexamined irritation, I felt no inclination to achieve a perspective within her subjective experience. Shame accompanying our exploration of this situation was inevitable for both of us. I resisted addressing my resentment. Ellen wanted me to say, "You effortfully meet my needs and show your appreciation of me with your payment. I dismiss this with my lackadaisical billing."

Instead, after several minutes, Ellen broke the silence, telling me that last weekend her sister had described her as belligerent. After a pause she continued, "I see why she said that." I felt, in her comment, recognition of my anger toward her. In her thoughtful tone I heard something of our work together. I realized, as well, that I needed her recognition at that moment and that she had served her mother in a similar way as a child. My emotional experience of this enactment made tangible for me her relationship with her mother and others in her life.

With her comment as a trigger, I appreciated how arduous it was for me to endure Ellen's selfobject entreaties, and I regained my equilibrium and independence (Steyn, 2013). I found a reinvigorated understanding of her insistence on her preeminence, her assumptions of our oneness and her efforts to dodge anticipated humiliations. Disentangling myself from my side of this enactment, her selfobject hunger repelled me less. I accepted how her psychic reality registered in me without feeling defined by it. Less ensnared in her selfobject claims (and problematic fee), I was freer to ask how she perceived my need and desire for her. Moreover, my tone no longer conveyed only what I already knew but also a discovery of my and her lived experience. This enactment entered into our discussions. In the weeks that followed we discussed "the reality" of her minimal copay and scheduled an increase in her fee. She observed that I accepted her perceptions around my lackadaisical billing. She observed as well that I did not share her perceptions. After telling me she did not know how she could reconcile this, she remarked, "I am seeing more about myself from the way you respond to me."

Because I no longer felt coerced to provide a selfobject function, I was able to refind Ellen's perspective. I survived for her *outside* my role as a selfobject. She felt this change in me. In this way, and not through meeting or frustrating a selfobject need, or a personal revelation to my patient, my separate subjectivity entered the treatment for her. We will return to Ellen later.

The self and recognition of the subjectivity of the other

Throughout this chapter, we have referred to self-experience as embedded within intersubjectivity. Others are our first reality. Recognition that comes from being held and seen by a parenting other is essential to feeling we exist. A further recognition that comes from being esteemed and loved is essential to feeling we are alive and related (Loewald, 1960; Stern, 1985; Sander, 1995). We internalize our experience of being recognized or unrecognized in order to conceive and retain a structured subjectivity that we call a self. Without ongoing engagement in an intersubjective matrix, even established internalized structures crumble. We seek recognition from others throughout our lives and battle with what satisfactions are possible, as others also demand recognition.

A child's healthy narcissism (a child's healthy development of a self) results in mature narcissism, not object love. The development of a self, and the development of intersubjectivity, as mutual recognition, steer nonlinear courses and are inextricably interdependent but, clinically, the distinction between the two is important. The conflict between our desire for recognition, with its consequent subjugation, and our desire for mutuality has no resolution (Benjamin, 1990). The conflict endures as a dialectic with the potential to introduce mutative, but frequently transient, understanding.

Kohut stressed that narcissism pursues its own line of development, distinct from the object libidinal line of development that culminates in object love (Freud, 1905; Kohut, 1971). Kohut made this distinction for a variety of clinical, conceptual and historical reasons (Kohut, 1966). An important clinical reason for this distinction addresses treatments that often unthinkingly attempt to dethrone narcissism and crown object love and concern for others. Such an aim splits off, represses or leaves unformulated the strivings of a grandiose self.

What does recognition of others mean to someone when the other is a selfobject or an object and not a separate subject? A fuller recognition of my subjectivity can come only from another whose subjectivity is independent of mine (Hegel, 1807). If the other is a subject within my control, primarily my selfobject or object, the other's recognition of me is not free. Desire for fuller recognition of my subjectivity and the allure of another's unique subjectivity vacillate with the sturdiness of my self-experience. When the cohesiveness of my subjectivity is perilous, my curiosity about the subjectivity of the person "responsible" for a selfobject function is out of reach.

Only when a sense of self is sufficiently firm, self-esteem is sufficiently reliable and disruptions to a sense of self have been hammered out thoughtfully, is a more in-depth and consistent recognition of another's subjectivity possible. Split-off and repressed omnipotent strivings feed an unstable sense of self, and the relentless search to satisfy selfobject desires obscures the subjectivity of the other. Employing a different theoretical framework, we fluctuate, sometimes moment to moment, between paranoid schizoid and depressive positions. We interpret attentive to a patient's immediate self-state.

How does recognition of the other enter usefully into a treatment, especially when a selfobject transference organizes the treatment? Our subjectivity, even when unrecognized, is inherently part of every treatment. Each time we articulate our empathic understanding and offer an interpretation to a patient, we tacitly hint at personal conflicts that made up our understanding. When a patient acknowledges we have understood, we also feel understood. Resistance, seen as a conflict between our patient's curative fantasies and our curative fantasies for the patient, is an encounter between two subjectivities (Schafer, 1983; A. Ornstein, 1995; Benjamin, 2004). How we understand and interpret resistance will deepen or diminish the experience of mutual recognition.

What we want to emphasize, however, is one particularly important way the recognition of the subjectivity of the other enters treatments characterized by selfobject transferences. A patient may first glimpse our subjectivity when she detects that her fantasies, desires and rage affect us and yet we are able to survive *outside* our role as her selfobject (Winnicott, 1969). When we fail to survive for her, as her selfobject but, more critically, as ourselves with her, because we are too defensive, angry or unmoved by her psychic reality, we reveal ourselves again, in how we recoup.

We may feel insincere and resentful when pressed into "responsibility" for a selfobject or empathic failure that we view as more complicated. We often tolerate that responsibility and, temporarily, our toleration can be our survival for a patient. Our patients eventually glean, however, that this prescription for responsibility is our failure to survive their discontents and hatred. When we fail to survive, our understanding ceases to be alive to our patient's and our own lived experience, as we described above in the vignette about Ellen.

Patients internalize how they affect us – when they affect us – especially how we handle surviving or failing them as selfobjects, as objects and as subjects. When we know, after weathering repeated disruptions and repairs, that the patient too can survive, then both patient and therapist can anticipate the work necessary to repair future disruptions (Wolf, 1988). In the course of a successful treatment we become more than reinstated selfobjects and new objects for a patient; we become new subjects. At times, in a treatment, we feel glimpsed at or seen. When patients reliably recognize their own subjectivity, they can reflectively acknowledge ours. In the process of our work to understand and interpret how we are selfobjects and subjects to our patients, we also change.

Ellen (continued): increased structuralization of a self and recognition of the other

Ellen began her analysis with a precarious sense of self. Her fragile claim to her own subjectivity made working through her selfobject transference a prerequisite for the development of her capacity to recognize my subjectivity. She achieved a more intricate, if tenuous, recognition of the subjectivity of others over the years of repairing disruptions in her selfobject transference relationship to me (S.O.). Early

Self-experience within intersubjectivity **185**

in our work, she would silence me: "Why do you talk when you know that I do not want you to?" She wanted a wise analyst who knew when to speak and when to remain silent, an expression of an archaic idealizing transference. She afforded me little recognition as a separate subject. She was dating women who drank. When they passed out, as when she silenced me, she could relax into a longed-for oneness with them, unthreatened by their differences that forced her to anticipate their desires and criticism.

A session we called "the *New Yorker* incident" spotlights a disruption and repair of her selfobject transference relationship with me that she incorporated years later into a more mature recognition of me. She slipped a copy of *The New Yorker* magazine from the waiting room into her bag, confident I would let her borrow it. Instead, I "preferred" that she return the magazine to the waiting room table, and she was offended. Years later she still remembered the *New Yorker* incident: "You got that you had hurt me and you thought about what I felt. You said, 'In supervising myself, I see better ways I could have responded to you.'" Now, she realized, she could use the way I thought about my impact on her to think about her impact on others. She remembered how she exalted me when she started analysis: "I admired you so I could feel enhanced. I relied on that, but I don't feel any more it is a real connection. You are different than that." She observed that, when she is hypervigilantly attuned to me to assure her specialness, it is impossible for her to reflect. "I find myself less watchful of you, so I can think about what you are saying and who you are."

Strengths and limitations of a self psychological approach

It is in four concepts that we see the strengths of using self psychology to find and track what is mutative in our work with patients. First, we listen with sustained attention from within the patients' perspective, working to enter how they inhabit their lives and experience us. To do this we have to inhabit our experience of ourselves with them. An interpretive process emerges in conversation with a patient from within an empathic stance, over time (Ornstein & Ornstein, 1996).

Second, narcissism is the expression of developmental desires for realization of one's subjectivity through recognition by others. We see its driving force in desires to feel seen and esteemed, in desires to idealize in order to find affective regulation and calm, and in desires to feel similarly and to belong. The child's original assumption of omnipotence is transformed into healthy narcissism through empathic frustration of or responsiveness to these selfobject desires by important others. This conceptualization of narcissism, as the development of subjectivity embedded in intersubjectivity, means that, in treatment, we do not approach narcissism as a defense or a pathological retreat from relationships.

Third, the selfobject concept clarifies why the balance between vitality and lifelessness hinges so exactly on how we hear and explain the patient's experience. The selfobject concept allows a therapist to track, in a field of emotional landmines, the therapist's impact on the patient. A selfobject is not fully self and not fully object or other. The selfobject experience is the catalyst for the development of subjectivity and transitional in the development of the asymptotic and often asymmetric recognition of subjectivity.

Fourth, self psychology provides an access to shame and hostile aggression that is experience-near and contextual to the treatment and extends our insight into the sources of cruelty. In this view, rage and violence are the expressions of disturbances in the self–selfobject experience with another person. As we have described, this conceptualization of narcissistic rage also offers us a way to understand some forms of ostensibly masochistic behavior. The study of individuals unable to accept their failures to achieve omnipotent perfection has led to an appreciation of the role of shame, as distinct from guilt, in unconscious motivation. Self psychology explores envy as a form of narcissistic rage. Guilt, shame and envy persist, however, as capacious terms for heterogeneous mental states that continue to require further conceptualization. Explorations of the capacity to recognize the subjectivity of another will lead to further elaborations of guilt and concern from a self psychological perspective.

Self psychology allows us to treat patients with narcissistic personality disorders that are otherwise untreatable. Although the purely neurotic patient in psychoanalytic literature is more cherished myth than reality (Glover, 1955; Cooper, 1986), as self psychological theory extended its domain to disorders of the self, including the neurotic patient, it ran into limitations. It became necessary to map the theory beyond the selfobject and examine conceptualizations of attachment, object, subject and intersubjectivity.

With its original focus on the vicissitudes of self-experience, self psychology undertheorized the force of our subjectivity on the patient's selfobject experience. At the time, psychoanalysts tried to eclipse their subjectivity when they analyzed patients. The use of countertransference to amplify empathy is inherently part of a therapeutic process. In our vignettes, we explicated working through our countertransferences, our subjectivity with a patient, within the context of sustained empathic immersion. In addition, self psychology undertheorized the development of recognition of another's subjectivity. A number of clinicians and theorists, influenced by self psychology, continue to study the subjectivity of the other in the development of the self (Stern, 1985; Boston Change Process Study Group, 2010; Atwood & Stolorow, 1984; Stolorow, Brandchaft & Atwood, 1987; Benjamin, 1990; Teicholz, 1999; Beebe & Lachmann, 2002).

References

Aron, L. (1996). *A Meeting of Minds: Mutuality in Psychoanalysis*. Hillsdale, NJ: Analytic Press.

Atwood, G. E., & Stolorow, R. D. (1984). *Structures of Subjectivity: Explorations in Psychoanalytic Phenomenology*. Hillsdale, NJ: Analytic Press.

Auchincloss, E. L., & Samberg, E. (Eds.) (2012). *Psychoanalytic Terms and Concepts*. New Haven, CT: Yale University Press.

Bacal, H. A. (1985). Optimal responsiveness and the therapeutic process. *Progress in Self Psychology*, 1: 202–227.

Bacal, H. A., and Newman, K. (1990). *Theories of Object Relations: Bridges to Self Psychology.* New York: Columbia University Press.

Balint, M. (1968). *The Basic Fault: Therapeutic Aspects of Regression.* London: Tavistock Publications.

Boston Change Process Study Group (2010). *Change in Psychotherapy: A Unifying Paradigm.* New York: W.W. Norton.

Beebe, B., & Lachmann, F. M. (2002). *Infant Research and Adult Treatment: Co-Constructing Interactions.* Hillsdale, NJ: Analytic Press.

Benjamin, J. (1988). *The Bonds of Love: Psychoanalysis, Feminism, and the Problem of Domination.* New York: Pantheon Books.

Benjamin, J. (1990). An outline of intersubjectivity: The development of recognition. *Psychoanalytic Psychology,* 7(Supp.): 33–46.

Benjamin, J. (2004). Beyond doer and done to: An intersubjective view of thirdness. *Psychoanalytic Quarterly,* 73(1): 5–46.

Bion, W. R. (1962). *Learning from Experience.* London: William Heinemann Medical Books.

Brenman Pick, I. (1985). Working through in the countertransference. *International Journal of Psychoanalysis,* 66(2): 157–166.

Cooper, A. M. (1986). Narcissism. In A. P. Morrison (Ed.), *Essential Papers on Narcissism,* pp. 112–143. New York: New York University Press.

Cooper, A. M. (1988). How does analysis cure? *Journal of the American Psychoanalytic Association,* 36(3): 175–179.

Fairbairn, W. R. D. (1952). *Psychoanalytic Studies of the Personality.* London: Tavistock Publications.

Ferenczi, S. (1913 [1952]). Stages in the development of the sense of reality. In E. Jones (Ed.), *First Contributions to Psycho-Analysis,* pp. 213–239. London: Hogarth Press.

Freud, S. (1893 [1955]). Studies on hysteria. In J. Strachey (Ed. & Trans.), *The Standard Edition of the Complete Psychological Works of Sigmund Freud,* Vol. II, pp. 1–306. London: Hogarth Press.

Freud, S. (1905 [1953]). Three essays on the theory of sexuality. In J. Strachey (Ed. & Trans.), *The Standard Edition of the Complete Psychological Works of Sigmund Freud,* Vol. VII, pp. 135–243. London: Hogarth Press.

Freud, S. (1908 [1959]). Character and anal erotism. In J. Strachey (Ed. & Trans.), *The Standard Edition of the Complete Psychological Works of Sigmund Freud,* Vol. IX, 167–176. London: Hogarth Press.

Freud, S. (1914 [1957]). On narcissism: An introduction. In J. Strachey (Ed. & Trans.), *The Standard Edition of the Complete Psychological Works of Sigmund Freud,* Vol. XIV, pp. 67–102. London: Hogarth Press.

Freud, S. (1917 [1955]). On transformations of instincts as exemplified in anal erotism. In J. Strachey (Ed. & Trans.), *The Standard Edition of the Complete Psychological Works of Sigmund Freud,* Vol. XVII, pp. 125–133. London: Hogarth Press.

Freud, S. (1923 [1961]). The ego and the id. In J. Strachey (Ed. & Trans.), *The Standard Edition of the Complete Psychological Works of Sigmund Freud,* Vol. XIX, pp. 12–66. London: Hogarth Press.

Gadamer, H.-G. (1975). Hermeneutics and social science. *Philosophy and Social Criticism,* 2(4): 307–316.

Gallese, V., Eagle, M. N., & Migone, P. (2007). Intentional attunement: Mirror neurons and neural underpinnings of interpersonal relations. *Journal of the American Psychoanalytic Association,* 55(1): 131–166.

Glover, E. (1955). *The Technique of Psycho-Analysis.* New York: International Universities Press.

Goldberg, A. (1999). *Being of Two Minds: The Vertical Split in Psychoanalysis and Psychotherapy.* Hillsdale, NJ: Analytic Press.

Hegel, G. W. F. (1807 [1967]). *The Phenomenology of Mind* (J. B. Baillie, Trans.). New York: Harper Torchbooks.

Joseph, B. (1983). On understanding and not understanding: Some technical issues. *International Journal of Psychoanalysis*, 64(2): 291–298.

Kernberg, O. F. (2004). *Aggressivity, Narcissism, and Self-Destructiveness in the Psychotherapeutic Relationship: New Developments in the Psychopathology and Psychotherapy of Severe Personality Disorders.* New Haven, CT: Yale University Press.

Kohut, H. (1959 [1978]). In P. H. Ornstein (Ed.), *The Search for the Self: Selected Writings of Heinz Kohut 1950–1978*, Vol. I, pp. 205–232. New York: International Universities Press.

Kohut, H. (1966). Forms and transformations of narcissism. *Journal of the American Psychoanalytic Association*, 14(2): 243–272.

Kohut, H. (1970 [1978]). Narcissism as a resistance and as a driving force in psychoanalysis. In P. H. Ornstein (Ed.), *The Search for the Self: Selected Writings of Heinz Kohut 1950–1978*, Vol. II, pp. 547–561. New York: International Universities Press.

Kohut, H. (1971). *The Analysis of the Self: A Systematic Approach to the Psychoanalytic Treatment of Narcissistic Personality Disorder.* New York: International Universities Press.

Kohut, H. (1972). Thoughts on narcissism and narcissistic rage. *Psychoanalytic Study of the Child*, 27(1): 360–400.

Kohut, H. (1977). *The Restoration of the Self.* New York: International Universities Press.

Kohut, H. (1979 [1991]). Four basic concepts in self psychology. In P. H. Ornstein (Ed.), *The Search for the Self: Selected Works of Heinz Kohut 1978–1981*, Vol. IV, pp. 447–470. Madison, WI: International Universities Press.

Kohut, H. (1984). *How Does Analysis Cure?* (A. Goldberg & P. Stepansky, Eds.). Chicago: University of Chicago Press.

Lachmann, F. M. (1986). Interpretation of psychic conflict and adversarial relationships: A self psychological perspective. *Psychoanalytic Psychology*, 3(4): 341–355.

LaFarge, L. (2015). The fog of disappointment, the cliffs of disillusionment, the abyss of despair. *Journal of the American Psychoanalytic Association*, 63(6): 1225–1239.

Lichtenberg, J. D. (1989). *Psychoanalysis and Motivation.* Hillsdale, NJ: Analytic Press.

Loewald, H. W. (1960). On the therapeutic action of psychoanalysis. *International Journal of Psychoanalysis*, 41(1): 16–33.

Loewald, H. W. (1973 [1980]). Book review: Heinz Kohut, *The Analysis of the Self.* In *Papers on Psychoanalysis*, pp. 342–352. New Haven, CT: Yale University Press.

Ogden, T. H. (1994). The analytic third: Working with intersubjective clinical facts. *International Journal of Psychoanalysis*, 75(1): 3–19.

Ornstein, A. (1991). The dread to repeat: Comments on the working-through process in psychoanalysis. *Journal of the American Psychoanalytic Association*, 39(2): 377–398.

Ornstein, A. (1995). The fate of the curative fantasy in the psychoanalytic treatment process. *Contemporary Psychoanalysis*, 31(1): 113–123.

Ornstein, A. (1998). The fate of narcissistic rage in psychotherapy. *Psychoanalytic Inquiry*, 18(1): 55–70.

Ornstein, A., & Ornstein, P. H. (1996). Speaking in the interpretive mode and feeling understood: Crucial aspects of the therapeutic action in psychotherapy. In L. Lifson (Ed.), *Understanding Therapeutic Action: Psychodynamic Concepts of Cure*, pp. 87–101. Hillsdale, NJ: Analytic Press.

Ornstein, P. H. (Ed.) (1978a). *The Search for the Self: Selected Writings of Heinz Kohut 1950–1978*, Vol. I. New York: International Universities Press.

Ornstein, P. H. (Ed.) (1978b). *The Search for the Self: Selected Writings of Heinz Kohut 1950–1978*, Vol. II. New York: International Universities Press.

Ornstein, P. H. (Ed.) (1990). *The Search for the Self: Selected Writings of Heinz Kohut 1978–1981*, Vol. III. Madison, WI: International Universities Press.

Ornstein, P. H. (Ed.) (1991). *The Search for the Self: Selected Writings of Heinz Kohut 1978–1981*, Vol. IV. Madison, WI: International Universities Press.

Ornstein, P. H. (1993). Chronic rage from underground: Reflections on its structure and treatment. *Progress in Self Psychology*, 9: 143–157.

Ornstein, P. H. (2011). The centrality of empathy in psychoanalysis. *Psychoanalytic Inquiry*, 31(5): 437–447.

Parens, H. (1979). Aggression: A reconsideration. *Journal of the American Psychoanalytic Association*, 21(1): 34–60.

Racker, H. (1953). A contribution to the problem of countertransference. *International Journal of Psychoanalysis*, 34(2): 313–324.

Rapaport, D., & Gill, M. M. (1959). The points of view and assumptions of metapsychology. *International Journal of Psychoanalysis*, 40(1): 153–162.

Reich, A. (1953). Narcissistic object choice in women. *Journal of the American Psychoanalytic Association*, 1(1): 22–44.

Sander, L. W. (1995). Identity and the experience of specificity in a process of recognition. *Psychoanalytic Dialogues*, 5(4): 579–593.

Sandler, J., Holder, A., & Meers, D. (1963). The ego ideal and the ideal self. *Psychoanalytic Study of the Child*, 18(1): 139–158.

Schafer, R. (1983). The analysis of resisting. In *The Analytic Attitude*, pp. 162–182. New York: Basic Books.

Schwaber, E. (1981). Narcissism, self psychology and the listening perspective. *The Annual of Psychoanalysis*, 9: 115–131.

Stern, D. B. (1997). *Unformulated Experience: From Dissociation to Imagination in Psychoanalysis*. Hillsdale, NJ: Analytic Press.

Stern, D. N. (1985). *The Interpersonal World of the Infant: A View from Psychoanalysis and Developmental Psychology*. New York: Basic Books.

Stern, D. N. (1992). One way to build a clinically relevant baby. *Infant Mental Health Journal*, 15(1): 36–54.

Stern, D. N., Sander, L. W., Nahum, J. P., Harrison, A. M., Lyons-Ruth, K., Morgan, A. C., Bruschweiler-Stern, N., & Tronick, E. Z. (1998). Non-interpretive mechanisms in psychoanalytic therapy: The "something more" than interpretation. *International Journal of Psychoanalysis*, 79(5): 903–921.

Steyn, L. (2013). Tactics and empathy: Tactics against projective identification. *International Journal of Psychoanalysis*, 94(6): 1093–1113.

Stolorow, R. D. (1975). Toward a functional definition of narcissism. *International Journal of Psychoanalysis*, 56(1): 179–185.

Stolorow, R. D., & Atwood, G. E. (1996). The intersubjective perspective. *Psychoanalytic Review*, 83(2): 181–194.

Stolorow, R. D., Brandchaft, B., & Atwood, G. E. (1987). *Psychoanalytic Treatment: An Intersubjective Approach*. Hillsdale, NJ: Analytic Press.

Stolorow, R. D., & Lachmann, F. M. (1984). Transference: The future of an illusion. *The Annual of Psychoanalysis*, 12(1): 19–37.

Stone, L. (1954). The widening scope of indications for psychoanalysis. *Journal of the American Psychoanalytic Association*, 2(4): 567–594.

Teicholz, J. (1999). *Loewald, Kohut and the Postmoderns: A Comprehensive Study of Self and Relationship*. Hillsdale, NJ: Analytic Press.

Trop, J., & Stolorow, R. D. (1992). Defense analysis in self psychology: A developmental view. *Psychoanalytic Dialogues*, 2(4): 427–442.

Winnicott, D. W. (1951 [1958]). Transitional objects and transitional phenomena. In *Through Paediatrics to Psycho-Analysis: Collected Papers*, pp. 229–242. London: Tavistock Publications.

Winnicott, D. W. (1969). The use of an object. *International Journal of Psychoanalysis*, 50(4): 711–716.

Wolf, E. (1985). The search for confirmation: Technical aspects of mirroring. *Psychoanalytic Inquiry*, 5(2): 271–282.

Wolf, E. (1988). *Treating the Self: Elements of Clinical Self Psychology*. New York: Guilford Press.

9

INTERPERSONAL PSYCHOANALYSIS

Eugenio Duarte

Introduction

Introducing someone to interpersonal psychoanalysis is much like introducing someone to New York City. You can never show someone *the* New York City but only *your* New York City – the things about it that you love and enjoy, and are special enough to share with someone else. Similarly, I cannot acquaint you with the one and only interpersonal psychoanalytic orientation, because such a thing does not exist. What I can do is introduce you to my own interpersonal psychoanalysis, because, as a particular way of thinking and working, interpersonal psychoanalysis, broadly speaking, is underpinned by certain core principles – but it cannot be pinned down. It defies singular definition, yet speaks to many therapists in uniquely meaningful ways. So, what I offer in this chapter are the ideas and approaches from the interpersonal orientation that I find most useful, special and exciting.

I will begin with key ideas that serve as the foundation for later, more specific applications of interpersonal concepts. One such foundational idea is the assumption of *participant observation*, which is the understanding that, as therapists, we influence what we observe. I will discuss how this basic idea evolved into the understanding that *one cannot not interact* with one's patient – that is, that the observing participation runs both ways and that analyst and patient are constantly acting on one another. This understanding necessarily changes our conception of the role of the analyst in the clinical encounter. I will also discuss how interpersonalists conceive of the analyst as *riding a wave* rather than steering a ship in the consulting room. Next, I will acquaint you with one of the most well-known products of the interpersonal orientation: the *detailed inquiry*. Following this review of core ideas will be key implications of an interpersonal approach, such as the importance of psychoanalytic humility and the natural fit between interpersonal psychoanalysis and multicultural competence. The chapter will conclude with an examination of

192 Eugenio Duarte

some limitations of the interpersonal approach and the benefits of integrating interpersonal ideas with those of other theoretical orientations.

Participant observation

Participant observation is a basic concept that underlies many of the more specific ideas and techniques that will be discussed later. Participant observation is not a technique but a guiding assumption that interpersonalists maintain about the nature of their involvement in their clinical work. As such, participant observation is something that either you believe to be the case in your clinical interactions or you do not – and I am a believer. The assumption of participant observation is the assumption that the analyst influences the patient's experience by virtue of observing it – in contrast to the more traditional assumption that one can observe a person or phenomenon without affecting the person or thing one is observing. From the perspective of participant observation, the analyst is unable, by design, to ever observe the patient "from the outside." One practical and important clinical implication is that, as therapists, we are limited in the degree to which we can generalize from what we see in the consulting room to what takes place in the patient's life outside the consulting room. We would make such generalizations only if we thought of ourselves as unobtrusive "flies on the wall," watching but not influencing our patients. The assumption of participant observation denies this mythical idea and forces us to accept the reality that we shape what we see.

To illustrate, if you are working with a patient who speaks rapidly and tangentially and even interrupts you throughout the session, you would not conclude that this patient's in-session behavior is a straightforward replica of his or her out-of-session behavior – at least not if you are someone who believes in participant observation. Instead, you would consider the possibility that the patient's rapid and erratic speech is elicited and maintained, in part, as a response to some aspect of your own behavior or mere presence. Your patient's unique speech patterns may be some kind of response to how you are participating with him or her. And, even if it can be established that this patient behaves this way with almost everyone in his or her life, it would still behoove you to wonder why the pattern recreates itself with you now and to wonder how your participation fits with that behavior. Working under the assumption of participant observation means giving up any claim to pure objectivity or neutrality. It means conceding – or, better yet, embracing – that you always have a role in co-creating the phenomena you observe.

In my day-to-day practice, the assumption of participant observation lies in the background of my awareness, while the details and nuances of the explicit interaction I am having with my patient are in the foreground. But foreground and background can swap places, particularly when the interaction takes an unexpected turn, leaving me puzzled about what is happening. In such a moment, I lean on my awareness of participant observation to help me make meaning out of the situation. For example, a male patient who struggles with eating problems tells me about all the progress he has made in the past week, bingeing less and eating more intuitively.

He feels proud of himself and hopeful about his ability to work through other difficulties he never felt he could resolve. After elaborating on these thoughts and feelings for some time, he pauses. After a minute of silence, he becomes a bit somber and changes topic to a recent argument with his partner, who criticized him for being at times unreliable and forgetful. My patient complains of feeling doubtful that he can improve enough to please his partner and worries about being dumped. I find myself puzzled by his sudden shift in topic and tone and wonder what just happened.

As I mentally scroll back through our interaction, I realize that I remained silent while he was talking about his recent accomplishments in the area of eating. At this point, my awareness of being a participant observer leads me to wonder whether my patient's shift in topic and mood were in some way a response to my silence. I tell him that I have noticed his shift and ask him what he thinks it is about. He tells me that he interpreted my silence as an indication that his accomplishments were not as big a deal to me as they were to him, which led him to wonder if perhaps he was undeservedly patting himself on the back. He then felt a bit ashamed and motivated to explore other areas of his life where he could still make improvement. He also tells me he felt disappointed by my failure to congratulate him, because it matters to him that I be proud of his accomplishments. What follows is a conversation about his long-standing wish for someone to be proud of him and how my characteristically placid way of responding to statements of accomplishment sometimes clashes with his characteristic need for laudation.

This example illustrates how even subtle, nearly imperceptible aspects of our behavior with our patients can have significant influences on what our patients say, how they feel and how they behave. It also demonstrates how explicitly attending to the participatory nature of your ongoing observation in the consulting room can illuminate subtle but important dimensions of the patient's experience and of the ongoing relatedness between patient and therapist.

The idea of participant observation thus teaches us that we can never totally neutralize our influence on the clinical exchanges in which we participate. However, we can make efforts to reduce it, and it is sometimes helpful to do so. That is, it is possible to stay out of the patient's way to some degree, which can be helpful for patients who need extra silence and space to formulate their thoughts and feelings. I find that one of the conditions that facilitates this reduction in the therapist's explicit influence is use of the couch. In my own practice, I recommend use of the couch to patients who have difficulties attending to and articulating their own thoughts and feelings in the presence of someone else, particularly someone whose opinion matters to them. Some patients cannot help but constantly monitor my facial expressions and nonverbal gestures for signs of approval or disapproval. Others find the sitting-up arrangement too reminiscent of casual conversations and unfavorable for exploring more primitive, inchoate experiences. Use of the couch – which moves me out of the patient's direct line of vision – can help such patients tune me out sufficiently that they can more easily hear themselves think and say out loud what would feel risky to say while facing me.

Use of the couch is only one way by which therapists can reduce their explicit influence. Another is, simply put, shutting up. When a patient is "on a roll" – a phenomenon that is difficult to define but recognizable to most therapists – the best thing is often to let her continue her flow until she reaches a natural stopping point, even if there are silent pauses along the way. Making comments or asking questions during these pauses may interrupt a process that is already under way that does not need the analyst's explicit assistance. A less extreme way of reducing one's analytic influence is by keeping one's comments and questions short. A simple "How did that happen?" or "Wow!" can serve as a useful reminder that you are actively listening, without disrupting the patient's associative flow. Such comments also protect the patient's autonomous thinking and associating by reducing the analyst's relative influence, though they don't eliminate it. A patient who I see twice weekly, on the couch, often says to me "Are you OK? I heard you breathe funny" or pauses altogether if she hears me shift in my chair. Such moments remind me that, in the end, I am not a neutral, unobtrusive observer but, rather, a participating one.

You cannot not interact

Although Harry Stack Sullivan (1970) made us aware of the impossibility of neutralizing our influence, he seemed to believe that the therapist can be aware of this influence and use it productively. He did not believe in objective, removed observation but he did believe that the therapist was the relative expert in the room on interpersonal relations and had a better grasp than the patient of what was happening during the clinical hour. In taking this position, Sullivan assumed greater power and clarity in the consulting room than later interpersonal analysts would claim to possess.

Since Sullivan's time, one of the most fascinating developments in interpersonal psychoanalysis has been its increasing embrace of mystery, uncertainty and surprise in the clinical encounter. Contemporary interpersonal psychoanalysts aim to be comfortable with and even embrace – more so than many of their predecessors – moments of not knowing what is going on. We embrace such uncertainty and mystery because we accept that we have unconscious motives and blind spots, just like our patients, and that we enter the clinical encounter as equally flawed human beings with our own needs, desires, fears and histories. And, despite our best attempts to privilege our patients' needs over our own, we sometimes behave in ways that unwittingly serve the latter.

In learning about and understanding these ideas, one of the individuals who has been most helpful to me is Edgar Levenson. Over the last five decades, Levenson (1972, 1983, 1991) has expanded Sullivan's ideas and written about how both members of the therapeutic dyad unwittingly act on and affect one other. Through his writings, Levenson has made me consider that we are always acting upon each other in the consulting room, always communicating to and behaving with each other in perceptible and imperceptible ways. His ideas are well captured by an aphorism popular among interpersonalists: "You cannot not interact" (Levenson, 2009).

Sensible though this assumption might seem at first blush, it is a radical departure from the assumption that guides the work of analysts and therapists with more classical or traditional orientations, namely that one can "turn off" one's influence on the patient or inoculate oneself from the patient's influence. Analysts who adopt these latter assumptions tend to lean on them most heavily during moments of strong countertransference. For instance, a male patient complains to his more classical analyst about his college-age daughter's interest in becoming an actor rather than a doctor just like him. The analyst finds herself feeling irritation at her patient's self-centeredness and empathy toward the unsupported daughter. She notices her irritation and fears speaking in a way that will unduly hurt her patient, so she remains silent. After ten minutes of such silence from the analyst, the patient moves from griping about his daughter's silly career aspirations to examining his own ambivalence about medicine as a profession. The analyst, feeling less irritated and a bit pleased by her patient's self-examination, comes out of her silence and makes comments about her patient's associations.

If the analyst in this scenario is one who operates by more traditional assumptions of mutual influence, it is quite likely that she will think her silence helped the patient and the process along. So might interpersonal psychoanalysts, but for different reasons. More traditional analysts might think that their emotional state at the time of their patient's paternal griping threatened to jeopardize their neutrality and render them incapable of nonjudgmentally interpreting their patient's experience. They would further assume that, by remaining quiet, they encouraged their patient to explore his own thoughts and feelings free from his subjective opinion, which in turn allowed him to arrive at a more genuinely introspective place on his own.

As an interpersonal analyst, I would not necessarily dispute that the analyst in this case made a good choice nor that the session moved in a useful direction as a result of her silence. In fact, I would be less concerned with judging the interaction in positive or negative terms and more interested in understanding what happened between the two participants and what motives were involved. What I would dispute is the analyst's assumption that her silence protected the patient from her private irritation. In my interpersonal view, the analyst's silence simply constituted a different form of active behavior toward patient and can be thought of as both a response to the patient's behavior and an outgrowth of the analyst's own motives, feelings and personhood.

Perhaps this kind of selfish griping is something the patient does frequently and maybe the analyst has grown tired of hearing it. Perhaps it reminds her of her own parents' discouragement of her pursuit of a doctoral degree in clinical psychology and her silence serves to passive-aggressively punish the patient for his repetition of the same crime. Perhaps this therapist once dreamt of being an actor herself but never pursued it and rarely thinks about it now, so in her silence she identifies with the unsupported daughter. Perhaps this analyst demonstrates more patience when her patient complains about matters that do not press on personal buttons the way this one does. All these possibilities illustrate the notion that the therapist's behavior toward his or her patient contains traces of his or her own experiences and motives. To be clear, what matters is not what precise motives and affects were silently operative in the clinical vignette but that there *were* silent motives and affects in play. Those factors are among the things an interpersonal analyst would be most attentive to in the service of understanding the evolution of the therapeutic relationship.

To offer another illustration, take something as concrete and seemingly technical as a suicide assessment. We have all been trained to ask more or less the same questions and clarify the same factors when a patient indicates suicidality. We inquire about quality and degree of ideation, intent, plan, means and lethality; precipitating events; protective factors; and possibilities of a safety plan. We may each have our characteristic ways of conducting such an assessment but we probably all have the same goals in mind: to find out exactly what is going on so that we might take the necessary steps to keep our patient safe. Therefore, when doing a suicide assessment, it is easy to feel that what we are doing is fairly standard and not much influenced by the ebbs and flow of the therapeutic relationship. One can feel like a technician executing a pre-packaged set of actions and feel OK with that, since one's singular focus is assessing and securing the safety of one's patient.

Yet, from an interpersonal psychoanalytic point of view, talking to your patient about her suicidality and making efforts to secure her safety constitute an interpersonal event, one that will make a significant mark on the trajectory of the therapeutic relationship and afford understanding that may be healing for the patient. An easy way to imagine this idea in action is to think about the last time you conducted a suicide assessment with an ongoing patient and ask yourself: What led you to ask about suicidality in that moment, of all moments? What were you feeling? What might your patient have thought and felt about you taking her expressions of hopelessness and hints of self-harm so seriously and literally? Do other people in her life do so? Is it typical, within the history of your relationship with this patient, for you to respond this way? And how typical is it for your patient to speak like this? Have there been times when you have responded differently to similarly ominous statements? How did you feel those other times and how was it different from how you feel now? Will the fact of this assessment influence whether and how your patient expresses similar feelings again in the future? Has this instance made her feel safe and supported enough to explore these feelings in more depth or will she censor herself next time to avoid triggering what she deems your exaggerated worry? How does she feel about having someone care so much about her safety and wellbeing? And how do you feel about having a patient whose safety is a concern of yours? Do you worry about her, or might her frankness in answering your questions put you more at ease?

An event such as this one, like any other, can be understood to have short- and long-term ripple effects on the overall course of the therapy relationship. What is tricky is that one can rarely predict when the effect of the event will be noticed or felt, and what the nature of that effect will be. I feel both daunted and somehow reassured by this fact. As an interpersonal analyst, knowing that I cannot know how any one interaction will affect the evolution of the relationship frees me to

Interpersonal psychoanalysis **197**

approach difficult moments with greater curiosity than fear about how things will unfold.

Riding the wave

I hope by now it is clear that interpersonal psychoanalysts are open to states of not knowing, mystery and uncertainty. Although we do make interpretations, ask questions and try to understand what is going on with our patients, we do not consider these activities to be the center of mutative action. Our approach is expansive rather than reductive. We are infinitely curious about the many layers of our patients' experiences. We understand psychoanalysis to be a process involving continuous deconstruction of the material into increasingly complex networks of meaning and we consider this process itself to be curative. In our view, what heals patients is not exploration in the service of eventual explanation but the exploration itself. As analysts, we are constantly turning over new stones with our patients. This process helps them, not because there are explanatory pearls waiting underneath such stones, but because patients who were never very curious about their own experience learn to be. They learn to see the stones and gain the courage to turn them over themselves.

To speak metaphorically, the interpersonal analyst is not so much steering a ship as riding a wave, not directing a process so much as protecting and supporting it. Even when we think we are being directive – for instance, by asking questions or commenting on specific aspects of the material – we understand that we are always under the influence of the ebbs and flows of the relationship and that our behavior is always shaped by past twists and turns. We take for granted that we can never step outside the ongoing flow of mutual relatedness happening between ourselves and our patients.

Viewing ourselves as servants of the analytic process rather than the other way around disposes us toward some surrender of control and some embrace of uncertainty and surprise. We do our best to act in ways that will be useful to our patients and to the analytic process but accepting that we are not ultimately in charge of how things evolve in the treatment gives us little choice but to approach new developments in the work, especially unpleasant or difficult ones, with curiosity rather than judgment. We aim to think of all developments as new data about which to be curious rather than critical.

To illustrate, while preparing this chapter, I had what felt like a "bad session" with an analytic patient I had been seeing for a few years. This session happened during a couple of weeks when I had been finding myself frequently annoyed and grated upon by the patient. He had a habit of canceling sessions via text with little notice, and had just done it again, and I felt irritated and devalued. When I saw him next, he sat down and launched right into a lengthy description of the unfortunate events that had made it impossible for him to attend. I sensed that he expected me to unquestionably accept this explanation and not wonder about possible unconscious motives on his part. But his story did not add up, despite his insistence that it should. I asked questions about those parts of the story that did not make sense to me. As I did, he became defensive and eventually angry. He felt I was accusing him of making lame excuses. I denied such an intention and tried my best to articulate my inchoate sense that something significant was happening between us vis-à-vis this pattern of last-minute cancelations. I tried my best to convey curiosity rather than accusation, but he seemed to experience me as doing the opposite. This discussion took up the whole session, and, when it ended, neither of us felt that anything had been resolved or gained. I felt generally bad, as though I had failed at doing my job and perhaps even inflicted harm on my patient and on the treatment.

Walking home that night, I wondered whether I had been too aggressive or hostile, whether I had acted out my countertransference rather than held it and processed it on my own for later understanding and therapeutic use. Perhaps I had lost my cool and taken his cancelation too personally. I considered all sorts of explanations, each of which implicated me as having behaved badly and led to the conclusion that I needed to make some kind of attitudinal and behavioral change. But then my interpersonalist self-state kicked in. I reconnected with my core interpersonal values and remembered what I hold to be true about the work we do: that analytic events and behavior are not good or bad but surprising or familiar; that the ongoing relatedness between us will inevitably take us in unexpected directions and evoke unexpected and even difficult reactions; that I could not claim to know, in any positivistic sense, what this thorny interaction meant, whether it should or should not have happened, nor whether I was the one who made it happen.

As I allowed my interpersonal values to wash over me and allowed myself to be less certain about what had just happened, I realized that I needed to take a similarly curious and open attitude to my ideas about what might happen next. That is, rather than think in terms of what I should or should not do next, I found my way to a more "Let's see what happens" stance. And, suddenly, I looked forward to my next session with this patient, not as an opportunity to correct for bad behavior on my part, nor to make things right, but as a chance to observe what effect the session had on him, how it compares with the effect it had on me, and what he and I will end up doing with those felt impacts together. I also looked forward to the chance to gain some understanding about what might have happened in the heat of the moment to explain my temporary loss of curiosity.

I do not mean to convey that interpersonalists do not constructively critique their own work and try to improve; we certainly do. What I mean to illustrate with this example is that, by seeing ourselves as servants and protectors of an unpredictable but healing analytic process, we strive to consider the multiple and complex meanings that any clinical moment might have without needing to control or fix the moment in question, even the difficult ones. Our belief in the healing power of expanding complexity is well captured by something the well-known interpersonalist, Darlene Ehrenberg, said to me one day in class during my analytic training.[1] I asked her how she ever knows whether the analytic process is moving along productively and she said, "When the patient starts having new associations, that's how you know you're onto something." What I learned from her is that my job is not to arrive at reductive explanations but to facilitate the emergence of fresh ideas

Interpersonal psychoanalysis **199**

and new paths, because that means the patient's ways of seeing his or her world are evolving.

Detailed inquiry

As interpersonal analysts, we get to ask questions. Curiosity is an important tool in the psychoanalytic process. By wondering about the details of a patient's life and being curious about those things we do not understand, we avoid premature conclusions and foster the patient's ability to think about his experience in new ways and see patterns he had not seen before.

Sandra Buechler (2004) teaches us that our questions are also interpretations. When I ask my patient about a particular thing, I am also conveying that such a thing is worthy of special consideration – perhaps more so than other things about which I am not asking at that moment. Levenson (1972, 1983), similarly, tells us that speech is behavior – that when we speak to our patients, we also act toward them, as do our patients when they speak to us. So, when I ask my patient a question, I am having an impact on him by way of directing him to wonder about a particular thing.

I value questions but that does not mean they are how I begin sessions. Typically, I allow the patient to start while I listen attentively to the material and see where it goes. My behavior may be limited to verbalizations such as "Hmm" or "Huh," a summary statement here or there, and an occasional reaction to what I am hearing. If I find myself moved or affected in a particular way by a certain part of the material, though, I may at that point ask questions and engage in a more explicit form of questioning that interpersonalists call the *detailed inquiry* (Sullivan, 1970; Levenson, 1991).

Usually, what prompts such a shift on my part is what Donnel Stern (2010) calls *chafing*. Something about what the patient is saying, or how she is saying it, leaves me with a funny feeling – the kind one has when events as they are told to you do not quite add up or make sense. As my mother likes to put it, "Two and two are not equaling four." Often, one does not even know why things do not make sense; one simply registers that they do not or that something is missing. Interpersonalists believe that this feeling emerges when patient and analyst traverse over dissociative waters. The material contains aspects tied to shame or anxiety for the patient, and so the patient narrates her life in a way designed to circumvent those areas. The funny feeling or chafing the analyst experiences is her way of registering the existence of these omissions or dissociated experiences. The patient does not leave out certain details on purpose; she simply engages in what Sullivan (1956) called *selective inattention* to those details. They are dissociated. To the patient, the narrative makes sense and flows seamlessly, but, to you, the analyst, whose personality and history are organized along different lines of awareness and dissociation from the patient's, it does not. So the detailed inquiry can help bring these anxiety- and shame-ridden bits of experience out of the darkness of dissociation and into the light of conscious awareness.

In my own work, when I feel the kind of chafing just described and have some idea of what seems to be missing from the story, I ask about the missing part, which kick-starts a progressive unfolding and expansion of the narrative into areas never before narrated. To illustrate, a male analytic patient in his early forties begins his second session of the week by announcing that he just lost his job. He says he did not see it coming and feels surprised and indignant. He assures me that the termination had nothing to do with anything he did wrong and that he was laid off, not fired, because his employer no longer had enough work for him to do. Over the next several minutes he seems defensive and insists on explaining the myriad ways that he did nothing to deserve being terminated. He also describes this event as yet another example of how things never work out for him despite his best efforts.

At some point, he off-handedly mentions that he tended to arrive at least 15 minutes late to work almost daily. When I ask about it, he insists that his lateness did not matter to his supervisor, who also tended to arrive late. When I ask if his supervisor ever brought his tardiness to his attention, he says he never even noticed it, which means it could not have possibly caused his termination of employment. He further mentions that on several occasions he made what others deemed off-color jokes in front of his supervisor. When I ask about these jokes, he complains that his coworkers lacked a sense of humor and cared too much about political correctness.

At this point, I begin to privately wonder about several things, such as: Why would his supervisor not ever address his tardiness? Is it because it would have exposed his own hypocrisy, since he also arrived late? Is it possible his supervisors did bring it up to my patient, who has somehow "forgotten" those discussions? Why was he always arriving late anyway? And why does he need to believe that his supervisor never noticed it? Have there been other occasions when he has sought comfort in the fantasy of invisibility? If so, what does he achieve by convincing himself that no one sees him misbehaving? Has he considered that bosses are often not held to the same standards of punctuality as employees? And how would he rate his overall performance at this job anyway? Was he really trying to do well at the job? If so, what were his incentives for making a good impression? And what jokes exactly was he telling? What did others find offensive about them, and does my patient truly not understand why that was so? Is it a cultural thing – that is, might his cultural identity include a conception of humor that is different from that of the mainstream culture?

Of these questions, I ask only a few of them aloud to my patient. When I do, they elicit more defensive explanations. After all, if he has left out from his story the details about which I am asking, it is for a reason: they do not fit with the narrative he wants to construct about his experience. For instance, when I ask why he was always late to begin with, he blames the inconsistent subway trains and hesitates entertaining other motives. If there were unconscious or dissociated motives at play, they may not be the kind he wants to know or reveal. Talking about them would disrupt his preferred way of understanding his life and prompt him to reorganize his experience in novel ways, taking into account information about his motives and feelings that he does not yet recognize as his own.

You might wonder why I would want to disrupt my patient's preferred way of narrating his life. After all, if it allows him to avoid feeling ashamed and guilty about an upsetting experience such as getting fired, why would I take that away? My aim is not to make my patient's life more difficult or painful but to increase his freedom and options for dealing with challenges. When I conduct a detailed inquiry into the nuances of how my patient handles difficult life events, I work from the assumption that he dissociates those experiences he does not know how to handle or make sense of any other way. I understand him to be suffering from a case of limited options and narrow vision, and I want to help him change that.

My questions led to a discussion about his anxiety about failure and a felt lack of power at the workplace. It was his fifth job in just two years, so he was starting to feel insecure about his professional and social skills. He really needed the job – for his bank account and self-esteem. He felt on pins and needles with his supervisor, afraid to make mistakes but also afraid to assert himself when his needs were not being met. To him, his supervisor held all the power in the relationship. He felt at his mercy, resentful about this arrangement and ashamed about his chaotic professional life. Arriving late and making tasteless jokes were the only ways he could have a conscious experience of being in control and immune from his supervisor's criticism while dissociating his desperate need to do well and earn his approval. Telling himself that no one was bothered by his misbehavior nor his humor allowed him to disown his awareness of the kind of professional danger in which he was placing himself.

The problem is that my patient had barely any conscious experience of the feelings and needs he was acting out through his problematic behavior. It was not until our detailed inquiry that he began to wonder about potential motives and feelings. He did not have any awareness that he felt desperate and insecure at work nor that he was behaving in ways to counter those feelings and produce opposite ones. In fact, he had never thought that his behavior was at all remarkable or worthy of attention – until I did. And, to return to how we started, this whole process was set off not by my having the conscious thought that his tardiness or jokes might be relevant factors in his firing but by listening to his story and registering a faint feeling that something about it was amiss. By following up on that feeling with questions into the details he was barely mentioning, we proceeded down a path that led through his pattern of silent rebellion and further down into his disowned feelings of inferiority and inadequacy. The ensuing discussion allowed my patient to become more aware of certain aspects of his emotional life at work and to reflect on the choices he had made to deal with those feelings in order to, ultimately, make more effective ones.

I am a fan of the detailed inquiry. One of the things that I have learned from using it so much is that in addition to the individual meta-messages conveyed by one's questions – i.e., "These are important details to examine" – there is a meta-meta-message also being communicated: "How you live your life is worthy of your curiosity." I find that some of my patients need time to get used to this kind of curiosity. They are not accustomed to thinking that banal details matter as much as they do to me. But once we have been working together for a while, and they have become accustomed to my taking such deep interest in the nuances of their lived experiences and interpersonal worlds, they are able to anticipate the kinds of questions I might ask or the kinds of details I might find worth examining further. They will relate a story and, before I can ask something, will say "I know what you're probably wondering..." followed by a question I would likely ask. I think there is reason to believe that, at some point during the course of the treatment, my patients start to wonder why they are not as curious about their lives as I am, or why their therapist needs to be the one to always ask certain questions. They eventually internalize my curiosity, it becomes their own and they start to pose questions to themselves that have not yet occurred to me. The gift of the detailed inquiry is not just the invitation to elucidate unexamined details of one's experience but to examine one's resistance to self-examination in general. The detailed inquiry offers a model for becoming more perplexed about oneself and using it to improve one's life.

Psychoanalytic humility

Use of the detailed inquiry rests on a guiding assumption that goes something like this: Who am I to explain this material or say what it all means? Human experience is too complex and layered to be simplified and reduced. For interpersonalists, there is no necessary endpoint to a detailed inquiry and no need for one. There is always something more to wonder about, always some detail that would add nuance to the story. The patient is better served by exploring and articulating the endless complexity of his or her experience than by reducing it to generalities. During my graduate training I tried my hand at offering patients grand explanations that tied their various experiences together, and, frankly, I was not very good at it. Even when I did manage to offer a compelling interpretation, patients were sometimes impressed but rarely moved.

Explanatory narratives, from an interpersonal point of view, often cause more trouble than good. Humans gravitate toward familiar narratives to make sense of lived experience, which can limit our ability to adapt to new, unexpected realities and our capacity to retain a flexible but stable sense of self in the face of changing circumstances. Psychoanalysis offers patients the unique opportunity to become aware of their preferred narrative tendencies and develop fresh ways of navigating and making sense of their changing worlds. A key point is that analysts are the suppliers not of such alternative narratives but of the curiosity necessary to formulate them.

This approach has important clinical implications. Freeing myself from the responsibility to tie everything together levels the playing field and invites the patient to share in the responsibility of articulating the meaning of his or her experience. When I refrain from explaining what I hear, I assume my patient has some kind of inner intelligence that he or she can use to make sense of what he or she is telling me. If I can resist the urge to explain, and stay out of my patient's way, this inner intelligence will supply the associations, fantasies, sensations and other bits of data that he needs in order to begin making meaning of otherwise dissociated experience.

Such a stance requires what I think of as rigorous psychoanalytic humility. By *psychoanalytic humility*, I mean an attitude of openness to surprise, comfort with not knowing, and willingness to be wrong when one ventures a guess. I offer myself to my patient as someone who will listen closely to what she has to say, attend to my associated thoughts and feelings, and offer them in the spirit of expanding rather than reducing our joint exploration. I understand myself to have no privileged knowledge about what a patient should do, how she should live or what an experience might mean to her. What makes this kind of humility rigorous is that it requires continuous discipline and effort to resist one's natural desire to explain or connect disparate pieces of material. I may share hypotheses and hunches pointing in some vague directions over others but I otherwise operate in a kind of welcome uncertainty and not-knowingness.

To illustrate, if a female patient tells me she is thinking of ending a two-year-long romantic relationship with a partner whom she has described as alternatingly kind and hostile, I likely have thoughts or fantasies about what outcome my patient might find most satisfying but I register those as artifacts of the ongoing relatedness between us rather than indicators of some veritable truth about my patient's best interests. If pressed, I may say to her something like "Well, you more often complain about your partner than praise her. Do you think this says something about what you want or what you should do?" or "You've never seemed too happy with this relationship, at least judging from the conversations we've had about it." But the spirit of such statements is not to lend an authoritative view on the rightness or wrongness of her choice of partner so much as to let my patient know the impression she has given me about her relationship – or, more accurately, the impression I have formed out of the data she has supplied me about her relationship. At best, I can hope she will use what I have shared of my own thoughts and feelings to expand her awareness of her own.

Multicultural awareness

The interpersonal approach is particularly well suited for clinicians who aim to practice in multiculturally competent ways. The interpersonal analyst continually tries to understand how the patient is shaped by her environment – people, places, things, events, customs, beliefs and values – in becoming who she is and in developing her idiosyncratic ways of dealing with life. Interpersonalists believe that a patient becomes who she is not in a vacuum but in the context of a rich family and social milieu, which includes cultural beliefs and practices. The interpersonal analyst is also interested in the details of the patient's life, such as where she was born and grew up; to what parents she was born and what their cultural, religious, ethnic, racial and gender identities were; what the migration patterns were in her family and the reasons and circumstances surrounding such migration; what kind of school she attended, how she performed and how that performance was received by loved ones; what the town was like where she spent most of her life; details about her religious upbringing and the degree to which she still adheres to those religious values; and how her culture of origin views the problems she seeks to address in treatment. These are just a few important considerations among many.

To illustrate, when a female patient in her late thirties complains that her room-mates never pay back the money she lends them nor volunteer to buy groceries for their shared home, I wonder about many things that could shape my understand-ing of her indignation. For instance, what are her views about money? What are some of her most significant experiences involving money? What did her parents teach her about money? How are moneylending and money collection regarded in her culture? What was her family's socioeconomic status growing up and what is it currently? How did her parents earn a living and how carefully, or not, did they guard their earnings? Did she get an allowance as a child and, if so, under what conditions? On what did her parents like to spend money growing up? How does the patient think her family and cultural background influence her current deal-ing with money generally and the situation with her roommates specifically? How does she feel about having roommates and are those feelings informed by her age? What are the ages of her roommates and are there issues of differential maturity at play between them?

These questions, when posed to my patient, prompt her to ponder how her interpersonal world – currently and historically – shapes her dealings with money and other matters that come up for examination. She can then, in turn, ponder how her current attitudes and behavior reflect her unique ways of inter-nalizing or improving upon what she unwittingly learned in her family of ori-gin. This way of approaching clinical material shows how the interpersonal view shares certain tenets in common with systems ways of thinking and working. Interpersonal and systems theories both view the individual patient as a player in a larger family system that nudges him or her to perform certain roles and serve particular interpersonal functions. Helping this patient become aware of such systemic forces and their impact on her individual experience expands her ability to understand the dynamics in which she is caught up that may otherwise seem inexplicable.

This kind of special interest in the impact of patients' cultural and family back-grounds is the hallmark of multiculturally competent clinical practice. In the United States, it is now standard to teach this kind of practice to all students of psychotherapy, who are required to complete various forms of diversity training and multicultural competence coursework. However, in my own experience as a graduate student and later a graduate instructor, the way such training is presented – typically in the form of special courses – can leave students with the impression that multicultural awareness is an add-on rather than a starting point for competent clin-ical practice. In my view, interpersonal psychoanalysis places cultural and familial influences at the center of its theories and practices and, therefore, gives it a more central rather than auxiliary place in clinical work.

Limitations

One limitation of interpersonal psychoanalysis is that, when applied to the exclusion of other approaches, one's approach can be "too interpersonal." That is, one can end up placing disproportionate emphasis on external events, especially interpersonal ones, and not enough on intrapsychic dynamics. This is a fair criticism, if one leans too much on upbringing, culture and other environmental factors in understanding how a patient came to be the way he or she is and not enough on internal or intrapsychic factors, such as unconscious fantasies, wishes and feelings.

Another limitation of interpersonal approaches concerns the risk of adopting an overly confrontational stance when a more patient one would be indicated. The detailed inquiry, in overzealous and misguided hands, can shut down rather than promote the patient's autonomous exploration and growth. Although identifying the holes in the Swiss cheese is a useful way to combat dissociation, sometimes rolling with the resistance can give the patient the space and time he needs to work things out on his own.

The healing power of a less involved, more "watch and listen," alternative approach is aptly depicted in the movie *Lars and the Real Girl* (2007). Ryan Gosling plays Lars, a painfully shy young man who avoids all social contact despite his deep and long-standing loneliness. He orders a plastic, life-size, anatomically correct doll from the Internet, names her Bianca, and develops a delusional romantic relationship with her. When he excitedly introduces Bianca to his community, they do not know what to do, especially when they realize that Lars thinks Bianca is a real person. One day Lars takes Bianca to the family doctor, Dagmar, who recommends Lars bring in Bianca for continuous weekly checkups. Dagmar uses these meetings to get to know Lars, Bianca, and their deepening relationship, without ever questioning Lars about his delusion. As the relationship between Lars and Bianca deepens, Lars looks happier, livelier and more engaged with people and the world around him. But then Lars and Bianca start having fights, through which Lars seems to live out past traumatic losses and pain. Throughout, Dagmar's stated approach is to join Lars in his delusion "until he no longer needs it." Eventually Bianca "passes away," Lars mourns her loss, and the movie concludes with Lars taking a romantic interest in a real-life coworker who has been interested in him for a long time.

This film raises questions for me about the nature of therapeutic healing and the diverse ways by which it can be achieved. When a patient tells me about doing things that I think clearly contradict reality, as I see it, my modus operandi is to inquire into selectively unattended aspects that I assume scaffold the patient's shaky grasp on reality. As I said before, I work from the assumption that attending to left-out details forces a reworking of the data into newer, more adaptive narratives that require less dissociation from my patient. But Lars' therapist did none of that. She never asked "Why does Bianca never speak?" nor "Why can't Bianca walk by herself?" Instead, Dagmar – along with the entire town – embraced Bianca as though she were a real person and took an interest in Lars and Bianca's evolving relationship. As a result, Lars felt more alive, became more engaged socially and ultimately gave up the delusional relationship for a real-life connection. So how might an interpersonalist think about the unquestioning approach taken by Dagmar?

First, despite my general belief in the power of thoughtful inquiry, in Lars' case it would have shattered rather than helped him. By joining Lars in his make-believe world, Dagmar and his loved ones helped him to open up about and work through the painful life experiences that created the need for such a defensive delusion in the first place. Such memories constitute the kind of data that interpersonalists try to help patients access and articulate through the use of detailed inquiry. Dagmar achieved the same end by different means. Perhaps her approach is a lesson in the power of thinking about long-term goals rather than short-term accomplishments. Dagmar did not immediately put her finger on the holes in Lars' Swiss cheese. Rather, she provided an unconditionally accepting space that allowed Lars to take important risks, face his fears of human connection and outgrow his primitive defenses at his own pace.

The lesson I took from this fictional treatment is that the detailed inquiry and other active interpersonal approaches need not be the proverbial hammer one takes to every nail that emerges in treatment. When a patient tells me something that strikes me as delusional, perhaps validating and learning about his or her version of reality will lead to more fruitful exploration and growth than questioning its validity. If I think in terms of the long-term rather than short-term trajectory of the treatment relationship, perhaps one day down the line such a patient and I will look back on this moment in our treatment and understand why it was important for us to jointly believe in a version of events that in retrospect does not make sense. Hopefully, such understanding will be more useful to him or her in the long run than having short-circuited it in the short run.

In general, I find it useful to complement my preferred interpersonal approaches with interventions and principles from other orientations, psychoanalytic and non-psychoanalytic, alike. Doing so does not threaten my sense of self as an interpersonal analyst, since I understand my interpersonal orientation to form the core of how I work no matter what interventions I use. To illustrate, a relatively new patient complained of experiencing intense anxiety in crowded spaces, and I saw fit to talk with him about mindfulness meditation practices. We spent an entire session discussing how meditation works and how it can be applied in different settings. In the next session, we discussed how the meditation strategies worked out. Although these interventions may be more characteristic of cognitive-behavioral or solution-focused than psychoanalytic approaches, my interpersonal principles informed how I thought about my use of them in this moment and their place in the evolving therapeutic relationship. Because this was only my third session with this patient and I was aware that it was his first therapy experience, I thought he might need to feel me out to determine my trustworthiness and that offering short-term strategies could, in addition to helping with his anxiety, help establish myself as someone he could count on for help. These interventions also gave me a way to start gauging how he might need to utilize me and this treatment, and how he might respond to different kinds of effort to be helpful. Implementing interventions from other orientations can create opportunities for learning something important about the patient and the kind of relationship that will be most healing to him. This kind of thinking is what makes me an interpersonalist, even if I momentarily act like a cognitive-behavioral therapist.

Conclusion

The aim of this chapter was to introduce the reader to key ideas and practices in interpersonal psychoanalysis. While no such introduction can ever cover all the necessary ground, I hope you now have an understanding and feel for the unique contribution that an interpersonal psychoanalytic perspective might make to your own clinical work. Interpersonalists take a unique interest in the endless richness and complexity of our patient's lived experiences, and we believe that the exploration itself is what heals. We care more about asking questions than finding answers, particularly about experiences that have never seen the light of curiosity. Interpersonal psychoanalysis not only helps patients learn how to be curious about unexamined aspects of their lives and their world, it also helps them to have the courage to attend to and articulate aspects of their experience that were previously too scary or threatening to look at. An interpersonal approach therefore offers patients the chance to be brave and the opportunity to become more flexible in how they understand and live their lives.

Note

1   Personal communication, 2013.

References

Buechler, S. (2004). *Clinical Values: Emotions that Guide Psychoanalytic Treatment.* New York: Routledge.
Levenson, E. A. (1972). *The Fallacy of Understanding.* New York: Basic Books.
Levenson, E. A. (1983). *The Ambiguity of Change.* New York: Basic Books.
Levenson, E. A. (1991). *The Purloined Self: Interpersonal Perspectives in Psychoanalysis.* New York: Contemporary Psychoanalysis Books.
Levenson, E. A. (2009). The enigma of the transference. *Contemporary Psychoanalysis,* 45(2): 163–178.
Stern, D. B. (2010). *Partners in Thought: Working with Unformulated Experience, Dissociation, and Enactment.* New York: Routledge.
Sullivan, H. S. (1956). *Clinical Studies in Psychiatry.* New York: W. W. Norton.
Sullivan, H. S. (1970). *The Psychiatric Interview.* New York: W. W. Norton.

10

RELATIONAL PSYCHOANALYSIS

Not a theory but a framework

Johanna C. Malone*

Introduction

> *There is no such thing as a relational theory, but there is such a thing as a relational point of view, a relational way of thinking, a relational sensibility, and we believe that it is this broad outlook that underpins the sea change that many of us recognize as breathing fresh life into our field.*
>
> *(Ghent, 2001)*

These words of Emmanuel Ghent framed the emergence of the relational movement within psychoanalysis, which challenged the status quo of the application of both theory and technique by emphasizing the primary importance of relationships for the development and experience of the human psyche. A psychoanalyst drawing on relational principles actively reflects on relational dynamics between self and other that are playing out both within a person's internal experience (intrapsychically) and external/environmental experience (interpersonally) in order to best understand and help patients. When attending to these dynamics, particular attention is given to how they emerged in the past and are now experienced in the present. There is also a value of the tensions between reality and fantasy, and between the interpersonal and interior domains that make up experience. A relational approach emphasizes that the analyst reflects simultaneously on these dynamics not only in the patient but also in his or her own experience. This means having an eye toward how the analyst's own characteristics are impacting the therapeutic process and relationship, and ways they may potentially be clinically utilized. Those who value a relational sensibility generally appreciate the inherent messiness of experience, which is made up of shifting patterns of order and disarray (Benjamin,

---

* I would like to thank Marilyn Charles, Patricia Harney, Gwendolyn Kelso and Stacey Novack for their generous feedback and thoughtful comments regarding this chapter.

1990; Bromberg, 1991; Knoblauch, 2008). In other words, when experience and people appear to be neatly summed up or packaged in formulations or diagnostic/theoretical categories, there is most likely a problem.

The relational framework differs from other theoretical schools of psychoanalytic thought, which center on a comprehensive model developed by a particular individual (e.g., Freudian, Kleinian) or a group of individuals (e.g., ego, self psychological perspectives). As a result, there is no single or unified "relational theory" (Mitchell & Aron, 1999; Ghent, 2001). Instead, relational psychoanalysis serves as a framework or set of sensibilities that can reorient psychoanalytic ideas around the centrality of relationships in the human psyche, whether it is relating to internalized objects or to people outside the self. Adrienne Harris (2011) believes some relational analysts are more drawn to what she calls the big "R" of relationality, which involves being connected to the deepening set of ideas within the particular tradition, while others may be more attracted to the little "r," which represents its hybridity of many strands of diverse interdisciplinary perspectives. Relational psychoanalysts therefore might present a wide range of theoretical orientations and even have strong theoretical disagreements while maintaining a common interest in understanding how relational dynamics in the past/present, experienced in external reality/internal fantasy and constructed between individuals, are always at play.

In this chapter, I will provide some initial background of the relational movement, followed by some important clinical ideas utilized by relational psychoanalysts in practice, including a "two-person psychology," intersubjectivity, multiplicity of self and the analyst's use of self. I will conclude by discussing some limitations of relational psychoanalysis and ways that recurring patterns of emphasis and de-emphasis within this approach may place relational clinicians at risk for certain clinical difficulties or blind spots.

Background

The emergence of the relational psychoanalytic movement was a necessary disruption to the field of psychoanalysis. As is common across most fields of study, whether within the arts or sciences, incoming generations are often able to spot and challenge limitations and unnecessary rigidity within older theoretical models and, by doing so, develop new ideas. The relational movement surfaced in the 1980s and 1990s when a group of psychoanalysts, primarily American psychologists (who were often unwelcome as trainees at many psychoanalytic institutes), challenged long-held ideas of Freudian psychoanalytic principles regarding drive theory and the authoritative stance of the psychoanalyst (Berman, 1997; Greenberg & Mitchell, 1983; Harris, 2011). The relational movement incorporated developments not only of theoretical change in psychoanalysis but also of aspects of a contemporary anti-authoritarian stance regarding social change in society (Altman, 1995; Cushman, 2015; Layton, Hollander & Gutwill, 2006). The result was a powerful wave of thinkers bringing new perspectives about the development of human experience and social justice. Voices from feminist and queer theory were able to challenge conceptualizations of sexuality and gender that were saturated with prejudice and oppressive themes (see, e.g., Butler, 1990, 2005; Dimen & Goldner, 2002; Corbett 1993, 2009; Harris, 2005). New ways of formulating race and culture emerged from this movement, with an eye toward enactments that go on between patient and analyst, and within the patient's and analyst's experience of themselves (see, e.g., Suchet, 2004; Tummala-Narra, 2004). Relational psychoanalysis also was influential in challenging themes of socioeconomic elitism that sometimes ran through psychoanalytic communities and aimed to reach a broader spectrum of patients, including those facing the challenges of poverty (Altman, 1995). As part of this, the relational psychoanalytic movement at the onset drew heavily on ideas of social constructivism (e.g., Hoffman, 1998) and critical theory (e.g., Foucault, 1976), which brought new perspectives into the meanings and definitions of experience, by emphasizing the ways experience is subjectively constructed by the individual in relation to broader culture and society rather than being firmly set in an objective truth (Layton, 2013).

Jay Greenberg and Stephen Mitchell (1983) first used the term "relational psychoanalysis" in their volume *Object Relations in Psychoanalytic Theory*. These authors drew upon two distinct schools of psychoanalysis – interpersonal psychoanalysis (primarily the work of Harry Stack Sullivan) and object relations theory (primarily the work of Ronald Fairbairn) and demonstrated how, despite their differences, both theories prioritized the common theme of human relatedness to the formation and expression of the human psyche. However, these two theoretical perspectives also stemmed from different intellectual traditions, approaching the importance of relationships quite differently. Interpersonal theories focused more "externally" on real-life human interactions, and object relations theories focused more "internally" on struggles with the internalized representations of people inside us. Sullivan's interpersonal perspective emphasized that people could be understood only in the context of relationships and that analysts themselves were participant-observers rather than possessing a truly objective perspective from which to understand the patient (Sullivan, 1940). Fairbairn's (1952) work reconceptualized early personality development as object-seeking rather than pleasure-seeking. Whereas early psychoanalytic structural theory viewed early fundamental motivations either as increasing pleasure due to the libidinal drive or as decreasing tension, he saw human beings as primarily seeking connections with others. Unlike some theoretical developments, the relational perspective is not simply an additive approach to understanding preexisting psychoanalytic theory but, instead, shifts the primary focus of human motivation itself onto the dynamic field of *relationships* rather than a preestablished set of drives (Greenberg & Mitchell, 1983; Mitchell & Aron, 1999). In this way, some relational conceptualizations are incompatible with, and alternative explanations to, previous psychoanalytic perspectives (rather than being integrative or extensions of older ideas).

Prior to the relational movement, the underpinnings of classical theory for understanding human development, the organization of internal life, and motivation were largely understood by Freud's model of internal drives (i.e., no big "R" relational perspective), for which there had been no unified broad-scale critique. Within psychoanalysis, the process of questioning established Freudian principles has often been a contentious one, evoking strong emotions tied to loyalty, identity and fears of challenge to a personally developed sense of expertise/knowing (Berman, 2013). This notorious intergenerational battle within the psychoanalytic heritage can be seen in the ways Freud interacted with his own colleagues who branched out in their thinking, thus moving away from Freud's models (e.g., Ferenczi, Jung, Rank).

Although Sándor Ferenczi's forward-thinking ideas were initially met with disapproval, they are now seen as foundational in the relational psychoanalytic movement (Harris & Kuchuck, 2015). While Freud is often referred to as the father of psychoanalysis, some have referred to Ferenczi as the "mother" of this intellectual tradition (Hoffer, 1991). Ferenczi (1932) did not shy away from looking at the analyst's own emotional involvement (i.e., controversially proposing that the analyst's decision to refuse to become emotionally involved within the treatment was itself hypocritical). His understanding of the impact of child abuse in the development of self-experience outlined in his paper "Confusion of tongues" laid the groundwork for understanding multiplicity of self and dissociative processes tied to actual trauma (as opposed to a distortion of reality: Ferenczi, 1932). Freud (1896) himself originally alluded to some important relational overtones of child abuse on psychological development and psychopathology but soon afterward rejected his own seduction theory. This is to say that, despite the radical nature of relational psychoanalysis, which challenged and disrupted the psychoanalytic community, one can actually trace its origins and developmental threads as a persistent undercurrent in the clinical practices and theorizing of many earlier psychoanalysts.

With a commitment to an anti-authoritarian stance and the questioning of long-held principles, the relational psychoanalytic movement breathed new life into psychoanalytic communities by shaking up the status quo and asking analysts and patients to wonder: What are we doing and why do we think it goes a particular way? In fact, the emphasis on "we" was a refreshing shift, which had commonly been either disapproved of or not readily theorized. Put simply, analysts were less inclined to think *with* their patients as opposed to *about* their patients. Thus, there was a need for psychoanalysis to include more theorized constellations of "I," "you," "they" and "us" than had ever been available with older models of countertransference and transference. For example, relational analysts might be thinking "What do you think about how you see me thinking about you? How does that relate to the ways we think together and in what ways do we each participate in this process?" Such questions emerge by considering the real relational dynamics unfolding between two people in the room, along with the internal dynamics of representations carried inside each individual participant, which can serve as lenses to guide and interpret the exchange. Through this approach, patients might understand what they project not only onto their therapists based on personal past experiences but also onto aspects of who their therapist actually is and how that may influence the therapeutic work (Aron, 1991; Gill, 1984). As a result, there are more ways of

212 Johanna C. Malone

understanding not only the patient as an individual but also the patient in relation to others.

To illustrate these notions more deeply, I will identify some important conceptual ideas that relational psychoanalysts hold in mind as they work. An effort is made to speak about them in plain language, without extensive use of psychoanalytic jargon, to offer clarity and accessibility. The ideas here are not meant to be exhaustive or complete but to serve as a starting place for those interested in relational psychoanalysis.

A "two-person" psychology

The relational movement of psychoanalysis shifted the emphasis of patient formulation from the innate to the experiential (Aron, 1990; Spezzano, 1996; Wachtel, 2007). By rejecting aspects of Freudian drive theory, the focus of relational psychoanalysis became more focused on the interpersonal context that led to the creation of the individual (Greenberg & Mitchell, 1983). That is, the mind of each individual develops and exists in the context of a relational matrix, and this relationship must be attended to and actively theorized in the context of psychoanalytic interventions. For the relational psychoanalyst, one is considering not simply the way the past determined the present but more the way the present relational context can be illuminated by past experience (Gill, 1995). This perspective has important implications for intervention, since insights into what happened in the past (while still important) may become less central as a mutative force in therapeutic action. Instead, experience in the context of new relationships (including the relationship with the analyst) becomes the more crucial vehicle of change (Benjamin, 2010; Stern et al., 1998). This reorientation evolved and integrated pieces of work from theorists across the history of psychoanalysis but also integrated a growing body of developmental research unavailable to psychoanalysts a decade before (see, e.g., the work of Beebe, Lyons-Ruth, Stern and Tronick).

Some notable early precursors to the relational movement are seen in the ways that analysts once thought about mother–child relationships and then attempted to apply these ideas to the understanding of work between adult patients and analysts. For example, Donald Winnicott's (1960) statement "'There is no such thing as an infant,' meaning, of course, that whenever one finds an infant one finds maternal care, and without maternal care there would be no infant" (p. 587) is foundational to knowing how the mind of a new person emerges in the context of another. It is not that the mother and the baby cannot be separated but, instead, that the infant relies on the parent and the mind of the parent to develop a mind of his or her own. Similarly, Hans Loewald's (1972, 1978) work reinterpreted many psychic structures that emerge out of the interactions between infants and their human environment, viewing instincts as relationally motivated rather than discharge-seeking. Finally, Heinz Kohut's (1984) work in self-psychology made contributions by considering the deficits of the early childhood relational environment and the need for new experiences within the context of attuned empathic connection.

Ongoing developmental research also made numerous contributions highlighting the importance of relationships, particularly caregiving relationships, to the development of the human mind. Attachment theory empirically demonstrated the ways in which internal working models (IWMs: representations of self and others) develop in the context of caregiver relationships and then continue to serve as guiding relational schemas across the lifespan (Bowlby, 1988). As with relational principles, these IWMs can be modified in the context of new relational experiences (e.g., with a romantic partner, therapist, etc.) and are not considered fixed internal experiences (Wachtel, 2010; Weinfield, Sroufe & Egeland, 2000). Like the development of IWMs, the child's own development of reflective functioning, or the ability to think about the mind and intentions of one's self, is also embedded in a relational process (Fonagy et al., 2002). Edward Tronick's (2003) work studying infant–parent interactions has demonstrated through observation that one cannot fully understand the infant's behavior without also taking into account the psychology of the parent. Finally, Beatrice Beebe and Frank Lachman's (2002) work has shown patterns of dynamic interplay within the parent–infant dyads that result in regulation, disruption and heightened affect.

Importantly, some relational analysts have been wary of the tendency to rely on generalized developmental metaphors when understanding individual patients (Mitchell, 1984; Westen, 2002). This stance in part stemmed from a reaction to older models of psychoanalysis, which risked infantilizing the patient by emphasizing his or her regression while simultaneously promoting the analyst's objective authority. Nevertheless, developmental theories and research, when used metaphorically rather than concretely, have much to offer relational clinicians as long as they continue to hold in mind that adult patients have psyches shaped by a great deal of relevant lived experiences in addition to those of early childhood.

Drawing on developmental theory and research, relational psychoanalysts began to note the ways that it was impossible to fully consider the mind of a patient outside the context of other relationships. Thus, there was a move from a one-person psychology (looking at the patient as an encapsulated separate personality organization that could be objectively assessed) to a two-person psychology (the self being seen in relation to others). This shift has essential clinical implications regarding the clinician's sense of how to understand the patient.

When applying a two-person psychological approach and thinking developmentally, one listens to a patient's story with an ear toward how experiences have been co-created by the participants (both in the past and in the present). This means that the patient's understanding of his or her own struggles and strengths were developed in the context of other people who participated in the experiences that unfolded. It also means that the analyst is a contemporary participant – meaning that the analyst's own psychology has an impact on the experiences of the patient during the course of treatment (and vice versa). For example, when listening to a male patient who was severely neglected by his mother in childhood describe his anger toward his wife, a one-person perspective might be primarily interested in the anger and the ways that the patient might be using anger to feel strong and in control in order to avoid the pain of weakness, vulnerability, shame, etc. A two-person perspective might focus more on how the present anger can be understood based on histories of old and new relationships and interpersonal motivations (e.g., receiving insufficient care or attention or fears of depending on someone and feeling humiliated, etc.).

In this example, the telling of this story to the analyst also exists in a two-person frame in which the analyst's past experience is the lens through which to understand the patient. There is no objective analyst. As the patient above is communicating the story about his wife and mother, he is also expressing with the analyst expectations of what it means to be heard, understood and helped in this new context. What unfolds for both the patient and the analyst is a relational matrix of past and present, reality and fantasy, internal experiences of people and external engagements with people. The analyst actively reflects on the transference/countertransference dimension in precisely this way in order to consider how interactions are being bidirectionally evoked based on *two* sets of developmental histories, so that they might be utilized in ways that may more successfully guide the treatment. All these levels of consideration reframe the way a patient is understood, as a being unfolding within relational motivations rather than existing within a current of competing drives.

Intersubjectivity and the third

Embedded within the concept of a two-person psychology is the overlapping "space" that emerges between individuals. In the psychoanalytic treatment there are two separate individuals, each with his or her own mind and inner words but, in the coming together a unique experience unfolds between them that belongs only to them. This is a place of intersubjectivity, or what in psychoanalysis might be known as the analytic *third*. There are many different definitions and variations of intersubjectivity and the psychoanalytic third (see, e.g., Aron, 2006; Benjamin, 2004; Britton, 2004; Ogden, 2004). What may be most important for a relational perspective is the way in which attending to the intersubjective space may enable analyst–patient dyads to both step outside rigid symmetrical binds and consider co-created dimensions that open up new ways of understanding the patient and her struggles. Jessica Benjamin (1988, 2004), for example, emphasizes the ways old binaries that are solely complementary can promote reliance on familiar sadomasochistic power structures of "doer and done to." Instead of clinging to familiar roles, the development of the psychoanalytic third allows movement into a new place where one acknowledges one's own participation and can also tolerate the other person's separateness. This draws upon Winnicott's (1971) description of a developmental shift from "object relating" to "object usage," in which the child experiences her own destructiveness toward the (m)other and sees that she can, amazingly, survive. In this process, the person experiences a sense of separateness from the other in which she gives up the fantasy omnipotent control and is then able to "use" the other. This entails loving and being loved by the object (mother) that survived being destroyed in unconscious fantasy. Applying this to the relational analytic context, Ghent (1990) describes this shift as moving from a place of submission to surrender in which there is an experience of "letting go." This shift involves vulnerability and risk for all involved and requires what Steven Cooper (2000) describes as a mutual containment that provides regulation from both dyadic participants.

Benjamin (2004) believes that, as part of therapeutic action, analysts must be able to step out of a binary into the third. This sometimes means being able to acknowledge that they not only are seeking to soothe and help the patient but also will inevitably hurt the patient through some aspect of truly being in a relationship. This sometimes occurs through the opening of old wounds. It is in this process of surviving the breakdown and restoration of intersubjective space by moving between a binary and a place of separate-connectedness that therapeutic work occurs. From this relational perspective, one begins to accept the relationship between loving and aggressive feelings that begin in the context of the parent–child relationship and then continue to evolve in other relational systems, including the analyst–patient relationship. Mitchell (1993) posits that the ability to love is an achievement that comes from the belief that we can repeatedly repair our relationships despite regularly expressing aggression and destructive feelings.

By reflecting on and being part of this intersubjective place of the third, the relational analyst is able to unveil existing maps of psychoanalytic terrain previously just out of view. Some of this might be quickly available and generally understood, while other aspects will be out of reach for some time, as part of what Samuel Gerson (2004) calls the "relational unconscious," which he considers the "reciprocal and mutual influence of minds upon one another" (p. 71). This means that neither analyst nor patient will ever have a full understanding or view of "the third" that is created between them. While such experiences may have to do with split-off parts of the self that feel insufficiently compatible with another person (Davies, 1996a), other aspects of the third may be out of focus or outside the primary tone of the expressed moment. Here the work of Thomas Ogden (1997) is particularly relevant, as he describes the analyst drawing on his reverie (i.e., thoughts, feelings, daydreams, physical experiences, mental images) to understand the intersubjective space and the experience of the patient. The reverie is a personal experience of the analyst but one that is infused with the experience of the patient and thus asymmetrically co-created. To use this reverie in service of the treatment, the analyst must allow himself to be in a state of not always fully knowing what is going on and remaining open to an emerging unfamiliar register of experience in order to better inform the intervention.

The clinical utility of this intersubjective analytic third in a relational psychoanalytic framework can take a number of different forms. When thinking about the third derived from the work of Winnicott (1971) and expanded upon by Benjamin (2004) and other colleagues, the therapist might be attending to moments of rupture and repair that emerge between the patient and analyst, not just in words but also in attunement and affective connectedness. These moments may be explicitly

216 Johanna C. Malone

talked about in terms of the meaning in the patient's life (past and present) or may be internally reflected upon by the analyst so as to inform their stance and future interventions. Additionally, analysts in this model maintain an ongoing place of reflection to think about not only the patient's mind and way of relating but also their own participation during breakdown and reconnection in order to think about how their own feelings and life experience are informing their responses. Relational therapists will also note not only moments of conflict in this approach but also the absence of conflict for more rigidly defined roles influenced by dynamics of submission and power.

Furthermore, when relational clinicians draw upon the analytic third, outlined by Ogden (2004) and heavily influenced by the work of Wilfred Bion, they may engage in what is often a much more private process of reverie in which they can allow the mind to drift while still being connected to the patient. Analysts will then use the reverie to have access to the analytic third in order to understand what is unfolding between themselves and their patients. Here the patient's unprocessed experiences (emotions, unformulated thoughts) are being taken in and experienced by the analyst in such a way that they can be reflected upon within a form similar to a daydream. Relational analysts may or may not share the content of reverie directly but, instead, use this separate place created jointly by the minds of both individuals to guide their work (Bion, 1962).

Given that relational psychoanalysis is not a theory in and of itself, it has the luxury (yet chaotic task) of being able to draw on multiple theories with an emphasis on the ways that human relationships result in variations of experiences of both painful conflict and pleasure. The ways in which relational analysts consider and utilize intersubjectivity may vary greatly in terms of the amount that they verbally communicate their own personal reflection and experience to their patients. However, more central may be the ways these analysts maintain a reserved area of reflection to understand the co-created space of the intermingled psyches, in order to guide their interventions and ways of being with the patient (Cooper, 2008; Cooper, Corbett & Seligman, 2014; Seligman, 2014).

Self-states and the multiplicity of the self

In addition to considering the intersubjective space between people, relational psychoanalysis has also broadened the ways one looks at the internal landscape within individuals. In particular, growing out of the interpersonal tradition, there is an interest in how configurations of personality might vary based on particular relationships. Sullivan stated, "For all I know every human being has as many personalities as he has interpersonal relations" (1950, p. 221, c.f. Bromberg, 1996).

The term *self-states* refers to the normative presence of shifting states of identity that develop and are maintained through dissociation (Bromberg, 1998). The study of self-states developed in part out of an interest in the impact of trauma and the role of dissociative processes in fragmented experiences of the self (see, e.g., Davies

Relational psychoanalysis **217**

& Frawley, 1994; Davies, 1996a). Some previous psychoanalytic models emphasized how traumatic experience becomes split off from awareness through the process of repression (a horizontal split), which meant that unacceptable or distressing material was defensively forgotten (either forever or temporarily) in order to prevent the flooding of the ego with anxiety. In contrast, a relational perspective tends to emphasize the additional ways trauma is managed through irreconcilable self-states, whereby experience may simultaneously be known and not known (Davies, 1996b). Some very early abuse may be known and not known because it occurred before it could be formulated in language and encoded in memory. This process of knowing and not knowing is facilitated through regulatory systems in the body that encode affective memory through nonverbal somatic processes (van der Kolk, 1994). Some dissociated material that has never been processed and organized in such a way that it can even be verbally articulated may be what Donnel Stern (1983, 1997) calls *unformulated experience*. This refers to "potential thoughts" that may become both known and spoken for the first time within the intersubjective field between patient and analyst through processes of imagination and spontaneity (Stern, 2010).

While traumatic experience may lead to dissociative self-states, multiplicity of self and dissociation are both normal and adaptive (Bromberg, 1998). Dissociation is a process that preserves continuity of self in the face of the incompatibility of the self and experience (Bromberg, 1996; Fischer et al., 1997). This process becomes problematic when different self-states are entirely cut off from one another and cannot be simultaneously accessed (despite the contradictions), and a person is forced to shift almost categorically between each self-state (which would include a different way of understanding people, the self and the world). Philip Bromberg (1993, p. 166) states: "Health is the ability to stand in the spaces between realities without losing any of them – the capacity to feel like oneself while being many." He uses the term "standing in the spaces" to refer to a subjective experience that does not feel fully containable within the "me" of whom a person believes themself to be (Bromberg, 1996).

Self-states are inherently relational and have their roots within the context of primary interpersonal contexts starting in infancy. Karlen Lyons-Ruth and colleagues (Lyons-Ruth, 2003; Lyons-Ruth et al., 2006) have demonstrated through longitudinal infant research the ways that some adult dissociative processes have their roots in disorganized attachment relationships characterized by ongoing inconsistency, emotional unavailability and role reversal. The relational perspective emphasizes that each dissociated self-state has a constructed version of reality (some overlapping and some distinct) based on particular experiences that may emerge in the context of psychoanalytic treatment (Davies, 1996a). Within each self-state there is a subjective experience of reality (including the minds of other people), and this experience shifts in subtle or dramatic ways depending on the relational world that surrounds a developing individual. For example, when children are faced with ongoing abuse, neglect, aggression or a sense of being chronically misunderstood, they must still find creative ways to relate to their caregivers. This means relating

218 Johanna C. Malone

both at times of being close, dependent on care and finding the best the caregiver can offer, and at other times of being violated, misunderstood, harmed or neglected. Dissociation allows a range of self-states to exist as a form of resilient adaptation to difficult situations. The dissociative processes may be less helpful and more problematic as the person grows and lives within different contexts. In more nurturing environments, a child may still have to face disruptions (e.g., parents' inconsistencies, occasionally surfacing unresolved pain or mild fluctuations in emotional availability) that result in more subtle forms of dissociative phenomena and self-states that can overlap or shift with greater fluidity.

When working with the idea of self-states clinically, the aim is to think about moments of coherence, lack of coherence and over-coherence that seem to unfold as the patient shifts in his or her affective stance, ways of communicating or ways of thinking about a problem. When faced with stress or a painful emotional experience a patient may act in ways that seem inconsistent with other moments. This inconsistency might be subtle or it might be more pronounced. The analyst gradually aims to enter into the experience with a patient in order to see the multiple realities of the patient's experience increasingly in relation to one another.

Relational analysts think not only about the multiplicity of the patient but also about the multiplicities within themselves (Bromberg, 1996). How might the way that a patient is acting tap into the clinician's own experience of relating to people? If a patient is in a hostile, angry state of mind and raging at the therapist, does the clinician respond from a self-state (internal organization of thoughts, feelings and strategies) in which he or she has received such treatment in the past? The relational analyst attends to the expression of the patient's self-state by reflecting on what is being activated in the patient (given his or her history) and how the analyst has contributed to the patient's response. However, the analyst is also thinking about her own experience that is guiding her responses. For example, does the patient's anger result in the analyst feeling in touch with her own experience of being hurt and afraid, aloof and disengaged, or retaliatory? The analyst might wonder about how this information could be useful for thinking about the patient (i.e., is it similar to something in the patient's own history?). Alternatively, the analyst might consider that this patient might finally be able to express rage toward someone who feels ineffective and far away, and the analyst might have to face a self-experience of being inept, helpless or a failure. In other words, the dynamic interplay between the dyad would be completely dependent on the history and present moment of not only the patient but also the analyst. This means an evaluation of how both participants are experiencing the reality and fantasy of who the other is, including their motivations and needs. One of the clear difficulties of this approach is that it is dependent on analysts drawing upon their own unconscious experience in ways to which they may or may not have ready access. It may often only be after the fact that they are able to reflect on the relational configurations that emerged through the lens of self-states.

The analyst's use of self

The emergence of a relational framework meant a new focus on the ways that the analyst uses and shares him- or herself within therapeutic settings. The analyst becomes much more than a transference object and unavoidably impacts the treatment and the therapeutic relationship through his or her unique personal characteristics and history. In this new mode, the analyst's verbal interpretations, although important, become contextualized as part of the unfolding spoken and unspoken aspects of the therapeutic relationship in which patients came to know and experience themselves (Beebe & Lachman, 2003; Lyons-Ruth et al., 1998; Stern et al., 1998). Interestingly, this shift is consistent with psychotherapy research highlighting that the therapeutic alliance is the key predictor of positive change across therapeutic modalities (e.g., cognitive behavioral, psychodynamic, supportive, etc.: Castonguay, Constantino & Holtforth, 2006). That is, regardless of your chosen theory, and whether it is within or outside psychoanalysis, the therapeutic relationship is fundamental to the patient's idea that he or she can change. In parallel to this, and consistent with a two-person perspective, is the recognition that, within the process of the analysis, both participants will need to affect one another and be changed by one another, as highlighted by Slavin and Kriegman (1998) through their consideration of "why the analyst needs to change."

This growing focus on the therapeutic relationship opened up room for further unpacking of ways that analysts could draw upon their experience. The analyst's participation in enactments came to be seen as inevitable rather than problematic (Maroda, 1998; Safran & Kraus, 2014). Within enactments, the patient and analyst pull each other into familiar ways of relating, but responsibility falls asymmetrically upon the analyst not only to be mindful of how they participate but also to reflect upon the implications of the interpersonal and intrapsychic processes that are simultaneously unfolding. Analysts need to actively consider the ways that they may be unwittingly repeating old traumatic or dysfunctional patterns (of their own and of the patient) in their responses or experience of a patient (Davies, 1994). For example, if analysts find themselves responding to a patient's repeated lateness with unspoken irritation and a sense that the patient "doesn't value the work," they may begin to realize that the patient is actually communicating anxiety about being close and being seen, while they themselves are feeling old anxious feelings of being devalued or forgotten. By reflecting on the enactment, analysts may be able to approach the patient's anxieties more directly and compassionately, while recognizing that their own irritation may not entirely belong to the patient. Relational analysts' insights about themselves most often will not be shared with the patient (but may be, depending on the apparent clinical utility), as the focus of intervention is not on understanding the analyst but, rather, on using the analyst's experience to understand the patient. Thus, the analytic dyad's willingness to be reflectively immersed in enactments is consistent with Stern's (2003) value of "courting surprise" and will likely allow for access to otherwise inaccessible self-states (Benjamin, 2010).

220 Johanna C. Malone

In keeping with the aforementioned spirit of anti-authoritarianism, relational analysts also challenged the previously neutral stance of the analyst, bringing to light both the artificiality and the impossibility of this concept (Greenberg, 1986). This meant room for new kinds of analytic expressiveness in verbal and nonverbal domains. There was an increased value on spontaneity (see, e.g., Hoffman, 1992, 1994) and a desire to think about ways of relating to patients that had previously been seen as unilaterally interfering with the transference (e.g., warmth, reassurance, humor, forms of self-disclosure). By opening up the padlocks that surrounded expressiveness, relational analysts had to grapple more directly with what their implicit and explicit communications to a patient meant, rather than denying that they existed. This movement also was consistent with analysts being willing to take a risk to be "seen" more as a person, in parallel to what they were hoping and expecting from their patient. Aron (1996) described some of this process as a movement into mutuality in which transformation results from processes of regulation and recognition, but also emphasized that, in this process, asymmetry remained. With this shift, analysts had a more complicated dance to follow in which they had to still leave room for evolving transferences and not eagerly try to over-establish themselves as a good object in the patient's life (Mitchell, 1988). For example, Cooper and Levit (1998) have explored the ways relational analysts sometimes move too quickly into trying to act as a new object in the patient's life, risking staleness and compliance, rather than leaving room for repetitive older patterns as the patient engages in a search for newness. They describe the goal of the work as, instead, engaging in a process in which there is an expansion of multiplicities of relating between patient and analyst.

A final development of the analyst's use of self that is central to the relational movement is analysts' use of their own reverie to better understand the patient's experience. Drawing on the work of Bion (1962), relational analysts actively reflect on how they feel and what it is like to be with their patients, and understand this to be part of the patient's communication. Rather than thinking of projective identification as something one-directional in which the patient is putting something (often toxic) into the analyst, relational analysts see the bidirectional nature of shared experience (Seligman, 1999). Consistent with Bion, this means that, through being connected, the analyst will "metabolize" the patient's experiences in order to create something that can be shared and taken back by the patient in a more usable form. This might mean bearing grief with a patient or taking in anger or pain and feeling it together so that it can be transformed.

Weaknesses and limitations

Earlier in this chapter the relational movement was described as a necessary disruption in the development that challenged existing norms of how analysts understood and interacted with their patients. As a result, many psychoanalysts today draw on relational principles without necessarily considering themselves to be relational psychoanalysts. However, the relational framework is filled high and deep with its

Relational psychoanalysis **221**

own potential blind spots or room for error. Stern (2014) believes that "every theory comes with the risk of losing the forest through the trees in a different way" but he objects to the idea of ascribing "inevitable excesses," arguing that the risks of one's perspective can be avoided if one is aware of them and willing to struggle with them. In addressing this vulnerability, Cooper (2007) emphasizes the need for all analysts, but particularly relational analysts, to utilize a "pluralistic third" that allows them to step outside their own theoretical approach in order to understand blind spots or angles of approaching and conceptualizing technique and formulation. This means a willingness to know and engage with a range of theoretical perspectives. The first analysts in the relational movement already had developed theoretical perspectives. Subsequent generations of clinicians, who begin by learning principles in the relationship framework, unsuccessfully try to use the approach as a theory in and of itself, as opposed to a lens through which to use, question and orient themselves within and across theories. Maintaining theoretical diversity, rather than constituting a theory in and of itself, allows for the necessary conflict or debate that makes relational work useful and alive. Relatedly, Tublin (2011) has highlighted the ways in which relational psychoanalysis has a somewhat underdeveloped language of technique. He attributes this in part to having the benefits of many theoretical approaches but then being faced with the problems that this ideological freedom brings, such that analysts must be more vigilant on the declared meaning of their own clinical choices.

Another common critique of the relational movement is that it prioritizes interpersonal interactions and experiences of external reality over internal phantasy and conflicts (Mills, 2005, in press). However, the salience of this critique rests largely on how any one particular analyst practices. The historical roots of the relational movement of psychoanalysis draw heavily from the ideas of object relational clinicians, including those drawing on the work of Fairbairn, Melanie Klein and Bion. When using the work of Fairbairn (1952), the relational analyst is apt to consider the internal conflicts and loyalties patients have, not only with those in their external world, but also the internalized objects or representations of people within. Similarly, drawing on Klein, relational psychoanalysts think about moments of aggression and reparation that occur not only in reality but also in fantasy. Malcolm Slavin (2016) has emphasized the existential dimension of relational work, in which patients are necessarily drawn into darker places that are not simply about experiences of trauma and external relatedness but also the struggle of being alive and of eventual dying. Finally, Bion's (1962) work, which highlights internal reverie and the process of container and contained, is fundamental to the analyst's use of self and to understanding the patient through the self. If relational clinicians ignore these other internal domains by focusing only on moments of external relating and reality-oriented interactions, they miss the opportunity for deeper connection and for helping the patient expand what is possible in life.

Relational analysts themselves have outlined ways in which the relational movement has at times risked overvaluing the spontaneous, expressive improvisational aspects of the analyst at the cost of internal reflection (Cooper, Corbett & Seligman,

222 Johanna C. Malone

2014; see also Aron, Grand & Slochower, in press a, in press b). In such cases, they make concrete recommendations encouraging relational practitioners to remember to slow things down within and outside the clinical moment and make space for quieter places of inner reflection and internal life. Seligman's (2014, p. 649) phrase, "to get involved while paying attention," is particularly useful in stressing the simultaneous action and reflection that is required of the analyst.

Conclusion

The emergence of relational psychoanalysis allowed for the articulation of broader ways of understanding patients' minds and lives and the nuances of the therapeutic relationship. It grew out of a spirit of needing to break down authoritarian structures and to move closer to the range of meanings that might unfold as the therapist and patient are immersed together in processes of relating. With this shift, the relational movement encouraged an active questioning of previous theoretical models, but also an ongoing recognition as to how a range of theoretical ideas can be useful for understanding not only the internal and external world of the patient but also the patient and analyst in relation to one another.

References

Altman, N. (1995). *The Analyst in the Inner City: Race, Class, and Culture through a Psychoanalytic Lens*. Hillsdale, NJ: Analytic Press.

Aron, L. (1990). One-person and two-person psychologies and the method of psychoanalysis. *Psychoanalytic Psychology*, 7(4): 475–485.

Aron, L. (1991). The patient's experience of the analyst's subjectivity. *Psychoanalytic Dialogues*, 1(1): 29–51.

Aron, L. (1996). *A Meeting of Minds: Mutuality in Psychoanalysis*. Hillsdale, NJ: Analytic Press.

Aron, L. (2006). Analytic impasse and the third: Clinical implications of intersubjectivity theory. *International Journal of Psychoanalysis*, 87(2): 349–368.

Aron, L., Grand, S., & Slochower, J. (Eds.) (in press a). *De-Idealizing Relational Theory: A Critique from Within*. New York: Routledge.

Aron, L., Grand, S., & Slochower, J. (Eds.) (in press b). *Decentering Relational Theory: A Comparative Critique*. New York: Routledge.

Beebe, B., & Lachmann, F. M. (2002). *Infant Research and Adult Treatment: Co-Constructing Interactions*. Hillsdale, NJ: Analytic Press.

Beebe, B., & Lachmann, F. M. (2003). The relational turn in psychoanalysis: A dyadic systems view from infant research. *Contemporary Psychoanalysis*, 39(3): 379–409.

Benjamin, J. (1988). *The Bonds of Love: Psychoanalysis, Feminism, and the Problem of Domination*. New York: Pantheon Books.

Benjamin, J. (1990). An outline of intersubjectivity: The development of recognition. *Psychoanalytic Psychology*, 7(Supp.): 33–46.

Benjamin, J. (2004). Beyond doer and done to: An intersubjective view of thirdness. *Psychoanalytic Quarterly*, 73(1): 5–46.

Benjamin, J. (2010). Where's the gap and what's the difference? *Contemporary Psychoanalysis*, 46(1): 112–119.

Berman, E. (1997). Relational psychoanalysis: A historical background. *American Journal of Psychotherapy*, 51(2): 185–203.

Berman, E. (2013). *Impossible Training: A Relational View of Psychoanalytic Education*. New York: Routledge.

Bion, W. R. (1962). *Learning from Experience*. London: William Heinemann Medical Books.

Bowlby, J. (1988). *A Secure Base: Parent–Child Attachment and Healthy Human Development*. New York: Basic Books.

Britton, R. (2004). Subjectivity, objectivity, and triangular space. *Psychoanalytic Quarterly*, 73(1): 47–61.

Bromberg, P. M. (1991). Artist and analyst. *Contemporary Psychoanalysis*, 27(2): 289–299.

Bromberg, P. M. (1993). Shadow and substance: A relational perspective on clinical process. *Psychoanalytic Psychology*, 10(2): 147–168.

Bromberg, P. M. (1996). Standing in the spaces: The multiplicity of self and the psychoanalytic relationship. *Contemporary Psychoanalysis*, 32(4): 509–535.

Bromberg, P. M. (1998). *Standing in the Spaces: Essays on Clinical Process, Trauma, and Dissociation*. New York: Psychology Press.

Butler, J. (1990). *Gender Trouble: Feminism and the Subversion of Identity*. New York: Routledge.

Butler, J. (2005). *Giving an Account of Oneself*. New York: Routledge.

Castonguay, L. G., Constantino, M. J., & Holtforth, M. G. (2006). The working alliance: Where are we and where should we go? *Psychotherapy: Theory, Research, Practice, Training*, 43(3): 271–279.

Cooper, S. H. (2000). Mutual containment in the analytic situation. *Psychoanalytic Dialogues*, 10(1): 169–194.

Cooper, S. H. (2007). Begin the beguine: Relational theory and the pluralistic third. *Psychoanalytic Dialogues*, 17(2): 247–271.

Cooper, S. H. (2008). Privacy, reverie, and the analyst's ethical imagination. *Psychoanalytic Quarterly*, 77(4): 1045–1073.

Cooper, S. H., Corbett, K., & Seligman, S. (2014). Clinical reflection and ritual as forms of participation and interaction: Reply to Bass and Stern. *Psychoanalytic Dialogues*, 24(6): 684–690.

Cooper, S. H., & Levit, D. B. (1998). Old and new objects in Fairbairnian and American relational theory. *Psychoanalytic Dialogues*, 8(5): 603–624.

Corbett, K. (1993). The mystery of homosexuality. *Psychoanalytic Psychology*, 10(3): 345–357.

Corbett, K. (2009). *Boyhoods: Rethinking Masculinities*. New Haven, CT: Yale University Press.

Cushman, P. (2015). Relational psychoanalysis as political resistance. *Contemporary Psychoanalysis*, 51(3): 423–459.

Davies, J. M. (1994). Love in the afternoon: A relational reconsideration of desire and dread in the countertransference. *Psychoanalytic Dialogues*, 4(2): 153–170.

Davies, J. M. (1996a). Dissociation, repression and reality testing in the countertransference: The controversy over memory and false memory in the psychoanalytic treatment of adult survivors of childhood sexual abuse. *Psychoanalytic Dialogues*, 6(2): 189–218.

Davies, J. M. (1996b). Linking the "pre-analytic" with the postclassical: Integration, dissociation, and the multiplicity of unconscious process. *Contemporary Psychoanalysis*, 32(4): 553–576.

Davies, J. M., & Frawley, M. G. (1994). *Treating the Adult Survivor of Childhood Sexual Abuse: A Psychoanalytic Perspective*. New York: Basic Books.

Dimen, M., & Goldner, V. (Eds.) (2002). *Gender in Psychoanalytic Space: Between Clinic and Culture*. New York: Other Press.

Fairbairn, W. R. D. (1952). *Psychoanalytic Studies of the Personality*. London: Tavistock Publications.

Ferenczi, S. (1932 [1949]). Confusion of tongues between adults and the child: The language of tenderness and of passion. *International Journal of Psychoanalysis*, 30(2): 225–230.

Fischer, K. W., & Ayoub, C. (1994). Affective splitting and dissociation in normal and maltreated children: Developmental pathways for self in relationships. In D. Cicchetti & S. L. Toth (Eds.), *Disorders and Dysfunctions of the Self*, pp. 149–222. Rochester, NY: University of Rochester Press.

Fonagy, P., Gergely, G., Jurist, E. L., & Target, M. (2002). *Affect Regulation, Mentalization, and the Development of the Self*. New York: Other Press.

Foucault, M. (1976 [1990]). *The History of Sexuality*, Vol. I, *An Introduction* (R. Hurley, Trans.). New York: Vintage Books.

Freud, S. (1896 [1962]). Heredity and the aetiology of the neuroses. In J. Strachey (Ed. & Trans.), *The Standard Edition of the Complete Psychological Works of Sigmund Freud*, Vol. III, pp. 141–156. London: Hogarth Press.

Gerson, S. (2004). The relational unconscious: A core element of intersubjectivity, thirdness, and clinical process. *Psychoanalytic Quarterly*, 73(1): 63–98.

Ghent, E. (1990). Masochism, submission, surrender: Masochism as a perversion of surrender. *Contemporary Psychoanalysis*, 26(1): 108–136.

Ghent, E. (2001). Relations: Introduction to the first IARPP conference. Paper presented at the first annual conference of the International Association for Relational Psychoanalysis and Psychotherapy. New York, January 18.

Gill, M. M. (1984). Transference: A change in conception or only in emphasis? *Psychoanalytic Inquiry*, 4(3): 489–523.

Gill, M. M. (1995). Classical and relational psychoanalysis. *Psychoanalytic Psychology*, 12(1): 89–107.

Greenberg, J. R. (1986). The problem of analytic neutrality. *Contemporary Psychoanalysis*, 22(1): 76–86.

Greenberg, J. R., & Mitchell, S. A. (1983). *Object Relations in Psychoanalytic Theory*. Cambridge, MA: Harvard University Press.

Harris, A. E. (2005). *Gender as Soft Assembly*. Hillsdale, NJ: Analytic Press.

Harris, A. E. (2011). The relational tradition landscape and canon. *Journal of the American Psychoanalytic Association*, 59(4): 701–736.

Harris, A. E., & Kuchuck, S. (Eds.) (2015). *The Legacy of Sándor Ferenczi: From Ghost to Ancestor*. New York: Routledge.

Hoffer, A. (1991). The Freud–Ferenczi controversy: A living legacy. *International Review of Psychoanalysis*, 18(4): 465–472.

Hoffman, I. Z. (1992). Expressive participation and psychoanalytic discipline. *Contemporary Psychoanalysis*, 28(1): 1–15.

Hoffman, I. Z. (1994). Dialectical thinking and therapeutic action in the psychoanalytic process. *Psychoanalytic Quarterly*, 63(2): 187–218.

Hoffman, I. Z. (1998). *Ritual and Spontaneity in the Psychoanalytic Process: A Dialectical-Constructivist View*. Hillsdale, NJ: Analytic Press.

Knoblauch, S. H. (2008). "A lingering whiff of Descartes in the air": From theoretical ideas to the messiness of clinical participation. *Psychoanalytic Dialogues*, 18(1): 149–161.

Kohut, H. (1984). *How Does Analysis Cure?* (A. Goldberg & P. Stepansky, Eds.). Chicago: University of Chicago Press.

Layton, L. (2013). Dialectical constructivism in historical context: Expertise and the subject of late modernity. *Psychoanalytic Dialogues*, 23(3): 271–286.

Layton, L., Hollander, N. C., & Gutwill, S. (Eds.) (2006). *Psychoanalysis, Class and Politics: Encounters in the Clinical Setting*. New York: Routledge.

Loewald, H. W. (1972). The experience of time. *Psychoanalytic Study of the Child*, 27: 401–410.

Loewald, H. W. (1978). Instinct theory, object relations, and psychic-structure formation. *Journal of the American Psychoanalytic Association*, 26(3): 493–506.

Lyons-Ruth, K. (2003). Dissociation and the parent–infant dialogue. *Journal of the American Psychoanalytic Association*, 51(3): 883–911.

Lyons-Ruth, K., Bruschweiler-Stern, N., Harrison, A. M., Morgan, A. C., Nahum, J. P., Sander, L. W., Stern, D. N., & Tronick, E. Z. (1998). Implicit relational knowing: Its role in development and psychoanalytic treatment. *Infant Mental Health Journal*, 19(3): 282–289.

Lyons-Ruth, K., Dutra, L., Schuder, M. R., & Bianchi, I. (2006). From infant attachment disorganization to adult dissociation: relational adaptations or traumatic experiences? *Psychiatric Clinics of North America*, 29(1): 63–86.

Maroda, K. J. (1998). Enactment. *Psychoanalytic Psychology*, 15(4): 517–535.

Mills, J. (2005). A critique of relational psychoanalysis. *Psychoanalytic Psychology*, 22(2): 155–188.

Mills, J. (in press). Challenging relational psychoanalysis: A critique of postmodernism and analyst self-disclosure. Conference proceedings of challenging the relational approach: A conference with Dr. Jon Mills, Bar-Ilan University, Israel, February 13, 2015. *Psychoanalytic Perspectives*.

Mitchell, S. A. (1984). Object relations theories and the developmental tilt. *Contemporary Psychoanalysis*, 20(4): 473–499.

Mitchell, S. A. (1988). *Relational Concepts in Psychoanalysis: An Integration*. Cambridge, MA: Harvard University Press.

Mitchell, S. A. (1993). *Hope and Dread in Psychoanalysis*. New York: Basic Books.

Mitchell, S. A., & Aron, L. (1999). *Relational Psychoanalysis: The Emergence of a Tradition*. Hillsdale, NJ: Analytic Press.

Ogden, T. H. (1997). Reverie and interpretation. *Psychoanalytic Quarterly*, 66(4): 567–595.

Ogden, T. H. (2004). The analytic third: Implications for psychoanalytic theory and technique. *Psychoanalytic Quarterly*, 73(1): 167–195.

Safran, J. D., & Kraus, J. (2014). Alliance ruptures, impasses, and enactments: A relational perspective. *Psychotherapy*, 51(3): 381–387.

Seligman, S. (1999). Integrating Kleinian theory and intersubjective infant research observing projective identification. *Psychoanalytic Dialogues*, 9(2): 129–159.

Seligman, S. (2014). Paying attention and feeling puzzled: The analytic mindset as an agent of therapeutic change. *Psychoanalytic Dialogues*, 24(4): 648–662.

Slavin, M. O. (2016). Relational psychoanalysis and the tragic-existential aspect of the human condition. *Psychoanalytic Dialogues*, 26(5): 537–548.

Slavin, M. O., & Kriegman, D. (1998). Why the analyst needs to change: Toward a theory of conflict, negotiation, and mutual influence in the therapeutic process. *Psychoanalytic Dialogues*, 8(2): 247–284.

Spezzano, C. (1996). The three faces of two-person psychology development, ontology, and epistemology. *Psychoanalytic Dialogues*, 6(5): 599–622.

Stern, D. B. (1983). Unformulated experience: From familiar chaos to creative disorder. *Contemporary Psychoanalysis*, 19(1): 71–99.

Stern, D. B. (1997). *Unformulated Experience: From Dissociation to Imagination in Psychoanalysis*. New York: Routledge.

Stern, D. B. (2010). *Partners in Thought: Working with Unformulated Experience, Dissociation, and Enactment*. New York: Routledge.

Stern, D. B. (2014). Relational psychoanalysis and the inner life: Commentary on Cooper, Corbett, and Seligman. *Psychoanalytic Dialogues*, 24(6): 676–683.

Stern, D. N., Sander, L. W., Nahum, J. P., Harrison, A. M., Lyons-Ruth, K., Morgan, A. C., Bruschweiler-Stern, N., & Tronick, E. Z. (1998). Non-interpretive mechanisms in psychoanalytic therapy: The "something more" than interpretation. *International Journal of Psychoanalysis*, 79(5): 903–921.

Suchet, M. (2004). A relational encounter with race. *Psychoanalytic Dialogues*, 14(4): 423–438.

Sullivan, H. S. (1940). Conceptions of modern psychiatry: The first William Alanson White memorial lectures. *Psychiatry*, 3(1): 1–117.

Sullivan, H. S. (1950 [1964]). The illusion of personal individuality. In *The Fusion of Psychiatry and Social Science*, pp. 198–228. New York: W. W. Norton.

Tronick, E. Z. (2003). "Of course all relationships are unique": How co-creative processes generate unique mother–infant and patient–therapist relationships and change other relationships. *Psychoanalytic Inquiry*, 23(3): 473–491.

Tublin, S. (2011). Discipline and freedom in relational technique. *Contemporary Psychoanalysis*, 47(4): 519–546.

Tummala-Narra, P. (2004). Dynamics of race and culture in the supervisory encounter. *Psychoanalytic Psychology*, 21(2): 300–311.

Van der Kolk, B. A. (1994). The body keeps the score: Memory and the evolving psychobiology of posttraumatic stress. *Harvard Review of Psychiatry*, 1(5): 253–265.

Wachtel, P. L. (2007). *Relational Theory and the Practice of Psychotherapy*. New York: Guilford Press.

Wachtel, P. L. (2010). One-person and two-person conceptions of attachment and their implications for psychoanalytic thought. *International Journal of Psychoanalysis*, 91(3): 561–581.

Weinfield, N. S., Sroufe, L. A., & Egeland, B. (2000). Attachment from infancy to early adulthood in a high-risk sample: Continuity, discontinuity, and their correlates. *Child Development*, 71(3): 695–702.

Westen, D. (2002). The language of psychoanalytic discourse. *Psychoanalytic Dialogues*, 12(6): 857–898.

Winnicott, D. W. (1960). The theory of the parent–infant relationship. *International Journal of Psychoanalysis*, 41(6): 585–595.

Winnicott, D. W. (1971). The use of an object and relating through identifications. In *Playing and Reality*, pp. 86–94. London: Tavistock Publications.

AFTERWORD

Marilyn Charles

Some years ago I was presenting a clinical case at a national meeting and was stunned by a statement from the audience: "I am just a candidate but…" In that moment, I realized that what I had thought was a relatively free and collaborative interchange of ideas in a receptive environment was severely constrained for those who felt themselves to be outside, at the margins. That statement continues to reverberate in me, even decades later. It reminds me that it matters to what extent we feel respectfully included in whatever conversation is taking place, and of the high price we pay in becoming so absorbed in our own intentions – whatever they are – that we fail to pay sufficient attention to those with whom we interact. As is evident from the contributions in this volume, that awareness of the particularity of an individual mind, being and moment is a key thread running through all psychoanalytic approaches. Psychoanalysis is built upon encounters with the mysteries of the human mind, spirit and imagination through the lens of the individual psyche. Recognition of that foundation helps us to keep in mind the primary and fundamental value of the individual as a guiding principle, as our patients thread their way through becoming more fully and adaptively themselves.

But that striking comment also reminds us of the importance of paying close attention to how we talk about our work with our colleagues. Psychoanalysis has its roots in a tradition of brilliant discoveries and interpretations that tend to amaze and obscure rather than instruct. Countering that tendency, the contributors to this volume hope, together, to offer models for a more experience-near introduction to clinical work, so that evolving clinicians can learn from others' experiences as well as their own. Psychoanalysis entails a journey, as we evolve in relation to our patients' struggles to make sense of self and other. The analyst's journey requires the type of deep curiosity in the face of life's mysteries that enables us to continue to engage with one another with respect, vitality and humility, to learn from and with one another rather than closing down the rich process of discovery.

Although psychoanalytic jargon can be obscure and difficult to penetrate, it also offers incredibly useful metaphors that can aid the clinician in this challenging work if we can be called to attention when our ideas fail us or our patients show preference for their own metaphors. Psychoanalysis is not for the faint of heart: it offers no rule books but, rather, an invitation into the complexities that lie at the heart of human experience. Psychoanalysis invites us to recognize patterns and to become curious about them as a means toward exploration that opens up further possibilities for meaning, learning and growth. In that process, the metaphors that evolve through our encounters with our theories and our patients serve as our best guides in helping our patients find their ways through their own journeys.

Psychoanalysis is a process that involves both pain and transformation, a hero's quest in which our technical tools – and personal experience – become the arsenal that enables us to tolerate what *we* might need to suffer as we accompany our patients on their journeys. It is inevitably a humbling experience, because we can never be entirely up to a challenge that is never truly *our* challenge but, rather, puts the patient into the position of increasingly becoming the subject of her own story, one that we are afforded the honor of witnessing. I hope that you, the reader, will have found enrichment and enlivenment in these pages that will serve you well as you continue in your own explorations into the mysteries of the human mind and spirit that are at the heart of the psychoanalytic journey.

INDEX

References to endnotes consist of the page number followed by the letter 'n' followed by the number of the note, e.g. 138n1 refers to note no. 1 on page 138.

Abend, Sandor 16
Adler, Alfred 45, 47
Akhtar, Salman 11
alchemy 45
American Psychoanalytic Association
10; *Welch v American Psychoanalytic
Association* 125
American Psychological Association (APA),
Division 39 (Psychoanalysis), and new
Middle Group issue 138n1
analyst: analysand-analyst typological
mismatch 46; analysand-analyst
unconscious communication (Freud)
20, 22; analyst as relative expert in
the room (Sullivan) 194; analyst-as-
reparative-mother (Winnicott) 109;
analyst as the authority (Kleinian theory)
90; analyst open to present moment
(Bion) 90; "analyst's desire" concept
(Lacan) 135; analyst's personality vs.
theory (Jung) 33; analytical ideals and
ideal analyst 97–98; constraints on
analyst's behavior (Freud) 25; Freudian
analyst's technical tools 25–26; listening
and even hovering attention 21–22;
myth of neutral analyst (Winnicott)
102–103; physicians vs. lay analysts
125; reverie 22, 79, 160, 215–216, 220,
221; subjectivity of 20, 25; use of self

219–220; *see also* countertransference;
interpersonal psychoanalysis (Eugenio
Duarte); relational psychoanalysis;
relational psychoanalysis as framework
(Johanna Malone); transference/
countertransference
"analytic couple" concept, and
psychoanalytic field theory 147,
150–155, 156
analytic frame: Barangers' approach 147–
148; Freudian approaches 25; Kleinian
approach 76; Winnicott's approach
100–101
"analytic third" concept 24, 34, 214–216
analytic time: Barangers' approach 148;
Freud's approach 123; Lacan's approach
123; Winnicott's approach 122
"analyzability" concept 26
Anderson, Elijah 133
anima/animus, Jungian concept 40–41
Antigone 130, 131
anxiety, and Freud's theory 17, 127
archetypal theory, and Jungian approaches
36–39, 47–49
Arlow, Jacob 12, 16
Aron, Lewis 220
Association for Psychoanalysis, Culture
and Society, and new Middle Group
issue 138n1

230 Index

atè (Lacan's concept) 130–132, 136–137
attachment theory 10, 79, 213
Atwood, George E. 150, 153

Bach, Sheldon 11
Balint, Enid 132
Balint, Michael 109, 168
Baranger, Madeleine and Willy 4, 146–150, 157, 161–162
Bass, Alan 85
"bastion" concept (Barangers) 149
Beckett, Samuel 137
Beebe, Beatrice 212, 213
Benjamin, Jessica 109, 126, 214, 215
Bernstein, Jeanne Wolf 135
"binocular vision" concept (Bion) 2, 92
Bion, W. R.: analyst open to present moment 90; analytic third and relational psychoanalysis 216; attacks on linking and denial 87, 88; beta and alpha elements 80, 157–158, 161; "binocular vision" concept 2, 92; Bionian field theorists 4, 6; "blind eye" and fear of knowing 78, 85; containing function 79, 221; "dreaming the session" notion 77; experience vs. authorized knowledge 3; and Ferro's field theory 146, 157–158; grid 5; Oedipus complex 78; passion and essential truths 77, 86, 87; preconceptions 37; and relational psychoanalytic movement 221; reverie 220, 221; Samuel Beckett, analysand of 137; symbolization and dreaming 80–81; tennis net metaphor 80–81; tensions between growth and evasion 77–78; territory of truth and lies 90; "waking dream thought" notion and Ferro's theory 157–159; *see also* Kleinian/Bionian perspective (Marilyn Charles)
bi-personal psychoanalysis 145, 146–147, 150, 156, 161; *see also* psychoanalytic field theory (Montana Katz); two-person psychologies
bodily ego (Freud) 13
Bollas, Christopher 9, 25
Bolognini, Stefano 20, 24
Brecht, Bertold 123
Brenner, Charles 11, 16, 22
British Middle Group (or Independent tradition) 125, 134–135
British Psychoanalytical Society 99, 122, 125
Bromberg, Philip M. 217
Brown, Norman O. 69

Buechler, Sandra 199
Busch, Fred 11, 23
Butler, Judith 64

Cambray, Joseph 49
castration: anxiety/fear (Freud) 12, 17, 48, 62; symbolic castration (Lacan) 62–64, 131
cathartic method 21
Charles, Marilyn 1, 75, 227–228; *see also* comparative psychoanalysis (Marilyn Charles); Kleinian/Bionian perspective (Marilyn Charles)
Chodorow, Nancy J. 11, 109, 126
Chused, Judith 11
Civitarese, G. 6, 158–159
Claudel, Paul 130
"close process analysis" 11
collective unconscious (Jung) 36
comparative psychoanalysis (Marilyn Charles): diversity, character, and binocular perspective 1–2; overview of chapters 2–5; psychoanalytic process and metaphors 5–6
complexes, Jung's concept 47–49
compromise formation, and Freudian approaches 17–18
conflict theory *see* modern conflict theory
Cooper, Stephen H. 215, 220, 221
Corbett, Lionel 2, 33; *see also* Jungian approaches to psychotherapy (Lionel Corbett)
couch (vs. sitting-up): and Duarte 193; and Jung 34
countertransference: and Barangers' field theory 146; and field theory 145, 151–152; and Freudian approaches 24–25; Freud's view 133; Jung's view 34; Lacanian perspective 135; Winnicott's countertransference hate 102–103, 107, 110, 133; *see also* interpersonal psychoanalysis (Eugenio Duarte); transference/countertransference
critical theory 210
cultural influences, and interpersonal psychoanalysis 191, 203–205

danger situations, and fears 16–17
Davids, A. 9
Davies, Jody M. 113
defense analysis 11
defense mechanisms: and Freudian approaches 17–18, 23; and Kleinian/Bionian perspective (defensive

organizations) 77, 82, 87–88; and
Kleinian literature 19–20
dependence, regression to (Winnicott)
103–106, 109
depression, as dysphoric affect 17
depressive position, Kleinian/Bionian
perspective 81, 82–83, 87, 89, 92
desire: "analyst's desire" concept (Lacan)
135; "desire of the Other" (Lacan) 131;
incest desire and Freud–Jung break
35; lost object, "cause of desire" and
representation (Lacan) 67; recognizing/
naming desire (Lacan) 70–71; subject
caught by desire of the Other (Lacan) 91
detailed inquiry, and interpersonal
psychoanalysis 191, 199–202, 205–206
developmental research/theory: and Jungian
shadow 40; and self-other differentiation
19; and two-person psychologies
213–214
Dinnerstein, Dorothy 109
dissociation 216–218
Doolittle, Hilda ("H.D.") 121
dreams: Ferro and dream function of
sessions 158–160, 161; Ferro and
"transformations in dreaming" 160;
Ferro/Bion and "waking dream thought"
notion 157–159; Freudian dream
interpretation 22–23, 135; Jungian dream
interpretation 42–45, 48; and Jungian
ego-Self axis 40; and Jungian shadow 40;
Kleinian/Bionian perspective 80–81, 92;
Lacanian perspective 92; *see also* reverie
drives: drive derivatives 16, 22; Freud's drive
theory 35, 70, 78; vs. object relations
theories 3; and psychoanalytic field
theory 146, 150, 155, 156; and relational
psychoanalytic movement 209, 210–211,
212; and structure vs. relational/structure
model 18–19, 27; and Winnicott 99,
109, 125
Druck, Andrew B. 11
DSM, pathologizing of homosexuality 125
Duarte, Eugenio 4–5, 191; *see also*
interpersonal psychoanalysis (Eugenio
Duarte)
dysphoric affect 17, 18

Eagle, Morris N. 11, 23
ego: bodily ego (Freud) 13; Freud's theory
10, 19; Jungian view 39–40
ego psychology 10, 19, 27, 70, 124, 146,
168; *see also* North American field
theories

Ehrenberg, Darlene 199
Eichenbaum, Luise 126
Eigen, Michael 51
Ellman, Steven J. 11, 22, 24
empathy: experiences within empathic
connection 212; and narcissistic
personality disorders 168–169; and
projective identification 167–168; and
self psychology 165–167, 174, 186
enactment: and Freudian approaches 20–21,
24; and Harry Stack Sullivan's theory
151; and memory 15; and relational
psychoanalysis 219
envy, Klein's theory 89–90
Epstein, Lawrence 113
"essential ambiguity" concept (Barangers)
148–149, 161
experiences: vs. authorized knowledge
3; within empathic connection 212;
numinous experiences 50–51

Fairbairn, Ronald 19, 154, 168, 210, 221
Fast, Irene 109
fears, and danger situations 16–17
Feldman, Michael 84
feminist psychoanalysis/theory 10, 64,
109–110, 126–127, 210
Ferenczi, Sándor 123, 133, 168, 211
Ferro, Antonino 6, 146, 157–160, 161–162
field theory: Bionian field theorists 4,
6; and Jung's view of the analyst 33;
see also psychoanalytic field theory
(Montana Katz)
Fink, Bruce 135, 137–138
Fosshage, James L. 150, 153–154
free association: and Freudian approaches
21–22; and Kleinian/Bionian
perspective 80
Freud, Anna 10, 16, 124–125, 138n1
Freud, Sigmund: and American analysts
125; analyst's behavior, constraints
on 25; analytic time variations 123;
Antigone story 131; anxiety 17, 127;
archaic remnants 36; bodily ego 13;
Bollas on 9; castration anxiety 12, 17,
48, 62; and colleagues, interactions with
211; countertransference 133; death and
resurrection of 9; despair and loss of
object 82; devotees of and their attitude
to his failings 123; dream interpretation
22, 135; drive theory 35, 70, 78, 146,
210–211, 212; ego 10, 19; fears and
danger situations 16–17; free association
method 21–22; and free clinics 5,

232 Index

122; and Hilda Doolittle 121–122; homosexuality 13–14, 125; hysterical symptoms, conflict and repression 16; id 10; incest desire 35; and Jung 35–36, 49, 211; and Jung's psychological types theory 45; and Lacan 2–3, 55, 121–122, 124, 125–126; libido 35; linguistic ambiguity and unconscious/conscious thought 58; memory 14–15; mother and pre-Oedipal period 124; *nachtr ä glichkeit* 133; narcissism 168, 169; and object relations theory 19; Oedipus complex 13–14, 36, 47, 65, 68; primal fantasies as phylogenetic endowment 37; psychoanalysis and idea of human subject 56; psychoanalytic process as chess game 148–149; Rat Man case 131; representation and interpretation 54; reputation of in 1950s 69; seduction theory 211; sexual theory 13–14; shame 178; superego 10, 19; symptoms, attachment to 137; "thing and word representation" 24; unconscious 11–13; unconscious and the Other concept 55–56; unconscious communication between analysand and analyst 20, 22; unconscious to unconscious 133; and Winnicott 99, 121–122, 125; Wolfman case 123; *see also* Freud, Sigmund, works by; Freudian approaches (Danielle Knafo and Seymour Moscovitz)

Freud, Sigmund, works by: "On beginning the treatment" 123; *Beyond the Pleasure Principle* 66–67; *The Ego and the Id* 10; *Inhibitions, Symptoms and Anxiety* 10; *The Interpretation of Dreams* 54; *Introductory Lectures on Psycho-Analysis* 37, 122; *Jokes and Their Relationship to the Unconscious* 54; "The Medusa's head" 48; "Mourning and melancholia" 19; *Project for a Scientific Psychology* 127; *The Psychopathology of Everyday Life* 54; *The Three Essays on the Theory of Sexuality* 124

Freudian approaches (Danielle Knafo and Seymour Moscovitz): about chapter 2; basic tenets and principles 9–10; brief history of post-Freudian era 10–11; contemporary Freudian vs. non-Freudian orientations 27; dream interpretation 22–23; free association, even hovering attention and reverie 21–22; internalization and relations with others 18–20; intersubjectivity 20–21; memory, repetition and enactment 14–16;

pre-Oedipal development 19; psychic conflict and compromise formation 16–18; psychosexual development 13–14; resistance and defense mechanisms 17–18, 23; technical parameters 25; technical tools of analyst 25–26; therapeutic action 26; transference/countertransference matrix 23–25; unconscious fantasy 11–13; weaknesses of Freudian perspective (acultural assumption of universality) 26–27; widening scope of psychoanalysis 26; *see also* Freud, Sigmund

"gap" concept (Lacan) 81
genograms 131
Gerson, Samuel 215
Gestalt psychology 146
Ghent, Emmanuel 208, 215
Gill, M. M. 18
"good enough" concept (Winnicott) 99–100, 132–133
Grand, Sue 109–110
Gray, Paul 11, 22, 23
greed, Klein's theory 89
Green, André 4, 13, 134–135, 136
Greenacre, Phyllis 133
Greenberg, Jay R. 18–19, 27, 210
Grotstein, J. S. 1
Guntrip, Harry 125

hallucinosis, transformations in 160
Halpern, Jeffrey 4, 165; *see also* self psychology and intersubjectivity (Jeffrey Halpern and Sharone Ornstein)
Harris, Adrienne E. 209
Hartmann, Heinz 10
hate: countertransference hate (Winnicott) 102–103, 107, 110, 133; infant's hate toward bad breast (Klein) 133
Heidegger, Martin 60
Heimann, Paula 133
Hermes *see* Lacan and the evolution of Hermes (David Lichtenstein)
Hermes Trismegistus 64
Hirsch, Irwin 150
"holding" concept *see* Winnicott's clinical contributions (Joyce Slochower)
homosexuality: *DSM*'s pathologizing of 125; Freud's view 13–14, 125
Hopkins, Lionda 123
Horgan, J. 9
Horney, Karen 123
humility, psychoanalytic 191, 202–203

Index **233**

hypnotic method 21
hysterical symptoms and repression (Freudian concept) 16

idealizing transferences 176–178
Imaginary, Symbolic and Real (Lacan) 128–130
incest desire, and Freud-Jung break 35
Independent tradition (British Middle Group) 125, 134–135; *see also* new Middle Group
individuation, Jungian view 41–42, 46
"interactive matrix" concept 154
intergenerational transmission 131
internalization and relations with others, and Freudian approaches 18–20
internal working models (IWMs) 213
International Psychoanalytic Association 122
International Winnicott Association (IWA) 124
interpersonal psychoanalysis: and psychoanalytic field theory 150, 151–153; and relational psychoanalysis 154, 210, 216; and Winnicottian model 109; *see also* interpersonal psychoanalysis (Eugenio Duarte)
interpersonal psychoanalysis (Eugenio Duarte): about chapter 4–5; detailed inquiry 191, 199–202, 205–206; limitations of interpersonal psychoanalysis 205–207; multicultural awareness 191, 203–205; "one cannot not interact" 191, 194–197; participant observation 191, 192–194; psychoanalyst as riding the wave 191, 197–199; psychoanalytic humility 191, 202–203; *see also* interpersonal psychoanalysis
interpretation: limits of (Winnicott) 101–102; and representation (Freud) 54
interpsychic communication 20, 24
intersubjective psychoanalysis 10, 33, 150, 153
intersubjectivity: and Freudian approaches 20–21; and relational psychoanalysis 214–216; *see also* intersubjective psychoanalysis; self psychology and intersubjectivity (Jeffrey Halpern and Sharone Ornstein)
introspection, and self psychology 165–167
Ireland, Mardy 135–136, 138n1

Jacobs, Theodore 11
Jakobson, Roman 60, 66

Joseph, Betty 79
jouissance (Lacan) 91, 137
Joyce, James 128
Jung, Carl G. 123, 211; *see also* Jungian approaches to psychotherapy (Lionel Corbett)
Jungian approaches to psychotherapy (Lionel Corbett): about chapter 2; alchemy 45; analyst's personality vs. theory 33; couch, use of 34; countertransference 34; dreams 42–45, 48; ego 39–40; Freud-Jung break 35–36, 45, 49; incest desire 35; individuation 41–42, 46; Jung's attitude to psychotherapy 33–35; libido 35; opposite-sex qualities (anima and animus) 40–41; persona 41; post-Jungian thought symposium 35–36; psychological types 45–46; psychopathology and complexes 46–49; *puer/puella aeternus* vs. *senex* 41; religion and spirituality 49–51; remembering and re-experiencing 35; shadow 40; synchronicity 49; transference 38–39; transpersonal Self 33, 39, 40, 42; unconscious 34–35; unconscious and archetypes 36–39, 47–49

Katz, Gil A. 20, 24
Katz, Montana 4, 145; *see also* psychoanalytic field theory (Montana Katz)
Kernberg, Otto 137
Khan, Masud 123
Kirshner, Lewis A. 138n1
Klein, Melanie: and British Middle Group 138n1; defense mechanisms 19–20; focus on infants' phantasies 124–125; focus on traumatized children 75; and Freudian tradition 10; infant's hate toward bad breast 133; projective identification 3, 5, 146; and relational psychoanalytic movement 221; total transference 77; unconscious phantasy 37, 77, 78; and Winnicott 99, 105; *see also* Kleinian/Bionian perspective (Marilyn Charles)
Kleinian/Bionian perspective (Marilyn Charles): about chapter 3; about Kleinian theory 75, 76–78; Bion's contribution to Kleinian approach 75–76; defensive organizations 77, 82, 87–88; depressive position 81, 82–83, 87, 89, 92; greed, envy and gratitude 89–90; paranoid-schizoid position 77, 81, 87; pre-Oedipal development 75, 78–80, 99; projective

234 Index

identification 77, 81, 83–84; symbol formation 85–87, 93; symbolization and dreaming 80–81, 92; transference and countertransference 77, 79, 83, 84–85, 87, 93; weaknesses and limitations of Kleinian perspective 90–92; *see also* Bion, W. R.; Klein, Melanie

Knafo, Danielle 2, 9; *see also* Freudian approaches (Danielle Knafo and Seymour Moscovitz)

Kohut, Heinz: books and papers 168; empathy and narcissistic personality disorders 168–169; experiences within empathic connection 212; mirror transferences 173; narcissism vs. object love 183; and psychoanalytic field theory 150; self, definition of 170; selfobject functions/transferences 165, 170–172; self psychology model 4, 153; shame and narcissistic rage 178, 179; unfolding nuclear self 39–40

Kriegman, D. 219

Kris, Ernst 10, 58–60, 70

Lacan, Jacques: alleged transgressions of 123; "analyst's desire" concept 135; analytic time and variable-length sessions 123; *atè* (family's madness or curse) 130–132, 136–137; castration, symbolic 62–64, 131; "desire of the Other" 131; "discourse without words" 56, 60; dream interpretation 92; and feminist psychoanalysis 126–127; and Freud 121–122; and Freud, "return to " 55, 65, 125–126; on Freud and American ego psychologists 124; on Freud and speech/language in psychoanalysis 2–3; "gap" concept 81; growing international reputation of 124, 134; on humanism 122; Imaginary, Symbolic and Real 128–130; and International Psychoanalytic Association 122; *jouissance* 91, 137; "mirror stage" (*stade du miroir*) 127–128; *Other* vs. mother 126; *parlêtre* ("speakbeing") 57, 60, 63; patient as subject of conversation 85, 90; political views of 126; pre-Oedipal development 125, 134; on psychoanalysis and integral experience 3; and Société Psychanalytique de Paris 125; "specific prematurity of birth" 127; subject caught by desire of the Other 91; transference 56–57; unconscious 68; unconscious and language 37, 126; on "whole beings" 122; and Winnicott 122; *see also* Lacan, Jacques,

works by; Lacan and the evolution of Hermes (David Lichtenstein); Lacan and Winnicott for beginners (Deborah Luepnitz)

Lacan, Jacques, works by: *Les Complexes Familiaux* 127; "The direction of the treatment and the principles of its power" 59; essay on E. A. Poe's "The purloined letter" 67–68; *Freud's Papers on Technique* 58; *From an Other to the Other* (*D'un Autre à l'autre*) 56; *The Language of the Self* 69; *On Feminine Sexuality: The Limits of Love and Knowledge* 63–64; "On the signification of the phallus" 63

Lacan and the evolution of Hermes (David Lichtenstein): about chapter 2–3; Hermes, boundaries, and psychoanalysis 53–54; Lacan, Hermes, and messages 55, 57; Lacan's "return to Freud" and representation/interpretation 54–55; lost object, "cause of desire" and representation 67; messages from the Other 55–56; objections to Lacan's theory 70; Oedipus and Hermes 64–69; psychoanalysis as unique human science 69–70, 71; psychoanalyst and the Other 56–57; recognizing/naming desire 70–71; speech and discourse 68, 69; speech and signifiers 57–60; subject and delusions of perfect attunement 61–62; symbolic castration 62–64; *see also* Lacan, Jacques; Lacan and Winnicott for beginners (Deborah Luepnitz)

Lacan and Winnicott for beginners (Deborah Luepnitz): about chapter 4; background on Lacan and Winnicott 122–124; Freud, Lacan and Winnicott 121–122; Freud, Lacan, Winnicott and analytic time 122–123; Lacan, Winnicott and feminist analysts 126–127; Lacan, Winnicott and politics 126; Lacan's *atè* (family's madness or curse) 130–132, 136–137; Lacan's concepts 125–126; Lacan's three registers (Imaginary, Symbolic and Real) 128–130; Middle Group and Winnicott 125, 134–135; mirror stage in Lacan and Winnicott 127–128; Winnicott's concepts 124–125; Winnicott's psychoanalytical approach 132–134; working in space between French and British traditions 134–138; *see also* Lacan, Jacques; Lacan and the evolution of Hermes (David Lichtenstein)

Lachmann, Frank M. 150, 153–154, 213
language: Lacan's view on speech/discourse 37, 56–60, 68, 69, 126; Levenson's view on speech 199; and psychoanalytic field theory 151, 156–157
Laplanche, Jean 57
Lars and the Real Girl (movie) 205–206
Lemma, A. 13
Levenson, Edgar A. 150, 151–153, 156, 194–195, 199
Lévi-Strauss, Claude 60
Levit, D. B. 220
Lewin, Kurt 146, 150
libido, and Freud-Jung break 35
Lichtenberg, Joseph D. 150, 153–154
Lichtenstein, David 3, 53; *see also* Lacan and the evolution of Hermes (David Lichtenstein)
Little, Margaret 122
Loewald, Hans W. 16, 20, 24, 26, 153, 168, 212
Lowenstein, Rudolf 10
Luepnitz, Deborah 4, 121; *see also* Lacan and Winnicott for beginners (Deborah Luepnitz)
Lynch, P. E. 13
Lyons-Ruth, Karlen 212, 217

Malone, Johanna C. 5, 208; *see also* relational psychoanalysis as framework (Johanna Malone)
mandalas 39
Marcuse, Herbert 69
meditation strategies 206
Medusa myth 48
memory: remembering and re-experiencing (Jung) 35; repetition and enactment (Freudian approaches) 14–16
Merleau-Ponty, Maurice 146
metaphors, and psychoanalytical process 5–6, 228
Middle Group: British Middle Group (or Independent tradition) 125, 134–135; new Middle Group 137, 138
Middlemore, Merell 133
mindfulness meditation practices 206
mirror stage/*stade du miroir* (Lacan) 127–128
mirror transferences 172–176
Mitchell, Juliet 64; *Psychoanalysis and Feminism* 126
Mitchell, Stephen A. 18–19, 27, 100, 150, 154–155, 210, 215
modern conflict theory 11, 16–18, 70, 145

Moscovitz, Seymour 2, 9; *see also* Freudian approaches (Danielle Knafo and Seymour Moscovitz)
mothers: and feminist psychoanalysis 109–110; and Lacan's theory 61–62, 126; and Winnicott's theory 62, 98–99, 102–103, 125, 126, 132–133
motivation, vs. drives 155, 156
motivational systems theory 150, 153–154
multicultural awareness, and interpersonal psychoanalysis 191, 203–205
Myers-Briggs Type Indicator 46

narcissism: and Freud 168, 169; and Kleinian/Bionian perspective 87–88, 89–90, 92; and self psychology 166, 176, 185–186; and self psychology (Kohut's views) 168–169, 172, 183; shame and narcissistic rage 178–182, 186
National Psychological Association for Psychoanalysis 125
new Middle Group 137, 138
North American field theories 146, 150–157, 161–162
Novick, J. and K. K. 88
numinous experiences 50–51

object relations theories: vs. drive model 3; and Freud 19; and Freudian approaches 24; and Freudian "castration anxiety" concept 62; and Jungian approaches 49; and Kleinian perspective 76; and narcissism 168; and North American field theories 150; and relational psychoanalysis 154, 210, 221
object usage (Winnicott's concept) 2, 5, 82, 107–108, 110, 214–215
Oedipus complex: Bion's theory 78; Freud's theory 13–14, 36, 47, 65, 68; Lacan's theory 65–66; superego as "heir to the Oedipus complex" (Freud) 19
Ogden, Thomas H. 22, 23, 24, 34, 215, 216
Orbach, Susie 126
Ornstein, Sharone 4, 165; *see also* self psychology and intersubjectivity (Jeffrey Halpern and Sharone Ornstein)
O'Shaughnessy, Edna 87
Otto, Rudolph 50

paranoid-schizoid position, Kleinian/Bionian perspective 77, 81, 87
participant observation, and interpersonal psychoanalysis 191, 192–194

236 Index

Pauli, Wolfgang 45, 49
persona, Jungian concept 41
Piaget, Jean 37
Pick, Irma B. 93
Pine, Fred 11, 19
Plato 38
postmodernism, and psychoanalysis 150, 151
pre-Oedipal development: and feminist psychoanalysis 110; and Freud 124; and Freudian perspective 19; and Kleinian/Bionian perspective 75, 78–80, 99; and Lacan/Lacanians 125, 134; and Winnicott 99, 124–125
projective identification: and empathy 167–168; Kleinian/Bionian perspective 77, 81, 83–84; Klein's theory 3, 5, 146
psychic conflict, and Freudian approaches 16–18
psychoanalytic field theory (Montana Katz): about chapter 4; development of field theory 145–146; Ferro's model 146, 157–160; field theories from North America 146, 150–157; M. and W. Baranger model 146–150, 157; models compared 160–162
psychoanalytic psychotherapy, vs. psychoanalysis proper 26
The Psychoanalytic Review, post-Jungian thought symposium 35–36
"psychological field" concept 146
psychological types, Jungian theory 45–46
psychosexual development, and Freudian approaches 13–14
puer/puella aeternus, Jungian concept 41

queer theory 210

rage, shame and narcissistic rage 178–182, 186
Ragland-Sullivan, E. 134
Rank, Otto 211
Rapaport, D. 18
reflective function 91–92
regression to dependence (Winnicott) 103–106, 109
Reich, Wilhelm 123
Reik, Theodor 22
relational psychoanalysis: as developed by Stephen Mitchell 150, 154–155; emergence of 10; and Jung's approach 34; and Lacan 70; and technical parameters 25; and transference 23, 219–220; and Winnicott 124; and Winnicottian model

110–114; *see also* relational psychoanalysis as framework (Johanna Malone)
relational psychoanalysis as framework (Johanna Malone): about chapter 5; emergence and theoretical underpinning 209–212; framework vs. theory 208–209; intersubjectivity and analytic third 214–216; self-states and multiplicity of self 216–218; "two-person" psychology 212–214; use of self by analyst 219–220; weaknesses and limitations 220–222; *see also* relational psychoanalysis
religion/spirituality, Jung's view 49–51
Renik, Owen 20
repression (Freudian concept) 16
resistance: and Freudian approaches 23; *see also* defense mechanisms
reverie, and analyst 22, 79, 160, 215–216, 220, 221
Riviere, Joan 98
Roosevelt, Eleanor 48–49
Rose, Jacqueline 64
Rudnytsky, Peter L. 138n1

sadomasochism, and "analytic third" 214
Sandler, Joseph 24
Saussure, Ferdinand de 60, 66
Schoonejans, Sonia 123
Schopenhauer, Arthur 138
Schwartz, Murray 134
"second look" concept (Barangers) 149
Segal, Hanna 76, 78, 80, 89
Self: Kohut's definition 170; self-other differentiation and developmental research 19; self-states and multiplicity of self 216–218; transpersonal Self (Jung) 33, 39, 40, 42; true vs. false (or caretaker) self (Winnicott) 104, 108, 125, 128; unfolding nuclear self (Winnicott) 39–40; use of self by analyst 219–220; "a word like 'self'" quote (Winnicott) 135
selfobject transferences 165, 170–172, 180, 184, 185–186
self psychology 10, 49, 114n1, 153; *see also* self psychology and intersubjectivity (Jeffrey Halpern and Sharone Ornstein)
self psychology and intersubjectivity (Jeffrey Halpern and Sharone Ornstein): about chapter 4; empathy or vicarious introspection 165–168, 174, 186; idealizing transferences 176–178; mirror transferences 172–176; narcissism as driving force 168–169, 185; self and recognition of subjectivity of the other

181, 183–185, 186; selfobjects, selfobject functions and selfobject transferences 165, 170–172, 180, 184, 185–186; shame and narcissistic rage 178–182, 186; summary 185–186

Seligman, S. 222

senex, Jungian concept 41

sexuality: psychosexual development (Freudian concept) 13–14; *see also* libido

shadow, Jungian concept 40

shame: and narcissistic rage 178–182, 186; Silvan Tomkins' conceptualization 92

signifiers, Lacan's concept 58–60

Slavin, Malcolm O. 219, 221

Slochower, Joyce 3, 97; *Holding and Psychoanalysis: A Relational Perspective* 110; *see also* Winnicott's clinical contributions (Joyce Slochower)

social constructivism: and relational psychoanalytic movement 210; and Winnicottian model 109

Société Psychanalytique de Paris 125

Solms, M. 9

speech *see* language

spirituality/religion, Jung's view 49–51

Squiggle game 136

Star Wars, archetypal imagery 38

Stern, Donnel B. 150, 155, 199, 212, 217, 219, 221

Stolorow, Robert D. 150, 153, 169

Strachey, James 98

structuralism, and intersubjective psychoanalysis 153

structural linguistics 60, 63, 66

structural theory 11

structure, and drive vs. relations 18–19, 27

subject, Lacan's concept 61–62

subjectivity: of the analyst 20, 25; *see also* intersubjectivity

suicide assessment 196

Sullivan, Harry Stack: devotees of and their attitude to his failings 123; field theory and enactments 150, 151; patient's "selective inattention" to details 199; personalities and interpersonal relations 216; and relational psychoanalytic movement 210; relational/structure model 19; therapist as relative expert in the room 194

superego (Freud) 10, 19

symbolization, Kleinian/Bionian perspective 80–81, 85–87, 93

symptoms: attachment to (Freud) 137; Jung's view 46

synchronicity, Jungian concept 49

systems theories 150, 153, 204

therapeutic action, and Freudian approaches 26

Tomkins, Silvan S. 92

transference/countertransference: and Freudian approaches 23–25; idealizing transferences 176–178; and Jungian archetypal theory 38–39; and Jungian complexes theory 47; and Kleinian theory 77, 79, 83, 84–85, 87, 93; and Lacan 56–57; mirror transferences 172–176; and relational psychoanalysis 219–220; selfobject transferences 165, 170–172, 180, 184, 185–186; and two-person psychologies 214; and Winnicott's theory 106–108; *see also* countertransference; enactment

transference neurosis 24

transpersonal Self (Jung) 33, 39, 40, 42

Tronick, Edward Z. 212, 213

Tublin, S. 221

two-person psychologies 10, 212–214, 219; *see also* bi-personal psychoanalysis

unconscious: Barangers' view 147, 149–150, 161; Freudian view 11–13, 55–56, 133; Jungian view 34–35, 36–39, 47–49; Klein's view 37, 77, 78; Lacan's view 37, 68, 126; relational unconscious 215; unconscious communication between analysand and analyst (Freud) 20, 22; unconscious metaphoric processes (North American field theories) 156, 161

Van der Kolk, B. 15

Verhaege, Paul 138n1

Welch v American Psychoanalytic Association 125

Whitman, Walt 122

Winnicott, Clare 133

Winnicott, D. W.: alleged transgressions of 123; analyst-as-reparative-mother 109; analytic time experimentation 122; and British Middle Group 125, 134–135; conscious fantasy vs. unconscious phantasy 77; containing function 79; drives 99, 109, 125; fantasying 6; and feminist psychoanalysis 126, 127; on Freud 125; and Freud, relationship to 99, 121–122; "good enough" concept 99–100, 132–133; hate in countertransference

238 Index

102–103, 107, 110, 133; International Winnicott Association 124; and Lacan 122; mind vs. brain 151; mirror stage 127; mothers 62, 98–99, 102–103, 125, 126, 132–133; narcissism 168; object usage 2, 5, 82, 107–108, 110, 214–215; "the Piggle" child patient 135; political views of 126; pre-Oedipal development 99, 124–125; and relational psychoanalysis 124; and self psychology 4; Squiggle game 136; "There is no such thing as an infant" 212; transitional object 132; transitional space 24, 67; true vs. false (or caretaker) self 104, 108, 125, 128; unfolding nuclear self 39–40; "a word like 'self'" quote 135; *see also* Lacan and Winnicott for beginners (Deborah Luepnitz); Winnicott, D. W., works by; Winnicott's clinical contributions (Joyce Slochower)

Winnicott, D. W., works by: collected works (2015) 123–124; "Fear of breakdown" 133; "Hate in the countertransference" 133; *The Maturational Processes and the Facilitating Environment* 99; *Playing and Reality* 134; "This feminism" 127

Winnicott's clinical contributions (Joyce Slochower): about chapter 3; analytical ideals and ideal analyst 97–98; categories of psychiatric illness 105; child and maternal holding environment 98–100; differences with Freudians and Klein 99; "good enough" concept 99–100; hate in countertransference 102–103, 107, 110; holding, false self defenses and regression to dependence 103–105; holding and shift to object usage 106–108, 110; limits of interpretation 101–102; mutuality, move toward 108, 114; psychoanalytic set situation 100–101; transference/countertransference 106–108; transitionality, paradox and illusion 105–106; true vs. false self 104, 108; Winnicottian model and critics 108–110; Winnicottian model and relational retheorizing of holding 110–114; *see also* Lacan and Winnicott for beginners (Deborah Luepnitz); Winnicott, D. W.

Wolf, E. 171